SEARCHING
FOR
STONEWALL
JACKSON

*A QUEST FOR LEGACY IN
A DIVIDED AMERICA*

BEN CLEARY

TWELVE

NEW YORK   BOSTON

Twelve
Hachette Book Group
1290 Avenue of the Americas, New York, NY 10104

twelvebooks.com

twitter.com/twelvebooks

First Edition: July 2019

Twelve is an imprint of Grand Central Publishing. The Twelve name and logo are trademarks of Hachette Book Group, Inc.

The publisher is not responsible for websites (or their content) that are not owned by the publisher.

The Hachette Speakers Bureau provides a wide range of authors for speaking events. To find out more, go to www.hachettespeakersbureau.com or call (866) 376-6591.

Library of Congress Cataloging-in-Publication Data

Names: Cleary, Ben (Ben C.), author.
Title: Searching for Stonewall Jackson : a quest for legacy in a divided America / by Ben Cleary.
Description: First edition. | New York : Twelve, [2019] | Includes bibliographical references and index.
Identifiers: LCCN 2018048735| ISBN 9781455535804 (hardcover) | ISBN 9781549119910 (audio download) | ISBN 9781455535798 (ebook)
Subjects: LCSH: Jackson, Stonewall, 1824–1863. | Confederate States of America. Army—Biography. | Generals—Confederate States of America—Biography. | United States—History—Civil War, 1861–1865—Campaigns.
Classification: LCC E467.1.J15 C55 2019 | DDC 973.7/3092 [B]—dc23
LC record available at https://lccn.loc.gov/2018048735

ISBNs: 978-1-4555-3580-4 (hardcover), 978-1-4555-3579-8 (ebook)

Printed in the United States of America

LSC-C

10 9 8 7 6 5 4 3 2 1

To my wife, Catherine, and my son, Alexander—
In gratitude for their love and support

Contents

SEARCHING
FOR
STONEWALL
JACKSON

CHAPTER 1

The Soundtrack of Southern Victory

It was supposed to be the battle that would end the war. Light-hearted congressmen and other Washington dignitaries drove out in their carriages to the Virginia countryside to see the show. The summer weather was uncharacteristically temperate. July 21, 1861, was the perfect day for a picnic.

Irvin McDowell's Union army made a leisurely progress to the battlefield, falling out for berry picking and discarding such weighty impedimenta of war as packs and even cartridge boxes. Their objective was Manassas Junction, a strategic railroad hub a few miles behind Bull Run: a slow, mostly shallow stream with a formidable southern bank where the Confederates were waiting. Each side had the same plan: Attack the enemy's right flank.

McDowell's actually worked. Feinting to his left near the spot where the Stone Bridge crossed the stream, he sent his attacking force around like a powerful right hook, crossing Bull Run to the northwest, then driving the Confederates southeast over the rolling Piedmont hills.

General Thomas J. Jackson was behind Bull Run on the Confederate right, waiting to participate in an attack that never materialized. Acting on his own, without orders, he moved toward the sound of the guns.

The northern Virginia traffic wasn't half bad. It only took one click for me to get through most of the lights on 234, the developer road that runs from I-95 northwest to Manassas. The site of the war's first big battle was also the first stop in my quest to gain a deeper understanding of Stonewall Jackson. I've been fascinated with him for years, ever since I found out he marched down the road in front of my house. An incredible fighter, complex and contradictory, he's a puzzle I've never completely put together. I'd recently been asked to write a book about him. I relished the task.

I stopped at the town's small museum, parking in the shade before going inside to check out the exhibits and ask directions to Manassas Junction.

Inside, the fighting's aftermath leapt out at me more than anything about the battle itself. *Battles*, actually—there were two on almost exactly the same field. First Manassas in July 1861; Second in August 1862. Jackson was a major player in both.

In one exhibit, local resident Marianne E. Compton wrote about coming back into her house, which had been turned into a field hospital: "All the lower part of the house was filled with wounded. We walked through a lane of ghastly horrors on our way upstairs. Amputated legs and arms seemed everywhere. We saw a foot…lying on one of our dinner plates."

"You see that?" A young mother near me pointed out a cannonball to her pre-kindergarteners. "Your granddaddy used to find those and roll them down the driveway." Then, more to herself than to her kids: "I guess he should have saved them."

I purchased a Manassas fridge magnet. Neither the cashier nor the docent knew the location of the junction. Less than a mile away, the reason for the town and the reason for the battle—it was like a tour guide in Rome not knowing the location of the Coliseum.

"Lived here all my life and never been to this museum," the young mother told them as I was leaving.

"Look out for your left, your position is turned," Captain Edward Porter Alexander had signaled Colonel Nathan "Shanks" Evans when he saw a strong marching column crossing Bull Run at Sudley Ford.[1] Evans interposed his small—900-man—force in front of 20,000 advancing Federals, buying time but ultimately being beaten back, as were other holding actions by Brigadier General Barnard Bee and Colonel Francis S. Bartow. The Confederates retreated from Matthews Hill, over Buck Hill, and up Henry House Hill, outnumbered and dispirited.

Jackson, on the Confederate right, moved here and there in response to confusing orders from the excitable General Pierre Gustave Toutant Beauregard, the "Hero of Sumter," who shared command with General Joseph E. Johnston. Finally intuiting that the fight was elsewhere, Jackson marched his 2,800 men to Henry House Hill, arriving there around noon. Southerners retreated past him as he placed his men behind the crest of the hill, an ideal defensive position.

General Bee rode up. "The enemy are driving us!" he told Jackson.

"Then, sir, we will give them the bayonet."

The shade had moved from my car, but the heat that came out was only moderately ovenlike when I opened the door. Perfectly evocative of the battle: a mere eighty degrees, mild for a Virginia summer, and a great day for the spectators who had come out from D.C. to watch the saucy Rebels get whipped.[2]

As I drove I reflected on the young mother's grandfather and his cannonballs, and on all the other stories I'd heard about exploding Civil War ordnance. A history teacher at the high school near my house lost a couple of fingers when he was drilling out a shell to remove the powder so he could sell the artifact through the mail. He was lucky: In 2008, a relic hunter named Sam White lost his life when a shell he was disarming exploded, sending shrapnel into him and into the porch of a house a quarter of a mile away.[3]

Like the cannonballs, long-dormant issues had become explosive because of the recent murder of nine African American parishioners at a church in Charleston, South Carolina. The massacre was particularly horrifying because the victims had opened their hearts to their attacker by welcoming him into their Bible study. The killer, Dylann Roof, a white supremacist, had been photographed with the Rebel flag. A national outcry arose to eradicate it, and other symbols of the Confederacy, from public life. Confederate statues were vandalized. Some officials called for them to be razed or relocated. In New Orleans, Mayor Mitch Landrieu said the first step was to declare them a public nuisance.

I turned on WPFW, "Jazz and Justice Radio," out of D.C. A talk show host asked her audience what they thought about the Charleston congregation forgiving the murderer. Her listeners wanted nothing to do with it.

"I'm tired of these people hiding inside their churches!" said one.

"We've got to be more militant!" asserted another. The host asked her to elaborate but she hung up.

I turned off the radio, distressed by thoughts of the tragedy as well as by the fact that a subject I loved—Confederate military history—had become a pawn in the culture wars.

I found an intriguing historic site near an elementary school and parked to look around.

The Jennie Dean Memorial was where the Manassas Industrial School for Colored Youth had stood until some fifty years ago. Civil War and African American historical sites are often as close geographically as the intertwining issues posed by both. Dean, a former slave, was an educator and church founder who died in 1913. I explored the five-acre site, looking at photos and models of spacious, handsome buildings endowed by Northern philanthropists, wondering if demolishing them had been politically motivated—local officials eradicating a source of black pride and symbol of interracial cooperation—or simply a necessity because of structural decay.

As I was getting ready to leave, I discovered a historic marker about Manassas Junction. With its map in my head, I walked to the tracks.

Railroad ties are shorter apart than a full stride, so you have to take mincing steps if you walk on them, or stumble along on the big stones of the roadbed if you don't. I alternated between mincing and stumbling, my awkward strides echoing my attempts to make sense of the issues surrounding Jackson, slavery, and the Civil War.

Slavery was the cause of the war. It was a terrible institution. But for most Confederates, protecting their homes and families was a far more powerful motivator. There was nothing abstract about it— "home" often meant their actual houses. To relate just one incident: When Captain Edward Stevens McCarthy of the Richmond Howitzers was killed by a sharpshooter during the Battle of Cold Harbor in 1864, his "men broke down utterly and sobbed like children." His cousin procured an ambulance and carried the body to the family home in Richmond, about a dozen miles away. After he returned, he sent word to the captain's two brothers. They walked into town, attended the funeral, "and walked out again to their posts the same night."[4]

As a teacher, I dealt with the legacy of slavery, first in the Richmond public schools, then in juvenile prisons. Every day I confronted its consequences, the result of the segregation and poverty into which slavery had evolved. These ranged from the merely sad (an elementary school teacher confiding that most of the inner-city students I took on a field trip had never left their neighborhoods) to the truly horrifying— an incarcerated young man talking about how he was traumatized when he saw his first dead body, a drug dealer splayed over an alley fence, but after he saw another, and another, and another, it didn't even faze him: "I just keep on steppin'."

And here was the junction, the two tracks coming together. It looks like nothing much today, just as it looked like nothing much in 1861. I took some photos with my phone while recalling a quote from historian Bruce Catton: "This war went by a queer script of its own, and it had a way of putting all of its weight down on some utterly unimportant little spot that no one had ever heard of before—Shiloh Church, or Chancellorsville, or some such—and because armies contended for them, those place names became great and terrible."[5] He was writing about Cold Harbor, a nondescript crossroads near where I live northeast of Richmond, but what he said applied equally to

Manassas: just a place where a couple of railroads came together, and where thousands of men died.

I started back to my car, suddenly worried about railroad detectives and Homeland Security—the junction is still an important part of national infrastructure—at the same time thinking I was ridiculously paranoid. The yard crew moving cars with the Norfolk & Southern switch engine paid me absolutely no attention. I was just some old white guy out where he shouldn't be.

What Jackson did at Henry House Hill was inspired. Other units rushed in to stop the Union charge but only slowed the Federals briefly until they were rolled up like the rest. The retreat turned into a rout, and Bee, Bartow, and the others spilled past Jackson and his men on the far side of the hill. There, somewhat protected from Union muskets and artillery, he waited for the Federals to come to him.

After his conference with Jackson, Bee went back to his men: "There stands Jackson like a stone wall! Let us resolve to die here, and we will conquer. Rally behind the Virginians!"

Like so much else about Jackson, the statement is controversial. Some historians say Bee spoke other words. Others contend he spoke out of annoyance rather than admiration: Jackson was anchored like a wall on the field, not coming to his aid. It's impossible to know— Bee was mortally wounded shortly thereafter. The salient point is that Jackson emerged from First Manassas as "Stonewall." And in truth, "the most famous nickname in American military history" is only partially apt. While Jackson could certainly hold a position, he became far more famous as the war went on for moving quickly and quietly, then suddenly striking from a point where he was least expected—more like the snake in the stone wall than the wall itself.

Coming onto the field, Generals Johnston and Beauregard took in the situation. They began reorganizing the confused soldiers they encountered and placing them in line with Jackson. Jackson himself rode slowly and confidently along his line, seemingly unconcerned that he was an easy target for the fire that had most of his men lying "flat as flounders"[6] on the ground. "Steady men, steady," he kept repeating. "All's well."

Among Jackson's many eccentric habits was his tendency to lift an arm into the air. This started at West Point with the belief that one arm was heavier than the other. To remedy it, "he would occasionally raise his arm straight up, as he said, to let the blood run back into his body, and so relieve the excess weight."[7] By the time of the war, the habit seems to have become associated with prayer, the uplifted limb amplifying and focusing his petitions, a broadcast antenna pointing toward heaven.

While talking to artillerist John D. Imboden, Jackson thrust his arm into the air. A moment later he caught a bullet or piece of shrapnel, and brought his bloodied hand down, the middle finger shattered.

"General, you are wounded," exclaimed Imboden.

"Only a scratch, a mere scratch," Jackson said. He wrapped his injured finger in a handkerchief and resumed riding quietly along his line.[8]

Confederate resistance, anchored by Jackson, continued to stiffen. The Southerners were aided by a curious lack of aggressive follow-through from Union general McDowell. For a few vital hours he did almost nothing to cement the victory that he strongly believed was within his grasp.[9]

The fighting raged back and forth. General Bee was mortally wounded. Bartow was wounded slightly and had his horse shot out from under him. Undaunted, he obtained another horse. "Boys, follow me!" he shouted, waving his cap over his head. He was shot again and died moments later in the arms of a fellow officer.

McDowell decided to apply more artillery pressure to Jackson's part of the line. He sent two Union batteries forward to try to fire into the Confederates from the flank. Federal captains James B. Ricketts and Charles Griffin advanced and took up a position close to the

Southerners and dueled with Jackson's artillery. Then Captain Griffin bravely but foolishly moved his guns even closer. James Ewell Brown— "Jeb"—Stuart was nearby. He sent word back to Jackson of their vulnerable proximity.

Jackson reacted with one of his characteristic expressions: "That's good! That's good!" He gave the word for Stuart to attack the battery. Stuart's horsemen charged into the infantry supporting the guns. The Federals broke and ran. Another Southern regiment, the 33rd Virginia, charged the artillery. In this early stage of the war, these Confederates were wearing blue. Confusion bought them time and contributed to the success of their assault. The guns were captured! But the Confederates couldn't hold them. The batteries would be captured and recaptured three times before the fighting was over.

McDowell outnumbered the Confederates two to one on this part of the field. Now he brought his numbers to bear with a massive assault. "Reserve your fire until they come within fifty yards!" Jackson instructed his men. "Then fire and give them the bayonet! And when you charge, yell like furies!"

The Federals crested the hill. Concentrated fire from Jackson's infantry and artillery sent them reeling back. They re-formed, tried again, and failed. A third charge brought them within a few feet of the Confederate line. This was also beaten back.

It was now 3:30 in the afternoon. The Union drive had stalled and stopped. Beauregard ordered a counterattack. Jackson's men spearheaded the assault. Confederates charged forward, "yelling like furies." The first Rebel yell was the soundtrack of a gathering Southern victory. While the fighting would surge back and forth for another hour, the tide had turned. Adding to the momentum, Confederate reinforcements arrived from the Shenandoah Valley on the Manassas Gap Railroad.

It was almost five o'clock when McDowell ordered a retreat. Inexperienced Federal troops did not have the skill for orderly withdrawal. Exhausted, with screaming Southern maniacs bearing down, the Union army's retreat became a rout. Confederate artillery urged the bluecoats along. Soldiers discarded weapons and knapsacks and anything else that would slow them down, then got tangled up with picnicking dignitaries, who were heading back to Washington as fast as they could travel.

The Confederates, equally exhausted and disorganized, did not press their advantage, and so the battle ended.

Jackson rode to a field hospital to get his wounded finger dressed. The surgeons, as usual, recommended amputation. Jackson remounted and rode away. He found Dr. Hunter McGuire, the head of his medical division, who told him he thought the finger could be saved and bound it up.

Jackson's arm was in a sling when he encountered Confederate president Jefferson Davis at Young's Branch, a modest stream near the foot of Henry House Hill. Davis had stood the suspense as long as he could, then took a train from Richmond to see how the battle was going. As he approached, he encountered stragglers who told him the day was lost. When he saw Jackson and other soldiers, he thought they were demoralized troops.

"I am President Davis," he shouted. "All of you who are able, follow me back to the field."

Jackson at first did not understand who it was. Dr. McGuire explained it was the president.

"We have whipped them!" Some say he spoke it to McGuire; others say he shouted it to Davis. "Give me ten thousand men and I will take Washington tomorrow."

Young's Branch wasn't very formidable when I visited in the summer of 2015. I crossed on a couple of flat rocks without getting my feet wet. There was an interesting wayside exhibit about Jackson, the meeting with Davis, and the 10,000 men with whom he was going to take D.C. The sound of the stream was a pleasant counterweight to thoughts of Jackson's aggression, only one part of his multifaceted character. I mulled over some of the relevant points as I continued on a path that traced Jackson's route to the military crest of Henry House Hill.

Jackson's piety was the stuff of legend, but his Christian principles did not keep him from killing Yankees or executing his own men. He'd started an African American Sunday school in Lexington, defying public opinion and Virginia law to teach slaves to read so they could study the Bible, yet he went to war to preserve the institution of slavery. An eccentric and ineffective professor at the Virginia Military Institute—"perhaps the worst teacher in the history of the institution," according to a talk I once heard by biographer James I. Robertson Jr.—he was suddenly the best of the best when war came, mounting astonishing campaigns that are still studied today. Another factor of his fascinating legacy: his synergistic relationship with Robert E. Lee. Their partnership was greater than the sum of its parts, reversing, for a time, the North's vast advantages in men and matériel. When Jackson died, Lee lost far more than a hard-hitting corps commander. His death presaged the death of the Confederacy.

I rested on a bench beside a swampy stream. Four cross-country girls ran past, their long, easy stride a mockery of my plodding. One of them was Asian, and I meditated briefly about what Jackson would make of our present-day diversity. As a profound student of the Bible, hundreds of scriptural exhortations against injustice would have seeped into his soul. In addition, he would have been very aware of the implications of stories like the one in Acts 8 that reveal that the first non-Jewish convert to Christianity was an Ethiopian.

A young black man ran past, shirt off, sweat streaming. At the height of fitness and getting fitter: A backpack filled with weights bounced and clanked as he ran. I gave him a fist up in sincere admiration. He returned my salute, albeit halfheartedly, and continued up the path.

Only a small percentage of battlefield visitors come to study the war. The National Park Service preserves over five thousand acres of land associated with First and Second Manassas. It's a rural oasis amid suburban sprawl, where miles of town houses, relentless traffic, and indistinguishable big-box malls create a hellish Nowhere that seems to go on forever. For many in the surrounding burbs, the history park is one of the only places to get away.

A latter-day beatnik with a Maynard G. Krebs goatee and a narrow-brimmed, jauntily feathered straw hat strolled past, shortly followed by a middle-aged man in a Walking Dead T-shirt with a yellow Lab on a leash. They exhausted my interest in present-day humanity.

I've had a deep and abiding interest in the Civil War in general and Jackson in particular since the mid-1980s. My mother died around the same time as my grandparents, along with several others who were close, and a huge void opened in my life. At the time, I was teaching a volunteer creative writing class at the old Virginia State Penitentiary in Richmond. The class met in the library, and during a break I idly picked Bruce Catton's *A Stillness at Appomattox* off the shelf. I opened it at random and started reading about Totopotomoy Creek, which is just down the hill from my house in Hanover County.

"Hey, can I borrow this?" I asked an inmate, Evans Hopkins, a former Black Panther with whom I am still friends. "It's talking about my neighborhood."

"You take that book," he said.

So, a stolen book from the penitentiary led me into the Civil War. I devoured *Stillness*, which was the third volume in a set, went back and read the first two, then read *Stillness* again. Catton writes from a Northern perspective. My interest deepened when I found books that took a Southern point of view. Everything I picked up seemed to be about places I already knew well or could easily visit. Jackson was intertwined with almost all of them.

He camped just over a mile away after he marched down the road in front of my house in 1862. His performance at the subsequent

Seven Days Battles was uncharacteristically mediocre, one of the first of a host of intriguing anomalies that, along with the local connection, kept me returning again and again to studies of his life. Years later, when I wrote a handful of articles for the *New York Times* "Disunion" series, three of the four were about Jackson. A New York editor, Sean Desmond, saw them and urged me to write this book. I jumped at the chance. I was, of course, eager to be published, but even more eager to undertake a project that would allow me to dig deeper into an interest that had consumed me for three decades.

I wanted to understand what drew me to Jackson, to the Civil War, and to the past; I wanted to understand Stonewall, his contradictions, secretiveness, and incredible fighting ability. From the beginning I knew I would need to do more than research him on the page. I would also go where he'd lived and fought. "In great deeds, something abides," said Joshua Lawrence Chamberlain. "On great fields, something stays." Ecumenically taking my cue from that great Yankee general, I would go to those great fields to try and find that something. I would, as he said later, "ponder and dream" in those places where "spirits linger...the vision place of souls."

Chamberlain's 1888 speech dedicating the 20th Maine monuments at Gettysburg is probably history's most eloquent assertion of the importance of battlefields. A less mystical version of the truism states that "you can't know the battle unless you walk the ground." Visiting and revisiting the sites is absolutely essential to understanding what happened there. What I didn't realize when I started was how much of the present gathers around these places. I would learn as much about modern America as I would about the past; as much about myself as I did about Jackson. And, of course, at the end, I would be left with more questions than when I started.

CHAPTER 2

After the Battle

The heavens weep over every bloody battlefield,"[1] wrote Jackson's youngest staff member, Henry Kyd Douglas. First Manassas was no exception. That night soldiers wandered the field in the rain looking for fallen comrades. For most, it was their first exposure to the grim aftermath of battle. Lanterns revealed mangled corpses whose ghastly contortions did not protect them from looting. Some of the wounded begged for water. Others cried, cursed, or screamed. It was a scene that would be repeated, with minor variations, throughout the war.

Rain continued the following day. The dead were buried in the mud. It was Monday, Jackson's letter-writing day. It would take more than a major battle to disrupt his routine. The pious Jackson would not write or even read personal letters on Sundays. He even disliked the thought of them being in transit on the Lord's Day, and therefore timed his correspondence accordingly. In his tent in the rain, nursing his wounded finger, he wrote his beloved wife, Anna, as well as his Lexington pastor, Dr. William S. White.

Both letters reveal the inner man. To Anna, he wrote that he knew exactly what he had done and exactly what he deserved, even though recognition for him was anything but universal at the time: "Whilst great credit is due to other parts of our gallant army, God made my brigade more instrumental than any other in repulsing the main attack. This is for your information only—say nothing about it. Let others speak praise, not myself."[2]

Jackson could be forgiven a healthy dose of ego—albeit masked—at this point in his career. He had spent a decade at VMI as a teacher, a profession for which he had no gifts. Then suddenly, with the war, he came into his own: commanding, organizing, fighting. He was world-class, and must have known it. Everyone would know it as the war went on.

The letter to Pastor White arrived when the entire South was in a fever to learn details of the battle. "Now we shall know all the facts!" proclaimed Dr. White to the crowd at the post office when he recognized Jackson's handwriting. "My dear pastor," he read. "In my tent last night, after a fatiguing day's service, I remembered that I had failed to send you my contribution for our colored Sunday school. Enclosed you will find a check..."

That was it, the "fatiguing day's service" the only mention of the battle.

A terrible teacher, but a pillar of his church and a man whose inner life was as rich as his public persona was one-dimensional, Jackson must have felt the power of his transformation, his meteoric rise, and the sudden certainty that he had finally found his calling and was excellent at it. Alone in his tent, rain pattering on the canvas—we can easily imagine the religious part of his personality struggling to integrate with the power surging through him.

Jackson owned six slaves. Two of them had asked him to buy them. A third was given to him by "an aged widow....Emma was a four-year-old orphan with some degree of learning disability." The others were wedding presents. Wrote S. C. Gwynne, "Jackson's relationships with his own slaves illustrate the relative complexity of a system that was often seen by Northerners in the stark terms portrayed in Harriet Beecher Stowe's 1852 book *Uncle Tom's Cabin*."[3] Jackson's detractors would have trouble fitting him into the Simon Legree mold.

"Jackson neither apologized for nor spoke in favor of the practice of slavery," wrote James I. Robertson. "He probably opposed the institution."[4]

⊂══▶

I followed the path out of the woods and crossed a grassy field, trying to imagine Jackson and his men deploying amid whizzing musket balls and exploding shells. An arc of artillery pieces approximated the spacing and position of his cannon. Their barrels were hot from the sun. A bluebird perched on the end of one like a gunsight.

I continued walking. Suddenly JACKSON pierced the horizon, the bronze statue rising out of the ground as I walked up the hill. Larger than life, on a ten-foot pedestal, he's the focal point of this part of the park and an active mystery. JACKSON—statuary inscriptions are inevitably all caps—doesn't look like Jackson. Hand on hip, cape billowing, he theatrically faces the long-vanished foe. His uniform barely contains the bulge of his muscles. Even his horse, Little Sorrel, looks like he's been lifting weights.

Joining the crowd around the pedestal I read: THERE STANDS JACKSON LIKE A STONE WALL. A kid giggled at his discovery that the horse was anatomically correct. Tourists took cell phone shots from all angles. A war bore rehashed the controversy of exactly what General Bee meant: Was Jackson heroically immovable under fire, or like a stone wall in his refusal to help?

Sculpted at the end of the Depression, with World War II looming on the horizon, the statue resembles Superman, who had just appeared in Action Comics #1. A hero for that time—each generation creates the heroes it needs—JACKSON looks like he could take on the Axis as he had the Yankees, then clean up the economic mess for good measure. Even more disturbing, he bears a strong resemblance to the grandiose heroes of pre–World War II Nazi and Soviet propaganda art.[5] I heard later that "Stonewall on steroids" was a characterization current among the rangers.

It was a while after I visited when I was saddened to read that on

October 4, 2017, Manassas's Jackson statue was vandalized. According to a Fredericksburg.com post for that day: "White paint was splashed on the granite base of the monument and the word 'Dead!' was added in gold spray paint."

The Confederacy makes a spectacularly easy target. Everyone who fought for it has been dead since the middle of the last century.

I walked to the visitor center, refilled my water bottle, then walked back past JACKSON and through the artillery line into the woods. There were hardly any pedestrians now and I alternated between thinking of the past and dreading the two-plus-hour drive home. I startled a couple of deer feeding in an adjacent field, then became aware that I'd been hearing traffic on nearby interstate Route 66 for some time. A sign for "Portici" pointed me toward a field on my left.

Portici was named for a town precariously located at the foot of Mount Vesuvius in Italy. Portici the town burned during an eruption in 1631. Portici the house burned several times before the war and the owner whimsically named it for the town. It was Joseph E. Johnston's headquarters during the battle, a hospital afterward, and burned for a final time in 1862.[6] A foundation remains today, accompanied by a National Park Service interpretive sign. The surrounding fields were being cut the day of my visit.

Captain James B. Ricketts led one of the artillery units mauled by Jackson on Henry House Hill. Wounded in the thigh, he was brought to Portici after the battle. His wife, Fannie, came from Washington to help him a few days later. "Oh, nothing, no words can describe the horrors around me," she wrote in her journal. "Two men dead and covered with blood are carried down the stairs as I waited to let them pass. On the table in the open hall a man was undergoing amputation of the leg, at the foot of the stairs two bloody legs lay and through it all I went to my husband." She nursed him there, and later in Richmond where he was sent as a prisoner until he was exchanged.[7]

Ricketts, just one bit of collateral damage from Jackson's success;

Portici, scene of horror and heroism, just one of the way stations along his route to the battlefield.

I was called back to the present by watching birds—swifts, I think—following the mower for the insects, chirping ecstatically as they flew. A herd of Harleys rumbled by on I-66. The war seemed long ago and far away as I walked back to the tiny parking lot, got in my car, and headed home.

CHAPTER 3

All Things Work Together

Jackson's reputation increased slowly after Manassas. At first, he had been part of the general glow of Southern victory, his pivotal role in the battle known to only a few. As the summer wore on, however, he was talked and written about more and more. The seed of what would become his legendary status grew. A big part of it had to be the nickname. No professional PR team could have created a better one.

His letters to his wife reveal the struggle between his humanity and his ideals. On the one hand, he knew exactly what he had done militarily and the part he had played in the victory. Opposing that was a Christian humility that, while perhaps innate, had been nurtured by years of prayer, meditation, and practice. Jackson had an ego, but he disciplined it even more sternly than he did his soldiers. "Let others speak praise, not myself," he had written Anna in an already alluded to letter immediately after the battle. He enlarged on that in a letter on August 5:

> It is not to be expected that I should receive the credit that Gen. Beauregard or Johnston would, because I am under them, but I am thankful to an ever kind Heavenly Father that He makes me content to await His own good time & pleasure for commendation, knowing that "all things work together for any good."[1]

The verse he alludes to at the end is from the eighth chapter of Romans: "And we know that all things work together for good to them that love God, to them who are the called according to his purpose."

The verse was Jackson's favorite. That he could believe it is both amazing and admirable. Even the short list of his personal tragedies is daunting: His father and a sister died of typhoid fever when he was two; his mother, following a difficult childbirth, when he was six. He lost his brother Warren at seventeen. For almost all of his life he was very close to his sister, Laura. The war drove a wedge between them and they never saw each other after its outbreak. A staunch Unionist, she expressed little remorse following his death in 1863.

Jackson's first child was stillborn; his first wife died after the birth. When he married again, the couple's first child, a daughter, lived less than a month. Personally, he suffered from a multitude of ailments—some imaginary, many real—throughout most of his life. Add to all this the not inconsiderable humiliation of a decade spent teaching at the Virginia Military Institute as "Tom Fool" Jackson, the butt of classroom jokes and the object of more than a few students' disrespect. While cadets had mixed feelings about him—biographer Robertson avers that "the number of opinions [were] equal to those that expressed them"—his classroom performance was so notorious that some alumni actually tried to have him removed in 1856.[2]

Jackson had to have been conscious of his ineptitude as a teacher, just as he was conscious, after Manassas, of his military prowess. Recognition would come in God's time—and if it didn't, he would find a way to accept it the way he had come to accept all the other trials of his life.

One way he always coped was through hard work. After his parents died, he lived with his uncle Cummins Jackson on a large farm. Although loving, the relationship was mainly one of benign neglect. Nor was there much opportunity for the ambitious Jackson in the mountainous area around Clarksburg in what was then western Virginia.

In 1842, when Jackson was eighteen, he was able to obtain a congressional appointment to the U.S. Military Academy at West Point. Country schooling had so ill prepared him that he barely passed the entrance examination. He started near the bottom of his class in all subjects. With what one fellow student described as a "terrible earnestness," he studied incredibly hard, working by firelight most nights long after lights-out at 10 p.m.

At that time, West Point had "one of the most demanding academic programs in America." His fellow cadets in the Class of 1846 were "some of the brightest and cultured young men in the nation." They included George B. McClellan and George Pickett. A. P. Hill and Ambrose Burnside graduated the following year. U. S. Grant's last year was Jackson's first.

In a conversation following Jackson's death, Grant praised his "indomitable energy" as a student, saying that Jackson was "a sterling, manly cadet [who] enjoyed the respect of everyone who knew him."[3] Respected, but also an occasional object of fun. One account has him wrestling with a difficult mathematical problem at the blackboard, sweating so profusely that "he threatened to flood the entire room."

Cadets marveled at his general oddness. Jackson suffered from dyspepsia, the Victorian term for indigestion. Many of his most famous eccentricities were dietary. He seems to have subsisted for long periods on stale bread and water or buttermilk. In later years, if invited to a dinner party, he would sometimes bring his own stale bread, to the distress of the hostess.[4]

Jackson's class rank rose slowly as his knowledge grew. At the end of four years, he was seventeenth out of fifty-nine. "More than one observer was convinced that had the West Point curriculum lasted another year, the pitifully prepared mountain boy of 1842 would have graduated at the top of his class."[5]

The aftermath of the battle was also a time of intense work. Unlike many Southerners, Jackson did not see First Manassas as decisive. It was indeed a Southern victory, but the fruits of victory did not come—most importantly the European recognition that the Confederates needed so desperately. Received wisdom on the topic said that Europe, England in particular, depended on the South. Textiles drove their economy. Without Southern cotton, the mills would stand idle. Cotton was King.

Not exactly. Southerners had overplanted the kingly crop, so European warehouses were full and the mills rolled on. In any case, for Europe, the moral issue of slavery trumped the economic loss, which actually occurred later, in 1862, when the surplus was depleted and the Union blockade became effective.[6]

Confederates also thought the battle had proved the superiority of Southern arms. Hadn't the cowardly Yankees turned and fled?

They had; but until that point they had fought bravely and well, almost winning the battle early on. Demoralized but resolved, they weren't going away. Volunteers poured in, and Lincoln appointed a new commander, the youthful and dynamic George B. McClellan, who showed real promise of being able to turn things around.

Far more than others, Jackson was preparing for a long, hard struggle and a different type of war. He drilled his men relentlessly and enforced strict discipline. Furloughs were granted liberally in most of the Southern armies. Not under Jackson. When Colonel Kenton Harper learned that his wife was gravely ill, he applied to Jackson for emergency leave to return home to Staunton. His request was denied. The desperate Harper appealed to Jackson personally.

"General, General, my wife is dying! I must see her!"

Relating the anecdote, Jackson staff officer Henry Kyd Douglas said, "A wave of sadness and grief passed over the face of the General but for a moment, and then in cold, merciless tones he replied, 'Man, man, do you love your wife more than your country?' and turned away."

Harper resigned from the army. His wife died before he could return home. Although Jackson biographer Robertson correctly classifies the story as "hearsay"—Douglas wasn't present—it has the ring of truth, particularly Jackson's moment of soul-searching before his pronouncement. Douglas concluded: "The wife died and that soldier never forgave Stonewall Jackson."[7]

One wonders if he ever forgave himself. This is the essence of Jackson: It's easy to penetrate beyond the stern exterior, but which of the layers beneath contain the real man? Or do they all? The more you study him, the more interesting he becomes. Even a cursory acquaintance gives the lie to any simple analysis, be it "Christian warrior," "military genius," or filmmaker Ken Burns's famous, overtly hostile "pious, blue-eyed killer."

Jackson is far more complex than any sound bite.

While Jackson could not go to see his own wife, Anna, she could come to him, for a ten-day visit in mid-September. Traveling by train, Anna was rightfully apprehensive to be the lone woman among masses of soldiers, and was relieved when a family friend, Captain J. Harvey White, happened up the aisle. Because of a miscommunication, Jackson did not meet her when she arrived at Manassas, and she continued on to Fairfax Station, which she found "converted into a vast military camp, the place teeming with soldiers, and the only house visible from the depot being used as a hospital."

They spent the night on the train, soldiers coming through the car to gawk at the novel sight of a female, until Captain White locked the doors. The next day Anna stayed for a while in a room that Captain White procured for her in the hospital. She said it was "dismal… the one small window in the room revealing the spectacle of a number of soldiers in the yard, busily engaged in [her emphasis] *making coffins for their dead comrades.*"

When Jackson arrived they attended—surprise!—a church service, which Anna declared "delightful." Indeed, the whole visit was suffused with the rosy glow appropriate to a reunited loving couple who had only been married slightly more than four years. Anna described it using words like "grand," "splendid," and "beautiful." Her mood even transcended a tour of the battlefield itself: "Much of the debris of the conflict still remained: the old Henry house was riddled with shot and shell; the carcasses of the horses, and even some of the bones of the poor human victims, were to be seen."[8]

The visit ended abruptly when the army was ordered closer to Washington. Jackson continued to pour out his heart to Anna in frequent letters. Official duties continued; clerical visitors were a welcome distraction. When the editor and Presbyterian minister Dr. William Brown came to visit, the religious conversations continued into the night when he "shared a blanket" with Stonewall. (Soldiers of the period frequently slept together for warmth, and, possessing different mores, were unselfconscious about it.)

Brown and Jackson were deep in conversation about the men and how to promote religion among them when the general suddenly broke off and started talking about himself. He confided that he often went out alone in the woods to pray: "I find that it greatly helps me in fixing my mind and quickening my devotions to give articulate utterance to my prayers, and hence I am in the habit of going off into the woods, where I can be alone and speak audibly to myself the prayers I would pour out to my God." He added that he kept his eyes open to keep from running into trees and stumps: "Upon investigating the matter I do not find that the Scriptures require us to close our eyes in prayer."

Jackson concluded that this religious talk therapy was "delightful and profitable." Overall, he spent a tremendous, almost monastic amount of time in prayer—in his tent at night, particularly before a battle; on the battlefield itself, where it was often remarked upon by soldiers; and throughout the day. "Whenever I take a draught of water I always pause, as my palate receives the refreshment, to lift up my heart to God in thanks and prayer for the water of life."[9]

Jackson had another similar and remarkable habit. As a professor, he spent an hour each night "in perfect abstraction," with his chair turned to the wall. Anna asserted that he was reviewing his lessons for the next day's teaching,[10] but the practice seems far more meditative than academic. He continued it, with slight variations, during the war.

The night before the Battle of Front Royal, in the Valley Campaign, General Richard Taylor wrote that he "watched Jackson. For hours he sat silent and motionless, with eyes fixed on the fire."[11]

The time spent in quiet contemplation—and active introspection—added to the stability and strength of Jackson's character. In prayer, aligning himself with the Christian tradition, he became part of a larger, sustaining whole, the "cloud of witnesses" mentioned in the twelfth chapter of Hebrews in the New Testament. Jackson lived in a religious age, and we in a secular, but there is much for even present-day nonbelievers to learn from him about coping with loss and finding a source of strength outside oneself.

Unlike Jackson, I am a haphazard believer. The certainty fades from my faith in times of crisis. I remember vividly how, when my mother died, I could see nothing beyond this life but a huge void. Holding her hand in the hospital, I thought that if I let go she would just drop off into the darkness.

Jackson wasn't afraid of death, his own or that of others. He was hurt terribly by his mother's loss, and that of his first wife, children, and others, but he transcended grief through religion. I have had glimpses of that kind of faith, but it's not something I live with day to day. His steadfast convictions are one of the main reasons I'm attracted to him.

Maybe I'd get something of Jackson's mojo if I immersed myself in his legacy.

Jackson's promotion finally came. In November 1861, he was made a major general and put in command of the western part of Virginia. It was a mixed blessing. He would be in charge of a huge area—six thousand square miles, the left flank of the Confederacy, threatened by Yankees from across the Potomac—but hardly any soldiers to defend it. Richmond must have thought him capable or they would not have given him the assignment. The bonus for the higher-ups was that it got an overly aggressive commander away from the capital. Jackson had made no secret of his impatience with Davis's wait-and-see-what-the-Europeans-will-do strategy. He had wanted to attack Washington in the aftermath of Manassas. Now he would have plenty to do in the Valley and be far enough away so as not to embarrass the administration.

To say that he had bonded with his men was an understatement. He was Stonewall. They were the Stonewall Brigade. Now it was time for him to say farewell to his brigade command. He spoke individually to groups of officers. Then it was time to address the troops. Mounted on Little Sorrel, he gave a moving speech, which ended:

> In the Army of the Shenandoah you were the First Brigade; in the Army of the Potomac you were the First Brigade; in the second corps of this army you are the First Brigade; you are the first brigade in the affections of your General; and I hope by your future deeds and bearing you will be handed down to posterity as the First Brigade in our second War of Independence. Farewell![12]

Many soldiers cried, and many reported that Jackson had tears in his eyes as well. His men cheered him with the Rebel yell as he rode away.

CHAPTER 4

Fearful Odds

Jackson's emotional farewell occurred on November 4. On November 5, the Stonewall Brigade was ordered to follow him to Winchester, the town that would be his headquarters in the Shenandoah Valley. They got the news November 7. Many of them expressed their happiness by getting spectacularly drunk en route, and the brigade dribbled intoxicated soldiers all the way to the Valley.

Jackson, with two aides, had traveled by train to Strasburg, where they disembarked, obtained horses, and rode what must have been an exhausting eighteen miles to Winchester, arriving at the Taylor Hotel around midnight.

The next day, Jackson quickly discovered that his work would be hindered by hordes of curious townspeople. He was grateful when a wounded officer, Colonel Lewis T. Moore, convalescing in Richmond, offered his house for a headquarters. "Alta Vista" was off the beaten path, close to Winchester's largest Confederate encampment, and only six blocks from the Kent Street Presbyterian Church. Jackson's office was on the first floor, his bedroom on the second.

Today, the Taylor Hotel is freshly renovated, consisting mostly of condos, with the exterior looking pretty much as it did during the war. A three-story brick building, it has a three-story porch along the front with railings and imposing white pillars, an Old South setting evocative of hoop-skirted belles and mint juleps—or, in Jackson's case, glasses of water. Plans on getting a peek at the inside were quashed when my wife, Catherine, and I discovered that the building's restaurant had recently closed. We contented ourselves with reading a wayside exhibit and staring up the windows of Number 23, the corner room where Jackson and his aides spent the night.

The Stonewall Jackson's Headquarters Museum—the Moore House—less than a half a mile away, was more welcoming. We visited several times with a different docent for each visit. The most personable was Joanne Roulette. Her interest in the Civil War started with visits to her grandfather's farm, which was part of the Antietam battlefield. Enthusiastic and vivacious, she is an accomplished visual artist who also makes period clothing for herself and the other interpreters.

Jackson spent much of the winter of 1861–62 at the Moore House. It was from here that he launched his campaign into northwestern Virginia, capturing Bath—now Berkeley Springs, West Virginia—and Romney. By no means a Southern mansion, the Moore House is a rather comfortable upper-middle-class Victorian home. Full of relics, evocative and moving, it is a place where an active imagination can slip easily into the past.

The desk on which Jackson worked is in his downstairs office, his prayer desk in another first-floor room. Touring, I touched both surreptitiously, but received no psychic jolt. Roulette made much of the wallpaper in his office, which Jackson described in a letter to Anna as "elegant gilt paper. I don't remember to have ever seen a more beautiful papering." Actress Mary Tyler Moore, a descendant of Colonel Moore, contributed funds to have the house turned into a museum. She had the paper, depicting colorful twining vines and leaves, replicated by a firm in California. Today the re-creation adorns the office walls.

Roulette departed from the Jackson script to tell a story about Mary Greenhow Lee, one of the "Devil Diarists of Winchester"—ardent secessionists who plagued Union soldiers with attitude and pen. Mary Lee defiantly flew the Confederate flag during one of Winchester's many Union occupations. She was finally prevailed upon to take it down. The Yankees afterward searched her house, looking for the flag.

"The flag could not be found," Roulette told our group. "Do you know why?" She raised her skirt to show the battle flag sewn to her petticoat, provoking first gasps and then laughter from the people on the tour.

There's a lighthearted quality to the war at this point. It was still something of a lark, the prevailing mood not so different from that of the Union soldiers who broke ranks on their way to Manassas for berry picking. The shocking casualties from Shiloh in the west and the Seven Days and other bloody 1862 battles in the east were well over the horizon. The actors were somewhat different too: In the South, generals P. G. T. Beauregard and Joseph E. Johnston remained at their zenith. In the North, Lincoln had promoted McClellan to overall command after his successes in southwestern Virginia. Sent to reclaim that lost territory, Robert E. Lee fought the Battle of Cheat Mountain in September, an action that, even according to laudatory biographer Douglas Freeman, ended "ingloriously."[1] In Lee's favor, it has been said that the weather was so bad that no one could have succeeded. One soldier claimed that it rained "thirty-*two* days in August."[2]

One of Jackson's big problems was keeping his soldiers, particularly the Stonewalls, out of Winchester. Whiskey and pretty girls, not to mention friends and family—the town was home to some of the men—were among the attractions. There were lots of comic episodes as the soldiers tried and succeeded in eluding Winchester's militia guards.

Private John Opie of the 5th Virginia tells of learning the password to leave the camp by eavesdropping on the sentinels. Chalk-drawn epaulets couldn't be distinguished from the real thing in the dark; the filched officer's saber was the genuine article: "and there was the full-fledged lieutenant—sword, shoulder-straps, and countersign. The objective point, Winchester; the attraction, the beautiful girls of the town."[3]

He relates another tale about a time when his officers obtained several kegs of "fine old rye" and didn't offer to share with the enlisted men. Opie and his cohorts pulled some pegs up from the back of the officers' tent, rolled out a keg, filled some buckets, and had their own party. They made a campfire "that resembled Vesuvius, and raised Cain; but, as the officers of the regiment were engaged in the same meritorious business, we escaped punishment."[4]

A much more serious business involved a drunken soldier, James A. Miller, who shot his company commander, Captain John Henderson. The bullet shattered Henderson's elbow and permanently paralyzed his right arm. A court-martial sentenced Miller to death by firing squad.

There were many calls for leniency. Among the hardest to resist for Jackson must have been the visit from Dr. James R. Graham, the minister of Kent Street Presbyterian Church, with whom he had already formed a bond, and Colonel John Preston, his chief of staff and an old Lexington friend and VMI colleague—actually the main founder of the institution. Dr. Graham wrote later that Miller's assertion that he would rather "die as a soldier on the field of battle, and not as a dog at the muzzles of the muskets of his own comrades" deeply moved the general: "His voice quivered and there was moisture in his eyes."

But Jackson let the sentence stand. "In this war we contend against fearful odds," Graham has him saying. "Our soldiers are brave, but undisciplined; and discipline is essential to success. In an army, resistance to lawful authority is a grave offense. To pardon it would be to encourage insubordination and ruin our cause."

While Jackson was no mean wordsmith, he always grew more eloquent when quoted by the Presbyterian ministers with whom he was invariably surrounded. Still, the sentiments, if not the exact words, were certainly his.

The story has a tragic coda. At Jackson's suggestion, a request for clemency was sent to Jefferson Davis, who pardoned Miller. Word didn't get back to Winchester, however, because the courier got drunk and didn't arrive until after the execution. No one blamed Jackson for Miller's death, but they almost killed the messenger when he finally arrived from Richmond: "He was met by a committee of infuriated citizens and warned to leave town immediately."[5]

Jackson was thinking of attacking Romney almost as soon as he arrived in Winchester.[6] Some 4,000 Union soldiers were stationed there, on the border between the United and Confederate states, only a little more than forty miles away. They were harassing the local secessionists— fewer in number than the Confederates liked to think—and protecting the strategic Baltimore and Ohio Railroad, which Jackson wanted to wreck. Worst of all, Federal soldiers in Romney could unite with others on the border, then maneuver southeast to threaten Winchester, which was not only his headquarters but the strategic key to the lower Shenandoah Valley. (The northern part of the Valley is counterintuitively called the "lower" because the Shenandoah River flows north.)

On November 20, Jackson sent a plan for what came to be called "The Romney Expedition" up the chain of command. He noted that it would involve the sacrifice "of much personal comfort" for his soldiers. That would turn out to be one of the great understatements of the war.

Richmond gave the plan lukewarm approval. One of its provisions involved General W. W. Loring bringing his 5,000 soldiers from the southwest mountains to join Jackson. Loring was a career army officer who had lost an arm and been brevetted for bravery in Mexico. His support for the project was as reluctant as Richmond's, and his participation was correspondingly lackluster. It took most of December for him to move his soldiers the two hundred-plus miles to Winchester. In the meantime, Jackson received word that the Federals in Romney had been reinforced, their numbers now 11,000.[7]

Anna arrived in early December, a welcome distraction from Jackson's frustration with the slow start of his offensive. Jackson had already become close friends with Reverend James Graham, the Presbyterian minister who lived only two houses away. Jackson and Anna would shortly move in with the Grahams, an arrangement Anna found especially congenial. "With the exception of the Romney expedition," she wrote, "there was nothing to mar the perfect enjoyment of those three blessed months."[8]

The expedition itself finally creaked into motion on New Year's Day. The morning was mild, in the fifties, so soldiers left their overcoats for the supply train wagons. These would be sorely missed as the temperature dropped through the afternoon. Confirming the cynical military maxim "Hurry up and wait," some units started ten hours behind schedule. The strung-out column covered only eight miles, camping at Pughtown, which is now Gainesboro. With their wagons miles behind, soldiers spoon-slept without cover on the frozen ground.

Route 522 travels northwest out of Winchester. Catherine and I bought gas at Stonewall Plaza, then drove a few miles to explore Gainesboro, an unincorporated cluster of houses off the main road. A dearth of commemorative signage signaled our approach to Union territory— in the Valley and the Tidewater, a Jacksonian sneeze rates a historic marker. In Clarksburg, West Virginia, the site of the house where he was born gets only a small plaque. There is a fine equestrian statue of him in full gallop in front of the courthouse. Hard-looking women smoke heavily nearby, awaiting the outcome of their trials.

Some soldiers must have slept in the hollows of the still-active Back Creek Quaker Cemetery overlooking Gainsboro. I parked, opened the gate, and walked past a mixture of well-tended markers and neglected tombstones leaning drunkenly this way and that. Southern heritage was invoked by a Confederate battle flag etched into the tombstone of a young man who had died at twenty in 2014. His family's votive offerings included his Mello Yello camo cap, a shotgun shell, and a picture of him with a trophy buck. Saddest of all was the pumpkin inscribed with a Sharpie: "We miss you Daddy," followed by the names of his two children. The second time I visited was right after Christmas when I noted the addition of a big jingle bell.

I couldn't help but think of young Confederate soldiers, many of whom had left wives and children at home and would die an equally untimely death.

Nearby was a stone with an incised banjo and guitar. A young man wrote about his grandfather: "I miss the smell of sawdust and the sound of van wheels on a dirt road, guitar picking beside a camp fire, your jokes and stories...I can never look at a river without thinking of you fishing...you had a creative, gentle spirit...the days I spent with you were the best in my life."

Part of the old man's arrowhead collection was also left by the marker. Itching to take one, I restrained myself, knowing it would be disrespectful. I did take photographs with my phone. The one of the grandfather's stone shows my reflection on the inscription. The epitaph reminded me of how close I was to my own grandfather. My interest in history has a lot to do with him, the relics I found in his fields and the stories he told when we were together. I meditated for a moment on how the richness of that relationship nurtured me—in contrast with the orphaned Jackson, who lacked not only doting grandparents, but mother and father as well. It's easy to see how their absence made him especially value home and family—"He was intensely fond of his home," wrote Anna, "and it was there he found his greatest happiness"[9]—but I also wondered if that early pain of loss was responsible, in a compensatory way, for his incredible willpower, self-control, and ambition.

It snowed on the soldiers the second day of the march. The temperature didn't rise above twenty-seven degrees.[10] Wagons carrying the food, blankets, and discarded overcoats were far behind. Wind blew snow into the men's faces. They suffered greatly, making only seven miles before going into another cheerless camp at Unger's Store.

Loring halted a few miles short of the assigned bivouac. Jackson was furious and ordered him to bring his men forward in the darkness. Furious himself, Loring obeyed, but not before bad-mouthing Jackson in front of his troops: "By God, sir, this is the damndest outrage ever perpetuated in the annals of history, keeping my men out here in the cold without food!"[11]

Sam R. Watkins, who fought under Loring, is the author of *Co. Aytch*, one of my favorite Civil War books. Wrote Watkins: "It was the coldest winter known to the oldest inhabitant of these regions. As [the soldiers] walked along icicles hung from their clothing, guns, and knapsacks; many were badly frost bitten, and I heard of many freezing to death along the road side. My feet peeled off like a peeled onion on that march, and I have not recovered from its effects until this day."[12]

The snow on the road was packed into a solid sheet of ice. Men and horses slipped, slid, and fell. Riders were injured; wagons and artillery stalled and stopped. Jackson got points for dismounting and personally putting his shoulder to the wheels. That was practically the only goodwill he accrued. Angry, disgruntled men muttered "Tom Fool Jackson" and worse whenever he passed.

He continued to have problems getting soldiers moving when he needed to. Before Romney, he wanted to attack the Union-held town of Bath. On the morning of January 3, with the temperature at seventeen degrees, he ordered the men to grab some rations from the supply wagons and get on the move. Richard Garnett, who had assumed command of the Stonewalls after Jackson, told the men to take the time to make fires and actually cook their food.

Riding back along the column, Jackson confronted him, demanding a reason for the delay.

"I have halted to let the men cook their rations," Garnett explained.

"There is no time for that."

"But it is impossible for the men to march further without them."

"*I* never found anything impossible with this brigade."[13]

To attack Bath, the soldiers needed to cover some sixteen miles on

January 3. They didn't. In late afternoon, advance troops encountered Union pickets about three miles outside of town. There was a minor firefight. The element of surprise—and the column's momentum—was lost.

Colonel William Gilham, former commandant of VMI, advanced his men tentatively toward the enemy. Jackson ordered him to get moving, but before he could make an attack, Loring ordered Gilham to halt for the night.

This led to another testy confrontation between Jackson and Loring. "If you should be killed," complained the latter, "I would find myself in command of an army of the object of whose movements I know nothing!" Jackson hadn't told Loring—or anyone else, for that matter—where he was going. He didn't now, and rode away without imparting anything further.

Three inches of snow fell on the sleeping soldiers that night. After digging themselves out the next morning, they were finally in a position to attack. Loring and the Stonewall Brigade were to go straight into Bath. The militia was to swing around and attack from the west.

When the militia encountered the Federals, both sides fired a volley, then fled in opposite directions.

Gilham, leading Loring's advance, stalled when he encountered rearguard resistance a half mile outside of town. He halted, did nothing, and didn't tell Jackson he had stopped.

Time passed. Finally, in midafternoon, Jackson himself rode forward to lead the charge. John H. Worsham was one of the soldiers Jackson gathered up and led into the town: "He ordered us to double quick, and we soon ran. This was a grand sight.... When we reached the top of a ridge, we could see the Yankees disappearing at the far end of a field, going toward the Potomac River."[14]

Almost the entire Federal garrison escaped because of the delayed and disorganized assault. Confederates looted what the Yankees didn't carry away. Later, Jackson ordered up his artillery and shelled the Federals in Hancock, a few miles from Bath on the Maryland side of the river.

CHAPTER 5

Icicles of Blood

Many members of the Stonewall Brigade spent the night in Strother's Berkeley Hotel, a favored treatment that did not go unnoticed by Loring's men, who gathered around outdoor fires, struggling not to freeze to death as temperatures dropped to eight degrees. It snowed again, the flakes "as large as goose eggs," according to Sam Watkins. He tells a macabre story about going to relieve an outpost in the middle of the night:

> There were just eleven of them. Some were sitting down and some were laying down; but each and every one was as cold and as hard frozen as the icicles that hung from their hands and faces and clothing—dead! Two of them, a little in advance of the others, were standing with their guns in their hands, as cold and as hard frozen as a monument of marble—standing sentinel with loaded guns in their frozen hands![1]

The anecdote has a tall tale quality that makes me question its veracity, though the war certainly has enough equally bizarre and horrible stories attested to by multiple witnesses. True or not, it has an iconic quality that somehow sums up the hardships of the campaign.

Henry Kyd Douglas, Jackson's young staff member, has a contrasting comic tale that may or may not be from the same night (the postwar reminiscences are hard to harmonize). Douglas's men were stationed near Hancock to guard against a Union counteroffensive. Deciding that there was really no danger, Douglas told his soldiers to get some rest. "In the middle of the night I felt moisture on my face and covering myself from head to foot in a blanket I slept soundly." Douglas woke early next morning "oppressed with heat. Rising up and throwing off my blanket, I scattered to the air and ground perhaps five inches of snow that had fallen on me."

The snow had insulated him from the cold. Douglas looked around. "The scene before me was a weird one. Great logs of men were lying in all directions, covered over with snow and as quiet as graves. Now and then one would break out and look around him with amazement." Then the company comedian woke up. "Great Jehosophat!" he yelled, rousing the rest of the sleepers. "The Resurrection!"[2]

The Confederates threw a few more shells into Hancock and, more productively, burned a B&O Railroad bridge and tore up track and telegraph lines. Jackson contemplated attacking across the river, but abandoned the idea when Union reinforcements arrived. He would return to Unger's, then attack Romney.

Berkeley Springs today is a charming town with lots of elderly buildings. Mineral-rich waters, which emerge from the earth at a constant seventy-four degrees, flow through the spacious lawns of the old spa before becoming the town's municipal water source. A picturesque gazebo overlooks the stream, which also flows through a natural stone "bathtub" used by Native Americans and George Washington.

There is a Civil War Trails marker by the downtown visitor center, but nothing about Jackson among the office's plethora of brochures. They do advertise a "thriving arts community," and multiple massage therapists with alphabets of credentials following their names. An annual "Festival of Light Psychic Fair and Alternative Healing Expo" has among its many attractions a "Crystal Alley" with "jewelry, crystals, essential oils, and fairy furniture." Fairy furniture?

This New Age airiness contrasts with the earthy good humor

of the Berkeley Springs Brewing Company, whose generous signature glass is decorated with a huge, unmissable "BS."

In other words: lots of local color, but barely a trace of Jackson.

James I. Robertson calls the day of the countermarch to Unger's "the worst of the campaign,"[3] which is saying a lot. It snowed again. Wind chill made the twenty-degree temperature seem like zero. "The march was a terrible one," wrote John H. Worsham. "The road had become one sheet of ice from marching over it." Horses and men slipped and fell, and again, there were lots of broken bones. To gain solid footing, soldiers led horses along ditches and through woods adjacent to the road. On hills, they cut small trenches across the roads for traction.[4]

The march continued into the night. Soldiers' icy beards glistened "like crystals" in the moonlight; icicles of blood hung from the horses.[5]

At Unger's, Jackson got the news that the Federals had captured Hanging Rock, a Confederate outpost between Winchester and Romney. The soldiers he rushed to the site discovered that, for no apparent reason, the Yankees had abandoned it and returned to Romney.

The soldiers called their bivouac at Unger's "Camp Mud." When they relocated a short distance away they called it "Camp No Better." They rested as best they could while the horses were reshod for the ice.

A couple of curious horses examined me as I read the Civil War Trails marker in the bottomland at Unger's. Uphill, their owner gave me a friendly wave from his golf cart. It was hard to imagine Confederate misery in this Sunday-supplement slice of rural America. "Hundreds of wagons and horses, thousands of men, and relentless snow and rain quickly turned these fields into a quagmire," read the marker. "During the campaign, some 2000 men, or almost a quarter of Jackson's force, became casualties not of bullets but of illness. Many became sick during the miserable bivouac here and slowly staggered back to

Winchester in small groups. An unknown number died of pneumonia and other diseases related to extreme exposure."

"Produce Today" said the sign at the actual Unger's Store— "A.C. Unger and Son General Merchandise." Neatly stacked firewood, nested baskets, apples fourteen dollars a bushel. Nobody home. "Surveillance cameras in use." I walked up the hill to snap a photo of Oakleigh Manor, a big white house with a picket fence overlooking the valley. Jackson stayed there, uncharacteristically not sharing the privations of his troops, during the second encampment. I could imagine him inside fuming at the delay.

It was a cold week indeed for Colonel William Gilham. Jackson brought charges against him for not attacking at Bath and then not notifying him of the inaction. He returned to VMI. "It is worth noting," writes Jackson biographer S. C. Gwynne, "exactly who Jackson had just pushed so abruptly out of the army." Gilham was Jackson's former boss at the Institute; also a longtime friend, yearlong roommate, and business partner. "He was the academic star of the institution, its most brilliant professor…smart, elegant, self-possessed, and enormously popular with cadets. He was, in short, everything that Jackson was not."[6]

The bottom rail was now definitely on top. Jackson had brushed Gilham aside, a trusted former superior with whom he had a close personal relationship. A storm was also gathering in regard to General Garnett, commander of the Stonewall Brigade, who was the subject of a scathing January 10 letter to Judah P. Benjamin, Confederate secretary of war: "My duty to my country requires me to say to you that General G. is not qualified to command a brigade." Jackson wanted Garnett replaced by Colonel Seth M. Barton of the 3rd Arkansas.[7] His request was ignored, perhaps shelved alongside the unacted-upon court-martial of Colonel Gilham.

Jackson had disliked Garnett from the start—for no discernable reason. His actions with both Garnett and Gilham seem petty and vindictive. There were no hovering Presbyterian clergymen to comment on his soul-searching—if there was any—so we can only speculate about what was going through his mind. He may have convinced himself that keeping Garnett in command would be detrimental to the Cause. I don't think he gave the demotion of Gilham even that much consideration. It wasn't personal. The man was a better educator than soldier. He didn't measure up and had to be discarded.

What's more telling is that Jackson himself didn't seem to dwell on the role reversal. In a little over a year and a half, he had gone from brevet major to major general; from an eccentric, if well-regarded, professor at a modest military college to "Stonewall Jackson, Hero of the South." His star would continue rising. While pleased by this, he does not seem to have given much thought to his rocketing rise to fame. His focus seemed always on the future, his thoughts on the tasks at hand.

Before the column could get under way, Jackson got news that the Federals had abandoned Romney just as they had Hanging Rock. Morale was mixed as the soldiers toiled toward their prize through sleet and snow. They cursed "Old Jack" as they marched through the mud, but cheered him when he came riding by.

Following the route today, roller-coaster hills alternate with spacious valley farms that bring to mind the ranches on the western slope of the Colorado Rockies: prosperous houses, big pickup trucks, cattle. G. F. R. Henderson, who wrote one of the first monumental biographies of Jackson, called it "the paradise of the grazier." He continued: "The farms which rest beneath the hills are of manorial proportions, and the valley of the beautiful South Branch [of the Potomac] is a land of easy wealth and old-fashioned plenty."[8]

Winter hid the land's milk-and-honey attributes from the soldiers, and Romney itself, when they arrived, hardly seemed worth the effort to reach it. "A hog pen,"[9] one soldier called it, though all were pleased with the stores left by the enemy.

CHAPTER 6

An Insubordinate Frenzy

Jackson wanted to strike deeper into Union territory, but the men were too demoralized, too worn out by the winter campaigning. He changed his plans. Loring would remain in Romney, garrisoned there to defend against Federals stationed in Cumberland, Maryland, some twenty-five miles away. The Stonewall Brigade—the better marchers—would return to Winchester, a central point from which they could respond in case the army of Nathaniel P. Banks crossed the Potomac and headed south.

Loring's men and the Stonewalls snarled and cursed at each other when the latter left Romney on January 23. It was a three-day march to Winchester. Charging ahead, Jackson and Little Sorrel covered the forty-three miles in one day. He stopped at the Taylor Hotel to clean up, then hurried to the Grahams', where he surprised his wife, "bounding into the sitting room as joyous and fresh as a schoolboy."[1]

Jackson had good reason to be pleased. Starting with almost nothing, in less than three months he had assembled an army and pushed it through a successful winter campaign that brings to mind the hardships of Napoleon in Russia. He had driven the Federals from his district. About a hundred miles of B&O Railroad track were destroyed along with a major bridge; large quantities of military stores had been captured. When he sat at the Grahams' cozy fireside that night, looked around the room, and declared, "Oh, this is the essence of comfort!" he had earned the right to a little R&R.[2]

The quiet interlude would not last. He had left behind in Romney what one writer called "an insubordinate frenzy."[3] Loring's men were furious at having to garrison a miserable outpost. Raw sewage ran in the streets. The Federals had abandoned a courthouse full of rotting meat. It was cold! It was wet! It was dangerous! The Yankees were right across the river!

Officers signed a petition begging to be relieved. Some lobbied the government at the highest levels. Colonel Samuel V. Fulkerson wrote to two Confederate congressmen, Walter Preston and Waller Staples: "The place is of no importance in a strategic point of view.... We have not been in as uncomfortable a place since we entered the service." Colonel William B. Taliaferro added a postscript: "The best army I ever saw of its strength has been destroyed by bad marches and bad management."[4]

Crazy Jack had dragged his soldiers through ice and snow for nothing. Then he had gone back to Winchester with the Stonewall Brigade, his pet lambs, leaving the rest of his army suffering in an exposed and vulnerable position.

Taliaferro, on furlough in Richmond, got a sympathetic hearing from Vice President Alexander Stephens, who "denounced the Romney expedition in the severest terms." Jefferson Davis was next: "The president expressed shock and surprise at what Jackson had done to Loring's brave soldiers."[5]

At this point, two facts are worth noting. First, the highest government officials were all too willing to believe in Jackson's incompetence; and second, both Fulkerson and Taliaferro had served on VMI's governing board and, like Gilham, now served under their former subordinate. "Perhaps they could not quite accept the idea of the eccentric science teacher's transformation," wrote S. C. Gwynne.[6]

Things came to a head at the end of the month. President Davis directed Secretary of War Benjamin to order Loring's withdrawal. Jackson got the two-sentence telegram on the morning of January 31: "Our news indicates that a movement is being made to cut off General Loring's command. Order him back to Winchester immediately."

Hindsight reveals that no Federal offensive threatened Romney.[7] Jackson knew this at the time, but didn't quibble. He answered the telegram within the hour.

> Hon. J.P. Benjamin, Secretary of War, Sir:
>
> Your order requiring me to direct General Loring to return with his command to Winchester immediately has been received and promptly complied with.
>
> With such interference in my command I cannot expect to be of much service in the field; and accordingly respectfully request to be ordered to report for duty to the Superintendent of the Virginia Military Institute at Lexington; as has been done in the case of other Professors. Should this application not be granted, I respectfully request that the President will accept my resignation from the Army.
>
> *I am, sir, very respectfully, your obedient*
> *servant, T. J. Jackson.*

The storm of protest that had emanated from Romney would be as nothing compared to the reaction to Jackson's resignation. Soldiers, politicians, ministers, friends—all were united in protest and in their appeals to him to reconsider. Indignant dignitaries lobbied Davis and Benjamin; Benjamin, as usual, wound up taking the blame.[8]

In the midst of it all, Jackson appeared both outwardly and genuinely calm. He spent much of the day with Reverend Graham. He was potentially free of a tremendous responsibility, the corollary of which was, in his mind, keeping his own counsel. Jackson, famous for his secrecy, was suddenly able to talk. "He spoke freely of almost everything connected with the war, the country and the church," wrote Graham. "Events of interest in his own life were related, and scenes he had witnessed and places he had visited during his time in Europe were described. While the household was in sore distress, and the troops in a sense of exasperation, and the whole town in a ferment, he was himself perfectly self-collected and serene."[9]

Not all of his thoughts were devoted to returning to the quiet life of a college town. Later that day, Jackson found time to slip back to headquarters and pen a letter to the governor of Virginia, John Letcher. He reiterated his desire to be ordered back to VMI; he also set out, in no uncertain terms, exactly what he thought of the order he had received from Benjamin. It was "abandoning to the enemy what has cost much preparation, expense, and exposure to secure...and is an attempt to control military operations in detail from the Secretary's desk at a distance....As a single order like that of the Secretary's may destroy the entire fruits of a campaign, I cannot reasonably expect, if my operations are thus to be interfered with, to be of much service in the field." He requested again to return to the Institute, then talked again about the successes of the campaign. He concluded: "I desire to say nothing against the Secretary of War." Then he did, emphatically: "I take it for granted that he has done what he believed to be best, but I regard such a policy as ruinous."[10]

Confederate congressman Alexander Boteler, fast emerging as a friend and confidant to Jackson, was sent from Richmond with instructions from Letcher, Benjamin, and Davis to talk Jackson out of resigning. Boteler arrived at Winchester in the afternoon, found Jackson ensconced in "domestic tranquility," sitting with Anna at headquarters, she sewing, both talking, "perfectly happy." Hardly the picture of a man at the center of a military/political firestorm. Boteler gave Jackson an importunate letter from Letcher, declined an invitation to tea because of a pending meeting with his own wife, then promised to return that evening. When he arrived at eight, "I found him alone and we were soon engaged in an earnest conversation upon the subject of my mission."

Passions ran high as Boteler appealed to Jackson's patriotism from several angles. "While arguing these and much other reasons as I thought might have some effect upon him, we both had risen from our chairs and were standing face to face." Others were making sacrifices for the Cause—how could Jackson refrain?

Jackson, "eyes flashing," paced the room. He stopped in front of

Boteler and spoke rapidly: "Sacrifices? Have I not made them? What is my life here but a daily sacrifice? War has no charms for me; I've seen too many of its horrors. My only ambition is to be useful....I left a very happy home, Colonel, at the call of duty, and duty now not only permits but commands me to return to it."

Undaunted, Boteler persisted. The two united in excoriating Benjamin—how could the secretary, at a distance of three hundred miles, presume to direct operations in the field? But now Boteler had assurances that Richmond would never again interfere with Jackson's command.

Jackson continued pacing. At a vulnerable crossroads in his career, he opened his mind to Boteler just as he had to Graham a few days before: "He burst into an impetuous torrent of speech in which he detailed his comprehensive projects with a Napoleonic fire and breadth of view." Both Graham and Boteler got to see the real Jackson; both said he was never more impressive than during these candid, expansive moments. He even proved himself prophetic: "The next news from Romney will be of the reoccupation by the enemy, who will then be in a position to operate effectively with Banks in his contemplated invasion of the Valley. When the spring campaign opens, the movement in this direction will be on both flanks as well as on the front. They want this valley, and if the Valley's lost, Virginia is lost!"

Boteler continued his efforts, but maybe Jackson had convinced himself. He formally withdrew his resignation two days later.[11]

For the Jackson enthusiast, Romney today is as disappointing as it was for the soldiers. Over and above the lack of legacy, there is a smallness about it, a depressing quality that is hard to characterize but extremely palpable. Funeral homes and used car dealerships predominate. Catherine passed on visiting the visitor center. I was in the back, looking at some Civil War exhibits, when a female voice penetrated my consciousness. Drifting down from upstairs, it was urgently telling the story of a recent suicide. A woman suffering from a debilitating illness had put the barrel of a gun in her mouth and pulled the trigger with her big toe. An impeccable housekeeper, she had wanted to minimize the mess, and so put down towels.

Feeling guilty for eavesdropping, and thinking the story might just be about a TV show, I tried to force my attention back to Minié balls and belt buckles. I blotted out something about the dog being inside with the corpse. Then, unable to help myself, I focused on the final tidbit concerning the miscreant husband: "And not a month later, he ran off with the nurse!"

At the front desk, when I asked the docent about Stonewall Jackson, she replied: "I think his headquarters was in one of those big houses out on Main Street." Thinking, uncharitably, that employment in the visitor center should require a more exact knowledge about a building only a block away, I left with Catherine and we walked past the Sheetz and down the main drag to view the large, comfortable house. We read the sign: "General 'Stonewall' Jackson used this brick home as headquarters when the confederates took possession January 14, 1862. He regarded Romney highly enough to resign from the army when ordered to fall back from the town. Later he reconsidered..."

Offended by the sign's jocular boosterism, I made some sour remarks, which Catherine wisely ignored, that started with the fact that Romney had been abandoned by both Union and Confederate armies.

At dusk, we explored Indian Mound Cemetery on the town's western edge. The cemetery has a deteriorating, if picturesque, tower "Dedicated to Jesus Christ," along with stunning views of the surrounding mountains. The mound itself is not spectacular, some seven feet high by fifteen in diameter. We next contemplated one of the oldest, if not the first, Confederate memorials in the United States. One hundred and twenty-five names are listed on the 1867 obelisk along with the inscription "The Daughters of Old Hampshire Erect This Tribute of Affection to Her Heroic Sons Who Fell in Defence [*sic*] of Southern Rights."

A melancholy wind sighed in the evergreens. I struggled to come to terms with the two warrior cultures—Native American and Confederate—spending eternity side by side. I finally imagined them enjoying a cross-cultural Valhalla, making war all day, then feasting all night while arguing vociferously about their respective fighting abilities, tactics, and so on.

"What a quiet, lonely spot," I said to Catherine after we got into the car. "It really makes you think about history, the passage of time, and all those things the Romantic poets wrote about. And we'd never have found it if we weren't out being history detectives."

"Be careful not to hit one of those stones while you're backing up," she replied.

Indian Mound Cemetery's Confederate monument was vandalized on September 16, 2017. The graffiti read, "Reparations now." Adds the September 19, 2017, *Hampshire Review*, "In addition to damage to the monument, papers were left behind with vulgar language."

Richmond's Confederate legacy has a discordant relationship with the city's current progressivism. Whites fled to the suburbs after integration, making the city minority-majority, with politics that reflect the shift. Monument Avenue is famous for its statues of Lee, Jackson, and others. There had been rumblings recently about having them removed. When I drafted this section in early April 2016, Chad Ingold, a candidate for mayor, focused on Jackson when asked his opinion on the matter: "How do I feel about removing Stonewall Jackson's statue from Monument Avenue? Bring your own hammer!" The sympathetic crowd erupted with raucous cheers. Almost immediately a photoshopped image of Ingold's head on hip-hop star MC Hammer's body started making its way round the Net.[12]

As far as I can tell, all of Richmond's Confederate monuments have been vandalized, most more than once. While I was working on a later draft of this manuscript, someone splashed several cans of red paint on the Lee monument along with the letters B. L. M.—Black Lives Matter. A. P. Hill's monument, in the city's Northside, was vandalized a few days later.

Richard Ashby, the brother of Jackson's cavalryman Turner Ashby, was also buried in Indian Mound Cemetery, though his body was later moved to Winchester. Turner Ashby, "the Black Knight of the Confederacy," was the beau ideal of the dashing Southern cavalryman. "In appearance," wrote Douglas Freeman, "Turner Ashby was dark, almost swarthy, suggesting the popular appearance of an Arab. To romantic Southerners he looked as if he had just stepped out of a Waverly novel."[13] The younger brother Richard was almost equally striking and larger-than-life. He and a small group of cavalrymen were ambushed by Federals on June 26, 1861. Wounded, he was stabbed and bayoneted after he had fallen, then lingered through seven days "of intense suffering."[14]

Turner was able to hunt down and kill some of his brother's assailants. At Richard's funeral "he stood over the grave, took his brother's sword, broke it and threw it into the opening; clasped his hands and looked upward as if in resignation; and then, pressing his lips as if in the bitterness of grief, while a tear rolled down his cheek, he turned without a word, mounted his horse and rode away. Thenceforth his name was a terror to the enemy."[15]

We left Romney after dark and headed for Winchester in misting rain. Terrible visibility. Impatient drivers followed too close because there was no place to pass—Route 50 is two-lane most of the way.

I had a couple of cars in my wake as I crested a hill and saw a car stopped, blinker on, waiting to make a left through oncoming traffic onto a dirt road. I slammed on the brakes and stopped in time. So did the guy behind me—but the guy behind him didn't.

I watched headlights in my rearview mirror coming toward me

with no diminution of speed. The person directly behind me tried to pull off but couldn't because there was no shoulder. Headlights came closer. We were going to be hit. I yelled an obscenity.

Then suddenly, at the last second, the man driving the speeding car yanked the wheel to the left and shot through a gap in the oncoming traffic. He made it to the dirt road, braking in a cloud of dust.

Moments later we were back on our way. I broke the silence after a couple of miles. "I wonder," I said. "How many people's last words are 'Oh shit!'"

In Winchester, we went to a Mexican restaurant on the pedestrian mall and soothed our jangled nerves with margaritas. I thought of Jackson at the Battle of Chapultepec during the Mexican War, continuing to fight after a cannonball passed between his legs, and at Manassas walking so calmly among the bullets that one memoirist said he was moving like "a farmer about his farm when the seasons are good."[16] Not me. Seriously shaken, I kept playing and replaying the scene in my mind. "Headlights of Death in my rearview mirror," I thought melodramatically, staring down at my refried beans. I believed I'd gotten over it after we showered and relaxed at the hotel, but the scene came back again and again when I woke in the early morning hours and couldn't go back to sleep.

I still lacked trust in what Jackson called "an ever-kind Providence." By immersing myself in his life and following in his footsteps, I hoped to gain some of his quiet confidence. It hadn't happened yet, I thought ruefully, watching replays of our near disaster until the morning light filtered in through the hotel curtains.

CHAPTER 7

A Dazzling Glimpse

Jackson stood up for himself, letting the bureaucracy know that he was not someone to trifle with. In the South in general and Virginia in particular, public opinion would shift from a view of him as peculiar, even "crazy," to respect for him as a hard-hitting, vitally important commander. The South had need of heroes. Losses in the west and along the East Coast, coupled with the fact that across the Potomac, McClellan was finally preparing to move the largest army ever assembled in the Western Hemisphere, 150,000-plus men,[1] led Jefferson Davis to write that "events have cast on our arms and hopes the gloomiest shadows."[2] He reflected the general mood—with a few exceptions.

It was anything but gloomy for Jackson and Anna, living with the Grahams at the Presbyterian manse in Winchester. Jackson could find relief from military affairs by discussing spiritual matters with Graham, or simply relaxing in the family circle. "The pleasure he found in domestic life was almost pathetic," wrote Douglas Freeman.[3]

Jackson was very taken with Alfred, the Grahams' three-year-old son, and delighted in giving him piggyback rides, "the performance provoking as much glee on his part as it did on that of the child." Throughout his stay, Alfred would call Jackson "Horse." It was also during this time that an event occurred that could figure prominently in that extremely slim, still-unwritten volume on the humor of Stonewall Jackson.

A group of people, including visiting officers and the Reverend Graham himself, were in the manse parlor. They started a playful mock battle, using the backs of chairs as artillery pieces. Their fun made so much noise that Jackson descended from his upstairs bedroom to see what was going on. Wrote Anna: "Taking in at a glance the broad humor of the occasion, he said, sharply: 'Captain Marye, when the engagement is over, you will send in an official report."[4]

"The memories of that sojourn in our 'war home' are among the most precious and sacred of my whole life," she continued.[5] Anna became pregnant sometime that February.

Jackson's calm happiness was astonishing considering the odds he faced. Across the Potomac, General Nathaniel P. Banks had 38,000 men poised to invade the Valley. He clearly had no thought of encountering significant resistance from Jackson's 5,000 or so Confederates. Yet in Winchester, Jackson, outnumbered almost eight to one, was relaxed, cheerful, and eager to have a go at Banks.

Confederate commander Joseph E. Johnston's devotion to the defensive was equal to Union commander George B. McClellan's caution, which made for a very slow dance indeed that spring in Virginia. Expecting an advance from the north, Johnston started abandoning his lines during the first week of March, actually moving back before McClellan moved forward. McClellan, who for nearly eight months had been fine-tuning and polishing the grand military machine that was the Army of the Potomac, marched out to Johnston's vacated works *after* Johnston had left, "to push the retreat of the rebels."[6]

The retreat didn't need pushing. And in the empty earthworks the soldiers—as well as the press—made the startling discovery that the fierce-looking cannon were actually "Quaker guns," logs painted black and mounted on wagon wheels to resemble heavy ordnance. "The fortifications are a damnable humbug and McClellan has been completely fooled," fumed the *New York Tribune*.[7] McClellan looked bad. So did Lincoln, for sustaining him. The general would have to do something soon.

When Johnston retreated, his generals were supposed to fall back with him. Jackson seized on an ambiguity in the orders and interpreted his instructions creatively. Anticipating a fight, he fortified Winchester, at the same time complying with instructions to leave by moving out his stores. On March 8 he wrote Johnston: "Though you desired me some time since to fall back in the event of yourself and General Hill doing so, in your letter of the 5th inst. you say, 'delay the enemy as long as you can.' I have felt justified in remaining here for the present."

The Hill he was referring to was Daniel Harvey Hill, his brother-in-law. Hill had finished retreating, so Jackson blithely asked for his services, along with those of his men. "And now, General, that Hill has fallen back, can you not send him over here? I greatly need such an officer." Jackson said his own men were "in fine spirits," and would be even happier if Hill's men reinforced them. Then, still under the guise of complying with Johnston's instructions to evacuate, he revealed what was really on his mind: "If we cannot be successful in defeating the enemy should he advance, a kind Providence may enable us to inflict a terrible wound and effect a safe retreat in the event of having to fall back."[8]

Anna was dispatched south, out of danger. She had to take the same train that carried the sick and wounded from the hospitals. "Some were so helpless that they had to be carried on the backs of their comrades—their pale, emaciated, and despairing faces and moans of suffering being pitiful and heart-moving beyond description. At Manassas there was a delay of an hour or more in transferring them to another train, and as I sat and watched the procession of concentrated misery, with my own heart so heavy and anxious, I was never so impressed with the horrors of war."[9] As with her earlier battlefield tour, she did not make the connection that Jackson had been directly responsible for creating many of those horrors, and would create many more before they saw each other again, thirteen months later, the following winter.

She left behind a husband who was not only happy—though distressed, of course, at her departure—but healthy as well. Once Jackson got into the field, the ailments, real or imagined, that plagued him throughout his life were barely mentioned. Like an engine that runs ragged at low speed but smoothes out as it accelerates, his body was responding to the overall rightness of a man finally doing what he did best. And the fresh air and exercise didn't hurt. "How God does bless us wherever we are!" he wrote Anna shortly after she left. "I am very thankful for the measure of health with which he blesses me. I do not remember having been in such good health for years."[10]

General Nathaniel P. Banks was a self-made man. He had started out working in a cotton mill at eleven, then found out he had a talent for public speaking, and wound up riding that talent almost to the top. He became Speaker of the U.S. House of Representatives, governor of Massachusetts, and contended for the 1860 Republican presidential nomination against Abraham Lincoln, who considered him for a cabinet post but instead made him a political general. Prior to the war, he had no military experience.

"Banks had more nicknames than any Civil War general," said historian Ed Bearss. "In the House they called him 'N.P.,' for 'Nothing Positive,' and 'The Dancing Master,' because he was something of a dandy. His nom de guerre was 'Commissary Banks.' The Confederates called him that because of the vast amount of stores they captured from him."[11]

He did wonderfully well as a politician; he probably would have been an adequate general—if he had gone up against somebody else.

Banks marched to within five miles of Winchester by March 7. A three-day stalemate ensued. Finally, an impatient Jackson decided to take the battle to the enemy. On March 11, he gathered his officers and proposed a night attack, as rare at this time as the winter campaign he had just completed to Romney. The plan was for soldiers to move south out of Winchester, get food from the wagons waiting there, rest for a few hours, then hurry back and surprise Banks on the north side of town. There was a full moon. It might possibly work.

Jackson visited the Grahams, who reported him in fine spirits. He ate with them, prayed with them, and alleviated their fears, which the whole town shared, of being abandoned to the enemy: "I don't expect to leave." At sunset he walked over to join his officers at headquarters, where his good mood was soon destroyed. The supply wagons, which were supposed to have been just outside of town, had mistakenly been sent eight miles south. The soldiers had followed them there to get their rations. His officers all concurred that if they marched back they would be too tired for the long-odds attack to work. Jackson had to agree.

He returned to the Grahams and asked the minister to follow him to headquarters. "He said he did not mean to deceive us by giving the impression that he would not abandon the town. He had intended to lead out his troops that night and hurl them on the camp of the enemy and drive such as were not captured and might survive back across the Potomac." Unable to accept the situation, Jackson blamed his officers. "They had exhibited so much opposition...as to forbid him to hope for its successful execution."

Agitated and still conflicted, Jackson paced the room. He paused before Graham. Then, "his face fairly blazing with the fire that was burning in his soul," he drew his sword halfway from the scabbard. "I may execute my purpose still," he said. "I have ordered my officers to return at half past nine."

Once again Graham witnessed the inner man, a sight few had been privileged to see. "His appearance, as he stood there and uttered those words, I can never forget. I was completely awed before him." But then the veil was drawn. Jackson resheathed his sword and slumped, dejected. "No, it will cost the lives of too many brave men," he said. "I must retreat."

He returned to the Graham house, where "he bade us a touching farewell."[12]

The Confederates retreated south under the full moon. Dr. Hunter McGuire rode with Jackson to a high place overlooking the column and the town. McGuire was from Winchester and felt terrible about abandoning it to the enemy, but when he looked at Jackson his own feelings were "arrested" by the general's emotional intensity.

McGuire echoes Graham in saying he was "awed," then continues: "Presently he cried out with a manner almost savage: 'That is the last council of war I will ever hold!' And it was—his first and last."[13]

Jackson had given both McGuire and Graham what writer Shelby Foote called "a dazzling glimpse into the secret corners of his mind."[14] It was something that happened far too seldom during the war. Commentators—and common sense—agree that Jackson kept his own counsel far too much. If he had shared a portion of his plans with Loring, for example, he probably could have avoided the open rebellion that ultimately led to his aborted resignation.

No one debates the necessity of secrecy in wartime. But news is a precious commodity when people's lives are at stake. Spreading and gathering it are survival skills. General Joseph E. Johnston relates a telling anecdote about a "secret" Confederate cabinet meeting about the withdrawal of the Southern army from Manassas. When he left the meeting and returned to his hotel, he met an acquaintance who eagerly asked if he'd heard the story, which was currently being discussed in the lobby, about the cabinet meeting that day concerning the withdrawal of the army from Manassas. Marvels Douglas Freeman: "An accurate report of what had been considered in the utmost secrecy, behind guarded doors, had reached the hotel almost as soon as Johnston had!"[15]

It goes without saying that if the information had reached the hotel, it had also reached the enemy.

The only sure way to keep a secret is not to tell anyone—a

strategy that is counterproductive in a fluid, reactive military situation. There is a happy medium between total secrecy and sharing enough information to make subordinates more effective, but Jackson wasn't a happy-medium kind of guy. As he did with so much else in his life, he took things too far, turning strength into weakness. He mystified his opponents, but kept his own officers baffled as well. As General Richard Ewell confided to General Richard Taylor, "[I] never saw one of Jackson's couriers approach without expecting an order to assault the north pole."[16]

McClellan had been in command of the Army of the Potomac since shortly after Manassas. His soldiers were well armed, well fed, impressively uniformed, and drilled to perfection—but outside of that, they weren't doing very much. Lincoln and the Union were becoming increasingly frustrated. "If General McClellan isn't going to use his army, I'd like to borrow it for a time," Lincoln said, echoing the general sentiment.

McClellan always wanted more men. Part of this was because Secret Service chief Allan Pinkerton magnified Confederate troop strength—sometimes to a fantastic degree. But in truth, Pinkerton's exaggerations found a willing audience in "Little Mac," and he was always ready to pass them on as one more reason to delay. McClellan firmly believed that he was vastly outnumbered by the Confederates. In actuality, the situation was reversed. According to S. C. Gwynne, "On October 15, McClellan's rolls showed 152,501 soldiers, of whom realistically only 100,000 or so were available to actively campaign. The 41,000 or so under Johnston at Manassas were subject to the same deductions for sick, absent, confined, etc."[17] In so many words: The odds were better than three to one in McClellan's favor.

Sometimes in the late winter it became evident, even to McClellan, that he would have to do *something* with the opening of the spring campaigning season. But a straightforward movement against a fortified enemy was not in his nature. He decided on a flanking maneuver.

He would attack Richmond from the east, transporting his troops by water from northern Virginia and disembarking at Fort Monroe, which was at the southern tip of the peninsula between the York and James rivers and still in Union hands.

Lincoln, a mere civilian, failed to see the brilliance of the plan, telling McClellan that he would face the same soldiers whether he attacked from the north or the east, and equally formidable fortifications. But he eventually acquiesced, on one condition: The general had to leave enough troops in Washington to protect the capital. McClellan gladly agreed. The Peninsula Campaign began.

Events that spring in the Shenandoah Valley would be inextricably interwoven with what was happening on the Peninsula. McClellan wanted troops from the Valley for the campaign against Richmond. Only a token force, he thought, was needed to keep Jackson in check. At this point, no one saw the strange professor with his tiny army as much of a threat.

Banks occupied Winchester on March 12. Jackson marched south and camped at Strasburg, about twenty miles away. He was followed by James Shields's division, some 9,000 Federals—more than double the number of soldiers in Jackson's army. Outnumbered, Jackson continued south for another thirty miles, passing the railhead at Mount Jackson to camp at Rude's Hill, a sort of natural fortress that rose a hundred feet above the valley floor. It was further protected by the North Fork of the Shenandoah River. The "moatlike expanse" of the river low ground was crossed by a single bridge, usable by the Confederates but "combustible enough to prevent Federals from securing it."[18]

Two interconnected and important events happened during the retreat. First, Virginia's Governor Letcher issued an executive order that gave Jackson and other commanders the authority to enlist militia units in their districts. That the Confederates would wait until almost the second year of the conflict to do this points to an extraordinary inefficiency of government that could only have hurt the war effort.

Jackson immediately mobilized the Valley militia. Though most of them were inexperienced, armed with shotguns, squirrel rifles, or no guns at all,[19] they increased his numbers and would be efficient soldiers once they were equipped and drilled. Outdoor life and farm labor were good preparation for the army. Added G. F. R. Henderson, "Men who had been used from boyhood to shoot squirrels in the woodland found the Federal soldier a target difficult to miss."[20]

Second, Jedediah Hotchkiss arrived with the Augusta County Militia. A native of New York State, Hotchkiss came south when he was eighteen for a walking tour of the Shenandoah Valley and quickly decided it was home. He began teaching to support himself, and by the time of the war he had a wife, two children, and his own boarding school, Loch Willow Academy, in a serene rural setting near Staunton in the upper Valley. He also made maps.

Hotchkiss knew Jackson from before the war, when he had been a visiting examiner at Washington College in Lexington. While there, he was a guest in the home of the college president, Dr. George Junkin, father of Jackson's first wife, Elinor. Jackson was also living with his in-laws at the time. The campus of the Virginia Military Institute, where Jackson taught, is adjacent to Washington College, now called Washington and Lee University.

Hotchkiss wanted to work for Jackson when he met with him at his headquarters to report the arrival of the Augusta militiamen, but he bided his time, probably planning to enlist the aid of Colonel William S. H. Baylor, of the 5th Virginia, who he knew respected his talents.

Jackson and Hotchkiss had more in common than previous acquaintance, and the potential for a productive partnership was definitely there. Devout and devoted to duty, both were abstemious Presbyterians who neither smoked nor drank. Furthermore, at this early stage of the campaign, Jackson must have been pondering how to use anything and everything, including the terrain of the Valley itself, in his struggle against the Federals. That an expert cartographer had just walked through the door probably seemed an obvious manifestation of the "ever-kind Providence" he was always writing about.

On March 16, McClellan called for Union troops from the Valley. But they were only going to Manassas—once the focus, now the sideshow—to help guard Washington in case the Confederates made a sudden lunge north. Still, for Banks, it would be closer to the spotlight of publicity on the Peninsula. That was where reputations would be made that could be turned into postwar political capital. And the clock was ticking: As it had been with Manassas the previous year, the feeling now was that the struggle for Richmond was going to be the great final battle that would end the war. There might still be a chance to do something before the game was over and the laurels distributed.

The Valley was even less important than Manassas. Banks would leave behind enough soldiers to rebuild and protect the Manassas Gap Railroad, which had been destroyed by Jackson, as well as "something like two regiments of cavalry" that would occupy Winchester and "thoroughly scour the country south of the railway and up the Shenandoah Valley."[21]

On March 21, a rainy Friday with highs in the mid-forties, Jackson received word from Ashby that Shields was pulling back from Strasburg. At the same time, Federal soldiers and loaded wagons were leaving Winchester and headed east toward the Blue Ridge. The movement of Valley troops to support McClellan had begun.

Characteristically, Ashby added that he was pursuing Shields's 9,000 men with three companies of cavalry and one of horse artillery. Jackson determined to follow "with all my available force."[22] But on the twenty-first, Shields was already back in his camp north of Winchester, having marched a Jacksonian twenty-two miles the previous day in driving rain.[23]

Jackson's men moved northward, some traveling twenty-seven miles on March 22. "We marched as only Jackson's men could march," wrote a Virginia private. Many fell out from exhaustion.[24] Ashby, meanwhile, had sent soldiers into Winchester disguised as farmers selling eggs. The intelligence they gathered, as well as reports from other sources, convinced both him and Jackson that the Federals had gone, leaving only a few regiments behind.

Ashby rode in to take possession of what he thought was an abandoned town. But Federals were there, though not in force. When the action started, Shields himself left his camp north of town, arriving on the scene with infantry and artillery. He was placing a cannon when he was hit by shell fragments that broke his arm and wounded his side. Colonel Nathan Kimball took command.

Ashby still thought that only a token force held the town and relayed this misinformation to Jackson, who was hurrying north at a punishing pace. By the time he reached the small hamlet of Kernstown, four miles south of Winchester, around 2 p.m. the next day, his numbers had dwindled to 2,700 infantry and 290 cavalry.[25] At first he ordered his exhausted men into bivouac. It was Sunday and Jackson had serious qualms about fighting on the Sabbath. He quickly changed his mind, however. The Federals had seen him and could bring up more men if he hesitated. The enemy had already posted artillery on the high ground west of the Valley Turnpike, and there was even higher ground west of that which was currently unoccupied and needed to be seized.

CHAPTER 8

Following the Footsteps

Pritchard's Hill, site of the Federal gun batteries, is formidable. Not a mountain by any means, but still an incredibly strong position from which to rain down shells on an enemy. Not something I'd like to charge, I thought, getting out of my car one cold, rainy Saturday morning at the Kernstown battlefield. Their brand-new visitor center is at the foot of Pritchard's Hill. It was a few days before the anniversary and I had driven up for a special tour.

To understand a battle, you have to read about it and visit the site, then do it again and again. You cut your work in half when you use an expert. Gary Ecelbarger, who was leading the tour, wrote the book on Kernstown—literally. Its title was borrowed from what Jackson said after he realized how badly he was outnumbered: "We are in for it!"

I queried the woman behind the desk with the most frequently asked battlefield question.

"The port-a-potties are right outside," she replied. Before I could escape, she pointed out the new, as yet unopened bathrooms in another building: "When you come back you'll be able to use them instead of the port-a-potty." She was even prouder of the thirty-five acres the Kernstown Foundation had recently acquired off the southeast corner of the battlefield.

If you're a history fan, it's wonderful to find enthusiastic preservationists and successful projects. It's disturbing to come up against the flip side: open hostility, destruction, and ignorance. I found myself contrasting the negativity I'd encountered intermittently over the years with the woman's upbeat enthusiasm as I walked across the blacktop in the sprinkling rain.

In 1990, a man named Oscar Via bulldozed a thousand yards of wonderfully preserved trenches from Grant's 1864 Overland Campaign because he thought it was holding up the rezoning—and sale—of his land. I knew those trenches. They were only a few miles from my house and I took their destruction personally. When I heard about it I drove over in the dark, walking through the woods with a flashlight and feeling sick to my stomach as I surveyed the damage.

A few days later, Via received a standing ovation when he walked into a gathering of locals. They were applauding the idea that a man should be able to do whatever he wants with his property, even if it involves destroying an irreplaceable piece of American history. In their minds, the present-day battle lines were clearly drawn: property rights versus preservationists; landowners versus Big Government.

Today, almost all of the farms in my part of the county have been replaced by subdivisions.

For many, historic preservation and history itself are part of an educated culture they don't understand and intensely dislike. Some elevate their ignorance into a virtue. I recalled a local man speaking to our planning commission against the efforts of a group trying to save part of the North Anna battlefield, also part of Grant's Overland Campaign. "How can this North Anna battle be important?" he argued passionately. "*I've* never heard of it!"

A harmonic convergence of time and treasure—not to mention luck—had taken place for me to drive up and enjoy my little Civil War tour at Kernstown. It was the culmination of hundreds of thousands of dollars in donations plus thousands of hours of volunteer time, all from people passionate about history. I resolved to make a contribution, or at least buy a book, even though my shelves were already groaning under three decades of war-related acquisitions.

"This is Gary Ecelbarger," a man from the Kernstown Battlefield Association was saying when I walked back into the visitor center. "He will entertain you and entertain your questions."

There were about twenty-five people in the group. There was a scattering of women and younger folks, but it was mostly comprised of the middle-aged white guys, like me, who are the mainstay of Civil War tourism. "Rebel: Heritage not Hate" read one man's ball cap. There was nothing else remotely political. Lots of North Face rain gear.

Many people come to the Civil War through genealogy. If you have a male ancestor who was here in the 1860s, it's a good bet that he fought in the war. Once you have his name, it's relatively easy to find his unit; research the unit and you find out where he fought. It's incredibly moving to go to a battlefield and walk the same ground your great-great-grandfather did in the 1860s.

Ecelbarger did an ancestor call. Several people were descended from soldiers who fought at Kernstown. He found out the units and told the person when their ancestor would be emphasized on the tour. Then he sketched in the background: Jackson's retreat from Winchester. "The last council of war I will ever hold!" Moving up the Valley: Strasburg, Mount Jackson, Rude's Hill.

"Meanwhile, on the Peninsula, McClellan had 100,000 men headed for Richmond. It was like moving the ninth-largest city in America—hard to ignore."

General Johnston's orders to Jackson: Keep Banks in the Valley so he can't reinforce McClellan. But don't actually fight.

Yeah, right! I thought to myself. *Jackson not fighting.*

Ecelbarger continued summarizing: Union commander James Shields retired from Strasburg back into his camp north of Winchester; his wounding on the twenty-second. "Shields was a feisty Irishman, a Mexican War veteran who was also wounded at Cerro Gordo, where the doctor passed a silk handkerchief entirely through his body. On the day of the battle Shields said, 'Jackson is afraid of me. There'll be no fight today.' "

I jotted down notes, facts, and bits of dialogue: Kernstown was the first battle in the Shenandoah Valley. "There were actually three battles fought on this land. Like Mark Twain said, 'History doesn't repeat itself, but it often rhymes.' "

It was Jackson's first and only defeat as an independent commander. "Though it turned out to be a strategic victory...but Stonewall didn't know it at the time. There are those who say he did, but if he had gone around after the battle saying, 'It was a tactical defeat but a strategic victory,' people would have said he needed a checkup from the neck up, if you know what I mean."

I relaxed. Ecelbarger had a sense of humor. The next two hours wouldn't be just a hard slog through facts.

Jackson was facing tough westerners. Many were marching barefoot and had spent the night before the battle sleeping without tents on the frozen ground. "And they were cocky," Ecelbarger continued. "One Ohio soldier knew exactly where Jackson was on the twenty-first. He wrote, 'Jackson and his force have fallen back upon Mount Jackson. It is more than likely we will mount Jackson before long and if he don't kick too high we will ride him out of that part of the country sure.' "

Ecelbarger knew his quotes by heart. Engaging enthusiasm and jokey, rapid-fire delivery—he almost made us forget we were going out in the cold rain.

Luckily for the group, it was only misting when we left the shelter and walked up Pritchard's Hill. We read the markers and took in the view, which was seriously impeded by fog. "This is the widest part of the Shenandoah Valley," said Ecelbarger, killing time while the slower people caught up. "It's thirty miles wide at this point. The Shenandoah River serpentines—I just wanted to use that word in a sentence—along the Blue Ridge over there."

The stragglers caught up. Ecelbarger started again: "Colonel Kimball had taken command from Shields. The Federals vastly outnumbered the Confederates. There were three thousand infantry and eighteen cannon, which would fire over seven hundred shot and shell from this hill. Ashby had three cannon, three hundred cavalry, and a hundred and twenty infantry.

"Ashby's over there saying, 'Good heavens!'—I actually cleaned that up, he probably said something else—'Good heavens! There's a lot more than four regiments here!'

"When he came onto the battlefield, Jackson didn't realize what he was up against, either. And for some reason, Ashby and Jackson didn't communicate during the battle. When Jackson did take in the situation, he sent some 900 infantrymen under Colonel Samuel V. Fulkerson to attack the cannon by flanking them from the Confederate left. He had an aide order General Garnett to support Fulkerson—without telling Garnett what Fulkerson was supposed to do."

Par for the course with Jackson's secrecy and dislike of Garnett, I thought.

"The assaulting Confederates, subjected to a terrible fire, keep coming." He gestured down the hill at the Confederate side, then up the hill at the Federal. "Several of Union lieutenant colonel Philip Daum's artillerists deserted their pieces when they witnessed the Southerners' dauntless approach. He rounded them up at the point of his sword, threatening to cut their heads off if they deserted again.

"With newfound courage, they returned to serve their guns."

Ecelbarger earned an appreciative chuckle. Bright eyes, big gestures—he was wearing only a light hoodie against the chill. I guess his zeal for history kept him warm.

"Now, what's the ratio recommended for a successful assault?"

"Three to one," responded a chorus of voices. These weren't first-time visitors.

"That's right!" exclaimed Ecelbarger, a pleased professor. "But Jackson, who's making the assault, is *outnumbered* almost two to one."

My fingers were numb. I kept taking notes.

"Now let's go walk the route of this mini–Pickett's Charge."

The rain picked up as we walked down Pritchard's Hill. "I think I'll wait in the car," a woman told her husband. The group noticeably diminished as we passed the parking lot and the visitor center. I confess I thought longingly of the center myself—it was warm inside and there were homemade cookies in the nice little bookstore—but, recalling Jackson's soldiers, I persevered.

We crossed the lowland meadow that still served as an active cow pasture. "Remember to look down," people advised each other. It seemed that every time I avoided a cow pie, I stepped in a puddle. Now my toes were frozen along with my fingers.

Ecelbarger halted on the far side of the battlefield's land. He talked about Jackson ordering Fulkerson to charge and the terrible fire his men endured. We started back, retracing their route. Ecelbarger paused close to where they finally veered off to seek shelter in a locust grove at the base of Sandy Ridge to the west. Sandy Ridge was unsecured by Kimball and actually higher than Pritchard's Hill, two facts immediately noted by Jackson, the former professor of artillery tactics at VMI.

The charge didn't accomplish its main objective—to flank the artillery on Pritchard's Hill—but it, along with a feint at the Union left by Ashby, distracted Kimball from something even more important: Jackson was moving his guns up Sandy Ridge.

I gave up taking notes when the rain turned my writing into blue blobs on the page. No one seemed disappointed when Ecelbarger decided to finish the tour inside. Thawing out in the visitor center, I munched an oatmeal raisin cookie and congratulated myself as I listened to Ecelbarger expound on the rest of the battle. Instead of three or four lengthy car trips and God knows how much reading, his presentation made it all clear, and I had the added "benefit" of just enough discomfort to get a hint of what the soldiers habitually endured.

I've never been drawn to reenacting, but putting myself through a little of what the soldiers experienced gives me a deeper appreciation of their lives. I've always especially wanted to redo some of the epic marches, but it's almost impossible now because of my age. Although I'm in decent enough shape for my sixties, there's no way I could push myself twenty-plus miles wearing a wool uniform in the summer heat while carrying a pack and musket. It also makes me somewhat wistful to remember that Stonewall Jackson, so ancient-seeming to his soldiers that they nicknamed him "Old Jack," was thirty-nine years old when he died, more than two decades younger than me.

Now I march in the car and fight on the page. But the big lesson of Kernstown applies to everyone: Keep going. A single defeat doesn't make a campaign. It can even be turned to your advantage if you continue pushing hard enough.

Jackson succeeded in placing fifteen cannon on the military crest of Sandy Ridge and opened fire on the Yankee artillery. Now the Confederates were firing down on the Yankees—with deadly effect. At about this time, Jackson's aide Sandie Pendleton climbed to a high point of Sandy Ridge to observe the enemy and realized that it was not the token force Ashby had reported. Jackson was severely outnumbered and more men were coming. Marching from north of Winchester, Colonel Erastus B. Tyler was almost at the battlefield with 2,300 additional soldiers. The shocked Pendleton rushed back to report. "Say nothing about it," admonished Jackson. "We are in for it!"

Kimball sent Tyler to attack the Confederate cannon on Sandy Ridge. They were attempting to comply when they encountered 200 Southerners Jackson had sent toward Pritchard's Hill on the same errand. There was a four-hundred-yard-long shoulder-high stone wall running east to west on Sandy Ridge. The Confederates, sheltered behind part of it, opened fire on the Yankees. Outnumbered by more than ten to one, the Southerners held their own, aided by the fact that Tyler's men were bunched together in a big rectangle. The soldiers in front were sitting ducks, while those in the rear couldn't shoot at the Confederates without hitting their own men. Under intense fire, amid the confusion of battle, the Yankees were unable to spread out into an effective attack formation.

Stymied on his left, Tyler realized that the western section of the wall on his right was undefended. He sent men to capture it. The Confederates realized the same thing at the same time. Both sides ran for the wall. The Confederates won, and started pouring close-range volleys into the Yankees.

Now both sides were feeding men into the fight: Garnett and Fulkerson on the Confederate right, Tyler's Federals from Pritchard's Hill. The close-in combat increased in intensity.

There are dozens of quotes from soldiers on both sides who insisted that Kernstown was some of the hardest fighting of the entire war. To cite just two corresponding examples of the action: Four men were killed or wounded carrying the regimental flag of the 2nd Virginia, and the flag itself was hit fourteen times. On the opposing side, five men fell carrying the American flag of the 5th Ohio. That flag was hit an astonishing forty-eight times. The staffs of both flags were broken.[1]

The Northerners were literally fighting an uphill battle, but they outnumbered the Southerners two to one. Jackson was hoping to hang on until sunset, then disengage. He might have been able to do it if his men hadn't started running out of ammunition.

A soldier from the 21st Virginia was headed for the rear when he encountered Jackson. The general asked what he was doing. The man said he had shot all his ammunition away and did not know where to get more. Wrote John Worsham, "Old Stonewall rose in his stirrups and gave the command, 'Then go back and give them the bayonet!' "[2]

Worsham didn't record whether the man turned around or continued on his way. Others certainly questioned the wisdom of using a knife in a gunfight. When they ran out of ammunition, they left.

General Garnett's men exhausted their cartridges late in the day. Hard-pressed by the enemy, he ordered his soldiers to retreat. Garnett also ran into a furious Jackson. "Why have you not rallied your men?" demanded Stonewall. "Halt and rally!" Garnett replied that he had ordered his men to rally until he was hoarse.

Other units had pulled back with Garnett. With bullets whizzing around him, Jackson rode back and forth trying to turn the tide. He grabbed a drummer by the shoulder. "Beat the rally!" he ordered. "Beat the rally!" But even Stonewall couldn't stop the retreat.

Disorganized Confederates left the battlefield and headed south. Kernstown was over.

—=——♩

I bought *"We Are in for It!,"* got Ecelbarger's autograph on the title page, and told him how much I'd enjoyed his tour. I drove into Winchester for lunch, then paged through the book while I ate fried catfish at Bonnie Blue, a funky upscale barbecue joint in a renovated gas station. *"We Are in for It!"* was a serious endeavor containing none of the funny asides that made the tour so enjoyable. I put it away for later study.

The fish was excellent, but I couldn't stop processing the battle. At one point Ecelbarger had compared its immediate aftermath to a *Simpsons* episode: "Marge says, 'What's the moral of all this?' Homer says, 'There is no moral. It's just about a lot of stuff that happened.' "

In other words, it took a while for the "fog of war" to lift and the actual results of the battle to register. Shelby Foote called the Shenandoah Valley a "corridor pointed shotgun-like at the Union solar plexus." Lincoln "quarter-faced at the news of the battle…and found himself looking once more down the muzzle."[3] It wouldn't be long before he diverted 25,000 men from McClellan's big push toward Richmond. Washington had to be protected.

Some of this had to do with Shields's post-Kernstown PR. Jackson's outnumbered men had fought so fiercely that Shields could get away with exaggerating their strength and throwing in a couple of absent generals for good measure. After stopping all outgoing correspondence so that his letters would be the first to reach the papers, he penned a series of grandiloquent, self-serving missives that boosted Jackson's numbers while boasting about how he himself had precisely directed winning maneuvers from his sickbed four miles away. "We have this day achieved a glorious victory over the combined forces of Jackson, Smith, and Longstreet," he telegraphed. "The enemy's strength was about fifteen thousand."[4]

According to some accounts, as early as that night Stonewall wasn't talking like he had lost—even in the midst of a retreat. Was he just in denial, or could he actually see the big picture better than any-one else? Henderson, in his giant, laudatory 1898 biography, paints the following picture:

> As he stood before the camp-fire near Newtown, wrapped in his long cloak, his hands behind his back, and stirring the embers with his foot, one of Ashby's youngest troopers ventured to interrupt his reverie. "The Yankees don't seem willing to quit Winchester, General."
>
> "Winchester is a very pleasant place to stay in, sir," was the quick reply. Nothing daunted, the boy went on: "It was reported that they were retreating, but I guess they were retreating after us." With his eyes still fixed on the blazing logs: "I think I may say I am satisfied, sir!" was Jackson's answer; and with no further notice of the silent circle round the fire, he stood gazing absently into the glowing flames. After a few minutes, the tall figure turned away, and without another word strode off into the darkness.[5]

The meal finished, I got a second glass of iced tea and looked through Ecelbarger for the anecdote, which is one of my favorites. I guess I shouldn't have been surprised when he discounted it in a foot-note. Henderson wasn't present and the literary flourishes are just too good: flickering firelight; the cheeky youngster's wordplay; a cloaked, brooding Jackson; oracular pronouncements; then the dramatic exit.

But Ecelbarger replaces the story with a similar one that makes the same point. Again, the young man at the campfire isn't afraid to speak out: "General," he said, "it looks like you cut off more tobacco today than you could chew." Stonewall turned toward the soldier, smiled, and replied, "Oh, I think we did very well."[6]

The ultimate takeaway is that many of his soldiers believed that Jackson—prophetically—knew Kernstown was an overall success even while he was retreating. To him, it wasn't "just a lot of stuff that happened," it was a victory that only seemed like a defeat. Stonewall knew it—but how?

"Always mystify, mislead, and surprise the enemy,"[7] Jackson famously said. He not only managed to mystify the enemy, he mystified his subordinates and peers, as well as those who study him today.

Ecelbarger includes a different perspective on the battle's aftermath from a surgeon of the 7th Ohio: "I tramped and hunted over the woods all night until daylight. Often I stumbled over dead bodies and fell down. Oh, what a sight, legs smashed, heads torn off, faces mangled, arms shattered, pools of blood, bowels protruding, and every conceivable mutilation."[8]

I remembered the title of S. C. Gywnne's chapter on Kernstown: "A Jagged Line of Blood." It comes from what some Union soldiers saw when they rode along the stone wall on Sandy Ridge the day after the battle: "Across the top of the wall, running its entire length, was a jagged line of blood, the residue of hundreds of Union Minié balls hitting Confederate skulls."[9]

James I. Robertson calls his own chapter on the battle "The Lessons of Kernstown." Jackson lost the battle, but barely slackened his momentum, and so turned a defeat into a victory. That's the lesson.

Consulting Stonewall like a self-help book, I started making a mental list of instances in my own life in which I could stop brooding on setbacks and persevere.

I stared vacantly out the window, then said some words Jackson wouldn't have approved of. Driving rain had turned to driving snow—and it was sticking. I paid the check, then ran to the car with my head down. I thought about getting a room and going home the next day—"Winchester is a very pleasant place to stay in, sir!"—but consulted my inner Stonewall and decided to tough it out.

I crept along at twenty for over an hour, clutching the steering wheel, squinting through whipping wiper blades to see the road. Every few miles I would apply my brakes to make sure I had traction. Finally, near Fredericksburg, the snow turned to rain. I relaxed as much as anyone can on I-95 and got home at dusk.

CHAPTER 9

Spirits of the Place

Jackson retreated without haste while the Federals pursued without enthusiasm. Skirmishing continued, but the Southerners moved mostly unmolested up the Valley. Jackson even had time to admire the scenery. "This is a beautiful country," he wrote Anna. "After God, our God, again blesses us with peace, I hope to visit this country with my darling, and enjoy its beauty and loveliness."[1]

March slipped into April. Forces were gathering against the Confederacy on all fronts. Fort Macon was under siege in North Carolina. Savannah was threatened in Georgia. Would the forts on the Mississippi be enough to protect New Orleans?

In Virginia, McClellan continued transferring troops from the northern part of the state to the Peninsula. He began moving toward Richmond on April 4.

During the relative quiet between battles, Jackson's military relationships stand out. They range from the ideal to the trivial, with the added bonus of providing revealing glimpses of the leader he might have developed into—had he lived.

It was cold the day after Kernstown, and the group of former militiamen had marched eighteen miles toward what they knew was a defeat. The wounded, with their mangled bodies and agonizing cries, passed them going in the opposite direction for more than an hour. Now here was General Jackson, a man rumored to be crazy, saying turn around and march the other way. No explanation. No elaboration. Turn around and march the other way. That was all.

One soldier snapped. He started shouting that the Federals were just over the next hill. They were coming at that very moment to cut them to pieces.

Panic swept the ranks. Three hundred and eighty recruits were suddenly in danger of becoming an unruly mob.

There were only a handful of officers. Jedediah Hotchkiss stood out because of the quiet authority with which he calmed the men and got them back into line. The march resumed; the danger passed.

Jackson noticed, although Hotchkiss didn't realize it at the time. The general had been considering adding the mapmaker to his staff. Hotchkiss's coolheaded, capable performance tipped the balance in his favor. Two days later, Jackson called him to his headquarters in an old stone house near Narrow Passage Creek. "I want you to make me a map of the Valley," he told him, "from Harpers Ferry to Lexington, showing all the points of offense and defense in those places. Mr. Pendleton will give you orders for whatever outfit you want. Good morning, Sir."

Although it was exactly what he wanted, the assignment must have fallen on Hotchkiss like one of Jackson's surprise attacks, a thunderbolt out of a clear blue sky. Still, he got right to work, performing a reconnaissance that convinced him that Jackson's late March bivouac at Narrow Passage could be easily turned by a flanking maneuver from the west. Jackson moved the camp. It was the beginning of a long and productive relationship. "The general himself acknowledged that much of his success was due to the efforts of Jed Hotchkiss," writes Hotchkiss biographer William J. Miller. "Theirs was an extremely productive partnership, each man complementing and enhancing the abilities of the other. To know the brilliance of Jackson, one must know the work of Hotchkiss."[2]

With the exception of a willful blindness related to ministers, Jackson's staff was one of his lasting legacies. Each member is an example of a productive partnership as well as a testimonial to his ability to pick talented subordinates, men who complemented and enhanced his endeavors. All were gifted. Most were youthful. Alexander "Sandie" Pendleton was an actual prodigy. He entered Washington College at thirteen already knowing Latin and Greek, helped his professors teach mathematics and Latin, and graduated at sixteen, first in the class of 1857. Many had distinguished postwar careers, like Dr. Hunter McGuire, who was later president of the American Medical Association, among many other accomplishments.

The worst thing Jackson did after Kernstown was court-martial Richard Garnett.

Garnett had retreated at the end of the battle because his unit's ammunition had run out and he was in danger of being enveloped. When he pulled back, Fulkerson, on his left, was suddenly unsupported and had to retreat as well. At the same time, added pressure from the Federals caused a general collapse of the Confederate line and the "loss" of Kernstown.

It was an understandable decision, and, in the greater scheme of things, not half as bad as Stonewall's own lack of communication and the fact that the ammunition needed at the front was miles away in the rear.[3]

Kyd Douglas wrote that the court-martial caused "great bitterness of feeling" among the officers and men of the Stonewall Brigade. "Their astonishment at his arrest was only equaled by their indignation." The officers all thought Garnett had made the correct decision: "I do not know an exception to this opinion." Several wrote letters of support for the trial; for weeks, the men themselves refused to cheer Jackson when he rode past, their condemnatory silence a direct contrast with the brigade's enthusiasm both before and after the affair. "Garnett had completely won the confidence and affection of its officers and men."[4]

Jackson listed seven charges, "from inaccurate to niggling," according to James I. Robertson.[5] The most serious of them was the sixth, which said he retreated when he should have held his position. That one, in the words of S. C. Gwynne, "carried more than a hint of an accusation of cowardice."[6]

As an admirer of Stonewall Jackson, one wants so badly for this episode to simply go away. He should have been magnanimous, particularly now when his star was on the rise—gracious in victory as well as in defeat. It's upsetting to see him living so little by the spirit of his Christianity. It was a pattern of petty vindictiveness exhibited throughout his career. Garnett was not the only one slammed with career- and reputation-ruining charges when Jackson should have been turning a critical eye on himself.

It is fitting that Garnett's court-martial should open in the aftermath of Kernstown, the defeat that acted like a victory. Jackson's reprehensible behavior had positive repercussions. In the future, no matter how tough things got, none of his officers "would even think of retreat without being ordered to do so."[7] The strength of Jackson's forward momentum turned faults into virtues, negatives into positives.

Richard Garnett was a brave, capable, and honorable man. That his courage had been called into question may have led to his death during Pickett's Charge at Gettysburg, where he insisted on leading his men toward the stone wall on horseback, making himself a conspicuous target for the Union defenders. His body was never found, and is presumed to be among the unknown dead from Gettysburg buried in Richmond's Hollywood Cemetery.

I had been going to Hollywood since I was a teenager, but I couldn't remember ever seeing Garnett's grave. The Gettysburg dead are among the 18,000 soldiers in the Confederate section. It was murderously hot and humid when we visited in early July, a few days after the anniversary of the battle.

My wife, Catherine, who has already appeared in these pages, is as fiercely private as she is intelligent, so it's a major concession to be allowed to insert her into the narrative. She accompanied me on many of my excursions. While not quite as enthusiastic—she doesn't read every interpretive sign multiple times while being eaten by mosquitoes in the broiling sun—she's usually extremely interested and often deeply moved. In any case, Hollywood, with its meandering roads, beautiful sculptures, and spectacular views of the James River, would inspire even the staunchest nonhistorian to engage with the past.

A ninety-foot-high granite pyramid dominates the Confederate section. It's made from enormous James River rocks, many with still-visible quarry marks. They were fitted together without mortar, leaving spaces for hand- and footholds that I used to take advantage of in my daredevil years.

The Gettysburg dead are northeast of the pyramid. We found Garnett without much trouble. He had a typical-looking headstone with a lengthy inscription saying his body was never found but was presumed to be among the Gettysburg unknown. REQUIESCAT IN PACE RICHARD BROOKE GARNETT 1817–1863.

The grounds crew had just gone over the area with weed eaters and there were clumps of grass on the base of Garnett's stone. Some zealous Confederate memorialists had placed hundreds of flags in front of various markers and the weed eaters had zapped many of them, leaving them soiled on the ground.

Flags in the dust. I thought of Garnett's riderless horse galloping out of the battle smoke of Pickett's Charge in the movie *Gettysburg*. One account said he got within twenty feet of the wall. My wife took a cell phone shot of me sitting in front of his marker.

We went over and sat in the shady little gazebo. She told me about the inscription she had read describing Rufus Weaver, who had exhumed the bodies of the Gettysburg Confederates—for $3.25 each—and sent them to Richmond and other points south. Two thousand and thirty-five came to Hollywood. Weaver was only paid for some of them and did the rest of the work at his own expense. General George Pickett, along with dignitaries and veterans, met each shipment at the train station and escorted it to Hollywood, a final slow charge to the cemetery.

Talking back and forth, we almost succeeded in conjuring up the procession. Next we spoke about Weaver, a Northerner, doing his bit for sectional healing. Then we fell silent. I thought about the Union cemeteries around Richmond, the thousands on both sides who came to the same end, and how fortunate I was to not have been called on to serve—though I deeply respect those who did. I came of age at the end of the Vietnam War and my Selective Service number was over 300 in a year they only drafted into the low teens. Would I be as interested in military history if I had actually been in combat?

Jackson was the quintessence of a soldier. His opposite in so many ways, I am anything but military. It's another reason I'm attracted to him. I dislike rules and routines and have spent much of my life trying to find ways to avoid having people tell me what to do. I was uncomfortable just visiting the Virginia Military Institute. A middle-aged man in a rumpled sweater, I felt profoundly conspicuous surrounded by starched and athletic cadets. Each greeting—and they all greeted me—seemed like a reproach to my unsoldierly demeanor.

"This is a really beautiful place," I said.

"You're right," said Catherine.

Two Gators drove up. A workman started a leaf blower. Catherine had to raise her voice to be heard over the roar: "So much for quiet contemplation." Avoiding the cloud of dust, we walked back to the car.

I quoted Joshua Lawrence Chamberlain in the first chapter: "On great fields, something stays."[8] Chamberlain was speaking about Gettysburg. Rude's Hill in the Shenandoah Valley is no Little Round Top: Jackson only camped there. Still, I felt that something of his spirit would remain in a place where he had spent time during an important period of the war.

I visited the site by myself shortly after the Hollywood excursion. There's a cluster of commemorative markers across from a tire store at the summit of Rude's Hill on State Route 11. The oldest is from 1927:

RUDE'S HILL
STONEWALL JACKSON'S CAMP GROUND
APRIL 2–16, 1862

A chest-high fence parallels the road with a bright new strand of barbed wire at the top; meadow and woods beyond. Jackson's headquarters was at the bottom of the hill—hills, really; the land sort of rolls—in a house that had been abandoned by a Danish Lutheran minister named Anders Rude. It took me a while to find the building because part of one wing had been removed since the picture on the marker had been taken. Then, when I found the house, I couldn't tell whether it was occupied or abandoned. I've never been one to just walk up and knock on doors, so I stared at it from the roadside, imagining the headquarters bustle of activity: soldiers in the yard, aides coming and going, Jackson inside issuing orders—or praying. It was here that he wrote his report on Kernstown, and here where the news settled in that his defeat had been a spectacular success, causing Lincoln to withhold and withdraw vast numbers of troops from McClellan. It was also here where he court-martialed Garnett.

The Shenandoah River's North Fork winds around the hill's base, adding to its defensibility. There are two bridges close by. Neither was there during the war. The wartime bridge was where the current concrete-and-steel structure carries Route 11 traffic across the river. To the west, the Meems Bottom Covered Bridge looks like it could be prewar, but isn't. It's the fourth one on the spot, the prototype having been constructed in 1867. More than postcard picturesque, it's genuinely beautiful, one of only seven covered bridges in Virginia. I parked beside a small red pickup in a pulloff under some trees and started over to look at it.

An older man in a yellow wife-beater was standing by a picnic table. He walked toward me, spoke, then quickly realized I wasn't "one of them Johnson boys," and apologized. We fell into conversation. He drove over every night to feed a cat, he told me. "I call her Stripe. She's a pretty little cat. I'd take her home but my wife won't let me 'cause I've already got five. Somebody dumped her here, I guess."

Having decided I wasn't threatening, Stripe jumped up on the picnic table to finish her dinner. The man talked about watching the deer at sunset, how they came out of the woods and followed the edge of the field. A benign genius loci, I decided. He made me feel peaceful. Like the bridge itself, he could have stepped right out of the nineteenth century.

Stripe finished eating and let me pet her.

"You see that bush?" The man pointed across the field. "This winter I saw a bear right there. *That one* wanted to chase it but I wouldn't let him." He pointed at his red pickup. "That one's" big black head stared out with a "Why don't you pay attention to me too?" look on his face. In spite of his canine smile, he looked like he could have given the bear as good as he got. "He's a devil," said the man appreciatively. "He kills every groundhog he sees."

"Do you know anything about Stonewall Jackson camping here during the Civil War?" The man looked like the type who might have done some relic hunting. "He had about six thousand men camped in these fields."

"No, I don't know anything about that." He pondered a moment. "But if you follow this road and take a left, you'll come to a camp where they can answer all your questions."

Back in my car, envisioning some improbable summer camp with veteran reenactors inflicting drill and hardtack on youthful Civil War enthusiasts, I turned on my headlights and drove through the bridge. There was no camp at my destination, and nothing remotely historical, just warehouses and a TV station's grouping of huge satellite dishes, listening to the sky for God knows what. When I drove back, Stripe and her benefactor were gone.

There was something else in the back of my mind about the bridge. I tried to remember it but couldn't until I got back to the motel, which was so economical that Social Services was using it to stash people with substance abuse problems. Painfully thin, they sat hunched in front of their rooms—smoking, smoking, smoking.

That was it: methamphetamine; a brutal murder; MS-13. A little research brought back the whole story: "Made in trailer-park labs and the backs of barns, crank is the drug of choice in rural America," said an archived article from the *New York Times Magazine*. "In the Shenandoah Valley, crank has been moved by a biker gang called the Warlocks, but MS-13 is simply outhustling the competition with its immigrant work ethic."[9]

On July 17, 2003, a fisherman and his son found a body near the Meems Bottom Covered Bridge. It was so badly decomposed that it was hard to tell whether it was male or female. Forensic investigation revealed that it was a young, pregnant Hispanic woman. She had suffered multiple stab wounds and "her throat had been slashed so violently that her head was almost completely severed."

It turned out to be seventeen-year-old Brenda Paz, "Smiley," a gang member and informant who was set to testify against MS-13 members in six states. She had been in the witness protection program in Minnesota, but had left voluntarily, lonely for her old gang associates back in Fairfax, Virginia. Shortly after she returned, a gang member told others he had seen her diary, which contained the names of police officers and the dates and times she was meeting them. Greenlighted for execution, she would be killed far from the gang's turf to avoid arousing suspicion.

Three gang members invited her to go fishing. One borrowed an SUV and they drove to Meems Bottom, probably parking in the same little pulloff I had used. Because she was pregnant, they helped her over the rocks to a secluded spot on the bank. Then they put a rope around her neck from behind and started stabbing her. Before she died, they told her she was being killed because she was a rat—a snitch. They tried to cut her head off but their knives were too dull.[10]

The story broke about the time I started working as a teacher in juvenile corrections, and I followed it closely because I had several

MS kids. Mostly they were pretty likable. Some of them even did their schoolwork.

I returned to Rude's Hill the next day. I reread all the markers, amused myself with the idea of Jackson buying a tire across the road— Michelin or Bridgestone, General?—then drove down to Meems Bottom. Stripe wasn't around, probably, in her feline wisdom, avoiding the young mother with her three kids splashing around in the river.

Their cheerful voices floated up to me as I walked through the bridge. I studied the amazing carpentry of the arched timbers, meditated on Brenda Paz, and played with the disturbing idea that the "something" Chamberlain said lingered on great battlefields was a template created by the violence, a pattern for more brutal aggression down the years, like the pheromone trail ants follow to a food source.

No, I decided, violence is an integral part of the human condition and could happen anywhere: Becket murdered in the consecrated cathedral, the Civil War soldier shot in a nondescript patch of woods. It is who we are.

A car came through the bridge. I hugged the wall. I could be killed in this beautiful bridge, I thought, and wind up a lonely shade wandering the riverbank with Brenda Paz and whatever Confederate soldiers had been shot nearby.

It was an easy place to die. I walked out of the structure as quickly as I could.

You can almost see Sir Walter Scott directing from the wings whenever Turner Ashby, "the Black Knight of the Confederacy," galloped onto the scene. He was brave to a fault, indefatigable and charismatic, and men "flocked to his banner" in spite of the fact that he wasn't much of a talker: "Those admirers who always remembered how he looked never recalled anything he said. He spoke best with his sword."[11]

That he was not notably articulate may have had something to do with his inability—or lack of interest—in enforcing discipline. Another factor was that his command had grown so large so fast and was spread out over so much of the Valley—and was so busy fighting—that the troopers would have been difficult for anyone to control. In the aftermath of Kernstown, Ashby had twenty-one cavalry companies under his command—or twenty-six, no one seems to know for sure.[12] With him, they acted like legendary heroes; away from him, less so. On April 16, about sixty of his troopers were captured in a couple of churches where they had decided to spend the night without posting guards. Three days later, a group of cavalrymen were assigned to burn a bridge. Too drunk on local applejack to carry out the work, they fled into the mountains at the approach of Federals, "to be seen no more for ten days."[13]

Still, Ashby continued as an object of worshipful inspiration, "to whom men and women were equally attracted."[14] Kyd Douglas related the story of a Union attack on Jackson's camp at Rude's Hill. Confederate defenders, watching approaching Union cavalry, were struck by the horsemanship of their leader, who was mounted on a milk-white steed. "It was beautiful," Douglas wrote of the tableau. "Distance lent enchantment to it, as it did on other occasions in my war experience."

As the group galloped closer, the Rebels realized that the man in the lead was Ashby, the horse his fabled Tom Telegraph. Far from leading, he was being chased.

A covered bridge spanned the stream in front of the Confederates. Pulling ahead of his pursuers, Ashby tried to burn the bridge. Time was too short. The Federals were upon him. "One shot from a horseman at his side cut into his boot, grazed his leg, and buried itself in the side of his charger. The next moment the avenging sword of the master came down upon the enemy and rolled him in the dust." In spite of his wound, Tom Telegraph bore Ashby to safety. Horse and rider "came sweeping over the plain." Behind Confederate lines, the horse "sank to the ground...his wound was mortal." Gazing into his eyes, Ashby stroked his mane and bade farewell. "Thus the most splendid horseman I ever knew lost the most beautiful war-horse I ever saw."[15]

But, as S. C. Gwynne icily pointed out, "In spite of his picturesque bravery, Ashby had failed to burn a strategically critical bridge."[16] Brave himself to a fault, Jackson valued discipline, organization, and efficiency to be of equal import. On April 24 he reassigned all but the advance and rear guards of the cavalry to two infantry regiments, effectively stripping Ashby of his command.

Ashby resigned. Jackson should have seen it coming. Less than three months before, he had done the same thing when confronted with an analogous situation. Now he faced a quandary: If Ashby left, he would lose an incredibly effective fighter. He would also probably lose most of the cavalrymen who followed him. But, Jackson being Jackson, reversing himself was not in his nature.

General Charles S. Winder had taken over the Stonewall Brigade when Garnett was court-martialed. He had only been with the Valley Army a short time, but he had made friends with Ashby, who was actually talking about challenging Jackson to a duel. Acting as a go-between, Winder persuaded the two to meet. Token concessions were made on both sides. Ashby returned to command.

According to Quartermaster John Harman, the affair ended "by Gen'l. Jackson backing square down."[17] But it was more complicated than that. Jackson had been diplomatic rather than rigid, putting the Cause for which he was fighting above his own personal standards. Displaying qualities of leadership beyond diligence and resolve, he showed inklings of the man he might have become.

Of course, he continued to lobby the War Department for the reorganization of Ashby's cavalry behind the scenes.

"It was right in this room where Jackson basically fired Ashby. And Ashby basically told him to 'Stick it.' "

Dan Goodson is the vice president of the Rockbridge Historical Society and the guide at the Miller-Kite House in Elkton, Jackson's headquarters while his men were camped in the Elk Run Valley from April 19 to 30. Back then the town was known as Conrad's Store. The camp provided a sheltered and safe bivouac with many advantages. The formidable South Fork of the Shenandoah was in front, the Blue

Ridge behind. A good nearby road—now U.S. 33—provided access to General Ewell. It could also be used as an escape route or as a way to join the fighting around Richmond.

Goodson has a cane and claimed he doesn't "get around much," but he became animated and mobile as soon as he started talking about history. "Then Jackson thought about what a good general Ashby was and sent word to him that he had made a mistake. That was something Stonewall rarely did."

We were in the parlor where the confrontation/reconciliation occurred. Late summer afternoon light through old wavy window glass gave a subtle radiance to the hardwood floors and polished dinner table.

"Ashby was sort of a partisan." Goodson gestured at a large portrait of the cavalryman. "He had extremely good generalship but didn't discipline his soldiers. Stonewall Jackson was a stickler for discipline."

Open only on Sundays in the summer, the Kite House is a museum from another era. Practically every object has a lovingly *typed* label. The guides actually allow visitors to touch the exhibits. I was able to handle an empty can of Stonewall Jackson Pork and Beans, certainly one of the oddest manifestations of admiration for the general I'd ever seen. There was a picture of beans on one side of the label, Jackson on the other.

Another advantage of being a private museum, said Goodson, is that they can fly the Confederate flag. There are two small ones on the sign out front. I let the conversational opening pass without any thundering salvos in favor of the Stars and Bars. I assumed he'd changed the subject, possibly believing he'd encountered an unsympathetic soul, but he picked up the thread a moment later and took it to an unexpected place with a story about the lost flag from one of the regiments of the Stonewall Brigade. A local elderly lady was a descendant of the soldier who put the flag under his shirt at Appomattox instead of surrendering it. Some years ago, a Pennsylvania antique dealer met her, told her that her relics were not worth much, and gave her $500 for the flag and some other memorabilia. Afterward, he approached the Historical Society and offered to sell them the flag for upwards of $100,000. They countered by asking for its loan, which was refused.

I made appropriate remarks about the dealer's deceitfulness and greed, then realized Goodson wasn't waiting for my reaction. He had a lot of good stories and just wanted to tell the visitor as many as he could. He encouraged me to view more exhibits and continued talking. There was a set of china that the lady of the house saved from the Yankees by hiding it under her bed and pretending to be sick, and an ancient horsehide—Goodson told me how schoolchildren loved touching it. "When the horse died the soldier asked for its hide. He was probably sleeping on the ground." Goodson fell silent while I read an incredibly sad letter informing parents that their seventeen-year-old son had died in combat. It was displayed with his coat, which was not part of a uniform and heartbreakingly small.

I started up the stairs to see the exhibits on the second floor. Goodson laughed when he heard me stop short: "What the—?"

There were about a dozen snakeskins draped over the third-floor stairway railing. "That third stairway just leads to a dead end. We put those up there to keep the kids from going up. But it just seems to make them want to go up more!"

After coming back downstairs, I asked Goodson about ghosts. He said a few things had happened, but they were "all like Casper, the friendly ghost." There were a couple of big sleigh bells on the railing beside us that I assumed were left over from Christmas events. He said that one night he was in the house alone, upstairs in the back room, when he heard the bells. Thinking there was someone in the house, he came down to investigate. The door was locked. He looked all around. No one was there.

"When you're by yourself in the house at night you always feel like there's someone with you. It doesn't scare you or anything. You just feel like there's someone there."

CHAPTER 10

God Blessed Our Arms

Jackson's chief of staff, the Reverend Robert L. Dabney, was a puzzle, an example of Jackson's selective blindness concerning men of the cloth. Jackson believed that if someone was good in the pulpit he'd be good at anything. A distinguished theologian, Dabney authored a shelf full of books, including the first monumental Jackson biography, which appeared right after the war. Jackson, terse to a fault in both spoken and written communication, makes an odd verbal pairing with Dabney, who never used a short word when a longer one would do.

Dabney was a professor at Union Theological Seminary, then in Farmville, Virginia, when he got the call to be on Jackson's staff. Thinking he could finagle the chaplaincy he preferred, the cleric traveled to Jackson's headquarters and tried to prove himself unfit for a staff job because of lack of military knowledge and ill health. Jackson was unmoved: "Rest today," he told him. "Study the Articles of War, and begin tomorrow."[1]

The following day Dabney appeared wearing a Prince Albert coat and beaver hat. Soldiers started jeering, more so when he opened an umbrella to protect himself from the sun. Taking in the situation, Jackson told his staff, "Gentlemen, let us ride!" and galloped off into the adjacent woods. When they emerged, "Major Dabney's umbrella had been reduced to tatters by the limbs and boughs of the trees, and his beaver hat knocked into a most unbecoming and hopeless shape." More appropriately uniformed the following day, Dabney gamely set about his administrative duties, while preaching as much and as often as he could.

Jackson liked "three o'clock men" on his staff—a.m., not p.m.— and one is always reading about him moving at "first light" or "early dawn," which actually meant "no light" and "before dawn." This was a trying ordeal for Dabney. "Industrious and hugely energetic as Dr. Dabney had always been," writes his biographer Thomas Cary Johnson, "he had also inclined to late rising in the morning, but when he entered the military family of Jackson, he entered a new sphere." Jackson's servant, Jim Lewis, cleared the table when Jackson finished breakfast and that was that. "Nor was any late comer served with even coffee and bread."[2]

It's amusing to contemplate Dabney, who wrote extensively in defense of slavery, trying to wrangle an untimely biscuit out of Lewis, the slave.

Dabney served Jackson as a sort of secretary, along with other military duties and preaching. He was not wanting in courage. Colonel Andrew J. Grigsby of the Stonewall Brigade colorfully delivered what was probably the general consensus of opinion when he said: "Our parson is not afraid of Yankee bullets, and I tell you he preaches like hell."[3]

One suspects that Dabney's most important function was as a like-minded companion for Jackson, a person who relished not just weekly but *daily* devotions, and with whom he could lose himself in the religious discourse that was his passion.

"Camp fever"—typhus—forced Dabney's resignation in August 1862.

These relationships serve as a backdrop for what would become the most profound professional alliance of Jackson's life, that with Robert E. Lee. Externally, the two were a study in contrasts: Lee was Anglican, from generations of landed Tidewater gentry; Jackson was Calvinist, a Scotch-Irish mountaineer whose ancestors had been transported for petty crimes. Even at Appomattox, Lee was invariably, though never ostentatiously, well dressed; observers of Jackson delight in describing his dusty, ill-fitting uniform, his "mangy cadet cap," and so on. Physically, Lee was impressive, a particularly imposing presence on horseback because of the little-known fact that his torso was disproportionately long in comparison to his legs. Observers were surprised to see a man of mere mortal stature when he descended to earth. Mounted on Traveller, he was magnificent, a figure from mythology, larger than life.

Meanwhile, Jackson, astride his own Little Sorrel, "a close-coupled thick necked ox-eyed creature,"[4] often looked like he was in danger of falling off.

The men made different first impressions. Jackson was usually characterized as "crazy," or at least off-putting; later came the respect that deepened into admiration and affection. Lee was charismatic from the start. Private Sam Watkins wrote of his first meeting with Lee: "His whole make-up of form and person, looks and manner, had a kind of gentle and soothing magnetism about it that drew every one to him and made them love, respect, and honor him. I fell in love with the old gentleman and felt like going home with him."[5]

Such comparisons are fun and could go on for pages, but what they boil down to is this: Though on the surface they were contrasting and improbable allies, Lee and Jackson were both smart, aggressive risk-takers. A palpable excitement vibrates behind the staid official correspondence that starts with Lee's April 21 letter to Jackson.[6] As it continued back and forth, it would seem at times that the two men were talking with one voice. They were like an old married couple, and it's easy to imagine them finishing each other's sentences.

At this point, General Joseph E. Johnston was in overall command. He had ordered Jackson to threaten Banks without risking an actual fight because of the Federals' vastly superior numbers—19,000 as opposed to Jackson's 6,000.[7]

Kernstown was Jackson not fighting.

Then, with Johnston preoccupied on the Peninsula, Lee, as

Jefferson Davis's military advisor, wrote Jackson not only telling him to fight, but giving him options. Jackson wrote back immediately. Of course he wanted to fight. His letter bristled with words like "attack," "opportunity," "threaten," and "advance." It must have been very gratifying to Lee after his association with the overly cautious Johnston.

Jackson was waiting for an opening to get at Banks. He continued: "It appears to me that if I remain quiet a few days more [Banks] will probably make a move in some direction...and thus enable me, with the blessing of Providence, to successfully attack his advance."[8] Lying in wait by Elk Run, he was so quiet that Banks, only twenty miles away in Harrisonburg, didn't know he was there. Jackson was gone, Banks wired the War Department. "There is nothing more to be done by us in the Valley."[9]

Lee wrote Jackson on April 25: "The blow, whenever struck, must, to be successful, be sudden and heavy. The troops must be efficient and light."[10]

This almost sounds like a continuation of the latter part of Jackson's famous "mystify" quote: "Never fight against heavy odds, if by any possible maneuvering you can hurl your own force on only a part, and that the weakest part, of your enemy and crush it. Such tactics will win every time, and a small army may thus destroy a large one in detail, and repeated victory will make it invincible."[11]

The two worked out a plan. Jackson started before he received Lee's final approval. If that bothered Lee, he never mentioned it.

Jackson would move south to the upper Valley where General Edward Johnson's small garrison, stationed west of Staunton, was being threatened by General Robert H. Milroy with the vanguard of John C. Frémont's 23,000-man army. Staunton, a vital crossroads and railroad hub, had to be secure; plus, if Jackson were fighting in the upper Valley, he could be attacked from the rear if it fell.

General Ewell would be summoned from east of the Blue Ridge, move to Elk Run Valley, and take Jackson's place observing Banks. Jackson would unite with Johnson, defeat Milroy, then return to the Valley and unite with Ewell to fight Banks.

Once again, Jackson was "mystifying, misleading, and surprising" not only the enemy, but his own compatriots as well. Ewell's soldiers reached Swift Run Gap on April 29 and looked down on the campfires of Jackson's soldiers in the Elk Run Valley. The next day, eager to visit with their compatriots, the astonished Confederates found only a deserted campsite. "Nothing met our gaze but the smoldering embers of his deserted camp-fires.... Gone he was, and whither for what no one could tell. Quietly, in the dead of night, he had arisen from his blanket, and calling his troops around him, with them had disappeared."[12]

Jackson probably did not even tell General Ewell where he was going. There were reports that after the mysterious disappearance of Jackson and his soldiers, Ewell either "cursed in anger or sat on a fence and sobbed in frustration." Considering Ewell and his relationship with Jackson, either or both are possible.

An excellent soldier, Ewell was as much of a character as Jackson. General Richard Taylor wrote of him: "Bright, prominent eyes, a bomb-shaped bald head, and a nose like that of Francis of Valois, gave him a striking resemblance to a woodcock; and this was increased by a bird-like habit of putting his head on one side to utter his quaint speeches."[13] The quaint speeches were uttered with a "twittering lisp"[14] and "his profanity was endless."[15]

Ewell's unlovely appearance would not keep him from marrying his first cousin, wealthy Tennessee widow Lizinka Campbell Brown, later in the war. He had fallen in love with her early on, and, when she married another, had sentenced himself to a life of bachelorhood fighting Apaches on the frontier. He and Lizinka became reacquainted during the war when her son, Campbell Brown, became his aide.

His soldiers called him "Old Bald Head," by all accounts with affection. Hunter McGuire characterized him as "brave, chivalrous, splendid, eccentric Dick Ewell, whom everybody loved." Like Jackson, he was fearless and aggressive. Taylor talks about him suffering palpably under the restraints of command, until a moment came when he thought he wouldn't get caught, then sneaking forward to fight alongside the skirmishers. "Having refreshed himself, he returned with the hope that 'old Jackson would not catch him at it.' He always spoke of Jackson, several years his junior, as old."[16]

He also shared Jackson's affliction of dyspepsia, and prescribed for himself a diet of frumenty, a sort of porridge/comfort food made from cracked wheat.

While Ewell languished at Swift Run Gap, Jackson marched south beside the South Fork of the Shenandoah. Kyd Douglas called it "a terrible march";[17] Private John Worsham wrote that it was "one of the most severe marches we had undertaken."[18] Both men had been through the snow, sleet, mud, and ice of Romney.

Frequent downpours softened the already muddy roads so that "when the artillery and wagons came along they sank up to their axles, and there was no way to get them out, unless the men put their shoulders to the wheels."[19] Jackson toiled himself, "covered with mud from cap to boots, encouraging soldiers and teamsters by word and example."[20] Slowly slogging along, the famous foot cavalry managed to cover only sixteen miles in two and a half days.[21] They turned east at Port Republic, seemingly to head toward Richmond, a fact that further depressed the weary Valley soldiers who thought they were abandoning their home to Yankee invaders.

Their spirits revived after crossing the Blue Ridge at Brown's Gap when they descended to a dry road and the sun came out. They continued marching to Mechum's River Station, west of Charlottesville on the Virginia Central Railroad. Jackson did a sort of triage, putting the least able-bodied men on several trains. A cheer went up when they jolted into motion. They were heading back to the Valley, not east toward Richmond.

All of this backing and forthing is hard to describe clearly. Meant to deceive the enemy, it also confuses the readers of today—and the writers.

Muddy, ragged Confederates received a hero's welcome when they detrained at Staunton midafternoon on May 4. When Jackson himself arrived a few hours later he had Ashby seal off the town. In spite of his concerns about security, good news came the next morning: The Federals still didn't know where he was. The men rested until May 7, then set off west to unite with Johnson and fight Milroy.

General Edward "Allegheny" Johnson was yet another character. An eye wound from the Mexican War left him with an involuntary wink, which either distressed or amused the ladies he came in contact with. A sharp-tongued Richmond socialite asserted that his head was shaped like an old-fashioned skep, or beehive, and that there were "three tiers of it...like the pope's tiara."[22] A lifelong bachelor, loud and gruff, he found solace with a series of widows, a fact that also did not go unremarked upon. Instead of a sword, he went into battle carrying a large, thick club, which earned him another nickname, "Old Clubby." Jackson thought him a good soldier.

The men under him had to be good soldiers as well. Shenandoah Mountain, where many of them had spent the winter of 1861–62, was a hard, if scenic, posting. Fort Johnson, named for the general, is on the top of the mountain, and is the entrance to Highland County, which advertises itself as "Virginia's Switzerland," both for its cool climate and its rugged terrain. There's a great interpretive trail through the old fort, with wayside exhibits featuring excerpts from the letters of Shepard Green Pryor, a lieutenant of the 12th Georgia Volunteer Infantry Regiment. A photograph of his wife, Penelope, features his five daughters arranged closely around her, all staring soulfully sweet into the camera. His photo shows a rugged-looking man with long wavy hair and a shovel beard. On April 9, 1862, he wrote Penelope, "It is sleeting now fast & sleet is about four inches deep now. Wee are faring badly now in tents I assure you. Cant stay by the fire much on account of the sleet."

It must have been a relief to the Confederates when they abandoned the fort on April 19 to move closer to Staunton. The Union subsequently occupied the fort, then quickly abandoned it as well. Despite the fact that it was a hardship posting, it's hard to imagine either side leaving such a strong position.

There's a beautiful view from the pulloff for Fort Edward Johnson, near the summit of Shenandoah Mountain about twenty-six miles west of Staunton. I admired the layers of mountains fading into the west over a soundtrack of trucks grinding their gears on adjacent Route 250. The vista must have been even more impressive during the Civil War when the trees had been cut to provide a clear field of fire. An interpretive wayside quotes from the diary of Major Frank B. Jones of the 2nd Virginia Infantry: "The Shenandoah Mt. Pass is grand indeed, you ascend to the very top of the mountain & from there you see as far as the eyes can reach, mtn. after mtn. in every variety of shape and grandeur."

Admiring the scenery and marching over it were two different things. "This is the meanest country I ever saw," groused Sandie Pendleton.[23]

Jackson moved west with General Johnson in the lead. On May 7 they quickly dispatched a Federal outpost on the eastern base of Shenandoah Mountain. Next they marched over the mountain, through Fort Johnson, to the vicinity of McDowell, then and now a small, quaint village near Sitlington's Hill. "The top of the hill resembled the back of a Bactrian camel," wrote historian William J. Miller, "the two humps rising 800 feet and 1200 feet above the bottomlands below."[24]

Milroy had overlooked the advantages of the high ground, but Jackson saw it immediately. After reconnoitering on May 8, he had Johnson deploy his men, some 3,000 in number, facing west on the dual humps of Sitlington's Hill. Jackson did not place his own 6,000 on the eminence because he thought Johnson's would be sufficient considering the strength of the position. He did not expect an attack that day for the same reason. His plan was to bring his artillery into play. He sent his scouts to find a route for the cannon.

Milroy, in the meantime, had called for reinforcements from his superior, General Robert Schenck, who had made a forced march of thirty-four miles in one day to join him. Schenck and Milroy were as uncomplementary a duo as Jackson and Ewell. Milroy, "the Gray Eagle of the Army," was hyperaggressive and militarily ambitious, with an amazing shock of stiff, upstanding gray hair that contrasted with his black beard. A staunch abolitionist, he wanted to punish the slaveholding Confederates. Schenck was a former congressman with a courtly manner. A scholar of the game of poker—and many other subjects—he would become known as "the Father of British Poker" while he was minister to the United Kingdom after the war. He even authored a book on the game in 1880.

Few gambling men would have bet on the Union in this engagement, though for a while it actually looked like they were going to win. Milroy's 2,300 soldiers were outnumbered and fighting uphill when they attacked at 4:30 in the afternoon, but the surprised Confederates had the advantage for only a short while before factors came into play that favored the Union. Wrote S. C. Gwynne, "Facing west, against a clear blue sky, the rebels presented neatly silhouetted targets, while the Union troops below were obscured in deepening shadows."[25]

Also, the Confederates were armed with outmoded smoothbores, which were only accurate to about one hundred yards. The Union's Springfield rifled muskets were accurate at three times that distance.[26]

In the Confederate center, in the dip between the camel's dual humps, the 12th Georgia bore the brunt of the attack because they could be fired on from two sides. The regiment's Shepard Pryor, who had suffered in the sleet at Fort Johnson the month before, was now enduring fire "as thick as hail and my best friends falling on both sides dead and mortally wounded."

Ordered to fall back, the 12th refused, screaming that they wouldn't run from the Yankees. Their colonel succeeded in evacuating one wing of the regiment. When he went to move the other, the first wing ran back to the front. Their bravery cost them dearly: Of the regiment's 540 men, 182 would be killed or wounded.

Jackson rushed more men into the battle just as the Confederates began to give way. The reinforcements were effective. According to Reverend Dabney: "The fire was now rapid and well sustained on both sides, and the conflict fierce and sanguinary."[27]

On the Confederate right, the Union 3rd Virginia faced the Confederate 31st Virginia. Both had been recruited from Jackson's birthplace in Clarksburg. Neighbors recognized each other. Wrote the 3rd Virginia's Andrew Price: "The 31st Virginia came close to the 3rd and saluted them, and called them by name, and proceeded with the slaughter."

General Johnson was wounded in the ankle and had to leave the battlefield. He would be out of the war for a year. General Taliaferro, who had brought up reinforcements, took command.

The Federals hung on until after dark, when they retreated to McDowell. Schenck and Milroy let their men rest until shortly after midnight. Then, leaving their campfires burning to deceive the Confederates into thinking they were still encamped, they retreated north and west toward Monterey and Franklin. Jackson allowed his men to rest until the afternoon of the following day before starting in pursuit.

General Imboden visited him the next day. He had to go to nearby Staunton, he said, and asked Jackson if he needed to send any telegrams. Jackson sat down, wrote out a half page, considered it, then tore it up. He wrote out another, shorter message, then tore that up as well. Finally he got it down to one memorable line: "God blessed our arms with victory at McDowell yesterday."[28]

Jackson wrote nine words; Southern newspapers wrote thousands. New Orleans had fallen on April 25. The noose was tightening everywhere, especially in Virginia with McClellan's vast army slowly inching its way toward the capital. The Confederates were desperate for good news and a hero. That Jackson was deeply religious and had a great nickname made the story even better.

Sober second thoughts were barely considered. Jackson had allowed himself to be surprised and the casualties were lopsided for an outnumbered force fighting uphill: Union, 259; Confederate, 416. But Milroy and Schenck had fled. Staunton and the upper Valley were safe and Jackson could return, unite with Ewell, and go after Banks.

He followed the Federals some thirty miles to Franklin. The Yankees set the woods on fire and shelled him through the smoke. Jackson decided he had chased them far enough. He started his return to the Valley on May 13.

The Sitlington's Hill trailhead is about a mile east of McDowell on Route 250. I pulled in beside a pickup truck with a Tea Party license plate, got my walking stick—a sawed-off hoe handle—and started reading the waysides. Dueling signage, as usual: One said ominously that the 1.5 mile loop would take two hours; the other promised "a steady incline approximately one mile long with spectacular views of the surrounding terrain."

"The climb is very steep and should be made with caution," warned the first, which gave me pause. I had injured a thigh muscle, which slowed me down considerably, actually making me limp when I exerted myself too much, which I was certainly getting ready to do. But when my inner Jackson whispered, "Never take counsel of your fears," I went ahead and started up the trail.

I met the Tea Party guy, a genial man about my age, a few minutes later. We were exchanging pleasantries when his granddaughter came around a corner and surveyed me with the look of a startled deer. He told me the trail was "steep...we didn't go the whole way," then followed her to his truck.

The next wayside talked about Hotchkiss guiding the Confederates: "As they approached bends in the road, Hotchkiss moved ahead and waved a handkerchief if the path was clear of Union soldiers." Lichen covered the text, so it was like reading through a greenish haze. When I went around a bend myself a few moments later it

silenced the road noise. Suddenly all I heard were singing birds and
wind in the trees.

The sky was overcast, the temperature mid-seventies. I counted
myself lucky—when I left Richmond it was in the mid-nineties. Highland County is a haven in other ways: There are no cell phone towers—
McDowell's Stonewall Grocery has an actual telephone booth—and
it's the only place I've been where you can autoscan for radio stations
through the whole dial without stopping.

Big hardwoods, ferny undergrowth, mossy stones. A yellow leaf
holding water from last night's rainfall. Whenever I thought I was okay
with the incline, the trail got a little steeper. If I paused to catch my
breath, the gnats and flies caught up with me. I fanned them futilely
with my hat. The trail got even steeper beyond a marker mentioning Confederates using ravines to come up the hill. Then suddenly it
opened on several acres of mountain meadow.

The timber had grown up, as it has on so many battlefields, so you
can only get glimpses through the canopy of the "spectacular views of
the surrounding terrain"—beautiful mountains, with more beyond. At
first I thought the field was predominantly purple, then I walked a few
steps and the thistles gave way to white Queen Anne's lace and blue
cornflowers. Bees and other pollinators happily worked the blossoms.

I continued to the higher of the camel's two humps. A warm
breeze, nice views, wildflowers—my main impression was of the beauties of nature rather than any blood-soaked legacy from the past. Then
I read the signs.

"Oh Dear, it is impossible for me to express my feelings," wrote
Lieutenant Pryor to his wife, Penelope. "When the fight was over and
I saw what was done, the tears came then free. Oh, that I never could
behold such a sight again. To think it among civilized people: killing
one another like beasts."

I remembered an account of Confederates piling up the bodies of
their dead comrades to shelter themselves from Yankee bullets. "The
ghastly faces of the dead made a sickening and lasting impression,"
remembered an artillerist who visited the next day.[29]

A quarter of the way down, the solitude started to get to me. Nature was wonderful, but for some reason, the impact of wartime horrors was intensified by its contrast with the bucolic scene. I hadn't seen anyone since Tea Party and his granddaughter hours before. It would be nice to encounter another human being and shake my gloomy thoughts.

Casting about for distraction, I made matters worse by remembering the warnings I'd read about "Bear Country." Dead soldiers were quickly forgotten as I scanned my surroundings for danger. On cue, there was a rustling in the underbrush. "I'm not scared!" I told myself as I prepared to "appear larger" and "remain calm." More rustling, and a spotted fawn appeared out of the bushes. We stared at each other until it decided I was harmless and walked away.

My good mood restored, I coasted downhill. Back at my car I was startled to realize that the exertion had helped, rather than hurt, my injured muscle. I got in my car and drove contentedly around the mountain into town.

There's a nice little museum behind the funeral home in McDowell. I had cheese and crackers and a bottle of water sitting on the front porch of the Stonewall Grocery.

Yankees and Confederates sleep together in the cemetery across from the Methodist church. Sheep grazed in a pasture on the other side. I was reading the historical markers when a church meeting let out and a man, who had to be the pastor, greeted me: "If you look at the front of the church you can see where the soldiers carved their names in the brick."

I walked over. Sure enough, I found 1862 B. CROSBY by the front door.

CHAPTER 11

An Unconscious Poet

Jackson had two bosses—Johnston and Lee. Ewell had three—the aforementioned two plus Jackson, that "enthusiastic fanatic" who gave him headaches and aggravated his indigestion. "I have never suffered so much from dyspepsia in my life," he confided to a niece while cooling his heels at Swift Run Gap.[1] Sticking to his post, he endured a fusillade of confusing and contradictory orders, watching and waiting, the two activities at which this explosive man of action least excelled.

But Jackson was on his way, pushing his men through yet another of those nightmare marches with which they had become so familiar. Torrential rains turned the roads to mud. Wagons got stuck, broke, and overturned. Firewood was soaked, like everything else. Some of the men were barefoot; others held their shoes together with twine.[2]

It was while his soldiers were slogging through the mud that Stonewall issued a new directive on marching. There were two main thrusts to the document. First: No straggling. Soldiers could no longer break ranks to fill their canteens from a roadside well or creek, and no soldier could leave the ranks at all unless it was a "case of Necessity" or they were confirmed sick by a "Regimental Medical Officer." Second: The men were to march fifty minutes, stack arms—which meant placing their muskets in an interlocking pyramid—then rest for ten.[3] The break was most rejuvenating if taken lying down.

The second rule must have been secretly satisfying to Jackson because it echoed the rhythm of the weekly Sabbath observances he held so dear: Work six days, rest one; march fifty minutes, rest ten.

Jackson's timing could have been better. One can easily imagine the reaction of a wet and hungry soldier to instructions on how to march after he had been marching all day. Still, as with everything else Jackson did, his mistakes—sometimes especially his mistakes—were converted by his forward momentum into strengths. These new rules provided the template for the metamorphosis of his already hard-marching soldiers into the famed "foot cavalry." And once again his favorite Bible verse seems preternaturally applicable: "All things work together for good...."

Jackson was upping his game in other ways. The twelve-month enlistments of seventeen soldiers of the 27th Virginia had expired. The recent Conscription Act passed by the Confederate Congress had extended their enlistments to three years. "Saying this was a breach of faith, they demanded their discharge, and laying down their arms refused to serve another day."

Colonel Grigsby referred the matter to Jackson. Reverend Dabney says his blue eyes flashed. "What is this but mutiny?" Jackson exclaimed. "Why does Colonel Grigsby refer to me to know what to do with mutiny? He should shoot them, where they stand."

He dictated an order to "parade the regiment instantly, with loaded muskets." The seventeen were disarmed and brought before them, then offered the choice of being shot or returning to the army. Dabney says that the seventeen "promptly reconsidered."

"They could not be afterwards distinguished from the rest of the regiment in their soldierly behavior; and this was the last attempt at organized disobedience in the army."[4]

What had happened to the eccentric, slightly befuddled VMI professor who was an object of fun to his cadets? And what had happened to the kind but stern commander who had patiently explained to the Reverend Graham why, as much as it pained him, he must let the execution of a man who had shot his commanding officer go forward?

It was a hard war, and Jackson may have been the hardest man in it. He would get harder still before things were over.

The sun came out when the soldiers entered the Valley. Suddenly it was spring. Back in the Alleghenies it had been "like mid-winter—not a bud nor blade of grass to be seen," according to an artillerist on the march. The man continued: "After the bleak mountains, with their leafless trees, the old Valley looked like Paradise. The cherry- and peach-trees were loaded with bloom, the fields covered with rank clover, and how our weary horses did revel in it. We camped the first night in a beautiful meadow."[5]

It must have been like Dorothy waking up to Technicolor in Oz. And now the junction with Ewell was imminent—as it needed to be. Banks had sent Shields east to join McDowell and was himself rumored to be preparing to move down the Valley. Lee kept urging Ewell and Jackson to combine their forces and crush Banks, and both of them were eager to do so. But on May 17, the two received orders from General Johnston that Ewell was to pursue Shields. Jackson had to stay in the Valley and "watch" Banks.

Jackson sent a message to Johnston asking him to reconsider, and instead of instantly complying, Ewell, who had spent his whole adult life in the military obeying orders, hesitated. He had indiscreetly raged against Jackson in front of various subordinates, calling him a "crazy fool," among other things. But he knew that Banks would be fatally outnumbered if he and Jackson united.

Ewell mounted his horse for an all-night ride of some thirty miles over Massanutten Mountain to Jackson's camp at Bridgewater. Somewhat surprised to find the general and his soldiers keeping the Sabbath rather than sharing his agitation, he went with Jackson to a nearby mill where the two of them conferred. They determined on what James I. Robertson called a path of "creative insubordination"—continue on their present course until Jackson got a response to his message to Johnston.

Jackson invited Ewell to hear Dabney preach. The irreligious Ewell must have agreed reluctantly, but probably gained some comfort from Dabney's topic, if not his homiletics: "Come unto me all ye that travail and are heavy laden, and I will give you rest."

There's a nice park beside the river in Bridgewater where this heavy-laden writer should have found rest. I lay down on a bench, but it was too hot to relax—that July was the hottest on record—so I got up and wandered around. The park has a pretty gazebo, swinging gliders, and a historical marker that mentions how the Confederates burned the bridge to keep the Yankees from using it. When Jackson and his soldiers arrived, they had to improvise a crossing using a series of wagons driven into the water and covered with boards for a walkway.

Tulip poplars trailed low-hanging branches in the river. Traffic noise and cicadas. A father and son played Pokémon Go, handing their iPhones back and forth. Mom drove up, parked beside Dad's pickup, and fussed loudly at the two of them, saying they should have been home. Subtext: *How come you guys are out having fun while I'm running errands?* Dad was unruffled: "Why don't you come over here with us?" His friendliness annoyed her even more. "I can't!" she exclaimed. "I've got ice cream in the car!" She drove off in a huff.

Trump was campaigning hard that summer, going from strength to strength, although at that point hardly anyone expected him to win. It was like he had poured gasoline on the nation's smoldering fires of racism and division. This snapshot of small-town domestic life—father-son bonding, Mom's ritual annoyance—was reassuring, giving me the feeling that a normal, Norman Rockwell kind of world still existed in the midst of all the craziness. Still, a sour note: All of a sudden I couldn't help but see Snorlaxes and Pikachus amid the Confederate ghosts with which my imagination had peopled the park. Then my playful irritation was subsumed into truly somber thoughts when I looked at the river and remembered that the bridge had been built by a crew of impressed slaves and free blacks—referred to as "black pioneers" in most accounts—who had no choice but to labor through the night in ice-cold water.

The father and son finished their game and drove off. I left a little later. Crossing the bridge, I found the natural amphitheater where Dabney preached. The owners kept the grassy slope well trimmed. It was easy to imagine the soldiers on the hillside during a Sunday service long ago.

The fifty-mile long Massanutten Mountain divides the Shenandoah Valley for about a third of its length. To the west flows the North Fork of the Shenandoah River. The South Fork flows to the east and the two join near the north side of the mountain close to Front Royal. Massanutten can be easily crossed at only one spot: New Market Gap, near its center.

On May 19, Jackson and Ewell started after Banks, who was at Strasburg, a few miles to the northwest of Front Royal. Ewell, on the east side of Massanutten, sent one brigade around the south side to Jackson. This had to have been a subterfuge to deceive observers that his whole force was uniting with Stonewall. Instead, the two armies swept northward on opposite sides of the mountain, Jackson starting out at his usual 3 a.m.

The brigade sent by Ewell consisted of Louisianans under General Richard Taylor, President Zachary Taylor's son and Jefferson Davis's brother-in-law. Educated at Harvard and Yale, Taylor was easily the best writer to cover the portion of Jackson's wartime career to which he was a witness, although historians vary in their estimation of his achievement. Douglas Freeman writes that he is "the one Confederate general who possessed literary art that approached first rank.... No firmer, more accurate pictures are to be found in Confederate literature than those Taylor penned of 'Stonewall,' of Ewell and of others less renowned."[6]

On the other hand, James I. Robertson avers that Taylor was "always portraying Jackson as an eccentric who spent most of his life on his knees, alternately praying and sucking lemons.... [Taylor] had a knack then—and a habit in his postwar memoirs—of manufacturing facts for a good story."

The biographer's ire seems far out of proportion to the offense. It's hard not to think that Taylor's real crime was being insufficiently reverent toward Robertson's hero.

Taylor's men put on a show for the Valley soldiers when they marched into camp, and he rises to a sort of martial poetry in describing it:

> Over three thousand strong, neat in fresh clothing of gray with white gaiters, bands playing at the head of their regiments, not a straggler, but every man in his place, stepping jauntily as on parade, though it had marched twenty miles and more, in open column with arms at "right shoulder shift," and rays of the declining sun flaming on polished bayonets, the brigade moved down the broad, smooth pike, and wheeled on to its camping ground.

Taylor settled his men into camp, then went to report to Jackson. Freeman rates Taylor's description of this iconic first meeting as "delightful." Robertson at first concurs, calling it "charming," before continuing far less generously: "Unfortunately, everything about the narrative has dubious overtones."[7]

Taylor found Jackson sitting on a fence.

> I saluted and gave my name and rank, then waited for a response. Before this came I had time to see a pair of cavalry boots covering feet of gigantic size, a mangy cap with visor drawn low, a heavy dark beard, and weary eyes—eyes I afterward saw filled with intense but never brilliant light. A low, gentle voice inquired the road and distance marched that day. "Keezletown Road, six and twenty miles." "You seem to have no stragglers." "Never allow straggling." "You must teach

my people, they straggle badly." A bow in reply. Just then my creoles started their band and a waltz. After a contemplative suck at a lemon, "Thoughtless fellows for serious work" came forth. I expressed a hope that the work would not be less well done because of the gayety. A return to the lemon gave me the opportunity to retire.[8]

Ewell had to call on Jackson again after receiving another message from Johnston. There was no wiggle room this time. He was ordered to either join General Richard Anderson to defend against McDowell, or to march to the aid of the main army in front of Richmond. Jackson's job was again to watch Banks.

Ewell found Jackson on the march and the two retired to a nearby patch of woods for privacy. This time Jackson determined to appeal to his new ally in Richmond, Robert E. Lee. He sent a courier to Staunton with instructions to send the following telegram: "I am of the opinion that an attempt should be made to defeat Banks, but under instructions just received from General Johnston, I do not feel at liberty to make an attack. Please answer by telegraph at once."[9]

No one was more of a stickler for following orders than Jackson. Except when he wasn't. Having already violated the chain of command, he countermanded Johnston's instructions to Ewell by writing on the message: "Suspend the execution of the order for returning to the east until I receive an answer to my telegram."

History does not record Lee's response. He didn't need to respond at all. Fresh orders arrived from Johnston that evening. He had reassessed the situation. The attack against Banks should go forward.

In the meantime, Jackson and Ewell received new information. A Union garrison, small and vulnerable, was stationed at Front Royal. They would attack there first. After defeating it, they would be on Banks's flank and move against him from the east.

Jackson crossed Massanutten from west to east at New Market Gap. Riding with him, their destination shrouded in mystery, General Taylor was deeply impressed by his reticence. He was more puzzled than ever when he thought about the fact that night that he was camped just a short distance from Conrad's Store, which he had left a few days earlier. He wrote fancifully: "I began to think that Jackson was an unconscious poet, and, as an ardent lover of nature, desired to give strangers an opportunity to admire the beauties of his Valley." He groused further about the hardship of riding in circles, taking in the scenery when he could have been gaining laurels on the Peninsula where the real fighting was going to take place.[10]

On May 22, Jackson shared with his chief commanders that they were going to attack the Union outpost at Front Royal with odds of sixteen to one in the Confederates' favor.[11]

That night, they camped just ten miles south of the town. They were already marching northward in a twelve-mile-long column when the sun came up. Everything looked to be in place for them to sweep into town when Jackson ordered a halt five miles from their objective.

Ashby had forwarded intelligence from one of his troopers about the number of soldiers in Front Royal and where they were camped. Lieutenant Walter Buck had grown up nearby and was intimately familiar with the townspeople and the terrain. The ideal person to send on a reconnaissance, he reported back that the Confederates were facing a force made up mostly of "one regiment of Marylanders."

When Jackson learned of this, he dictated written orders to an adjutant to bring his own Marylanders forward to spearhead the assault: "Colonel Johnson will move the First Maryland to the front and attack the enemy at Front Royal. The army will halt until you pass."[12]

Although his officers had been trying to keep it from him, Jackson undoubtedly knew that there was trouble in the regiment. This was another dispute about whether the soldiers were to serve for one year or three. Some wanted to join the cavalry; others just wanted to go home. Half the regiment laid down their arms, refusing to serve any longer. They were arrested. The rest, though they had not participated, were in turmoil as well. Their colonel was disgusted. Bradley T. Johnson had helped raise the regiment in 1861. A Princeton graduate, he had been a lawyer before the war.

When he received Jackson's order, he assembled the entire regiment and read it to them. Then, rising to rare rhetorical heights, he claimed he was going to have to return the order to Jackson because the 1st refused to meet the enemy. But "If I can get ten good men, I'll take the Maryland colors with them and will stand for home and honor." As for the rest, "Never again call yourselves Marylanders! No Marylander ever threw down his arms and deserted his colors in the presence of the enemy—and those arms and those colors given you by a woman!"

The woman he referred to was Hetty Cary, "the most beautiful woman of her day and generation," according to Kyd Douglas.[13] The regimental flag had been made for the unit by the secessionist "Ladies of Baltimore"—undoubtedly mothers, sisters, and sweethearts—and smuggled to them by Cary just before Manassas.

Home. The flag. A beautiful woman. If the soldiers didn't rise to the occasion, "You will wander over the face of the earth with the brand of coward, traitor, indelibly imprinted upon your foreheads, and in the end sink into a dishonored grave, unwept, uncared for."

"The men in ranks cheered," wrote Colonel Johnson. "The men under guard pleaded with tears to be allowed to return to duty, ran back miles to the wagons, got their guns and rejoined their regiment." The Marylanders sang as they marched to the head of the column, cheered for twelve miles by their fellow soldiers.[14]

CHAPTER 12

A Talent for Retreat

A fter orchestrating this inspiring bit of military theater with the Marylanders, Jackson turned his attention elsewhere. Cartographer Hotchkiss and engineer Keith Boswell were on a scouting mission to learn more about Banks and the country to the west, vital information for Stonewall's next move after he dispatched the Front Royal Yankees. Passing the Marylanders to the front, which took several hours, diverted his men while they were waiting, as well as building everyone's spirits.

"Wheat's Tigers" were to the left of the 1st Maryland. Shock troops on steroids, these mostly Irish American "wharf rats" were as prone to fight off the battlefield as on, and were noted for discarding their muskets at Manassas in favor of Bowie knives. They were just barely controlled by their colonel, Chatham Roberdeau Wheat. Six foot four in a time when the average man was five foot eight, the 275-pound Wheat had been shot through both lungs at Manassas. When the doctors told him his wound was mortal, he said, "I don't feel like dying yet." He didn't, recovering and returning to fight with the army eight months later. A soldier of fortune, he'd fought in Mexico and Cuba before the war and was with Garibaldi in Italy when hostilities started and he returned home.

Jackson modified his battle plans during the wait. Instead of moving against the enemy in two columns with his entire force, he would attack piecemeal along Gooney Manor Road, later wisely renamed

Browntown Road. This way, any Federals who escaped would not know his true numbers. He dispatched his cavalry to tear up track on the Manassas Gap Railroad to prevent Banks from reinforcing Front Royal. They were also directed to cut telegraph lines to keep word from getting back to him about the attack.

The fog of war was already thick around Front Royal because of the cavalry screen coupled with the all but impenetrable barrier of Massanutten. The fact that Jackson could halt so close to town for so long, and be casual about it, was a testament to the efficacy of both. Even more successful as a cloaking device was the Union conviction that Ewell and Jackson were miles away.

Front Royal Confederates knew exactly where he was. Kyd Douglas was with Jackson on an eminence overlooking the town when he saw "the figure of a woman in white" emerge and run toward the heights waving her bonnet, keeping a hill between her and the town. Jackson sent him to meet her, and, moments later, Douglas was startled to realize that "the romantic maiden" with the "tall, supple, and graceful figure" was his childhood friend Belle Boyd.

Nearly exhausted, Boyd spoke to him with her hand pressed against her heart: "I knew it must be Stonewall when I heard the first gun." The Confederates vastly outnumbered the Union garrison, she said. "Tell him to charge right down and he will catch them all."

Her exit was as dramatic as her entrance: "I raised my cap," writes Douglas, "she kissed her hand and was gone."[1]

Sadly, historians—many of whom actually seem to relish the idea of ruining a good story—agree that Jackson probably already had the information she conveyed.[2] Yet she's always mentioned, a pleasant interlude in the narrative, as welcome a diversion for the reader as it must have been for the hot and dusty soldiers who watched her come and go.

Lieutenant Boswell appeared and reported, overestimating Banks's numbers at 12,000—more than twice the number of soldiers actually stationed at Strasburg. Jackson told him to make two maps—one for

him and one for Ewell—of the country between Front Royal and Winchester. The attack began—finally—at around 2 p.m.

For the Union guards, it was a hot and lazy afternoon. "In the
Luray Valley to the south was no sign of life, save the buzzards sailing
lazily above the slumbrous woods."[3] The first Yankee whom Colonel
Bradley Johnson encountered was a sentinel taking his ease in a shelter made from a blanket and a couple of fence rails. The man got up,
"looked at the strange sight coming out of the woods, sheltered his
eyes from the sun, then made a grab for his musket, but before he could
fire, the cavalry was on him." Other pickets were captured before they
could give the alarm.[4]

The Confederates swept forward. Federals abandoned the town
with little resistance. A Union train pulled in. At first the Confederates
feared it brought reinforcements. When they discovered it was a supply
train, some of the Tigers tossed out the engineer and started playing
with the whistle. They would lose momentum again when they came
to the Union camp with its opportunities for plunder.

A Mississippi soldier managed to take advantage of the camp's
bounty while continuing to advance. "As I ran over one of their small
[breakfast] fires, I picked up a hot frying pan which was still on the
fire, threw the hardtack in it, placed my little finger over the spout
of the coffee pot, and carried the breakfast of that Yank over a mile
before I got a chance to eat a mouthful."[5]

Union colonel John R. Kenly rushed his infantry and two rifled
Parrott guns to high ground north of town. Richardson's Hill commanded a meadow over which the Confederates would have to pass
to reach the bridges beyond. Kenly's men fought bravely, not realizing
how badly they were outnumbered. "I prepared to hold the position as
long as possible," Kenly wrote later. "For I was certain that if I did not
check Jackson's advance...Banks was lost."[6]

General Taylor took advantage of a lull in the firing to ride
down to the river to get a better look at the Union position. His horse,
thirsty from the march, started to drink. Taylor was noticed by Federal

riflemen. "Instantly a brisk fire was opened on me, bullets striking all around and raising a little shower-bath." Knowing that his men were watching, he tried to look unconcerned.

"A provident camel, on the eve of a desert journey, would not have laid in a greater supply of water than did my thoughtless beast. At last he raised his head, looked placidly around, turned and walked up the bank."[7]

The Confederates came on slowly and steadily. Jackson was often out in front of the skirmishers. "His eagerness all through the campaign was surprising," wrote John Worsham, "and his escape from death was almost a miracle."[8]

They were hampered by their lack of rifled cannon. When Stapleton Crutchfield, Jackson's new chief of artillery, ordered up cannon, they were twelve- and six-pound smoothbores, easily outranged by the Federal Parrotts. Confederates were pinned down behind a stone wall at the foot of Richardson's Hill—and elsewhere. "The shells [came] quicker than I thought two guns could shoot," said a cavalryman.[9]

Frustrated with the one-sided battle, Jackson exclaimed, "Oh what an opportunity for artillery! Oh that my guns were here!" He turned to an aide: "Order up every rifled gun and every brigade of the army."[10] So much for keeping his numbers secret. Miles to the rear, the guns and the infantry would be slow in coming.

The Federals faced growing pressure from the Confederates as the afternoon waned. The sheer weight of numbers began to tell. Confederates closed in from the east and south.

North of the Federal position, the Shenandoah River forms a sinuous Y with its two branches pointing west. The main north–south road crossed both branches behind Richardson's Hill, the Manassas Gap Railroad crossed one. Around 4 p.m., Kenly saw Confederate cavalry coming in from the west. He had been flanked. He put his camp to the torch, limbered up his Parrotts, and hurried his men over the South and North Fork bridges. He took up a position on Guard Hill, the ridge to the north of Richardson's Hill and the forks of the Shenandoah. He was quickly in danger again of being enveloped by the Southerners.

And now Confederate artillery, firing from his just-vacated position on Richardson's Hill, had him within range.

He had tried to set fire to the North Fork Bridge, but green timbers and recent rains prevented the flames from catching. He sent Sergeant William Taylor to refire the bridge. This attempt was successful, although Taylor was wounded in the hand while he worked. Many years later, almost at the turn of the century, Taylor would earn the Congressional Medal of Honor for his bravery.

Taylor's heroic efforts only slowed the Confederates, who quickly extinguished the flames. Enough of the structure remained sound for several companies of cavalry to gingerly make their way across. Others forded the river. Kenly retreated north from Guard Hill. Jackson directed Major Thomas S. Flournoy to follow the Federals with about 300 cavalry. A few foot soldiers followed in their wake.

Retreating north, Kenly hoped to turn west and unite with reinforcements he expected from Banks. Unfortunately, Banks didn't receive Kenly's report and request until 5:45 p.m. The reinforcements started toward him—on the wrong road—at about the time Rebel horsemen, approaching on the west, cut him off from moving in that direction.

Kenly made a stand at Fairview, a stone house on a plateau some five miles north of Front Royal. At this point he had approximately 850 men, whom he deployed on both sides of the road. He sent cavalry galloping toward the advancing Confederates. A moment later they came galloping back. They charged through their own men, some of whom mistook the horse soldiers for Confederates and fired on them.

Picture-book "Charge of the Light Brigade" cavalry assaults were being phased out even in this early part of the war because of the lethal firepower of the rifled musket. No one shared this knowledge with the members of the 6th Virginia Cavalry, who attacked Kenly's men that evening at around 6:30 p.m. Galloping along the road, Company B crested the plateau ahead of Companies E, A, and K, who were advancing through woods and fields. In the lead, the eighteen-year-old color bearer, James H. "Dallas" Brown, was the most conspicuous target among many. A Federal volley devastated the troopers, killing or wounding twenty-three of the company's thirty-five horsemen. Dallas Brown died with twenty-one bullet wounds, fourteen in the arm that held the flag.

The rest of the 6th hit the Federals moments later. Attacking with pistols and sabers, the Southerners made up in ferocity what they lacked in numbers. With no time to reload, the Northerners fought back with clubbed muskets and bayonets. Kenly was hit by a musket ball. Then he suffered a saber blow to the top of his head. His adjutant, Lieutenant Frederick Tarr, was slashed across the face. Throwing up his right arm to shield himself, he took a second cut to the elbow. A third destroyed a thumb joint of his left hand, while a fourth, hitting the top of his head, penetrated to the bone. Remarkably, both men survived.

Mounted heroics prompted the normally reticent and uncomplimentary Jackson to utter a superlative, telling his staff that he had never in all his experience of warfare seen a cavalry charge executed with such gallantry. The fight segued quickly from slaughter to surrender. Jackson captured 700 infantrymen, including 20 officers. He also captured the two rifled Parrott guns that had pinned down his men, two locomotives, and a wealth of stores.

Wrote General Taylor: "Late in the night Jackson came out of the darkness and seated himself by my camp fire. He mentioned that I would move with him in the morning, then relapsed into silence.... For hours he sat silent and motionless, with eyes fixed on the fire. I took up the idea that he was inwardly praying, and he remained throughout the night."[11]

Praying certainly, but undoubtedly also planning, weighing his options and trying to discern the mind of his enemy. It was a night reminiscent of his teaching days at VMI, when for an hour or more each evening he would turn his chair to the wall and silently rehearse his lessons for the next day. Jackson was trying to figure out how to get at Banks.

It was frequently remarked that Robert E. Lee knew the minds of his opponents, almost as if he sat in on their councils of war. While Stonewall didn't have his gift, it didn't take a wizard to figure out what Banks could do. The Union commander had four options: hunker down in his Strasburg defenses and wait for Stonewall to attack; cut his way out through whatever Confederates were between him and the Blue Ridge; or run, either north to Winchester or west to Frémont.

There was high ground in Winchester that could be fortified and defended. It was also the next step to the Potomac and safety. It was clearly the best choice, but Banks himself wasn't yet to the point when he could even begin weighing options. In a sort of catatonic stupor, he completely rejected his predicament.

Colonel George H. Gordon was a Mexican War veteran and a former classmate of Jackson's at West Point. His picture of the situation was crystal clear. Visiting Banks in the early evening, he found the general "spiritless and dejected." Gordon urged an immediate withdrawal to Winchester. Instead of answering him, Banks kept repeating, "I must develop the force of the enemy."

Depressed by the general's unresponsiveness, Gordon left. News from the front continued trickling in. At ten o'clock Gordon decided to try once more. Again, all his remonstrances met with the same refrain: "I must develop the force of the enemy."

An exasperated Gordon reiterated that it was time to go. "It is not a retreat," he argued, "but a true military movement to escape from being cut off; to prevent stores and sick from falling into the hands of the enemy."

"Retreat" hit a nerve. Banks rose from his seat. "By God, sir, I will not retreat!" he said passionately. "We have more to fear, sir, from the opinions of our friends than the bayonets of our enemies."

Finally Gordon understood: "Banks was afraid of being thought afraid."[12] In the early stages of grief, he was mourning the death of his postwar presidential career. Gordon had witnessed denial and anger; acceptance wouldn't come until morning.

Banks moved at dawn. Before he left, he took time to pen a letter to his wife that closed with a plaintive "Good Bye."

Banks set fire to supplies he couldn't carry away. In addition to hundreds of wagons and thousands of soldiers, his miles-long column included ambulances as well as the ambulatory sick and wounded. Bringing up the rear were panic-stricken civilians, Union sympathizers black and white, along with more wagons piled high with their earthly goods and topped with children, who thought the whole thing was a lark.

Feeling his way forward, Jackson acted as though he knew what Banks was doing. He sent cavalry to two places on the Strasburg-Winchester portion of the Valley Pike, and himself moved with Ewell's soldiers toward Winchester. He left the Stonewall Brigade at Front Royal as insurance, in case Banks tried to break out to the east.

Jackson halted at Nineveh after marching only three miles and waited for particulars of the situation to come clear. Shortly before noon, he received news from a courier that Confederate cavalry under General George H. "Maryland" Steuart had struck the Union column at Newtown, today's Stephens City, about halfway between Strasburg and Winchester. This was confirmation that Banks was fleeing north on the Valley Pike. Jackson divided his forces. Ewell continued toward Winchester. Jackson, with infantry, artillery, and Ashby's cavalry, would hit the Federals farther south.

The unaptly named Middletown is a third of the way between Strasburg and Winchester, not half. Jackson got to high ground overlooking the town shortly after 3 p.m. Miles of wagons, along with cavalry, were passing north through town, their passage constrained by stone walls on either side of the pike.

Confederate artillery unlimbered on the high ground. Confederate infantry deployed north, preparing to hit the Federal cavalry from the east.

It was almost like target practice for the Confederate gunners. Shells plowed into the cavalry. Union officers urged the troopers to stay in formation. It was hard to move anyway because teamsters had abandoned their wagons, blocking the road. They finally scattered, some galloping to the west, raising an enormous cloud of dust; others north, toward a bend in the road and a stone wall behind which Louisiana troops were waiting.

Sabers drawn, the Federal troopers charged through the dust cloud into a trap. Infantry shot them from behind the wall, artillery from the high ground. Soldiers and horses fell in a confused, writhing heap. "Never did a host receive a more mortal thrust," wrote Reverend Dabney. "At every fierce volley, the troopers seemed to melt by scores from their saddles; while the frantic, riderless horses, rushed up and down, trampling the wounded wretches into the dust."

Wounded men tried to crawl to safety as the attacks continued. Others simply fled and looked for places to hide. More charges added to the pile. A Vermont soldier, stunned when his horse was shot from under him, braced to be trampled by the next charging company: "But I was spared and when I arose from among that mass of dead and dying I found that I was only a prisoner in the rebels' hands."

The Confederates took some 200 prisoners and acquired about as many horses. Dabney said the townspeople, emerging after the action, exalted "with uplifted hands" over the carnage. Like a Greek chorus, he has them exclaiming: "Behold the righteous judgment of God, for these are the miscreants who have been most forward to plunder, insult, and oppress us!"[13]

Maybe. But the God of Battles was about to give the Federals a break. Jackson, hearing artillery to the south, assumed that most of Banks's army was still between him and Strasburg. Actually, he had just annihilated the next-to-the-rear guard. Now he turned south where only a small remnant remained.

It took him an hour and a half of probing and fighting to understand his mistake. It was 5:45 before he finally headed north.[14]

Piratical tendencies of some Southerners hindered the pursuit from the beginning. "The gentle Tigers were looting right merrily," wrote General Taylor, "diving in and out of wagons with the activity of rabbits in a warren; but this occupation was abandoned on my approach, and in a moment they were in line, looking as solemn and virtuous as deacons at a funeral."[15]

Ashby's men were completely in character as well. Some requisitioned captured Yankee horses and took them to nearby farms—or their own homes—for safekeeping.[16] They were so intent on plunder that they became useless militarily. Ashby himself couldn't control them. "Forgetful of their high trust as the advance of a pursuing army," a still-irate Jackson wrote in his official report months later, "[they] deserted their colors and abandoned themselves to pillage."[17]

In pursuit of Jackson, wrote James I. Robertson, "It had taken Banks thirty days to cover the sixty-seven miles from Winchester to Harrisonburg."[18] Now, according to Shelby Foote, "Banks was showing a real talent for retreat."[19]

Once he surmounted his mental stumbling block and started, he moved with speed and dispatch. It helped that his troops were fresh, while Jackson's men had been marching hard for days. Hungry Confederates found it difficult to pass wagons full of delicacies and supplies, though few were as lucky as the Union soldiers who stuck bayonets into the flames and pulled out sizzling hams.[20]

For the Southerners, the night was surreal. They marched exhausted through an area many of them had grown up in, seeing familiar scenes illuminated by burning wagons and littered with grisly remnants of war. When they passed near his house, Private Seth Barton slipped away for a drink of milk or water, "which I needed very much to help me in this long march [that] had continuously kept up since five o'clock in the morning and it was then one o'clock the next morning." When he tried to open the gate, it hit something so that he couldn't pass through. "Looking down I discovered a dead Federal soldier with a bullet through his head, and his head against the gate.... I made no further effort to get in but hurried on to join my slowly moving company."[21]

Federal rearguard action also slowed the Confederates and kept them on edge. Jackson, secure in his knowledge that only a predestined bullet would kill him, rode in front as his men marched through the night. He was indignant when a volley from an ambush north of Newtown sent Southern cavalry galloping toward the rear in such dangerous confusion that artillerymen had to dive under their caissons to keep from being trampled. "Shameful!" scolded Jackson. "Did you see anybody struck, sir? Did you see anybody struck? Surely they need not have run, at least until they were hurt!"[22]

Jackson was shot at more than once. As General Taylor rode with him, darkness and fatigue engendered a sort of magical thinking, and he found himself believing that "Jackson was invulnerable and that persons near him shared that quality."[23]

Jackson's "iron will" pushed the pursuit until well past midnight. Around three, Colonel Fulkerson rode out of the darkness. "My men are falling by the roadside," he told Jackson. "Unless they are rested, I shall be able to present but a thin line tomorrow."

"Colonel, I yield to no man in my sympathy for the gallant men under my command," said Jackson, "but I am obliged to sweat them tonight so that I may save their blood tomorrow."

Remembering Kernstown, he was racing for the high ground south of Winchester. But he must have suddenly realized that at the rate he was going, when he got there he wouldn't have anything to fight with. Reversing his own quotable pronouncement, he told Fulkerson: "You shall, however, have two hours rest."[24]

CHAPTER 13

The Lion's Mouth

Lincoln and Secretary of War Edwin Stanton had just finished a meeting with Generals McDowell and Shields at Falmouth, a little north of Fredericksburg. They had decided to send the 40,000 soldiers stationed there due south for a coordinated attack with McClellan. The combined thrust from the north and east would be decisive. Richmond would fall.

Everything changed with the May 23 news of the Federal defeat at Front Royal and Banks's retreat. Jackson had to be dealt with and Washington protected.

Now McDowell would remain in place to protect the capital. Shields was to retrace his march to the Valley, where Frémont would join him from the west for a combined attack against Jackson. Once again, Stonewall had relieved the pressure on Richmond, but at the cost of putting his own head in the lion's mouth.

Not surprisingly, Jackson and Ewell were moving against Winchester at early dawn on Sunday, May 25. Equally unsurprising was that Banks had arrayed his men in a two-and-a-half-mile-long battle line on the hills south of town—Camp Hill to the east, Bowers Hill to the west. There was thick fog on the battlefield. When Ewell attacked on the Confederate right, his men encountered stiff resistance from Federals firing from behind stone fences. The attack stalled. Meanwhile, on the left, Jackson sent forward the Stonewall Brigade under General Winder. They drove off Federal skirmishers from a hill in front of Bowers. Jackson placed artillery on the hill. They came under enfilading fire from Federals on their left as they dueled with the Union cannon on Bowers Hill. In spite of the crossfire, the Confederates forced the Union artillery to pull back. The Federal batteries found a more secure position and continued firing. The Stonewalls advanced, only to be pinned down by infantry and artillery fire. Then Jackson saw Union troops moving to flank him on his left. He countered by sending Taylor around to the Union right.

Taylor noticed Jackson riding with him shortly after he started to move. "This was not the place for the commander of the army," he wrote, "and I ventured to tell him so; but he paid no attention to the remark." The flanking column attracted the attention of the Union gunners, but the Southerners were somewhat protected by the base of the ridge. The fire became more effective when the soldiers emerged from its shelter. "Many men fell," wrote Taylor, "and the whistling of shot and shell occasioned much ducking of heads in the column."

"What the h— are you dodging for?" Taylor exclaimed. "If there is any more of it, you will be halted under this fire for an hour."

It is certain that Taylor, who was noted for the fluency of his swearing, cleaned up the quotation for his nineteenth-century audience. But he had forgotten that Jackson was beside him. *And* it was the Sabbath. "I shall never forget the reproachful surprise expressed in Jackson's face. He placed his hand on my shoulder, said in a gentle voice, 'I am afraid you are a wicked fellow,' turned, and rode back to the pike."[1]

Taylor got his men in place, a long gray line that extended for a thousand yards. They started forward, Taylor riding in front with drawn saber, turning occasionally on his horse to make sure his men were aligned. "They marched up the hill in perfect order, not firing a shot!" wrote John Worsham. Taylor gave the order to charge, "and to and over the stone wall they went!"

"This charge of Taylor's was the grandest I saw during the war," he concluded. It was not without cost. An Indiana sergeant glanced over the stone wall while reloading. His senses sharpened by the intensity of combat, he saw a battlefield panorama that could "never be effaced from memory." In close formation, the Southern soldiers were hard to miss. "Some dropped all in a heap, some turned half way round and fell sideways, some fell forward, some backward, some fell prone on the ground, while others caught themselves on their hands. A still larger number were dropping their guns and starting to the rear, most of them clapping both hands to the place where they were hit."[2]

In spite of their losses, Confederate numbers and momentum prevailed. The rest of the Southerners followed Taylor. Simultaneously, Ewell was successfully attacking on the Confederate left. According to Worsham, "The enemy broke and ran in all directions."[3]

Jackson, in front of the line, had been holding up his hand, probably in prayer. He exulted when he saw what was happening, waved his cap in the air, and shouted, "Now let's holler!"

The Rebel yell echoed across the battlefield. The Federals retreated through Winchester, with Jackson himself in pursuit. Jed Hotchkiss, who was with him, finally prevailed upon him to stop.

Women shot at the Yankees as they raced through town. One was shot and killed after she fired on an officer. Those who lacked firearms threw boiling water. Crowds of Southern sympathizers emerged to welcome the Confederates. Young women offered food, hugs, and kisses. Union sympathizers followed the Federals out of town. Not only were the Southerners distracted, but they couldn't fire on the Yankees for fear of hitting civilians.

The Yankees emerged on the north side of Winchester and kept going. Jackson himself came to the edge of town around 10 a.m. Just as he had called out for artillery at Front Royal, he now called out for cavalry: "Never was there such a chance for cavalry; oh that my cavalry were in place!"[4]

But Ashby's men had melted away on the march. Jackson tried to pursue with infantry, but in addition to fighting, his men had marched a hundred miles in the past seven days. They were exhausted. After a couple of hours, he improvised a last-ditch effort at a mounted pursuit by ordering gun crews to mount their unhitched artillery horses, but the animals were as tired as the men, and Jackson was forced to turn back to town.

He visited the Grahams at the Presbyterian manse, his home away from home, for about an hour. Then he went to the Taylor Hotel, fell onto a bed, and, without taking off his boots or spurs, fell instantly to sleep.

"You just passed it," said Catherine as we traveled north toward Front Royal. I managed the turnaround, then eased back into the barreling traffic on U.S. 340, the "Stonewall Jackson Highway." I turned in at Asbury Chapel and parked her Volvo in the shade.

This was the spot where Jackson halted to pass the 1st Maryland to the front. I tried to envision the twelve-mile-long column of dusty Confederates with Jackson in the lead, but was only able to summon up a sigh for the loss of what must have once been a tranquil, bucolic setting. Asbury Chapel is still picturesque, with its white clapboard, tin roof, and a steeple that, for some unknown architectural or ecclesiastical reason, is beside the sanctuary instead of on top of it; but it's almost impossible to focus on anything but the rushing traffic.

I lost my nostalgic mood when I read the Civil War Trails marker about the bloody floorboards that were revealed when the church was reconstructed in the early twentieth century. Tranquility was as rare in the past as it is today.

We pulled out of the lot and took a quick turn onto Rocky Lane.

"So why are we on this road?" Catherine said sharply.

I tried to make my voice sound like a PBS narrator: "We're on a quest for the past." I slowed to navigate between a pothole and a tree root. "No, seriously, we're looking for a Civil War Trails marker."

"This is turning into a Civil War trial. Your history quest better not mess up the undercarriage of my car."

I tried to jolly her out of worrying: "Rocky Lane—sounds like a professional wrestler."

Silence.

I slowed down even more: "I'll be very careful."

We emerged unscathed from Rocky Lane and found the Belle Boyd marker in the parking lot of another church. My toured-out wife stayed in the car.

Feeling her unstated thoughts, I read the marker quickly, got back in, and started driving. "It said she shot a Yankee soldier who tried to raise the Stars and Stripes over her house."

"So she was a *real* femme fatale."

"Right. It also says she wasn't beautiful but was so attractive she could make a monk break his vows of celibacy."

"What does all this have to do with Jackson?"

"She gave him information about the Northern troops in Front Royal, but historians say he already had it."

"Oh."

"She went on all these lecture tours after the war. Died penniless in Wisconsin." Musingly: "I wonder how the skill set for being a spy harmonized with the one for self-promotion."

"It sounds like it didn't."

"I guess it didn't."

Prospect Hill Cemetery, as its name suggests, overlooks Front Royal. Southerners used it ineffectually as an artillery position during the battle.

While I am very familiar with the Civil War cemeteries near my home in central Virginia, I have only a cursory acquaintance with those in the Valley. Each comes as a small shock when I explore or reexplore it. The sheer volume of death from the war: The Confederate section of Prospect has 276 soldiers. That doesn't seem so overwhelming until you add in Winchester, Harrisonburg, Staunton, and the others throughout the Valley...

Prospect is slightly evocative of Stonehenge, with tombstones of the 90 known soldiers encircling the obelisk marking the mass grave of

the 186 unknowns. THEY DIED IN THE CAUSE OF HONOR AND JUSTICE
reads the inscription.

Honor and justice? Six hundred and twenty thousand killed during the war; countless others maimed; the damage to families incal-
culable. Cities, towns, and hundreds of square miles of farmland
devastated. Factor in the suffering of the animals and that's a high
price indeed for honor and justice. Or slavery. Or the Union...or anything else for that matter.

My melancholy reflections about Americans killing Americans
were somewhat alleviated a few stops later when I found a humor-
ous inscription describing Front Royal during the war. It was "quite
rural," wrote a soldier. "The principal objects of interest are two small
churches and the town pump."

Front Royal was anything but rural when we visited. The bridges
over the two forks of the Shenandoah were being replaced by new,
massive structures that can handle the ever-increasing traffic. Bull-
dozers, cranes, and raw earth completed the picture. A short distance
ahead, we turned down a gravel road and found the markers for our
next stop, Guard Hill, in a pocket park near a boat landing. When
I returned from reading them, my wife was bending over by the car.
"Hey you," she said gently. "Hey you."

It was a small, long-haired black cat. He fled when I approached.

"Doesn't like males."

"Probably abused."

She was able to pet him after I walked to the far edge of the parking lot. He fled the second I changed direction and started back to
the car.

It was late afternoon when we got to Fairview. The last stop on the
driving tour was an unoccupied stone house, joined at the hip to a
couple of two-story wooden structures of equal size. It was here that
the charge of the 6th Virginia cavalry broke the Federal resistance.
Dabney Eastham was with Company B, the one that had been almost

completely wiped out when it led the attack. The marker said that Eastham "was believed to be mortally wounded and was left lying in the yard. The next morning, when his father arrived from Rappahannock County to claim his son's body, he found that the grass and mud had clotted his wound and saved his life. To avoid opening the wound, the sod was taken up with him when he was carried into the house. Eastham survived and left descendants in Rappahannock and Warren Counties."

He was literally saved by the sacred soil of the South.

The site of so much drama, Fairview is currently an island of the past between U.S. 522 and the valley of industry that's just beyond a screen of trees. The "fair view" is now of Sysco Northeast Redistribution, a truly big-box building at least a quarter of a mile long. It is only one of many such monumental edifices along the row.

The North certainly won, I thought, in that the North represented the industrial way of life and the South the agrarian. Today this highway and those factories, warehouses, and distribution centers represent jobs and security—prosperity, even—to the folks who live nearby. Yet something had been lost...

I let that percolate while I took some photos with my phone. The evening light was lovely, giving the stones of the ancient house a sort of glow. I imagined Fairview filled with life before the war, all that quotidian vitality, then one incredible day of violence followed by weeks of intense suffering. Afterward the agricultural rhythm reasserted itself: seedtime and harvest, years of quiet country life, until the farm stopped being profitable or it was just too much work and the heirs moved on.

"I want that cat," Catherine said when I got back in the car.

"Yeah, I do too." I realized I had already named him Stonewall.

We found a Petco and bought food, litter, and a cardboard carrying case. It was almost dark when we got back. I walked down the boat ramp while Catherine tried to cajole Stonewall into the case.

I was studying the remains of the nineteenth-century bridge when I saw a cat by the water. Looking around, I saw another. A third in the underbrush. Watching. I couldn't get close. Ferals.

I saw a couple more when I walked up the ramp. They were different from Stonewall. Even though he was skittish, he had obviously been around people. Maybe his owners had dumped him here thinking he would just blend in.

He wouldn't get in the case, even with the wet food inside. When Catherine tried to pick him up, he scratched her and fled into the bushes.

The next day wasn't nearly as successful. We trekked between Strasburg and Winchester and found only a few markers. We were looking for the First Battle of Winchester. I speculated that it got lost because there was just so much fighting in the area. Several sources say that the town changed hands seventy-two times during the war—thirteen times in one day.

Our efforts at cat hunting were equally unsuccessful. Stonewall came out and greedily devoured some food, but, leery from the day before, wouldn't allow Catherine to get close. We gave him the rest of the food and left him to fend for himself.

CHAPTER 14

A Lost Battlefield

I can't understand battles or troop movements from just reading about them. I have to go to the places and walk the ground, usually more than once. I visited the Valley at least a dozen times while researching this book. A bus tour with Ed Bearss and Jeffry Wert was among my most memorable trips.

Jeffry Wert has written nine substantial books on the Civil War along with dozens of articles. Personable and knowledgeable, he's an engaging tour guide. But Ed Bearss is a force of nature, a historical hurricane. It was definitely his show. He talked almost nonstop for the whole three days of the tour in his signature growl, Wert spelling him only occasionally with some apt quote or observation. All of Bearss's information was accurate, every anecdote telling. Not bad for ninety-three. The frightening thing is that he's said to be able to do the same for all the major Civil War battlefields. He knows the Revolutionary War too, and, after our tour, he was going to lead an excursion to Normandy to discuss D-Day. He's also impressive in other ways: You never quite forget that he can barely use his left arm because it's still debilitated from when he was wounded by Japanese machine-gun fire during World War II.

"G! U! T! S!" Bearss drove his metal hiking pole into the ground to emphasize each letter. Next time he spoke louder and punched the ground harder. "G! U! T! S!"

It was a cool, rainy day in late May. Bearss was standing on Bowers Hill in Winchester, under a dripping evergreen tree, talking to the handful of Stonewall Jackson's Valley Campaign Tour participants who hadn't retreated to the bus. "You asked me why Taylor's men charged the guns on this hill?" A third and final time: "G! U! T! S!"

"When he saw them ducking their heads because of artillery fire, he told them, 'If you don't stop dodging I'm going to halt you under this fire for an hour.' He had just executed two of the Tigers and they had drawn beans to see who would shoot him. Now he's telling them to take this hill and they did. Taylor was an inspiring leader. But even the most inspiring leader needs good men.

"They were down where those water tanks are." He gestured with the hiking pole.

The tanks were fenced off. Bearss looked around at the comfortable suburban houses behind him and the nondescript office building across the street. "This is one of the lost battlefields," he said. "A preservation failure."

"I do not remember having ever seen such rejoicing as was manifested by the people of Winchester as our army yesterday passed through the town in pursuit of the enemy," Jackson wrote Anna on Monday, May 26. "The people seemed nearly frantic with joy; indeed, it would be almost impossible to describe their manifestations of rejoicing and gratitude. Our entrance into Winchester was one of the most stirring scenes of my life."[1]

His soldiers were equally gratified. Suddenly everything they had been through was worthwhile: "He had led us three weeks as hard as men could march," wrote John Worsham. "[But] to accomplish so much with so little loss, we would march six months! The reception at Winchester was worth a whole lifetime of service."[2]

Winchester wasn't the only place rejoicing. The South was starving for good news, and Jackson was it. "Southern editors trumpeted the success and polished it for all it was worth," wrote historian Robert K. Krick.[3] Hailed by the *Richmond Daily Dispatch* as a "military genius,"[4] Jackson provided a welcome diversion from McClellan's army, which was so close to the city that Union soldiers set their watches by its church bells. Lee added his praises to the chorus, then politely asked for more: "We rejoice at your brilliant success. If you can make demonstrations on Maryland and Washington, it will add to its great results." Jackson's own men, who had marched and fought so incredibly hard for him, thought him even greater than before. One Maryland soldier even went so far as to refer to him as "My earthly God." Jackson the man had become Jackson the legend.

The day after the battle, Monday, May 26, was "devoted to a religious rest." Since the men had fought and marched through the Sabbath, Jackson ordered them to suspend all military activities so that they could "recognize devoutly the hand of a protecting Providence in the brilliant successes of the last three days."[5] Church was at four.

There was much to be thankful for. Jackson had chased Banks clean out of the South. In doing so he had sustained 400 casualties, a fraction of his opponent's 2,019. Such vast quantities of arms and supplies had been captured that it took days to list everything and a week to haul it all away. Sutler's stores went first. "It was a strange sight," wrote Dabney, "to see the rough fellows, who the day before had lacked the ration of beef and hard bread, regaling themselves with confectionery, sardines, and tropical fruits."[6] Banks got a new nickname: Commissary Banks. Half a million rounds of ammunition, sugar, salt, hardtack, clothing, cannon, cattle—the list goes on. So many hospital supplies were captured that Sandie Pendleton thought they exceeded the amount in the entire rest of the South.[7] Probably the most satisfying gleaning for Jackson were the 9,345 stands of small arms. A "stand," wrote S. C. Gwynne helpfully, "consisted of a rifled musket, bayonet, cartridge belt, and ammunition box."[8]

Washington got a good scare. Secretary of War Stanton immediately called for help, telegraphing the governors of thirteen Northern states: "Intelligence from various quarters leaves no doubt that the enemy in great force are marching on Washington. You will please organize and forward immediately all the militia and volunteer forces in your state." After the first shock, Lincoln saw it as more of an opportunity than a threat. He ordered Frémont to move on Jackson from the west with his 15,000 men. McDowell was to come from the east with 21,000. Other nearby forces, including Banks's demoralized but still usable 7,000, brought the total that could be brought to bear against Jackson to 54,000.[9]

Jackson had 13,000 men,[10] maybe less. Gary Ecelbarger makes the eye-opening assertion that "discipline in his army had been so lax as to allow incredibly high rates of desertion in three weeks—more than fifty percent in his own division." He concludes an objective assessment of Jackson's strengths and weaknesses during the three days from Front Royal to Winchester with the following: "Jackson's dominance at maneuver, his refusal to allow obstacles to paralyze his momentum, and his insurmountable determination, outshone his tactical shortcomings and split-decision miscues to conquer his adversary and overcome adversity."

Jackson showed a seldom-used characteristic, reasonable caution, when he marched on Harpers Ferry later in the week and judged it too strongly defended to attack. Had he lived, this quality, balanced with his drive and aggression, would have made him even stronger and more effective militarily.

Having made his presence known on the border, and aware that he was overextended, he turned back south, leaving the Stonewall Brigade to make a final demonstration against the town.

Jackson knew that armies were converging to cut him off from the relative safety of the upper Valley. Frémont was moving toward him from the west—with great difficulty. Lincoln ordered him to move to Harrisonburg, forty-one miles southeast. If successful, this would have put him in Jackson's rear, ready for a hookup with Shields. But Hotchkiss had wrecked the road between Franklin and Harrisonburg, burning bridges and blocking the roadway with boulders and felled trees. With his men on half rations or worse, Frémont decided to march to his supply base in the north rather than push straight through to the Valley.

When he discovered what had happened, Lincoln was furious. "I see that you are at Moorefield," he telegraphed. "You were expressly ordered to march to Harrisonburg. What does this mean?" Instead of replying honestly that the road Lincoln wanted him to take was impassable, the Pathfinder—he had acquired the nickname from pre-war explorations in the West—quibbled over protocol: "In executing any order received I take it for granted that I am to exercise discretion concerning its literal execution according to circumstances. If I am to understand that literal obedience to orders is required, please say so."

Ill-humored correspondence in the same vein flashed back and forth over the wire for several days. After marching up and down mountains in rain and mud, Frémont's 15,000 men forded the swollen South Fork of the Potomac, holding their ammunition over their heads and grasping a cable stretched across the river. The department's medical director ordered a day's rest when he inspected the weary men after the crossing. Lincoln wasn't pleased about that either.

Coming from the east, Shields moved much more quickly in spite of the fact that many of his men were barefoot. His first destination was the small Confederate garrison at Front Royal.

The dire situation, compounded by his own fatigue, caused Jackson to behave erratically. Before sending his men back south, he observed an artillery duel with Generals Charles Winder and Arnold Elzey. General Elzey mentioned the big Federal guns on the heights overlooking the town. "General Elzey, are you afraid of heavy guns?" said Jackson. The artillerist who reported the conversation[11] does not remark on the tone, but it must have augmented Jackson's statement into an accusation of cowardice, made worse by the fact it was done in front of one of Elzey's peers. Elzey was by all accounts an extremely brave officer. It was a serious lapse of protocol, in addition to being out of character.

What Jackson did next was equally odd, though more understandable considering his fatigue: He took a nap. His friend and confidant Alexander Boteler found him stretched out beneath a tree, the cannons still booming nearby. A descendant of George Washington portraitist Charles Willson Peale, Boteler continued the family legacy with his hobby of sketching. He was completing a likeness of Jackson when he looked up to see that the general had awakened. Jackson asked for the drawing and examined it. "My hardest tasks at West Point were the drawing lessons," he told Boteler candidly. "I never could do anything in that line to satisfy myself—or indeed, anyone else."

Jackson continued after a pause. "Colonel," he said, "I have some harder work than this for you to do. If you will sit down here now, I will tell you what it is." Jackson told Boteler that he wanted him to go to Richmond and ask for 40,000 reinforcements with which he could "raise the siege of Richmond and transfer this campaign from the banks of the James to those of the Susquehanna."

As effective as he had been in the Valley, Jackson had to know that this was pure fantasy with McClellan so close to the Confederate capital. But what happened next was even more astonishing: Boteler asked Jackson what his situation was—and Jackson told him.

"McDowell and Frémont are probably aiming to effect a junction at Strasburg, so as to head us off from the upper Valley, and they are both nearer now to it than we are. Consequently no time is to be lost. You can say to them in Richmond that I will send on the prisoners, secure most, if not all, of the captured property, and, with God's blessing, be able to baffle the enemy's plans with my present force, but that it will have to be increased thereafter as soon as possible."

This was the opposite of Jackson's openness with Reverend Graham in the wake of his resignation following the Romney crisis. At that point, it was a sudden release of pressure that caused him to be candid. Now, with two armies closing in, the stress was incredible. Yet Jackson dropped his guard to let a friend know what he was thinking. The small relief he got from speaking freely must have comforted him as he faced the challenges ahead. In any case, later, when Boteler left for Richmond, the wall went up again.

Shields overwhelmed the Confederates at Front Royal, surprising them in spite of warnings of his approach from interrogated prisoners. The officer in charge, Colonel Zephanier T. Conner, lost his nerve and fled to Winchester. Before retreating, the Confederates set fire to the train depot, railroad cars, and a warehouse filled with captured supplies.

Storm clouds gathered. Rain began to fall. Firefighting Yankees, along with heavy rain, kept the flames from spreading to the town. The Federals were able to save much, including a couple of railroad cars' worth of muskets—a dangerous job since the loaded muskets fired when they were heated.

The rain was falling on Jackson as well. South of Harpers Ferry, he decided to board the one-car train taking Boteler to Winchester. When it started moving, Jackson put his arm on the seat back in front of him, leaned over, and fell asleep. Sandie Pendleton accompanied him. He and Boteler stayed alert, looking out the windows for Yankee cavalry.

They had traveled a little more than halfway to Winchester when Boteler spied a Confederate horseman signaling the train. He woke Jackson, who told the engineer to stop. The courier passed a note in through the window. Jackson read it, tore it up, and told the engineer, "Go on, sir, if you please." Then he again put his head down and went to sleep.

The note was from Jed Hotchkiss. It said that Front Royal had been taken. Shields was only eleven miles from Strasburg. The main body of Jackson's army was forty-four miles away. The trap was closing, but Jackson seemed unconcerned.

That night, at the Taylor Hotel, Jackson sent for Colonel Conner. "Colonel, how many men did you have killed, sir?"

"None."

"How many wounded?"

"None, sir."

"Do you call that much of a fight?" Jackson had him placed under arrest.[12]

Another of Jackson's revealing, out-of-character moments happened later that night. Boteler came calling and, mindful of the fact that he was soon to depart on a ninety-mile horseback ride in the rain, ordered two whiskey toddies sent up to Jackson's room. He offered one to Jackson, who of course refused: "I never drink intoxicating liquors."

"I know that, General," said Boteler, then alluded to his strenuous upcoming journey along with Jackson's far more arduous task of moving an entire threatened army: "A stimulant will do us both good."

Jackson, no doubt thinking the Calvinist equivalent of "Why the hell not?," picked up the glass and slowly sipped about half the drink. "Colonel," he said during a lull in the conversation. "Do you know why I habitually abstain from intoxicating liquors?"

Jackson answered his own question after Boteler shook his head. "Why, sir, because I like the taste of them. When I discovered this to be the case, I made up my mind to do without them altogether."

Boteler departed. At 3 a.m. on May 31, Jackson woke Hotchkiss and told him to go get General Winder and the Stonewall Brigade. Jackson said he would wait for the brigade in Winchester if he could, "but if I cannot, and the enemy gets here first, you must bring it around through the mountains."

Hotchkiss noted that, in spite of the task before him, or perhaps because of it, Jackson was "in fine spirits."

The task was daunting: 2,300 prisoners had to be moved, along with eight miles of wagons carrying captured supplies, before the soldiers started to march. The head of the column would be in Strasburg almost before the end of it left Winchester, and the Stonewall Brigade was far behind, starting late with farther to march. Frémont was closing in from the west, Shields from the east. According to S. C. Gwynne, it was to be "one of the most stirring footraces in military history."[13] Of course it rained heavily, although, following the first torrential downpours, it cleared off for a couple of days.[14]

The fifteen-mile-long column was strung out and vulnerable, as inviting a target as existed during the war. Frémont got within four miles of the Valley Pike—and stopped. No reason given. Shields, after his striking success at Front Royal, halted as well. Pondering his options, waiting for supporting troops to come up, he was attacked by Ashby's cavalry north of town. That settled it. The best thing to do was stop and wait.

"Shields's main problem now was, in fact, fear; his own, of

Jackson's growing legend," wrote S. C. Gwynne. Shields looked even worse two days later when he sent a dispatch to the War Department saying he hadn't gone to Strasburg because he "dare not interfere with what was designed for Frémont. His failure has saved Jackson." Two facts should be remembered here: Shields said earlier that Jackson was afraid of *him*; also, he had blatantly stolen credit for the victory at Kernstown from Colonel Kimball, even though he had been convalescing in Winchester with a broken arm during the battle. "A more barefaced series of Irish romances I never read," wrote a disgusted Federal soldier at the time.[15]

You can almost hear lugubrious theme music whenever Jackson's other opponent plods into the narrative. S. C. Gwynne on the Pathfinder: "There was something of the loser about Frémont, something that suggested only bleakness and indecision and hardship and misery and none of the glory and clarity that soldiers craved." I could feel more sympathy for Frémont were it not for the 1846 Sacramento River Massacre in which hundreds of Native Americans, including women, children, and babies, were slaughtered by his men. In some ways he personifies Hannah Arendt's phrase "the banality of evil."

Shields, the aggressive braggart, and Frémont, the tentative hasbeen, were both within striking distance of Jackson when paralysis hit. The rain came back shortly thereafter, the Confederate weather heralding what Robertson called "probably the rainiest week of the war."[16] Jackson waited for the Stonewall Brigade. Frémont started a halfhearted artillery duel with Ewell. Shields didn't do even that.

The Stonewalls thought the game was up when they heard the cannon. They were elated when they arrived in Strasburg safely. They had marched forty-five miles in two days without rations. One regiment, the 2nd Virginia, covered thirty-six miles in a single day.[17]

Jackson's united army headed south while darkness fell. One artillerist wrote that the Confederates had "slipped through the jaws of the closing vise like a greased rat."[18]

CHAPTER 15

The Dead Thick as Blackbirds

Hail mingled with rain that night, as hardships of the march mixed with feelings of triumph and relief. The Confederates had won the race, but they weren't out of danger. Hesitant to hit Jackson's flank, Shields and Frémont were emboldened at the sight of his back. The Pathfinder's cavalry harassed the Confederate rear. Ashby, who had been relieved of command—again—because of his poor showing at Winchester, was riding with the rear guard when it was attacked by Federal horsemen. Their shout that they were "Ashby's cavalry!" fooled enough Confederates to momentarily mask their identity. Ashby himself obviously wasn't taken in, hiding in a thicket while startled Southern cavalry stampeded into Southern infantry, some of whom fired on their own men in the darkness and confusion.

As chaos rolled south through the column, Ashby emerged and assembled enough stragglers for an ambush. When the Federals came galloping back, the concealed Confederates hit them with a devastating volley. Ashby mounted the stragglers on the captured horses—instant cavalry!—and rode to Jackson's headquarters, where he was rewarded for his initiative with the resumption of his old command.

General Taylor, whose Louisianans had been among those nearly trampled by the startled horsemen, took up rearguard duties. He says the darkness was so profound that "the white of the pike alone guided us." Harassed throughout the night, they heard rather than saw the attacks coming, and gauged the effectiveness of their firing by the light from their muzzle flashes.

Shields, to the east, took a page from Jackson's playbook and decided to travel south to Luray, cross Massanutten at New Market Gap, and hit the Southerners on the flank. Jackson, who had used the gap himself less than two weeks before, correctly divined his purpose and sent cavalry to burn the three bridges that would have allowed him to cross the swollen South Fork of the Shenandoah.

The rain-soaked race continued. Shields marched south on the east side of Massanutten; Jackson, pursued by Frémont, on the west. On the morning of June 3, Ashby received word that he had been promoted to brigadier general. That afternoon, Sandie Pendleton took the occasion of the promotion as an opportunity for some heart-to-heart advice: Since he was now a general, an even more valuable officer, he should expose himself less to the enemy. Ashby responded strangely, with an example of magical thinking that was patently untrue. "He was not afraid of balls that were shot right at him," Kyd Douglas quoted him as saying, "for they always missed their mark. He only feared those random shots which always hit someone for whom they were not intended."[1]

Ashby had another close call that day. His cavalrymen were getting ready to burn the bridge at Meems Bottom, the same task he had been about when he lost Tom Telegraph. Again, they were closely pursued by the Federals. Again, Ashby lost a horse during the rear-guard action. But this time his soldiers had thoroughly prepared the structure, stuffing the sides and underside of the covered bridge's roof with straw and dry wood, then scattering gunpowder and shells through the straw for good measure. Their sabotage was successful, and Confederate infantry cheered as the final cavalryman galloped through the burning bridge.[2]

The rain was especially torrential that night. Because his men were sleeping in the wet woods, Jackson himself resolved to do so, even though he and his staff had been offered dry accommodations at a nearby house. Directing that his tent be pitched in a hollow between two hills, the general retired early. In the night, water gathered and rushed down the two hillsides and through his tent. In the morning, Jackson appeared in a damp and bedraggled condition. Douglas confessed that the staff, who had not wanted to sleep rough themselves, were "amused and perhaps a little gratified" at the general's discomfort. He went to have a look at the tent. "All through it the water was still flowing and various small articles of apparel and furniture were floating about like little boats."

Even after that, it was hard to get the general to seek shelter the following night, an example of his famous resolve devolving into simple hardheadedness. The staff finally prevailed upon him to go into the town of New Market and set up headquarters in a house.[3]

Frémont had pontoons with him, and by the morning of the fourth, he succeeded in setting up a bridge at Meems Bottom, even managing to get some cavalry and infantry across. Jackson put his men on alert, but the heavy rains caused the North Fork to rise an incredible twelve feet in four hours. Frémont's soldiers cut the bridge's south bank ropes before it could be swept away, and the structure swung over to the northern bank, leaving part of his army stranded. Jackson's men rested, damply, in the rain.[4]

After passing through Harrisonburg, Jackson left the easy-traveling Valley Pike and turned southeast. His wagons quickly became mired in the mud. It was slow going, even with forty men from each regiment detailed to help. His immediate objective now was Port Republic, about fifteen miles southeast of Harrisonburg. Here, the confusingly named North and South rivers flowed in from the west, coming together to form the equally puzzlingly named South Fork of the Shenandoah, which flowed off northeast. The configuration was of a sort of serpentine Y lying on its side, the two branches being the North and South rivers. Most of the Port Republic village was between the Y's two branches. A defensible (and burnable) bridge crossed the North River; it was the only way the two Union forces could unite. There was high ground to the north, which afforded good positions for artillery.

Jackson had now passed south of Massanutten, which until then had separated the pursuing columns of Frémont and Shields. As at Strasburg, the danger was that they would crush his army between them like the jaws of a vise, or that they would combine and fight him with stronger numbers.

The heavy rain, which favored the defensive, slackened, then turned completely Union, stopping altogether by June 6.

There was rearguard cavalry action outside Harrisonburg. A British soldier of fortune, Sir Percy Wyndham, in command of the 1st New Jersey Cavalry, had vowed to "bag Ashby." A colorful character, with plumed hat, ornate spurs, and ten-inch mustachios, Wyndham had led a charge against the Confederates in which few of his men participated. The captured colonel, spitting mad at what he called his men's cowardice, was being escorted to the rear when he ran across his old compatriot Roberdeau Wheat. The two had fought together under Garibaldi in Italy. They had a brief reunion, then Wyndham was taken to Jackson's headquarters at the Kemper House in Port Republic.

It was during this interview that bad news came to Jackson. In a further cavalry action, Ashby had been killed. He had been leading his soldiers when another horse was shot out from under him. Continuing on foot, he shouted, "Charge, men! For God's sake, charge!"

A moment later he was shot dead—by an aimed or random musket ball, no one could tell. "It was late at night when news of Ashby's death came," wrote Hotchkiss. "After this Gen. Jackson walked the floor of his room, for some time, in deep sorrow, greatly moved by the sad news."[5]

Soldiers bore the body to the Kemper House. There was a brief funeral there the next day. Following the ceremony, Jackson spent some time alone with the body. It is tempting to speculate on his thoughts. Ashby was as different from him as was Wyndham, though far more congenial. They were both brave to a fault, and with both of them disregard for personal safety led to their deaths. But Ashby was from a different era, chivalric, with personal courage the main component of his leadership. Failure to discipline his soldiers had hurt the Valley

Campaign on several occasions, and irked Jackson personally, so much so that he tried to block his promotion. But the final verdict on Ashby had to have been that his incredibly successful fighting outweighed any faults. "As a partisan officer I never knew his superior," Jackson wrote in his report ten months later. It is interesting to note that this praise came after his fighting alongside Jeb Stuart, a cavalryman whose friendship and abilities he also valued highly. The unaccustomed string of superlatives continued: "His daring was proverbial; his powers of endurance almost incredible; his tone of character heroic, and his sagacity almost intuitive in divining the purposes of the enemy."[6]

Part of Jackson's mind must also have been devoted to selfish thoughts, militarily speaking. He needed Ashby. The cavalry were the eyes of the army, and Ashby's charisma held the cavalry together. Without his intuitive sagacity in "divining the purposes of the enemy," Jackson was flying blind.

Exactly how blind was proven the next morning. It was Sunday, June 8. Jackson and Dabney were enjoying the Sabbath calm and discussing the possibility of holding divine services when a horseman rode up and announced that the Federal cavalry was close by. Jackson sent a message to Ewell, whom he had placed in a rearguard position at Cross Keys, a village between Harrisonburg and Port Republic, so that he would not bring on an engagement there until this situation was resolved.

Jackson was strategically vulnerable. His wagon trains were separate from the army and so lightly guarded that they may as well have not been guarded at all. Headquarters at the Kemper House was unguarded as well. It was also poorly sited, far from the soldiers' camp and a full half mile from the vital North River Bridge. These oversights of positioning were probably due to the debilitating fatigue of the campaign. Sandie Pendleton had written his mother the day before, "Gen. Jackson is completely broken down."[7]

Jackson and his staff were waiting in the yard of the Kemper House for their horses when they heard two cannon shots. A rider appeared and reported: Federals had forded South River and were in the village! "Go back and fight them!" Jackson said.

Gunfire. Jackson started toward it. Federal cavalry appeared. Jackson must have weighed the odds of successfully fighting mounted men on foot, because when Jim Lewis arrived a moment later with Little Sorrel, he got on and galloped off. He and most of his staff escaped under fire across the covered bridge. His late-sleeping artillery chief, Colonel Stapleton Crutchfield, was captured along with another aide. Crutchfield tried to hand over his sword, but the Union commander said he was too busy to take it. Then a rider galloped up and said that Jackson's whole wagon train was "just up yonder," ripe for capture.

"Is that so, Colonel?" asked the Union officer.

"You must find that out for yourself," answered Crutchfield. The Federal correctly interpreted his evasion and sent a squadron to take the wagons.[8]

Jackson, meanwhile, had succeeded in getting Confederate infantry and artillery moving. William T. Poague of the Rockbridge Artillery, who had known Jackson before the war in Lexington, said that he "never saw Jackson as much stirred up at any other time."[9]

With his troops in action, Jackson moved to the edge of the high ground to survey the situation. A Union cannon had unlimbered on the far side of the bridge. A battery of the Rockbridge Artillery arrived. "Fire on that gun!" Jackson commanded.

Poague and his gunners insisted that the cannon was Confederate. Its crew were wearing blue, but many Confederates were wearing captured Union overcoats.[10] Even Jackson was wearing his old blue VMI coat. Momentarily convinced, Jackson yelled to the Federals, "Bring that gun up here!" They answered with a shot that buried itself in the hillside nearby.

The case of mistaken identity was resolved. "Let 'em have it!" yelled Jackson. Confederate artillery opened on the Union piece, which was quickly abandoned. Southern infantry charged down the hill. In the midst of the action, a Southern soldier was surprised when Jackson "dropped his reins on the horse's neck, raised his face and both hands to heaven, and engaged in silent prayer."[11]

"The God of battles heard," wrote Dabney, for whom no

Jacksonian prayer went unchronicled. Before "he had withdrawn his uplifted hands the bridge was gained, and the enemy's gun was captured."[12]

Federal infantry reinforcements arrived late even as the Federal cavalry were making their escape. Jackson personally oversaw the placement of ten additional guns on the high ground. They opened a deadly fire on the enemy, so unrelenting that the Southern cannoneers had to pour water from their canteens on the barrels of their pieces to cool them. The infantry retreated out of range—and then some.[13]

Port Republic was clear. But before the Confederates could congratulate themselves on their narrow escape, sounds of battle were heard to the west. Ewell was fighting Frémont at Cross Keys.

Ewell had an extremely strong position, on top of a ridge with open country in front and his flanks protected by woods. He thought his center was weak, and so placed four batteries there. An artillery duel, with no particular result, began around 10 a.m. General Arnold Elzey, who had recommended the overall position to Ewell, directed the Southern cannonade. "He rode among the gunners," wrote Douglas Freeman, "with fine contempt for the enemy's sharpshooters and their shell."

His horse was wounded. He paid no attention when he was warned he might be next. The scenario was the same as had resulted in the death of Ashby just two days before, except this time, after his poor animal was actually killed, Elzey was only wounded.[14] Historian James McPherson, in his monumental study of the Civil War era, *Battle Cry of Freedom*, noted that because Civil War generals led from the front instead of the rear, their chances of being killed in combat were 50 percent higher than those of privates.[15] General "Maryland" Steuart was also wounded that day at Cross Keys.

General Isaac Trimble, a combative sixty-year-old West Point graduate, commanded the Confederate right. Frémont's infantrymen mounted halfhearted attacks along the line throughout the day—with one exception: that of the 8th New York against Trimble.

Hungarian-born Julius Stahel, colonel of the 8th, sent his brigade of mostly German immigrants in perfect formation up the hill. He made the fatal error of not sending out skirmishers, so he had no idea what he was advancing into. Thirteen hundred Confederates were waiting behind a split-rail fence on high ground in front of woods. Lying down, they had stuffed leaves in the lower spaces between the rails to better conceal themselves. Most were armed with out-of-date smoothbore muskets, problematic as a general battlefield weapon, but still deadly at close range. Their killing efficiency was increased because many of the soldiers were firing "buck and ball"—three or more pieces of buckshot along with their musket balls. They had orders not to shoot until the Yankees, about 500 in number, came within point-blank range. One colonel even threatened "that if any man fired before he gave orders to fire, he would have him shot."[16]

The Southerners later described the New Yorkers coming up out of the declivity in their front: "first they could see the tops of the flags, then the flags themselves, then the men's heads."[17] The Federals were about forty yards away when the order to fire was given. The Confederates rose and discharged their weapons with immediate and devastating effect. "The poor Germans fell all across each other in piles," wrote one Confederate. "I never saw men double up and fall so fast," echoed another. The retreating survivors "went so fast down the hill you might have played marbles on their coat-tails." There was a second volley, then a third, though most of the Southerners could barely see through the battle smoke. They gave chase for a bit, voicing the Rebel yell, then decided it was more important to hold their position and returned to the fenceline.[18]

About 100 of the New Yorkers were wounded; 80 were mortally wounded or killed outright. "The dead and wounded yankees was lying in the field as thick as black birds," wrote a young Georgian. At least 74 were taken prisoner.[19] Half of the Federal casualties from the day's fighting were the result of the 8th's doomed advance. According to one historian, "it drained all of Frémont's initiative."[20] While Ewell and Trimble pushed forward, the Pathfinder was more focused on continuing his long-range artillery duel. Wrote Shelby Foote: "Out in the buckwheat the wounded New Yorkers lay under this fire, crying for water. Their cries decreased as the day wore on and Frémont continued his cannonade.

"In essence," he concludes, "that's all there was to the Battle of Cross Keys."[21]

CHAPTER 16

Their Backs to the Mountain

There was a revealing Jackson moment back at Port Republic, though exactly what it revealed is hard to say. Around noon, he was waiting with General Winder and other officers for a possible attack from Shields or for news of the fighting at Cross Keys. For a long time he looked down at the ground, cap low over his eyes, either in meditation or from simple tiredness. He emerged from his deep study to tell a Maryland officer, McHenry Howard, that he liked having Maryland troops under his command. Then he spoke in a low voice to Reverend Dabney: "Major, wouldn't it be a blessed thing if God would give us a glorious victory today?" Howard continued, "And I saw his face with an expression like that of a child hoping to receive some favor."[1]

A few hours later, Jackson made up his own mind that Frémont was routed and sent word to Ewell to press forward. Then he started preparing to fight the following day.

⎯⎯

That night, Jackson summoned a steady stream of officers to Port Republic for face-to-face instructions for the attack against Shields's Federals. He also directed the placement of a small force to delay Frémont when he approached from Cross Keys. He ordered the North River Bridge, by which the Pathfinder could cross and attack him in the rear, prepared for burning. Some sources speculate that

Jackson planned to defeat Shields early, then turn and destroy Frémont midmorning.

After moonrise at midnight, Stonewall briefly supervised the construction of a wagon bridge by black pioneers over the swollen South River. Southerners were to cross it in the morning to fight against Shields to the northeast. At 4 a.m., when a colonel came to report to Jackson that the wagon bridge was finished, he found the general asleep. He was the only person that night who reported him not awake.[2]

The bridge proved to be a rickety affair. Planks were laid on the wagons at crazy angles and were attached without nails. Soldiers refused to cross after some fell in the water. They were finally persuaded to cross single file.

Jackson started toward the enemy in the fog at early dawn, along with General Winder and most of the Stonewall Brigade. Setting out, they passed headless Federals, grisly remnants of the previous day's cannonade.[3] Up ahead, Union artillery waited for the Confederates. Six cannon were placed on the "Coaling," a level, clear-cut, ninety-foot-high spur of the Blue Ridge that took its name from its use as a charcoal manufactory. From this dominant position a wall of infantry, as well as more artillery, stretched southwest behind a split-rail fence to anchor on the swollen South Fork of the Shenandoah.

Jackson, his judgment clouded by impatience and fatigue, underestimated the strength of the Union position. He sent 500 men against the Coaling. They were repulsed by canister while the soldiers he sent against the rest of the line were hit by musket and artillery fire. Hunkered down or retreating, the Southerners continued to take punishment as the rest of the army came piecemeal to the battlefield, hindered by the bottleneck at the makeshift bridge.

Jackson saw his plan to defeat first Shields and then Frémont evaporate. He sent couriers to his rear guard at Cross Keys, instructing them to hurry to the battlefield and burn the North River Bridge when they crossed.

Taylor arrived with his Louisianans. "Delightful excitement," he quoted Jackson as saying, then continued: "I replied that it was pleasant to learn he was enjoying himself, but thought he might have an indigestion of such fun if the six-gun battery was not silenced."

This odd exchange, which brings to mind two Brits having a jolly good chat at a cricket match, is yet another example of Jackson's personality distorting under the stresses of the campaign.[4] He sent Hotchkiss to guide Taylor through the woods to the Coaling.

Winder started forward. His men fought their way almost to the fence before they were forced back. The Union counterattacked. Winder's men were running out of ammunition. They wavered, then fell back. Federals pressed their advantage. The battle was on the verge of being lost when Taylor emerged from the woods in sight of the Coaling. Rather than coming out behind the position, as he had planned, he was still south of the cannon, with Union infantry on his right flank.

The Louisianans heard battle action receding and Union cheers. They correctly read the signals. The situation was dire—no time for redeployment. Charging through a ravine, they took the guns. But the Union surged back. Taylor sent troops to neutralize the covering infantry, then charged again. Again they were victorious. But the Federals counterattacked a second time! Fighting was savage, hand-to-hand. "Men beat each other's brains out with muskets which they have no time to load."[5] Cannoneers used their rammers as clubs. Artillery horses were bayoneted and had their throats slit with Bowie knives so that they could not draw away captured pieces. The Federals recaptured the guns.

The Confederates withdrew to the woods beyond the ravine. They were exhausted, their numbers depleted. Orders came to go forward for the third time. "Eyes swept up that fatal slope, now gray with southern dead." There was a lull in the fighting. Soldiers on the rest of the field watched to see what would happen. Then the Federals on the western part of the battlefield turned toward the Coaling. "Wheeling to the right, with colors advanced, like a solid wall [they] marched straight upon us," writes Taylor. "There seemed nothing left but to set our backs to the mountain and die hard."[6]

At that moment, Ewell, with impeccable timing, appeared through the woods. He was quickly followed by Cross Keys reinforcements. "Men, you all know me," he shouted. "We must go back to that battery." The Louisianans cheered. Joined by Ewell's men, they made a third attack "over the ground already strewn with their fallen comrades." This final attack was successful.

When further reinforcements arrived, there was little for them to do but marvel at the carnage. "It was a sickening sight," wrote a Virginia soldier, "men in gray and those in blue piled up in front and around the guns and with the horses dying and the blood of men and beasts flowing almost in a stream."[7]

Confederates turned the Union guns to fire on their former owners. With the Coaling in Southern hands, the pressure on Winder eased. He started forward with every man he could muster from the battlefield. The Union line held, then wavered, then broke. The Federals, who according to all accounts had fought bravely and well, retreated in good order. The Confederates pursued, firing their field pieces whenever they got the chance and capturing many prisoners.

In the aftermath, Jackson rode up to Ewell, placed his hand gently on his arm, and said, "General, he who does not see the hand of God in this is blind, Sir, blind!"

Perhaps the hand of the Almighty would have been even more obvious to Jackson if he had attacked in force instead of dribbling his soldiers in piecemeal. He outnumbered the Yankees more than two to one.

The Pathfinder showed up after the battle was over. Wrote S. C. Gwynne, "Somehow it was perfectly in keeping with Frémont's character that he should arrive, bayonets bristling, on the ground across the South Fork of the Shenandoah, where he could only watch helplessly as the Confederates marched their prisoners to the rear."[8] With misdirected pique, he brought up his guns to shell the Confederates who were helping the wounded, in the process killing and injuring soldiers of both sides. Jackson wrote an irate letter to Union general McDowell about the incident shortly thereafter.

Port Republic, and with it the Valley Campaign, was over. Of course, it rained. Jackson returned to an earlier camp between the South and Middle rivers. Douglas Freeman wrote poetically: "In a lush and beautiful country, Jackson rested his men, held a day of thanksgiving, and with the humblest of privates participated in brigade communion."[9] They had much to be thankful for. Wrote James I. Robertson:

> During the period from March 22 to June 9, 1862, Jackson had no more than 17,000 ill-equipped troops at hand. Yet those self-styled foot-cavalry marched 670 miles, won five battles and numerous skirmishes, demoralized three Union armies totaling more than 65,000 men, and created near-consternation among high-ranking Federal officials. Three times Jackson's unexpected successes caused President Abraham Lincoln to suspend plans for sending a full corps lying idly at Fredericksburg to reinforce Maj. Gen George B. McClellan in front of Richmond.

Summarized Douglas Freeman: "Rarely in war had so few infantry achieved such dazzling strategic results."[10]

After Port Republic, Shields and Frémont retreated down the Valley. The Pathfinder was ordered to Harrisonburg. He went twenty-five miles farther, to Mount Jackson, putting even more distance between himself and Stonewall. Shields was ordered to Richmond. Lincoln had had enough of this crazy sideshow in the Valley. The Confederate capital was his most important objective. "It is the object of the enemy to create alarms every where else and thereby divert as much of our force from that point [Richmond] as possible," he wrote Stanton on June 8, finally figuring things out on the next-to-last day of the campaign. Almost simultaneously, Lee and Davis came to the same conclusion as

Lincoln and Staunton. Jackson himself would be summoned to Richmond shortly.[11]

Jackson was famous throughout the South and unquestionably a hero to his army. Yet, as before, a pettiness emerged in his moment of triumph. He wound up snapping at his long-suffering quartermaster, John Harman, when the latter had the temerity to observe that many of the discarded weapons he had scavenged from the battlefield were Confederate. "In a towering rage," Jackson asserted that his soldiers would never throw away their muskets.

Furious himself, as well as sure in his knowledge about muskets, Harman submitted his resignation. In an act showing how highly he valued Harman's abilities, Jackson apologized and the resignation was withdrawn.

The commander of the Stonewall Brigade, General Winder, also resigned. His soldiers had been horribly mangled because of Jackson's poor decision making in the early morning of June 9. He had also requested a furlough after the battle, which was refused.

Taylor acted as the peacemaker. He visited Jackson and spoke persuasively on Winder's behalf. He wrote that he observed Jackson closely as he spoke. "I caught a glimpse of the man's inner nature. It was but a glimpse. The curtain closed, and he was absorbed in prayer. Yet in that moment I saw an ambition as boundless as Cromwell's, and as merciless."

I have thought long and hard about his statement. Jackson was indeed human, and, having just conducted a legendary military campaign, could be forgiven ambition. But I think what Taylor saw was power. Jackson had been an obscure professor at a small college less than a year and a half before. Now he was the Hero of the South, one of the best in the world at a trade he had really only practiced since the war's beginning. It must have been like riding a lightning bolt. No wonder he prayed.

That night, Taylor got a note from Winder. Jackson had visited him and they had reconciled. His resignation was withdrawn.[12]

The Valley cemeteries are what stick with me more than anything else from researching the campaign. They just go on and on. I thought Richmond, where I live, was full of Confederate dead, but the Valley rivals even those numbers. There are cemeteries up and down the Shenandoah, most well tended and in heartbreakingly beautiful settings. Winchester's Stonewall Cemetery, with 2,500 Confederates, is only one of many. Turner Ashby is there—he's buried with Richard. There are crossed cavalry sabers on the monument to THE BROTHERS ASHBY.

The site of Ashby's actual death is on a pleasantly wooded hillside east of Harrisonburg. It overlooks a panorama of James Madison University's playing fields. I parked beside what must be an obstacle course for the institution's ROTC, heavily fenced and coyly unlabeled, like it's supposed to be some vital part of national security. Thoughts of Boris and Natasha sabotaging a rope bridge mingled with the somber observation that I was probably the only person for days who had visited because of an interest in Ashby.

There are generations of markers along the winding path, the oldest a cenotaph from the nineteenth century surrounded by black wrought-iron railings. I was alone until a dog walker passed through the parking lot. "A living dog is better than a dead lion," I remembered from Ecclesiastes. Ashby, a human lion, bravest of the brave—gone. But at least not forgotten, I thought, contemplating the hefty chunk of granite inscribed with his name.

If the war hadn't intervened, he would—like Professor Jackson—surely have remained obscure, a businessman or a farmer, one of thousands in the Valley. But was his sacrifice worth it? But what else could he have done, really? Like Jackson, he was a born warrior, fulfilling his destiny. Fighting is part of the human condition, whether we like to admit it or not. We don't really need a reason. The Greeks fought over Helen for ten years...

Historic sites are supposed to be like churches or museums. You learn a few facts, then linger in a quiet place where you can think about history or meditate on life in general. My mind was jarred into another track when I inadvertently glanced at the back of one of the signs. ROAD AND SITE IMPROVEMENTS MADE POSSIBLE BY THESE FUNDS DONATED IN 1992. It was followed by four columns of names. Marveling, I counted: 135 individuals and organizations. All to preserve just this tiny portion of the past. And that was over a quarter of a century ago. How many had worked on it since?

CHAPTER 17

The Tired Man

Lee and Davis were as protective of their capital as Lincoln and Stanton were of theirs, but they still sent Jackson 8,000 men at the end of the Valley Campaign in early June 1862. "We must aid a gallant man if we perish,"[1] a hard-pressed Lee declared, thinking that perhaps with a final thrust Stonewall could clean out the Valley and scare Lincoln a fourth time into diverting troops from Richmond. Hoping for a response from Washington, Lee played up the transfers, making sure that Jackson's reinforcements were seen marching to the train station by Union prisoners about to be paroled. He also appealed to the Richmond newspapers not to mention the movements, which "all but guaranteed their publication."[2]

But Lincoln didn't take the bait. He had stopped playing Jackson's Valley game. Richmond was the target now—if he could only get McClellan to move. Unfortunately for him, the weather was Confederate: Gray skies and rain gave Little Mac another excuse to stay bogged down.

Jackson dispatched Boteler with a second appeal for 40,000 men for an invasion into Pennsylvania. This wasn't going to happen with 120,000 Federals right outside Richmond. Lee wanted Jackson to clean up the Valley with the 8,000 soldiers already en route, then come help defend the capital. He played with this idea of a second Valley Campaign until he digested the information in the report Jackson sent along with Boteler: Shields and Frémont were too far away for Jackson to fight them quickly, and he wasn't sure he could hold the lower Valley if he defeated them. The Federals weren't doing much anyway: "The enemy in the Valley seem at a pause," Lee wrote Davis.[3] It was time for Jackson to come to Richmond.

The rains had stopped, the roads were drying, and there was something else: General J. E. B. Stuart, showy and capable, had turned a cavalry reconnaissance into a romp that encircled McClellan's entire Grand Army before returning with the vital information that the Federal right flank was "in the air"—meaning that it was anchored to no natural position of strength—and thus ripe for turning by Jackson when he thundered down from the Valley.

Thundered, that is, after he had moved quietly down to his jumping-off point on McClellan's flank. On June 17, Lee wrote Jackson to come quickly; in addition, "to be efficacious the movement must be secret."[4] He didn't have to tell Jackson twice, although moving 18,500 men surreptitiously was a major undertaking for even the masterfully secretive Stonewall. The most famous man in the Confederacy was also tasked with attracting no notice as he traveled to a council of war that would take place on the far side of Richmond.

Even high-ranking subordinates weren't in on the plan. General Chase Whiting had just arrived in Staunton with some of the reinforcements. Jackson sent for him. Whiting rode the fifteen miles to Jackson's camp near Weyer's Cave. Their meeting was cordial, but included nothing specific beyond instructions to return to Staunton and await orders. Whiting was furious. "He didn't say one word about his plans....I believe he hasn't any more sense than my horse!" he fumed to General Imboden that night. A second explosion occurred the next day when he was ordered to backtrack with his soldiers to Gordonsville. "Didn't I tell you he was a fool, and doesn't this prove it? Why, I just came through Gordonsville day before yesterday!"[5]

Jackson even tried—unsuccessfully—to deceive Hotchkiss. He called for him on the night of June 17 and quizzed him for an hour on the country between Port Republic and Lexington. The fake delivered, he called for him again a little while later to innocently ask for information that would help him understand the fighting that had just occurred east of Richmond. Hotchkiss answered questions and the two huddled over maps for an additional two hours. Jackson then rode to Staunton. He started the army moving east in the early morning hours of June 18.

The soldiers crossed the Blue Ridge, Hotchkiss and Jackson among them. On the mountainside in the dark, surrounded by 18,500 men, they were unable to locate their own headquarters. "General," said Hotchkiss, "I fear we will not find our wagons tonight."

Professor Jackson saw a teachable moment. "Never take counsel of your fears," he told Hotchkiss earnestly.[6] He was preaching to the choir. Hotchkiss was already brave. At McDowell, he had preceded the soldiers up Sitlington's Hill, waving his handkerchief at the bends if the next section of road was clear of Yankees. Still, the maxim stuck with him. It also served as an overture to the upcoming campaign. The outcome of the Seven Days would be largely determined by one powerful man—McClellan—listening to his fears. The Union commander believed the Southerners, whom he outnumbered two to one, actually had twice as many men as he did. He also believed that as soon as the invincible Stonewall Jackson arrived on the scene, he was doomed. Because of McClellan's active imagination, Jackson's reputation would be as much of a factor during the fighting as either the man himself or his army.

Jackson's soldiers began boarding trains on the Virginia Central Railroad at Mechum's River Station near the eastern edge of the mountains. There were ten or so trains with eighteen to twenty makeshift cars apiece.[7] Federals had destroyed vital bridges over the South Anna River in May, isolating the better rolling stock on the far side of that stream miles away. Stonewall's men had to travel on the cars that could be pulled together from the accessible parts of the line. "The soldiers, and officers especially, complained heavily and curses thick and fast fell upon us," remembered railroader Carter Anderson.[8] The trains picked up men marching in the rear, moved them to the front, then reversed themselves and repeated the process, which Anderson called "riding and tiring." The soldiers not riding traveled on parallel roads, as did wagons and artillery.

Lee had given Boteler a letter for Jackson, then told him mysteriously to go to Charlottesville and await orders. "I asked no questions," Boteler wrote later, though he suspected that "great events were on the gale." When he arrived at noon, he found that "a dozen trains of empty cars had passed through some hours before to the Valley." Confederate pickets sealed off the perimeter so no one could leave. The sleepy college town was "in a fever of excitement."

Boteler had not been long at the station before he heard an incoming train. "As it came thundering up to the station I saw, as I expected, it was filled with troops, who not only fully occupied the interior of the cars, but likewise their roofs, and, in fact, seemed to cover them all over like clusters of bees." Carter Anderson says that fully 2,000 men were on each train.[9] Jackson was in the first car. "Glad to see you, jump in!" said the general, extending a hand. "Got a pencil?" He proceeded to give the politician/soldier a to-do list, which he extended by telegram the following day.[10]

When they arrived in Gordonsville, the next major stop on the line, soldiers speculated that they were going to attack McDowell near Fredericksburg or march on Washington itself. "None of us had a single thought of Richmond," wrote John Worsham. "Why then send Whiting's division to the Valley to join Jackson?"[11]

Carter Anderson adds that Jackson increased the deception by having "everybody, citizens and soldiers, figuring out the best roads to Washington."[12]

Reverend Dabney had been put in charge of moving the army while Jackson went on ahead. The assignment would quickly prove too complex and difficult for the clergyman, as soldiers and wagons were strung out for twenty-five miles along the route. He became ill with diarrhea, probably as a consequence of the overwhelming task. No one else, not even Ewell, knew where the army was going, or when it was supposed to get there.[13]

Jackson continued to the small station of Frederick's Hall in

Louisa County. There he spent a quiet and rainy Sabbath at the home of Nathaniel W. Harris, a prominent citizen. When his hostess asked what time he would like breakfast, he replied, "Have it at your usual hour and send for me when breakfast is ready." But when she went to waken him in the morning he was long gone, having left at 1 a.m. to meet with Lee in Richmond.

Jackson traveled as secretly as his fame would allow. He had only three men with him, all of whom were instructed to address him as "Colonel." Curiously enough, one of them was Harman. It seems their frequent arguments masked a real affection and regard. This is even more impressive in light of the fact that just over two months before, Jackson had denied him an extension of a furlough after he went home too late to be at the deathbed of two of his children who succumbed to scarlet fever. Time with a critically ill third child was refused because of "the interest of the service," as was leave to go to the funeral.[14]

Jackson obtained a pass from Whiting for the unnamed colonel and removed his general's stars for the trip. He used a series of commandeered horses, and finished at Lee's headquarters, the Dabbs House east of Richmond, at 3 p.m., having covered a distance normally reckoned at fifty-two miles in fourteen hours.

The time for the trip seems long, a little less than four miles per hour, only slightly better than a good walking pace. It makes me think that Jackson rode a good deal farther, probably trying to avoid people who may have known him and/or to deceive possible observers. In any case, when he dismounted at the Dabbs House, he looked like a man who had spent a hard half day in the saddle—dusty and worn. Lee was busy, he was told, so he slumped against a fencepost, head down, cap low over his eyes as though to continue concealing his identity.

When General D. H. Hill rode up, he was surprised to see his brother-in-law, who he thought was still in the Shenandoah Valley. A hard-fighting general, Hill, yet another dyspeptic, was an old Lexington friend who had played a major role in Jackson's conversion to Presbyterianism. The two were invited in. Offered refreshments, Jackson accepted only a glass of milk.

Two more generals soon arrived: A. P. Hill and James Longstreet. The former would later have major conflicts with Jackson; the latter would be, for armchair generals and devotees of the Lost Cause, perhaps the most controversial figure of the war.

Hill, nicknamed "Little Powell" for his slight frame, was a combative general who always wore a red shirt into battle. He was an early suitor for Ellen Marcy, whose father forbade the match in favor of the high-achieving George McClellan. After graduating second in his class at West Point, McClellan had a stellar prewar career as a military officer and railroad executive, which culminated with the presidency of the Ohio and Mississippi Railroad in 1860. There are many amusing stories about McClellan's soldiers thinking that Hill's frequent and savage attacks against them were designed to settle a grudge based on his rejection. "My God, Nelly, why didn't you marry him?" they are reputed to have said as Little Powell's Confederates came at them yet another time with that fiendish Rebel yell.

George and Ellen were very close. They had two children and, when separated, wrote each other daily. While treasured by historians, it would have been far better for his reputation if McClellan's overly candid correspondence had been destroyed.

Hill was also happily married. He and his wife, the beautiful Kentucky widow Kitty McClung, had four children. Sister of Confederate cavalryman John Hunt Morgan, the devoted Kitty stayed with Hill whenever possible in the field. But his success as a family man and military commander was undercut by the gonorrhea he contracted at West Point. Though he believed he had been cured, he was often sick during the war, and was so ill when he was killed just a week before Appomattox that he probably would have died shortly thereafter anyway.

Biographer Jeffry D. Wert asserts that James Longstreet "was the finest corps commander in the Army of Northern Virginia; in fact, he was arguably the best corps commander in the conflict on either side."[15] But for many his reputation was defined by his disagreement over tactics with Lee at Gettysburg, not to mention the fact that he became a Republican after the war, an affiliation that, in the South of that day, meant something far different than it does in the present. He was also outspokenly critical of Southern sacred cows—most notably Lee himself—in his postwar writings.

At the time of this war council, Longstreet had recently lost three of his children in one week to scarlet fever. Wrote Shelby Foote: "Grief had given him a stolid and ponderous dignity, augmented by a slight deafness which he could sit behind, when he chose, as behind a wall of sound-proof glass."[16]

Though diplomatic and courteous to an extent that made superficial observers nickname him "Granny Lee," the Southern commander was definitely in charge of the Dabbs House council of war. The plan was his, and he outlined it in an upstairs room before withdrawing to let his subordinates work out the details.

The outnumbered forces in Richmond could not withstand a siege. Therefore the Southerners had to switch to the offensive. Stuart's ride had confirmed that McClellan's right was vulnerable, unanchored and separated from the main army by the rain-swollen Chickahominy. The 35,000 Federals there, under Major General Fitz-John Porter, would be the target when the battle opened. The four generals, along with forces under Brigadier General Lawrence O'Bryan Branch and Stuart's cavalry on Stonewall's left flank, would bring a total of about 65,000 men to bear—one of the rare situations in the war when the Confederates outnumbered the Yankees.

In the meantime, south of the river, a token force under Major General J. B. Magruder and Major General Benjamin Huger would hold fast against the rest of the Union army, 25,000 against 70,000. They would bristle aggressively, employing the subterfuges for which Magruder, whose hobby was amateur theatricals and whose nickname was "Prince John," was famous, making themselves seem like a huge army on the verge of attack. "If McClellan and his generals understood what Lee was doing, and acted on it," wrote S. C. Gwynne, "they would have little trouble smashing Richmond's defenses."[17] Lee was gambling everything on the hope that they wouldn't.

The four generals undoubtedly raised the possibility during the four-hour meeting, about which little is actually known. Lee undoubtedly answered it as he had earlier answered Jefferson Davis, by saying that, as an engineer, McClellan's first impulse would be to protect his lines of communication, which extended back to his supply base at White House on the Pamunkey River.[18] Nor was he prone by nature to make an aggressive counterpunch. In any case, the grand strategy was set.

Jackson would open. How soon could he get in place? The twenty-fifth, he said. Longstreet, more familiar with Hanover County's meandering, muddy roads, urged him to take another day. Jackson agreed, and June 26 was set. With only the meeting time for recovery, Stonewall rode forty additional miles to return to his army on the march, arriving in Beaver Dam Station in Hanover County at 10 a.m. on June 24.

At the home of a local citizen, drying his clothes by a bedroom fire, Jackson did something that for him was very strange: He read a novel. For the Presbyterian deacon, indulging in this kind of light entertainment was surprising, shocking even, and it was remembered and remarked upon by Dabney years later.[19] It continued the pattern of out-of-character behavior resulting from fatigue.

Discarding the book, Jackson got a little sleep, then made a few halfhearted attempts to get his disorganized command back on schedule. His soldiers actually covered twenty miles the following day, June 25, but that only brought them a short way west of Ashland, a small railroad town twenty miles north of Richmond. Their objective, Slash Church, was six miles farther along.

The twenty-fifth was the official opening of the Seven Days. McClellan wanted some high ground for his artillery that was just a little bit closer to Richmond and so did something that was even more out of character than Jackson's novel: He became aggressive. The daylong Battle of Oak Grove was the result. Lee must have been dismayed—all his calculations were based on McClellan keeping up his glacial pace—but then he seems to have shrugged it off as an aberration and decided to proceed as planned.

He was right to do so. McClellan gained only six hundred yards of ground and didn't even follow up on that small success. The battle is often overlooked because the frontal assault was so unlike McClellan, and because it was overshadowed by Lee's offensive over the following days. The battlefield is also a preservation failure, almost impossible for historians to study and interpret: Much of the ground on which it was fought is now occupied by the Richmond airport.

Something else happened on the twenty-fifth. McClellan's men had picked up a Confederate deserter the day before who spoke, with great precision, of Stonewall's movements down from the Valley. A former slave also came into the lines with a story that Beauregard, currently ill and over a thousand miles away,[20] had arrived in Richmond. Espionage Chief Allan Pinkerton had been telling McClellan for weeks that the Rebels numbered 180,000–200,000.[21] Other rumors of the invincible Confederate host flew thick and fast.

McClellan took counsel of his fears. A Confederate attack was imminent! Jackson was marching toward his flank! "I regret my great inferiority in numbers but feel I am in no way responsible for it," he lamented to Stanton that night. "I will do all that a General can with the splendid Army I have the honor to command & if it is destroyed by overwhelming numbers can at least die with it & share its fate."[22]

It was as if Oak Grove, following the three-month slog up the Peninsula, had expended his last ounce of aggression. He shifted his mind-set from offense to defense. The stage was set for his infamous "change of base."

If McClellan could have seen Jackson he probably would not have acted so precipitately. The general had not slept during his down-and-back ride to the war council. Afterward he slept little if at all, and regularly passed up opportunities for rest. By dawn on the twenty-sixth, the day he was to open the battle, Jackson had slept only eight hours in three and a half days.[23] His performance was intermittently affected. It was as though there were two Jacksons: the bold, decisive commander, and the man who was bone-weary, misdirected, and confused. The two vied for control. Most of the time, the tired man won.

The section of the Tidewater into which he was moving would have challenged a man at the top of his game. Roads and streams wander haphazardly through indistinguishable fields and vista-blocking forests. Country byways change their names as they travel between crossroad communities with maddeningly similar nomenclature. Hundley's Corner, for example, where Jackson went into bivouac on June 26, is just two miles from Old Polly Hundley's Corner. Among the landmarks he was directed toward the following day was "Cole Harbor." There are, in fact, two *Cold* Harbors: "Old" and "New."

Compounding the problem was the lack and/or inaccuracy of maps. It wasn't just Jackson's problem. "The Confederate commanders knew no more about the topography of the country than they did about Central Africa," fumed Richard Taylor, still indignant when he wrote about it years later. "Here was a limited district, the whole of it within a day's march of the city of Richmond, capital of Virginia and the Confederacy, almost the first spot of the continent occupied by the British race, the Chickahominy itself classic by legends of Captain John Smith and Pocahontas, and yet we were profoundly ignorant of the country, were without maps, sketches or proper guides, and nearly as helpless as if we had been suddenly transferred to the banks of the Lualaba."[24]

Jed Hotchkiss, whose help would have been invaluable in this situation, had been directed by Jackson to return to the Shenandoah and continue work on his map of the Valley. In addition, Lee's orders were confusing—which is what one would expect from a commander who had only been in charge of the army for a little over three weeks.

Jackson soldiered on. When he realized he was behind schedule, he directed that his troops begin their march on the twenty-sixth at 2:30 a.m. instead of three. The column didn't actually get under way until 8:00. Dabney blamed the delay on the "julep-drinking officers"; the officers in turn blamed Dabney.[25]

CHAPTER 18

Men Falling Continually

Jackson was six hours behind schedule by 9 a.m. on June 26. Bridges were out, streams swollen, roads muddy—but drinking water was scarce. The day grew hot. The officers allowed the men to break ranks and fill their canteens from nearby wells. Progress was slow. Around noon, they halted to rest and eat. A little later, Jackson encountered Jeb Stuart. At the time, the two were certainly the most famous soldiers in the Confederacy, Jackson for his Valley Campaign, Stuart for his "Ride Around McClellan." A more contrasting pair could scarcely be imagined. Jackson, silent and secretive, careless of dress, was invariably described as rumpled and dusty; Stuart, flamboyant to an extreme, was caped like a superhero, with plumed hat, yellow sash, and gauntlets. Stuart's entourage included a banjo player, Jackson's a clergyman. Introvert and extrovert, Calvinist and cavalier, the two would become fast, if improbable, friends. Excellent soldiers above all else, they were all business as they conferred in the yard of an old white house owned by a local physician.

Stuart sent riders ahead to seize the bridge over Totopotomoy Creek. Federals set fire to the bridge as they retreated. Southerners put out the fire and repaired the bridge. Jackson's soldiers arrived at the creek around 3 p.m.

After crossing the creek, a steep but climbable road led out of the forested ravine to open fields and Pole Green Church. His objective, Hundley's Corner, was less than a mile away. For Jackson, this last fraction of the march seemed to be the hardest. He deployed skirmishers to flush out nonexistent Yankees from the woods, then shelled the hillside to accomplish the same end. It took two hours for the head of his column to reach Hundley's Corner, where he was supposed to rendezvous with A. P. and D. H. Hill for the general advance. The Hills weren't there, but the sound of guns and musketry could clearly be heard from the west in the direction of Mechanicsville. A big battle was clearly in progress. The Jackson of the Valley would have seized the initiative, rushing his men toward the sound of the guns. Instead he made camp and waited to be told what to do.

Jackson spent the night at a house called Laurel Meadow. According to a locally published history: "General Jackson did not sleep in the room assigned to him but spent the night in the dining room writing dispatches."[1] Not only did his fatigue affect his judgment on military matters, it kept him from seeing the obvious fact that, more than anything else, he simply needed to rest.

It is here that my personal path intersects with Jackson's quite literally: His army marched past my house on June 26. The fact had a tremendous impact when I discovered it some three decades ago, and has had a hold on my imagination ever since. Astonishingly, it had passed out of local knowledge, at least the local knowledge I was acquainted with growing up, so that when I found out, it was a revelation. Suddenly I wasn't living in a dull, boring enclave of truck farms and woods, slowly being suburbanized by Richmond's white flight. I was on the landscape of a great drama, where history had been made at tremendous, bloody cost.

I sometimes imagine them even now, when I go up to the end of my driveway to fetch the mail. There's Stonewall on Little Sorrel instead of a soccer mom in an SUV; Jeb Stuart guiding him, rather than the harried FedEx guy or the plumber in the pickup smoking a Marlboro Light. Behind them, the miles-long gray column marching into battle. One account says it took the whole day for them to pass.

One day in the early 1970s, I helped my grandfather dig a cherry stump out of his front field. The tree had been gone for years, but the resilient wood of the stump survived and he was tired of plowing around it. I was down in the hole, hacking at roots with a grubbing hoe, when I found the rusted blade of a shovel. What was it doing there, three feet down and thirty from the road? Did somebody die on the march and a gravedigging soldier leave it after he broke the handle?

I wish Granddaddy had saved it. He saved tons of useless stuff, a lot of which I still have. But he didn't save that. A lost object with an unknown story, it surfaces in my mind sometimes when I walk up to the road and think about Jackson marching by.

There are so many body stories. Most recently, a man from my church told me about a former neighbor who had unearthed a Confederate some years ago in the subdivision on the far side of Totopotomoy Creek, less than a mile from my house and a little farther along Jackson's route of march. They were digging a ditch to pour a concrete footing for a garage when they broke through a coffin and saw a pair of feet. The cement truck was on the way and they didn't have the time— and perhaps not the inclination—to disinter the body, so they pushed the feet back up out of the way and continued with their project.

The man from my church had since moved. Still in Hanover County, he relocated to another battlefield: Haw's Shop, an 1864 precursor to Cold Harbor. "I have two graves on my property now," he said to me matter-of-factly. "They're everywhere."

A. P. Hill had an impetuous, combative personality. He had waited all morning for Jackson to appear so that he could start the attack. Then he waited through the afternoon. Finally, around 3 p.m., about the time Jackson was shelling nonexistent Yankees on the creek bank, he'd had enough. "Rather than hazard the failure of the whole plan by further deferring it,"[2] he started forward. Lee, on the heights overlooking the Chickahominy, thought Jackson had finally arrived. He didn't realize what Hill had done until later.

Lee didn't communicate with Jackson. Jackson didn't communicate with Lee. Neither Lee nor Jackson had communicated with Hill. Nevertheless, the Battle of Beaver Dam Creek, the beginning of Lee's Seven Days offensive, had finally lurched into motion.

After crossing the Chickahominy on the Meadow Bridges, Hill easily drove the Yankees through Mechanicsville. Continuing his advance, he encountered the enemy on high ground behind Beaver Dam Creek. It was an incredibly strong position, one that the Confederate engineers had earlier scouted for themselves. They considered it "absolutely impregnable to a front attack"[3]—and that was before the Federals fortified it with gun emplacements, rifle pits, and trenches.

Attacking first on the Union right, Hill's soldiers crossed "level meadows...where even every occasional scattered shade tree had been previously cut down by the enemy to give a free field of fire."[4]

Federal cannon took advantage of the shooting gallery. Infantrymen entrenched in front of the artillery waited until the Rebels were within easy musket range before firing. The Confederates who were left charged down into the creek bottom, where they encountered felled trees whose outward-pointing branches formed an almost impregnable abatis. A color bearer remembered wrapping his flag around its staff before trying to crawl through "this entanglement of tree tops, saplings, vines and every other conceivable obstruction, under a heavy fire....My flag was riddled in this battle, having been pierced with ten bullet holes through its folds, while a splinter was torn out of the staff about six inches above my head."[5]

The creek itself was "an open swamp eighty or a hundred yards wide in which man or beast mire to the waist."[6] Few got that far. Pinned down, the men of Hill's Light Division suffered 544 casualties.

Jackson was supposed to draw Fitz-John Porter out of his entrenchments by sweeping around and behind his right, the flank that was "in the air." Beaver Dam Creek wasn't supposed to be attacked headlong. But now it had been, at tremendous cost. And the attacks would continue. As the day faded, writes historian Stephen W. Sears, the battle "took on a life of its own that defied logic. Like a whirlpool, it drew more and more men into its vortex."[7]

Acting on his own, impetuous like his commander A. P. Hill, General W. D. Pender attacked the center of the Federal line near Ellerson's Mill. While the Union position was formidable throughout its length, assaulting on the right could be justified because Jackson was supposed to be flanking there at any moment. There was no reason at all to attack the center. One of Pender's units, the 38th North Carolina, lost 152 out of 420 men.

With Pender obviously in trouble, D. H. Hill, Lee, and President Davis all ordered General Roswell Ripley's brigade in to help. Private Edgar Allen Jackson, of the 4th North Carolina, had an experience similar to the other Confederates who had attacked the Federals on the high ground that day. "We had to march about a mile before getting to the Battle field," he wrote home a few days later, "the shells and round shot passing over our heads with their peculiar whizz."

The officers dismounted and led the soldiers on foot. "As we approached nearer the bullets flew by us in torrents." The officers ordered the soldiers to lie down, then rise up and charge. "We go with a yell; we proceed half way down the hill halt and exchange shot for shot with the yankees, who had the very best of covering. We were exposed to the galling fire of two batteries and a long line of yankees behind earthworks."

As he writes, the memory of the experience is so intense it makes him switch from the past tense to the present. "I have fired once and now trying to ram down a ball which fits too tight—men are falling around me continually—I see one of our company rise up and try to get to the rear he is wounded in the thigh. For nearly half an hour our boys load and fire, firing by the light of the enemy's guns. We are ordered to retreat but it is not heeded, again our colonel who lies wounded orders us to retreat; it is not heeded, the third time is the command given we rise up and slowly retire behind a hill and try to rally our sadly thinned regiment."[8]

The 1st North Carolina lost 142 men; another of Ripley's brigades, the 44th Georgia, lost 355.

Beaver Dam Creek was a series of costly Confederate mistakes. But now Lee had the initiative. The fight was on, and Jackson, even though he hadn't done anything yet, was poised on the Federal flank. McClellan thought he had fought Jackson on the twenty-sixth. That night, he found out that Jackson was still out there, unbloodied, ready to fall on his vulnerable right.

At first Little Mac had been triumphant over Porter's easy repulse of the Confederates. After midnight, the victory began to taste like ashes in his mouth. In the early morning hours, he started moving his vast army, along with all its attendant supplies, food, ammunition, herds of cattle even, south to the James River. There, at Harrison's Landing, it would be safe under the shelter of his gunboats' heavy artillery. He wasn't retreating, he reasoned, he was "changing his base." It was, in the face of a powerful enemy, "one of the most difficult undertakings in war."[9]

In a rearguard action, he ordered Porter to withdraw to Boatswain's Creek, another of the Tidewater's meandering, swampy streams with easily defended high ground on its opposite bank.

At the time of the war, Mechanicsville consisted of six houses, two of which were blacksmith—mechanic's—shops. I've heard it said that the road coming out from Richmond was so bad that two blacksmiths were needed to fix the many wagons that broke down on their way out of town. I've also heard that the smiths kept the road that way because it was good for business. There was a beer garden as well, along with a few residences.

The village is equally humble today, and equally representative of small-town America. The Mechanicsville Drug Store features an old-time lunch counter—I'm partial to the limeades—and no one raises an eyebrow when a patron walks in with a holstered sidearm. The

NRA types mix uncomfortably with residents of the group home a few blocks away who come in to get refills on water and leave mumbling incoherently to no one in particular. An ancient, nonfunctioning telephone booth is preserved near the front of the store.

I get my shirts done at the cleaners nearby. The changes in ownership are also emblematic of seismic demographic shifts. The surly, entitled white lady who always acted like I was interrupting her favorite TV show was replaced a few years ago by a succession of enterprising Asian immigrants. The current owner always acts like he wants my business. His wife takes care of their young daughter on the premises; a grandsire with little English is also usually present.

And of course there are the mechanics. We used to take our cars to the same man who serviced my grandparents' vehicles. Then we inherited my mother's Volvo. My grandparents' mechanic didn't work on "foreign" cars, so we started going to another shop nearby. This second mechanic had a dog named Brakeshoe who had actually been born in the grease pit; he also told me about Pappy, a hermit who lived in the woods behind the shop and collected aluminum cans from the roadside for extra money. After I heard about him, I looked for Pappy when I drove down Mechanicsville Pike. I used to see him inching along the shoulder, hunting the ditches, lips moving in conversation with an invisible interlocutor, an enormous bag of cans on the hood of his ancient, blistered automobile.

The National Park Service site commemorating Beaver Dam Creek is a couple of minutes away from the village by car. Today there's a strip mall, apartments, and a subdivision along the route where Edgar Allen Jackson, whose letter I quoted earlier, came under fire from "shells and round shot" and bullets that flew by "in torrents." I had an ancestor with Edgar Jackson's unit, the 1st North Carolina Infantry. Martin White also fought in the park. It's amazing to stand between the interpretive signs and the swampy creek and know you have a family connection with someone who was there, then read the letter describing what it was like.

The war is a huge story that's right in front of me, all the time.

Stonewall Jackson marched in front of my house. An ancestor fought six miles away. I have a trench in my woods and I've found Minié balls in my backyard. It's hard to imagine not being drawn to the past.

I drove over to Beaver Dam Creek while I was writing this. Standing on the bank, pondering the contrast between the site's peaceful present and hellish history, I was startled to see a cat emerge from the undergrowth with a mouse in her mouth, walking with that high-stepping gait they sometimes affect when they've just captured prey.

What was going on with Civil War sites and cats? I remembered the little black longhair we'd wanted to adopt up in the Valley... then all the ferals watching me from the undergrowth. Then I imagined being watched by other, unseen eyes. Suddenly the bright, sunny day seemed spooky. I've never seen a ghost, but if any place would be haunted it would be a battlefield...

More spooky thoughts: Beaver Dam Creek, which should never have been fought, was like a series of falling dominoes that just missed me at the end: A. P. Hill got too excited and jumped the gun; Jackson got too tired and dropped the ball; Pender went in when he shouldn't have; then Davis, Lee, and D. H. Hill all decided Ripley needed to go in and help Pender. They deployed the 1st North Carolina and it got cut to pieces. If one of its many dead had been my ancestor, I wouldn't be here.

Thinking that there was a reason I usually brought Catherine along on these jaunts, I decided to re-anchor myself to reality by inspecting what remained of the Union lines across the creek. I walked over a footbridge and passed an old millpond. At the top of the hill I wondered just what the contractor was thinking when he built that house directly on the remains of a trench. Further explorations in the subdivision made me doubly aware of what a strong position Porter held, and how foolish and brave the Confederates had been to assault it.

The cat had finished her mouse by the time I returned. She walked up and allowed me to pet her before she strolled back into the bushes to try her luck again.

CHAPTER 19

Bloody Ground

The following day, June 27, probing Confederates pushed back the few Yankees who were left at Beaver Dam Creek, the rear guard for the rear guard. Continuing forward, they passed corpses of those who had died in the previous day's assault. Some, knee-deep in mud, were still standing.

The Confederates expected to find the Federals at Powhite Creek, the next in the series of marshy tributaries of the Chickahominy. Gaines' Mill was on the Powhite, giving its name to the battle because it was the Confederates' first objective and because it was five stories tall, the largest structure in the surrounding countryside. Also, "the Battle of Boatswain's Creek," where the battle was actually fought, didn't have much of a ring to it.

Dr. Gaines and his mill were also memorable to the Yankees because the Federals camped near it during the siege. When soldiers died from fever, they buried them on the property; Gaines, an ardent secessionist, told them that when they left he was going to dig up the bodies and feed them to his hogs.[1]

The Federals had retreated to the next stream to the east, Boatswain's Creek, mentioned above. It was another strong position, made only slightly less formidable because Porter's men had not had time to entrench the way they had at Beaver Dam Creek. They did what they could, digging in as much as time allowed as well as piling up plundered fence rails and anything else that would stop bullets, even knapsacks. The line formed an almost two-mile-long crescent that arched toward the Confederates as it followed the ridge. Some 27,000 men were deployed in step fashion: the first line near the creek bottom, then two succeeding lines higher up. There were ninety-six cannon on the high ground. Because of the elevation, the three lines of infantry, as well as the artillery, could shoot simultaneously without fear of hitting their own men. And the Confederate slope was long and gentle, giving the Yankees more time to aim and fire. According to Confederate Private John Worsham, "This was the strongest point I saw occupied by either army during the war."[2]

Jackson, meanwhile, was finally on the scene. After accidentally shelling some of Maxcy Gregg's South Carolinians, in the van of A. P. Hill's forces, he met with Lee at Walnut Grove Church. The generals conferred out of earshot of their staffs. Both groups noted the contrast between the two. Jackson, the Hero of the Valley, was dusty and travel-worn. He stood with cadet cap removed to reveal a startlingly white forehead. Lee was seated on a cedar stump. Impeccably though not ostentatiously uniformed, he was unaffectedly aristocratic.

Jackson's assignment was unchanged from the previous day: Flank Porter out of his position. In other words, get around and behind him so that he had to fall back. After concluding his interview with Lee, Stonewall started toward his objective: Old Cold Harbor, a crossroads tavern near Porter's right and rear. After obtaining a local guide from one of Jeb Stuart's cavalry units, Jackson told the man he needed to go to Cold Harbor—but he offered no further details. His habit of doling out information on a need-to-know basis dovetailed unfortunately with the confusing nomenclature of the region: As mentioned earlier, there were two Cold Harbors, Old and New, and they were more than a mile apart. The guide started leading him, by the quickest and fastest route, toward the wrong Cold Harbor.

After an hour, Jackson heard firing ahead. "Where is that firing?" he asked the guide. A testy exchange ensued in which Jackson learned that Gaines' Mill was straight ahead. "But I do not wish to go to Gaines' Mill," said the angry general. "I wish to go to Cold Harbor, leaving that place on the right." It had to be on his right so he could flank the enemy.

"Then the left hand road was the one you should have taken," said the now-frustrated guide, contending with Jackson's secretiveness for the first time. "Had you let me know what you desired, I could have directed you in the right direction at first."[3]

Losing valuable time, the column had to backtrack a mile and a half. Other Confederates, meanwhile, had found the Federals behind Boatswain's Creek. They were assaulting piecemeal, mostly on the Confederate right, and paying a heavy price.

About a quarter of a mile into the woods at the NPS Gaines' Mill Battlefield site, there is a small clearing with a granite monument to the troops of the euphoniously named general, Cadmus Marcellus Wilcox, whose luxuriantly muttonchopped likeness is etched into a granite marker memorializing him and his soldiers. Beside the marker, a wayside exhibit tells the story of Private Banbury Jones of the 11th Alabama, one of Wilcox's units, who were attacking on the Confederate right. His story vividly conveys the intensity of the fighting.

Private Jones picked up the regimental flag after the previous color bearer had been shot thirteen times. Then Jones was himself shot through the right arm, both legs, then the left arm. "The flag dropped and was given to a third man despite Jones' plea to tie the flagstaff to his body as he was still able to walk."[4]

There are seldom any visitors to the site. Trees muffle the sounds of the nearby interstate and of the jets landing at the Richmond airport. When I walk the trail and get to the marker, I usually take a moment to reflect on the astonishing valor of the men on both sides. That, and their incredible suffering. One story I can't get out of my mind is from Alabama private W. A. McClendon, who talks of seeing a mortally wounded comrade with blood hemorrhaging from his abdomen: "In his delirium he made an unsuccessful attempt to stop the hole with the stopper from his canteen."[5]

Though outgunned, Confederate artillery fought valiantly. A cannon belonging to South Carolina's Pee Dee Light Artillery grew so hot from firing that it bent at the trunnions—the protuberances attaching the weapon to the gun carriage—and had to be abandoned.[6]

Seeing the futility of the struggle, around 4:30 p.m., A. P. Hill ordered his soldiers to stop firing and lie down on the ground. "These brave men had done all that any soldiers could do," he wrote later. Others were also pinned down. Most held their ground. Some continued to attack.

Not far away, near the center of the Southern line, Roberdeau Wheat, who cheated death when he recovered from his Manassas lung wounds, had a premonition before he led his Louisiana Tigers into battle. When aide Moxley Sorrel offered him a drink from his flask, he said, "Moxley, something tells old Bob that this is the last drink he'll ever take in this world and he'll take it with you." He was shot in the head shortly thereafter while leading the attack. Without their leader, the Tigers stopped fighting. "They have killed the old Major," said one, "and I am going home. I wouldn't fight for Jesus Christ now!"[7]

The Tigers were disbanded not long afterward. Wheat's final wish was to be buried on the field. He was, for a while, until his father had the body moved to Hollywood Cemetery, where he could more easily take care of the grave.

Private McClendon wrote that the battle was so loud he could only tell he had fired his musket from its kick against his shoulder.[8] South Carolina sharpshooter Berry Benson said of the firing, "For hours, absolutely unbroken by a pause, it was like the steady falling of water."[9]

The Union line held. Reinforcements swelled their numbers to 35,000. At first they were triumphant, then hard-pressed. Many were exhausted; ammunition was running low. Porter called for more men, but McClellan sent only a couple of brigades, approximately 2,000 men. Prince John was putting on such a show in front of Richmond that McClellan, taken in, saved most of his forces for the attack he thought was coming south of the Chickahominy. Military bands played, men cheered, infantry came out and put on an aggressive show of force, then artillery did the same. My favorite story has Magruder marching a small group of soldiers around and around in a circle for hours. Visible through a break in the trees, they made Union observers think that thousands were gathering for a massive assault.

Southern attacks continued. They were wearing down the Federals, but at terrible cost. The afternoon waned toward sunset. Lee needed to get his whole force into the fight. The biggest problem was on the Confederate left. Where was Jackson?

Stonewall's men, bedeviled by poor communication and counter-marching, were only just now trickling onto the battlefield. He encountered Lee near the Confederate center. "Ah, General," the patrician commander said, in what could have been his usual diffident politeness, a veiled rebuke, or both: "I am very glad to see you. I had hoped to be with you before." Jackson mumbled inaudibly and tossed his head in a gesture that could have meant almost anything. "That fire is very heavy," Lee continued. "Do you think your men can stand it?"

"They can stand almost anything," answered Jackson. "They can stand that!"[10]

Lee gave him instructions for bringing his soldiers into action. The plan was for a general assault all along the line with 60,000–65,000 men. It would be Lee's largest attack of the war, three times the size of Pickett's Charge at Gettysburg.[11]

Again, his plan showed the similarity of the two men's strategic vision: "Never fight against heavy odds," Jackson had said, "if by any possible maneuvering you can hurl your own force on only a part, and that the weakest part, of your enemy and crush it."

Stonewall had been lethargic during the day. Now he was vital and engaged. Adrenaline and devotion to duty overcame fatigue. Dabney recalled the animated Jackson in near-biblical terms, writing that his "fiery spirit fairly broke from his customary restraints and bore him away with a tempest of passion by which his face and person were literally transfigured."[12]

The time for action had arrived. Jackson sent word to his division commanders: "Tell them this affair can hang in suspense no longer. Sweep the field with the bayonet!"

On the Confederate right, Lee encountered the formidable presence of General John Bell Hood, commander of the Texas Brigade. Bearded and muscular, the sandy-haired, six-foot-two Hood is often described as a "giant." Lee outlined the situation and the urgent need to dislodge the enemy. "This must be done," he told Hood quietly. "Can you break his line?"

"I will try," Hood said simply.

"May God be with you." Lee turned and rode away.

There doesn't seem to have been any particular signal to start. It's doubtful one could have been heard. The line surged forward around 7 p.m. Hood was leading the 4th Texas, a brigade made up also of Georgians and South Carolinians. He ordered them not to fire until he gave the command. They started forward.

The Rebel yell, sounding "like forty thousand wild cats," echoed across the battlefield. A gap developed in the Southern charge. Hood wheeled his men to fill it. Soon they were in front. When they reached the ridgeline, they "were welcomed with a storm of grape and canister from the opposite hill side" while the entrenched Union infantry "poured deadly and staggering volleys full in our faces."[13] The undaunted 4th Texas charged down the hill. They reached the creek, still without firing, and helped each other across. Then, wrote Hood, "amid the fearful roar of musketry and artillery, I gave the order to fix bayonets and charge.... The Federals, panic-stricken, rushed precipitately to the rear."[14] Suddenly, the advantages of terrain were with the Southerners—defenders higher up could not fire on their attackers without hitting their own men. The Confederates "flew toward the breastworks." Clearing them, they finally fired, "and slaughtered the retreating devils as they scampered up the hill."[15]

The 4th Texas suffered staggering losses. Half would fall during the attack, as well as all of the unit's field officers. Only Hood himself would survive unscathed. Years later, he wrote about being approached after the charge by Major John C. Haskell, son-in-law of General Wade Hampton. The major "won my admiration by his indomitable courage: just after my troops had broken the adversary's line, and I was sorely in need of staff officers, he reported to me for duty, sword in hand, notwithstanding one of his arms had by a shot been completely severed from his body. I naturally instructed him to go in search of a surgeon."[16]

Nearly simultaneous breakthroughs occurred elsewhere on the line. Some of the close-range fighting was hand-to-hand. A group of Alabama soldiers, thinking they might not get to participate, dropped their heavy rifles and continued charging with only their bayonets. Federal artillery plowed the Confederates with double-shotted canister before limbering up and retreating. Many didn't escape. The Southerners captured twenty-two cannon during the retreat.[17]

Some Federals moved back in good order; others surrendered; some simply fled. Roiling battle smoke merged with twilight on the plateau. Wrote one Confederate: "It was the only field I had seen on which the smoke of battle rested, through which the setting sun shown red and dim."[18] Panic spread. Scenes comic and bizarre punctuated the confusion. An exultant Confederate, his pants thin and ragged, leapt onto a captured field piece as though he were riding a horse. He jumped off faster than he had gotten on. The gun, which had been firing for hours, was nearly red-hot. A New York newspaper correspondent recalled seeing a galloping horse "carrying a man's leg in the stirrup—the left leg, booted and spurred."[19]

In an attempt to save the guns, Jeb Stuart's father-in-law, the Federal brigadier general Philip St. George Cooke, ordered a cavalry charge. Southerners recalled actually feeling the earth shake. Flash of sabers, thunder of hooves...Confederates emptied saddles with one massed volley. They shot more horsemen as they closed, then finished off others with their bayonets. One hundred and fifty of the 5th U.S. Cavalry's 250 enlisted men were casualties, along with six of the seven officers. There were no Confederate casualties. Wrote an Alabama corporal: "We...taught them a lesson that when infantry are fighting they should keep out of the way."[20]

Federals retreated across their military bridges over the Chick-ahominy, burning them after they escaped. Confederate momentum stalled. Exhausted from the charge, the Southerners found themselves encumbered by prisoners. Two Union regiments, the 4th New Jersey and the 11th Pennsylvania, were captured whole. Wounded comrades needed to be found or helped. Another distraction: The battlefield was scattered with full Union knapsacks, up-to-date muskets, non-worn-out shoes, and everything else the Confederates lacked.

Night fell. Southerners bedded down among the wounded and the dead. Wrote one Confederate cavalryman: "The fact that the sufferers are of the enemy makes a great difference in the horrors of a battlefield. There is, of course, something soothing in seeing a good harvest by the dread reaper when they are not on our side." His satisfaction waned as the hours wore on. "Still," he added, "to hear even enemies groaning and praying around you all night is not agreeable."[21]

Heros von Borcke was a big man (six foot four) with a big sword (thirty-six inches) and sweeping mustachios. A Prussian cavalry offi-cer, he ran the blockade in 1862 and fought for the South as part of Stuart's colorful entourage until he was severely wounded late in the war. He was sleeping beside Stuart on the battlefield when, around midnight, he felt a hand on his shoulder. Grasping the hilt of his sword, he demanded to know who it was. "General Jackson," came the mild reply. Von Borcke got up and offered Jackson his blankets. "I left them alone, these grand warriors," he writes in the everyday nineteenth-century prose that approaches poetry, "...and wandered about, medi-tating on the stirring events of the day. I was deeply impressed by the blackness of the night and the profound stillness of the slumbering camp. Here and there a camp-fire shed a red glow around, and the still-ness was only too mournfully interrupted by the groans of wounded and dying men, who, not many hours before, had been full of health and hope."[22]

Stonewall may have slept afterward, or he may have continued his earlier pattern of busying himself throughout the night. Even if he did sleep, it would not have made up for all the nights he had been deprived.

⊷

"Around this crossroads is bloody ground," reads the old granite-based marker where the battlefield of Gaines' Mill overlaps the battlefield of Cold Harbor. Besieged twice, Richmond was attacked by McClellan in 1862 from the east, then by Grant from the north two years later. Battles from the two campaigns describe similar arcs from northwest to southeast, with the Seven Days closer to the city. Interestingly, in one of the ironies with which the war abounds, Gaines' Mill, "Lee's First Great Victory," was fought over much the same ground as his last, Cold Harbor. "Bloody ground" is an apt description, with 15,000 casualties from the first and 18,000 from the second. Many of the soldiers who fought in the second battle were veterans of the first. Some reported seeing human remains, disinterred from shallow graves by weather or scavengers, when they returned to their old battleground in 1864.

Antietam, the war's bloodiest day, began at dawn; 23,000 men were killed, wounded, or captured. Gaines' Mill amassed 15,000 casualties in a battle that only began midafternoon.

⊷

Since before World War II, the National Park Service has preserved some sixty acres of the Gaines' Mill battlefield. With the help of the Civil War Trust, they were recently able to add over three hundred more. "I've had an interest in the property for sixty years," said Richmond-area stockbroker Bob Giles. "When I was a boy, I roamed its woods and fields as a relic hunter. Once, down by Boatswain's Creek, I ran my detector over a fallen log and got eight readings. At least eight bullets hit that tree—that'll give you an idea of the intensity of the fighting.

"I later discovered one of my ancestors, John Rudder, had fought on that very ground."

Giles had a pivotal role in preserving the land when it came on the market in 2010. A childhood friend, Wayne McDougle, owned the property. With the help of National Park historian Robert E. L. Krick, Giles was able to persuade McDougle that preservation was "the highest and best use of the property, both for the nation and the world."[23]

The older part of the battlefield features the 4th Texas's breakthrough trail and Fitz-John Porter's headquarters, the Watt House. The house, while substantial, is far smaller than many homes in the nearby subdivisions. It was used as a field hospital after the battle. I visited it as a boy on a tour with my summer day camp. The camp director, who was driving us around in a repurposed school bus, told us that after the battle, piles of amputated limbs were as high as the bottoms of the windows on all sides of the house. While I've never been able to find that fact in a period account, a Watt relative did visit the house a few months after the battle and wrote:

> Even in the corners of the yard there were graves, and bordering it was a long trench, in the garden was another trench said to contain forty dead. The house, what a wreck! The walls and roof were torn by shot and shell, the weather-boarding honeycombed by Minié balls, and every pane of glass shattered. And the floors!—grandmother's immaculate floors! From garret to cellar there was scarcely a space of flooring as large as a man's hand that did not bear the purple stain of blood.[24]

The damage was repaired after the war. The house is not open to the public. Some years ago, I visited when a ranger friend of mine lived there. Morbidly curious, I examined the floorboards. Completely normal-looking, they had been replaced sometime in the intervening years.

I was often stationed at Gaines' Mill when I worked part-time as a seasonal ranger. Once, I was giving a tour to a man in his late middle age who acted as though he still wielded the authority he had left behind when he retired. It was just the two of us. I outlined the

Peninsula Campaign using the map of the exhibit, then talked about the Seven Days. I was just warming up to Gaines' Mill when he interrupted: "Wait a minute!" He had a "gotcha!" tone in his voice. "You're talking Seven Days, but there are only six listed on the sign. What's the seventh?" He folded his arms and gave a satisfied smile.

I didn't want to get into the whole Oak Grove/Richmond airport thing and had a sudden inspiration: "You're right!" I said. "On the seventh day, Lee rested."

Taken aback, he literally blustered: "Why, that's actually funny! You couldn't have thought of that. There's no way you could have thought of that!"

With the exception of the occasional annoying visitor, it was a great job, especially if you enjoyed being outside and talking about history. Most of the people I met were grateful for my time and the little bit of information I gave them. Like me, they had all fallen under the spell of the war in varying degrees and for various reasons. They really did come from "all walks of life." Some only visited once. Others came over and over.

"I just helped you with your landscaping," said the trucker, laughing. The park road is really not much more than a paved trail, and when he drove his rig through it ripped off branches. He told me he was from Baltimore and that he always stopped by after he dropped off his load. "Anything new?" he asked, glancing at the books and maps for sale in the shelter.

"Not really," I answered. He looked over the exhibits, then walked to the desk.

We chatted, then he told me he had a room in his house full of books and paintings devoted to the Civil War.

"How'd you get interested in this stuff?" I asked.

"I had a dream when I was six or seven. I was lying on a battlefield, wounded, pretending I was dead. A Confederate officer rode up

on his horse. He knew I was faking. He stabbed me with his bayonet."
The trucker shivered. "I had that dream over and over. I can still feel
the cold steel going in."

One day a woman came in to the shelter saying she was "just
going in to visit Mama." I thought she was talking about using the
park road to get to the small cluster of houses on the other side. Then
she asked about putting up a plaque. I assumed it was for an ancestor
who had fought there. It turned out to be for her mother. "She was a
good ol' southern lady, really into the Civil War and reenacting. She
told us, 'When I die, just sing "Dixie" and scatter my ashes in that old
Confederate trench at Cold Harbor.' So that's what we did."

Jackson himself may have been the first tourist. He visited the Gaines'
Mill battlefield the day after the fighting. Riding over the ground
where Hood had charged, he said, "The men who carried this position
are soldiers indeed!"[25]

Resting, gleaning, burying the dead—the army caught its breath on
June 28. Lee focused on McClellan's next move. Was he still planning
to attack Richmond? Or retreat? If he was going to retreat, would it
be back down the Peninsula the way he had come? Or south to the
James River and the shelter of his gunboats? Lee sent Stuart to destroy
track and make observations on the Richmond and York River Railroad, the line that supplied the besieging Federals from their base at
White House on the Pamunkey. While Lee waited for information, a
huge dust cloud appeared behind the shield of trees across the Chickahominy. The Federals were on the move—but going where? A courier arrived from Stuart: The Federals had burned the railroad bridge
over the Chickahominy. McClellan had abandoned his base at White
House along with the rail line that daily brought the six hundred tons
of supplies needed by the army. He was definitely retreating, probably

south toward the James. A change of base would save him from an ignominious flight back the way he had come. But still Lee hesitated, the situation not yet clarified in his mind. In spite of the uncertainty, he went to bed that night at a reasonable hour. Reports have him asleep by 11 p.m.[26] Unlike Jackson, he was taking care of himself.

CHAPTER 20

The Prize Within Their Reach

The next morning, June 29, Lee ordered Magruder to attack the Union rear guard near Savage's Station, a stop on the Richmond and York River Railroad. Jackson would support him on the left and Huger on the right.

Stonewall was to repair one of the Chickahominy bridges that had been burned by the Federals, cross, then fight alongside Magruder on his way down to White Oak Swamp, "a troublesome miniature of the Chickahominy,"[1] that was also on the route of the Union retreat. Jackson's work on the bridge was almost finished when, in midafternoon, he received an order addressed to Stuart from Lee's aide Colonel R. H. Chilton. Stuart was to watch the Chickahominy bridges. If the Federals tried to cross, he was to alert Jackson, who would "resist their passage until reinforced."[2]

Lee was sending mixed messages: Attack in the morning; watch and wait in the afternoon. They were also selective: He didn't share the fact with Magruder that Jackson had to stay in place in case there was a Federal counterthrust.

Shortly after Jackson received the Chilton directive, General David Jones, who was to fight on Magruder's left close to Jackson, rode up and asked Jackson when he was coming. Jackson said he had "other important duty to perform."[3]

One can easily imagine the effect of this reticence on Magruder. Normally high-strung, he was already reacting badly to medication his doctor had prescribed for indigestion. Now, without Jackson, he was going to have to actually attack a vastly superior Union host rather than just pretend that he was going to do so. And as the situation developed, he would not have Huger's help either.

Retreating Federal soldiers were meanwhile spectacularly destroying anything that could not be carried away. Bonfires bigger than barns consumed food and supplies. A Bostonian said that one such conflagration was as large as Faneuil Hall. Whiskey from stove-in barrels flowed in flaming rivers, burning the lips of soldiers who got down on all fours trying to salvage a drink.

Ewell's aide, Campbell Brown, saw dense smoke rising from the burning stores at Savage's Station. His column halted near the partially destroyed railroad bridge over the Chickahominy. Shortly thereafter, riding off to deliver an order, he heard "the most fearful explosion." Next, "the woods between us and the river were filled with falling shells." A preliminary bombardment, he decided. The Yanks were going to cross the river. Brown rode off to tell Ewell the news. He found the general coming toward him at full gallop. Behind him was "a dense white column of smoke...[and] a roaring in the direction of Savage's Station, growing momentarily louder & clearer." The Federals had blown up one ammunition train, then decided to make better use of another by sending it back toward the Confederates, blasting away. Suddenly it appeared, coming toward them at full speed. Fearful it would jump the gap in the trestle, they had their men take shelter, but it careened off the bridge and into the water, hissing fiercely and still sending off shells left and right.

"It was," concluded Brown, "one of the grandest sights I ever looked at."[4]

An entire Union field hospital with 2,500 patients was abandoned at Savage's Station. Medicines were poured down wells or mixed together into revolting, unsalvageable concoctions. The walking wounded walked away. The rest were left to their fate.

Confederate gleaners had a field day. Stuart went to White House after reconnoitering to the east. There, von Borcke found him sitting in the shade, "regaling himself with iced lemonade, which he shared with me, and which fell upon my tongue like nectar." He added: "Ice, lemons, crushed sugar, and many other dainties and delicacies, which we knew only by recollection, were heaped around us in large piles, for the benefit of anyone who would reach out his hand to take them." Another Confederate cavalryman also remembered "buckets of iced lemonade," as well as "pickled oysters, eggs roasted in blocks of salt, canned beef and ham, French rolls, cakes and confectionary of all sorts, and last but not least, boxes of delicious Havana cigars, and coffee."[5]

On a more prosaic level, the Confederates replaced almost every piece of equipment that could be upgraded. "Knapsacks were captured by thousands," wrote South Carolina sharpshooter Berry Benson, "while the whole Confed. army refitted itself with blankets, rubber clothes, tent flies, haversacks, and canteens. So that in the middle of the war and later, to see equipment of Southern make was somewhat of a curiosity."[6]

At first, Jackson assigned the bridge building to Dabney. The clergyman was as out of his depth as he had been when directing the march from the Valley. After a reality check, Jackson gave the job of reconstruction to Captain Claiborne R. Mason, a sixty-two-year-old engineer with whom he had worked in the Valley. His "African Pioneers"—a euphemistically named company of impressed slaves who labored with quiet and almost completely unremarked-upon efficiency—soon had the task in hand. Both sides used black labor for practically everything early in the war. While Lincoln had the highest motives for the Emancipation Proclamation, which would be issued later in the year, there was also a practical corollary: If the slaves were freed, they would no longer help the Confederacy.

Momentarily superfluous, Jackson eased Little Sorrel over the Chickahominy and rode south a short distance to the Trent House, which had been McClellan's headquarters until just hours before. It must have had something of the eerie feel of an empty football stadium after the big game. There were ashes from the huge campfire near which McClellan had informed his generals that he was changing his base. Thaddeus Lowe had launched his balloons from here. There was also a signal station.

Dabney either accompanied Stonewall or came through a little later. He writes that there were "extensive bowers, ingeniously woven of cedar boughs, which had surrounded the headquarters where M'Clellan had recently resided, in a village of canvas, provided with every appliance of luxury. Here also was his telegraph office, whence lines diverged to each corps of his army and to Washington, with the floor littered with the originals of those fictitious dispatches with which his government was wont to delude its people."[7]

McClellan's columns wended their way south toward the James. His 100,000 soldiers—now somewhat diminished in number—were accompanied by "281 pieces of field artillery and 26 heavy guns of the siege train, something over 3,800 wagons and ambulances, and 2,500 head of beef on the hoof."[8] McClellan went on ahead without leaving anyone to command the rearguard action, and things proceeded haphazardly. One corps, Brigadier General Samuel P. Heintzelman's, headed south without clearing the movement with anyone. Brigadier General Edwin V. Sumner formed a defensive line with Brigadier General Israel B. Richardson near Savage's Station. Sumner, a grizzled old army man, was nicknamed "Bull"—"in full, 'the Bull of the Woods'— because of the loudness of his voice; he had a peacetime custom of removing his false teeth to give commands that carried from end to end of the regiment, above the thunder of hooves."[9] Despite his aggressive nickname, Sumner deployed only ten of his twenty-six regiments. Outnumbered and unsupported by both Jackson and Huger, Magruder likewise sent in less than half his men. The battle began around 5 p.m. and ended inconclusively by nightfall.

Afterward, Lee was revealed in a puzzling and unflattering light when he received word of Jackson's absence from Magruder. He had just finished writing an uncharacteristically strong reprimand to Prince

John when aide Walter Taylor rode up and related the "other duty to perform" story. Letting his earlier words stand, he added to the message, "I learn from Major Taylor that you are under the impression that General Jackson has been ordered not to support you. On the contrary, he has been directed to do so and to push the pursuit vigorously."

Why then had Lee sent the earlier communiqué via Chilton? And why drop the hammer on Magruder, who had actually fought, rather than Jackson, who hadn't? In any case, around 3:30 a.m.—probably because he had received some prodding from Lee, though there is no record of it—Jackson himself rode to Magruder's headquarters and told him the Valley soldiers would be on the move by daylight. Relieved, Magruder went to bed. Jackson, who had earlier slept fitfully, if at all, probably didn't.

I had forgotten what an incredible preservation failure Savage's Station was until I stood on the Meadow Road Bridge and looked down at the twelve lanes of interstate and feeder roads covering the Confederate position. The farm next to I-295 was for sale. That would complete the destruction by turning the Union position into subdivisions as well. There is a grove of historic markers by a pulloff near the bridge in front of the farm that's for sale: four state markers, badly rusted, from the 1920s and '30s; a granite-based Freeman marker from the same era; and a state-of-the-art Civil War Trails sign complete with map. "Private Property" and "No Trespassing" decorate the farm gate if you run out of things to read.

Battlefields are often fought over again years after the fact because they are inherently desirable—vital crossroads, well-drained high ground, and so on—to both generals and developers. I was imagining the field before me sprouting suburban houses when a woman in a black Yukon pulled into the turnaround.

"Pardon me. Do you come here often? Do you know what happened to the flag?"

I told her I hadn't been there for years. She said a large Confederate flag had flown until just recently on the private property on the other side of the fence. I walked over and saw the hole where the flagpole had been.

"I drive past here all the time and all of a sudden the flag is gone."

I didn't know anything about it.

"I think we're going to lose all our statues on Monument Avenue, the way things are going."

I agreed that would not be good.

She was obviously from the neighborhood, so I asked her about living near the battlefield. She started telling relic-hunter stories. They used to come in her yard and go onto nearby farms without permission. To make matters worse, they didn't cover up their holes. "I had holes in my driveway that could have ruined my car. And if you have a hole in a field and a cow steps in it and breaks their leg you have to shoot the cow.

"I heard them talking one night. I opened the window and they were right outside. If I had dropped a rock I would have hit one in the head."

Another time, a hunter rubbed salt in the wound by bragging to her about getting top dollar for a buckle he'd found on her land. Later, pregnant, she was home sick in bed during the day when she heard them.

She had left the garage door partially open. She snuck out under it and took their pictures. "They said, 'What are you doing?' I said, 'Now I've got evidence!' That finally scared them off. They never knew that the pictures didn't turn out."

None of the relic hunters I've known have had such flagrant disregard for private property. A secretive lot, their main sin is the air of superiority they assume while guarding the location of their hunting grounds. That, and a somewhat cavalier attitude toward human remains.

"If you're a relic hunter, sooner or later you're going to dig up a body." The man, a National Park Service volunteer, had hunted for many years, stopping only recently because his age made it harder to get around in the woods.

"Did that happen to you?"

"There was hardly anything left. I just covered it back up."

"Where was that?"

Silence.

Changing the subject, he told me about a farmer's gang plow hitting a shallow grave and scattering bone fragments over the field the way a storm scatters boat wreckage over the surface of the water. He wouldn't say where that happened either.

"If you see a guy at a relic show with a row of buttons and a belt buckle, it's a pretty good bet he found a body."

Lee rode up to Magruder's headquarters around dawn the next day with a new plan. Jackson was to march to White Oak Swamp Bridge, where they would cross and attack the enemy's rear guard. Jackson got his men under way. They seemed in no particular hurry, taking time to scoop up over 1,000 Federals left behind during the retreat. There were further delays at Savage's Station, where his men gathered some of the vast quantity of stores left undestroyed by the enemy.

Arriving at White Oak Swamp around noon, he found the bridge burnt and the Yankees on the far side of the stream. Some of his artillery was already in place. Working behind a screen of trees, he continued a clandestine deployment, placing his guns at the top of the rise overlooking the swamp. Twenty-three guns opened on the Yankees a little before 2 p.m. "It was as if a nest of earthquakes had suddenly exploded under our feet," a Vermont soldier remembered.[10] Mules being watered at the stream trampled soldiers as they stampeded up the bank. Men and horses fled in all directions.

Federal artillerists withdrew their cannon, although three were left behind. Confederate cavalrymen, accompanied by Jackson and D. H. Hill, waded their horses across the stream and tried to secure the guns. They were met by determined musket and artillery fire and had to withdraw. The generals returned the way they had come. The cavalry made too large a target and rode downstream a quarter of a mile where they found an unguarded crossing.

Sharpshooters and artillery fire stymied Confederate efforts to rebuild the bridge. Cavalry colonel Thomas Munford sent word to Jackson of the unguarded crossing he had found, telling him that infantry could cross there and be on the enemy's flank. Jackson gave no response.

The action settled into a desultory artillery duel. Federal cannon fired from the high ground behind trees on the opposite bank. Wrote artillerist Porter Alexander: "When these new batteries opened, the Confederate batteries were ordered to open fire in their direction *guided by the sound*, for the forest in their front completely hid them from view. And, for all the rest of that day, that absurd farce of war was played, our guns firing at the enemy's sound & their guns firing at ours."[11]

Alexander continued, relating a story told to him on "several occasions" by General Wade Hampton. The general went exploring downstream with some of his staff. They found a way across the swamp and were soon able to unobtrusively observe the enemy's flank. Hampton went back and reported to Jackson, asking permission to cross with his own brigade and attack the enemy. Jackson told him to build a bridge. Hampton said no bridge was necessary but he would build one, and he did. Reporting back to Jackson upon its completion, he found the general sitting on a log, head down, cap over his eyes.

> When H. reported Gen. J. raised his head, looked under his cap brim, & said "H m-m?" (that unspellable interrogative). Gen H. repeated about his having built the bridge, Gen. J. said, "Um-h-m-m" (the unspellable assertive) and resumed his first position. Gen. Hampton waited for further remarks, until the situation seemed awkward, and then went back to his brigade.[12]

Eventually Jackson rose from his log, wandered over to a large oak tree, sat down beneath it, and, in spite of the artillery duel, fell asleep. Maryland Confederate McHenry Howard was riding in advance of his unit when he encountered Jackson's staff. The general was nearby, asleep in spite of the shelling. "With the exception of this slow firing," he wrote, "everything seemed to be quiet and it looked to me as if on our side we were waiting for Jackson to wake up."[13]

He did wake up that evening long enough to go to supper with his staff, but fell back asleep during the meal with a biscuit between his teeth. Waking up later, he rose and delivered an almost Shakespearean exit speech: "Now gentlemen, let us at once to bed, and rise with the dawn, and see if tomorrow we cannot do *something*."[14]

Porter Alexander thought that at Glendale, Southerners had their best chance of the entire war to win their independence: "The Confederacy at this moment was about in its prime & had more men available than ever before or after. And think of the moral shock to the North of the destruction and capture of McClellan's entire army....Never, before or after, did the fates put such a prize in our reach."[15] While other commentators don't go quite so far, all see it as a major missed opportunity. Just a few days before, the measure of success had been raising the siege of Richmond. Now it was total victory and independence. The huge Union column, 62,000 men, was funneling from two roads into one on its retreat to the James. Lee planned to bring almost all of his army into play, pin down the Yankees north and south of the crossroads, and destroy the center.

But Jackson, north of Glendale, was himself pinned down by fatigue at White Oak Swamp. Major General Theophilus H. Holmes, to the south, had come under a devastating bombardment by land and water, from well-placed rifled cannon on high ground as well as gunboats on the James. Huge shells from the latter knocked down trees and blasted giant craters in the earth, with a destructive efficiency that was no doubt deeply gratifying to General McClellan, who had boarded one of the boats, the *Galena*, at about 4 p.m. and would remain out of touch with his command until the final battle of the campaign the following day.

Lee ordered Magruder away from Glendale to support the immobilized Holmes, then ordered him back. With marching and countermarching, he would not fight that day. Major General Benjamin Huger—pronounced "You Gee"—was closest to Glendale and was supposed to attack the center, opening the battle. Instead, he got caught up in a "battle of the axes." The Federals blocked his road by felling trees. He decided to cut a new road parallel to the first, which took almost the entire day. His contribution was another halfhearted artillery duel, which the Federals won.

Finally, around 4 p.m., Lee ordered Longstreet to attack. He went forward with A. P. Hill's men, who were facing the same Pennsylvanians under George McCall whom they had fought earlier at Beaver Dam Creek and Gaines' Mill. Vicious and confusing combat seesawed back and forth. "It was desperate & bloody," wrote Porter Alexander. "It involved, I believed, more actual bayonet, & butt of gun melee fighting than any other occasion I know of in the whole war."[16] The climax came near sunset when soldiers of the 11th Alabama struggled for the six guns of Battery E, 1st U.S. Artillery, under Lieutenant Alanson M. Randol.

When the charging Alabamians were halted by canister, Union infantry rushed forward in a spontaneous counterattack. Then, fighting in front of the guns, they suddenly gave way, running back toward the battery so that the cannon couldn't fire on the Southerners.

Soldiers fought around the guns with bayonets and clubbed muskets. Shot by a Federal captain, Confederate lieutenant T. J. Michie retaliated by killing the man with his saber, then fell dying himself from five bayonet wounds—three in the face. The 11th's color bearer, Charley McNeil, leapt onto one of Randol's 12-pounder Napoleons waving the regimental banner, then was shot down. His nephew,

William McNeil, tried to raise the flag but was shot dead. The flag was captured.

Exhausted, both sides retreated, leaving dead and wounded around the guns. The Confederates retook them a final time, held them, then turned one of the pieces on the enemy and fired until dark.[17]

Capable and pugnacious Brigadier General Phil Kearny wandered into a group of Confederates in the twilight. Unrecognized, he was asked by a youthful Southern officer, "What shall I do next, sir?" Kearny, with enviable presence of mind, replied, "Do, damn you, why do what you have always been told to do!"[18]

Kearny safely made his way back to Union lines. General McCall, less fortunate, was captured when he stumbled into almost the same situation. "Not so fast," said the Virginia private who grabbed McCall's horse's bridle as he was preparing to ride away.[19]

Union and Confederate casualties were almost equal: 3,797 for the North, 3,673 for the South.[20] More than a third of Southern forces had not been engaged. The Army of the Potomac would make it safely to the James.

CHAPTER 21

A Melancholy Field

There are times when Malvern Hill makes me sick to my stomach. It shouldn't—it's probably the most beautiful of the Richmond battlefields, and the fact that it's tucked away in the countryside southeast of the city makes it incredibly undervisited. Usually you can park, read the exhibits, and take a selfie with a cannon before a single car passes on State Route 156.

But sometimes the solitude adds to the sadness. There's no distraction from the terrain, a perfect, blank canvas for imagining what happened there in the late afternoon of July 1, 1862.

The Federal cannon were at the top of the hill, which is a long, gentle slope, so slight that sometimes you can't even tell you're climbing. The Confederates charged toward the guns—a distance of about half a mile—going in piecemeal so the Yankees could focus on one or two units at a time. According to a Park Service sign: "Union artillery blasted the attackers with canister—tin cans filled with cast iron balls. The effect, at close range, seemed to make men disappear." If they managed to avoid the artillery, there were some 13,000 infantry waiting to finish the job, and more in reserve. Even the gunboats from the James got in on the act, firing their huge shells—the soldiers called them "lamp posts"—with terrifying, though usually inaccurate, results.

D. H. Hill got it mostly right. "If General McClellan is there in strength, we had better let him alone," he told Longstreet while the two of them were talking a couple of miles north of the battlefield. Longstreet, whom commentators often credit with preternatural insight, got it mostly wrong: "Don't get scared," he told Hill jocularly, "now that we have got him whipped."

McClellan was definitely whipped *and* definitely still dangerous, especially at the top of the natural shooting gallery that is Malvern Hill, "one of the strongest positions held by either army during the war," according to an NPS wayside.

Lee was frustrated because the opportunity of Glendale had slipped away. Malvern Hill was the last stop before the Army of the Potomac got to the shelter of its changed base at Harrison's Landing, his last chance to strike a blow, even if the possibility of total destruction was no longer on the table. Frustration clouded his judgment and a series of misunderstandings compounded his mistakes—with fatal results.

The plan called for a converging artillery bombardment from the Confederate left and right. When General Lewis Armistead, in an advanced position, saw that it was effective, he was to go forward "with a yell." Other infantry would follow for a Gaines' Mill–type general assault.

But because of the narrow roads, Confederate cannon only came into play one battery at a time. As soon as they unlimbered, massed Federal artillery zeroed in and blasted away. Fighting close to their homes in Richmond, Colonel Willy Pegram's Purcell Artillery got a battery into action around three o'clock. By four, only one cannon remained in operation, with Pegram himself helping to serve it. Other batteries, on both the left and the right, didn't fare much better.

Jackson, on the left, personally directed the placement of batteries, dismounting and helping to roll the cannon into place himself. Major John G. Gittins, passing on the battlefield, left an unforgettable portrait of Stonewall in action: "[He] was giving orders to a battery which was actually being destroyed by the concentrated fire of McClellan's artillery. He sat erect on his horse, in this hurricane of canister and grape; his face was aflame with passion, his eyes flashed, his under jaw protruded, and his voice rang out sharp and clear. Before he was entirely obscured from our view, the soldiers would turn, at brief intervals, to look back on him, as if for the last time. And indeed it was the last time for many of us."[1]

"Instead of one hundred guns, not more than twenty had been turned on the Federals at the same time," wrote Douglas Freeman. "The preparatory bombardment, in short, was little more than a bloody farce, a futile sacrifice of some of the finest youth of Virginia."[2]

More sacrifices were to come.

Prince John's troubles didn't end with the stinging rebuke from Lee over Savage's Station. He had spent the Battle of Glendale exploring little-known corners of the Virginia countryside as he marched and countermarched, trying to find his way to the battlefield. Confusion continued the day of Malvern Hill, when he was ordered to follow the "Quaker Road." Locals called two byways that name. One led to the battlefield, the other didn't. As fate would have it, Magruder's guides led him on the wrong Quaker Road, which delayed his arrival until four o'clock. Then he was given Lee's order to attack after Armistead had "charged with a yell." Three of Armistead's brigades were far in front of the Southern lines. Magruder did not know that their advanced position had nothing to do with a successful bombardment. It was rather because they had assaulted a group of annoying Federal skirmishers, then continued forward until they were pinned down in a ravine.

A little before this, Lee had received reports describing successful attacks. He quickly sent Magruder more instructions to follow up. Ordered twice into battle, Prince John obeyed.

The positive reports, it would later be revealed, were false.

Huger's troops were closest to hand. But when Magruder sent Major Joseph Brent to request them, the South Carolinian was in a confused and offended state. His soldiers and his authority had been trifled with, he thought, and told the major that some of his brigades "have been moved without my knowledge by orders independent of me, and I have no further information enabling me to answer your enquiries." He would offer nothing more, of conversation or of troops, so Magruder went forward with what he could put together, about 5,000 men.[3]

So began the series of unfortunate assaults—haphazard, inadequate, disjointed—that characterized the Confederate side of the Battle of Malvern Hill.

"Union artillerists rejoiced at their opportunity and delivered cannon fire of unprecedented violence on the Confederate infantry," wrote Richmond National Battlefield Park historian Robert E. L. Krick. Not only the artillerists. According to James J. Hutchinson, a soldier with the 5th Alabama Infantry fighting under D. H. Hill, "As we came fully in sight of the Federal batteries, not 400 yards to our front, the open space behind them became black with troops, thousands of whom issued from the woods in their rear. It was madness to go on."[4]

But they did go on. The 3rd Alabama was also fighting under Hill. Wrote Douglas Freeman: "The colors of the 3rd Alabama were both a target and a symbol.... Six men were shot down carrying the flag, the staff itself was shattered, and the bunting literally cut to bits. The seventh color-bearer brought off only a part of the staff."[5]

The 3rd bore the tragic distinction of having the highest losses of any Confederate regiment that day, with 200 dead and wounded. The 2nd Louisiana was second, with 182.[6]

Seventeen-year-old private Edwin F. Jemison was among the 2nd's casualties. You've probably seen his picture. It's appeared in countless books and articles, even a television commercial for insurance. According to former NPS historian Ashley Whitehead, "His haunting, very youthful face" has made him "the poster child for wartime lost innocence." The picture is reproduced on a wayside exhibit beside the trail that follows the Confederate charge up the western side of the battlefield. The sign says that Jemison was "killed...near this spot." Further research reveals he was decapitated by a Union cannon shell.[7] At least one account has his headless body continuing to run, still holding his rifle, the blood fountaining spectacularly from his neck.

Thirty-five thousand Confederates took part in the attack; roughly 5,600 would be killed, wounded, or captured. Remarkably, the Confederates managed to inflict some 3,000 casualties on the Federals. While no Southerners actually got to the guns, some got close enough to effectively fire their weapons. According to Robert E. L. Krick: "A few Confederate brigades got within revolver range. It's pretty frightening to think of what they endured just to get there and to have this opportunity to engage in a firefight with opposing Union infantry."[8]

Darkness brought an end to the fighting, though the artillery continued pounding the Southerners until around ten that night.

Rain began to fall. Jackson was riding back to his headquarters when he came upon Brigadier General Isaac R. Trimble leading his men toward the battlefield. The aggressive, sixty-year-old Marylander was preparing for a night attack: "I am going to charge those batteries, sir."

"I guess you had better not try it," said Jackson. "General D. H. Hill has just tried it with his whole division and been repulsed. I guess you had better not try it, sir."[9]

Robert E. L. Krick calls Malvern Hill "one of the most ill-managed and uncoordinated major assaults of the entire Civil War."[10] Douglas Freeman, who saluted Lee's statue on Monument Avenue every morning on his way to work at the *Richmond News Leader*, blamed subordinates, calling a chapter on the battle in *Lee's Lieutenants* "Malvern Hill: A Tragedy of Staff." Others blame Lee. He certainly did not look like the Good Gray General that night when he sought out Magruder, finding him about to lie down on his blankets and go to sleep.

"General Magruder," he asked him, "why did you attack?"

"In obedience to your orders," said Magruder, "twice repeated."

Wrote Freeman: "Lee said nothing in reply, for there was nothing to say."[11]

D. H. Hill provided the perfect coda to the battle: "It was not war," he wrote later, "it was murder."

But no matter what it was, it was not as important as the bigger picture: The Army of the Potomac was decisively defeated in the Peninsula Campaign, the siege of the capital lifted. A disappointed Lee would have done well to remember his own advice to Stuart before his famous "Ride": "be content to accomplish all the good you can without feeling it necessary to obtain all that might be desired."[12]

The rain stopped around midnight. Jim Lewis found some relatively dry ground where Jackson could lie down. He arranged his blankets for him. Jackson ate a small meal and fell asleep.

A group of apprehensive generals found him at around 1 a.m. Thinking that McClellan would attack in the morning, they were worried that they were too weakened to adequately resist. No one wanted to wake the sleeping general. Instead they squatted around him, related Dabney with redeeming humor, like so many frogs making conversation. Finally, someone propped him up and yelled their questions in his ear. He didn't wake immediately. They continued trying until, momentarily roused, Jackson said, "McClellan and his army will be gone by daylight," and went back to sleep.[13]

Remarkably enough, they were. McClellan had won a decisive, punishing victory, then retreated. Jackson proved prophetic once again.

Fog covered the battlefield. It dissipated with the morning sun. Cavalry general William W. Averell had been left atop Malvern Hill as part of a token rear guard. According to Averell:

> Our ears had been filled with agonizing cries from thousands before the fog was lifted, but now our eyes saw an appalling spectacle upon the slopes down to the woodlands half a mile

away. Over five thousand dead and wounded men were on the ground, in every attitude of distress. A third of them were dead or dying, but enough were alive and moving to give to the field a singular crawling effect.[14]

Jackson was busy that morning. Starting before dawn, in the drizzling rain and fog, he supervised the placement of the Confederate dead in rows beneath blankets and oilcloths. "Jackson gave the operation a degree of personal attention which surprised me," wrote cavalryman W. W. Blackford. Jackson hurried his workers along so fast that they did not even have time to rifle through the pockets of the dead, which resulted in not a few mumbled curses when Old Jack was out of earshot. Next "he made the men pick up every scrap of clothing and caps, and every piece of human flesh scattered around, such as legs and arms, etc. etc."

Jackson worked until "the dark bloodstains, soaking the ground, alone marked the numbers who had fallen." Now the magnitude of death did not seem so overwhelming: "Jackson had swept his dust into piles, like a good housewife, and the floor looked clean though the piles were still there."

The work completed, Blackford could not contain his curiosity and asked Jackson the reason for his actions.

"Why," said he, "I am going to attack here presently, as soon as the fog rises, and it won't do to have the troops march over their own dead, you know; that's what I am doing it for." Then, I thought, if you are crazy, there is surely "method in your madness" for it would have been a most demoralizing preparation for battle for men to have marched over the field as I first saw it that morning.[15]

I've been to Malvern Hill at least a hundred times. I went back while I was writing this. I was only a short distance from my car when it started to seem like the battlefield itself was angry with me. I kept walking, aware that that was the kind of magical thinking that occurs when you're out by yourself with a storm brewing. Early March: coming in like a lion. Dark gray clouds charged across the sky; intermittent light snow; wind so fierce it almost blew off my stocking cap.

After crossing the road, I took notes in my black composition book from an exhibit near the easternmost cannons. The Federals had "two to three dozen cannon," the exhibit said. Across the road, another sign said twenty-nine. Not far from that: forty.

I finished my notetaking and walked north on the path by the edge of the field. I stopped at a spot where a man on the Internet said he had heard ghostly voices. He wouldn't hear anything today over the roaring of the wind. It even drowned out the recorded message in the small open shelter at the top of the hill. I knew D. H. Hill was saying, "It wasn't war. It was murder," but I couldn't hear him.

The temperature dropped. The sky was full of fast-moving clouds and virga. I wanted to walk the entire trail, but didn't want to get soaking wet and catch a cold. I backtracked to the parking lot, getting in my car just as the snow got serious.

Jackson would have soldiered on, I reflected. That was his big mistake during the Seven Days: He pushed himself beyond the limits of human endurance. It had always worked before, both for him and his men—until he went beyond the possible. His most famous maxim—"You can be whatever you resolve to be"—is actually carved into stone above the entrance to Jackson Barracks at VMI. But it's only true up to a point. You can't ignore the fact that human beings *need* rest and sleep.

The fascinating thing was that the mistakes didn't matter. A. P. Hill attacked too soon at Beaver Dam Creek; Jackson pushed himself so hard he couldn't function; Lee and practically everyone else messed up at Malvern Hill—but the Confederates had seized the initiative, the magic X in the equation. It wasn't enough for Southern independence, nor was it enough to end the war; but it was decisive, at least for a while.

And of course I know that the mistakes did matter to the men who died, as well as to their friends and relatives. I turned my windshield wipers on against the snow. Cold and gray—the perfect day to reflect on the 35,000 casualties of the Seven Days.

Willis Church was on the left of the road as I drove north. A handsome brick building fronted with four white wooden pillars, the church burned in 1946 and was rebuilt in 1947. Part of its mission today is as a hostelry to cross-country cyclists.

Willis Church was a Union hospital after the Battle of Glendale, then a Confederate hospital after Malvern Hill. Confederate J. P. Jordan wound up there after Glendale. His story is emblematic of the sufferings of many of the wounded of both sides. It also has some darkly comic turns that make it stick in the mind.

First, Jordan's hip was bruised when his canteen and haversack were shot away. Then his collarbone was broken by a musket ball. Trying to get to safety, he was shot again through the foot. "I then threw away my knapsack and gun and tried to get away on one leg, but had gone a short distance only when a voice cried 'Surrender!' and this I promptly did. My captor was a good natured Irishman, who kindly gave me permission to ride on his back."

The Irishman carried him to his regiment. Moved afterward to the yard of Willis Church, Jordan met a Federal surgeon who tried to frighten him by brandishing one of his instruments and threatening amputation. The doctor then apologized, sort of, by saying he had heard that Confederate soldiers never got frightened. Wrote Jordan: "I told him that he had a Confederate soldier there who was worse scared than he had ever been in his life."

He was interrogated by General Fitz-John Porter, who expressed regret that he was probably dying and added that, since he was, he should have no compunction about answering questions. "I had no intention of dying at that time," wrote Jordan, "and no intention of telling him the truth." After misleading Porter, he was approached by a

Federal nurse who wanted to desert and asked for his help. Jordan said he would gladly help him if he could have some water. The canteen the nurse brought him was his first drink since he was shot.

When rain threatened, the nurse found Jordan a place inside the church. He got no sleep that night because a Federal officer "whose nose had been shot off and was very angry" spent the entire night walking up and down the aisles of the church wishing for "a Confederate soldier on whom he could vent his wrath." The light was dim, however, and Jordan's "so-called uniform" was so dirty he couldn't be identified as Southern.

A friend found him the next afternoon. He procured Jordan a seat in a horse-drawn vehicle going into Richmond. "This ride to Richmond over such roads as we had at that time was the most horrible of my life."

Whenever a wheel dropped into one of the road's deep ruts, all the injured passengers would fall together in a heap. "Some of us were wounded in the arms, some in the legs, and some, like myself, in the arm and the leg....If it had not been so sad, the scene would have been ludicrous in our efforts to help each other back on the seats."

He finally made it into town. "The hospitals being full, we were carried to a vacant storehouse where I was laid on a shelf."

The next day, "a good woman" gave him some food, his first in three days. Later his brother, who was stationed in the city, found him. "What few clothes I had were ragged and dirty, and the bandages on my wounds were filthy.... My hair had not been trimmed for a year. I had never been handsome at best and at this time surely would have made a good scarecrow."

His brother got him cleaned up and into a good hospital. Jordan survived the war and wrote about his experiences when he was seventy-four.[16]

The Glendale National Cemetery is just north of the church. I parked between the road and the stone wall surrounding the graves. The battlefield park has an intermittently open visitor center in the old superintendent's lodge, an attractive two-story house with a mansard roof. I remember being startled once when I was working there in late November—this was back in the 1990s when the park had lots more money to spend on part-timers than it does now. When I walked out at the end of the day it was cold, almost dark, and I was surrounded by graves.

It was pretty much the same mood now. Snow swirled. The rope beat the flagpole like a frantic alarm. I walked back to the huge, ancient cannon pointed at the sky. "United States/National Military Cemetery/Glendale/Established July 14, 1866/Interments 1192/Known 234/Unknown 958."

It brought back one of the most common experiences of working as a ranger: An eager visitor comes in at the culmination of his or her ancestral pilgrimage. A forebear was killed in one of the Richmond battles. Now they want to find his grave.

Sometimes you can locate it. Much more often, you can't, and the person leaves disappointed, closure denied.

The number of unknowns is staggering—889 in two mass graves at Cold Harbor National Cemetery, for example. The Union dead were reinterred in national cemeteries around the city after the war. There are five in Richmond, seventy-four nationwide. Of their 305,492 Civil War interments, about 45 percent are unknown.[17]

Confederate numbers are comparable. Soldiers are buried all around the city. This was partly because of the nearby battles and partly because of the city's hospitals. There were hundreds of military hospitals in and around Richmond. Some were used only for a while, like Willis Church; others were used throughout the war. Chimborazo was the largest hospital in the world at the time, treating about 76,000 patients. For reasons lost to history, it was named after an Ecuadorean volcano, which turned out to be an appropriate nod to the eruption of injury and death that occurred during the war.

Hollywood has the most Confederate interments, 15,000 to 20,000, according to National Park historian Robert E. L. Krick.[18]

Because of the tremendous number of burials and the chaotic conditions in wartime Richmond, historians do not like to speculate on Hollywood's number of Confederate unknowns. Oakwood Cemetery has about 17,000, with "some 8,000 unknown," according to the state historical marker. Even my church, Emmanuel Episcopal north of Richmond, has eighty-six—twenty-eight unknown and two others identified only with initials.

As mentioned earlier, Hollywood, with its winding roads, ancient trees, and beautiful statuary, is the scenic Southern cemetery from central casting. Oakwood is its workmanlike opposite, a mostly flat and functional expanse of grave after grave after grave. A few are marked with monuments, but most are only numbered with small granite squares. Years ago, I read about a visitor who was horrified to discover a bony elbow protruding from an embankment. The Sons of Confederate Veterans adopted Oakwood in 1999 and it has been much better tended on their watch.

During the war, all the cemeteries were frenzied hubs of activity. "More than 75 men a day were buried here in 1862 for several weeks after the Seven Days Battles," I read on one of Oakwood's interpretive signs. Northerner John Trowbridge toured right after the war on a day like the one I visited Malvern Hill. "Wild winds swept it and shook down on it whirling leaves from the reeling and roaring trees," he wrote. He pronounced it "a melancholy field,"[19] a description apt for all of them, whether scenic and well tended or neglected and forlorn.

CHAPTER 22

Leaving Richmond

In spite of Jackson's explanation, and generations of biographers' acceptance of it, his cleansing of Malvern Hill seems more of a psychological ritual than a necessary preparation for battle. Of course, even his combat-tested Valley soldiers would have swallowed hard at the sight of a hillside littered with scattered limbs and decapitated bodies, particularly since they expected to encounter the same massed artillery that had caused the bloodshed a little way up the road; but Jackson had never been one to spare their feelings before. His actions seem more like an effort to impose order on the deadly chaos of the previous week, as well as an attempt to soften the impact of the Confederate losses resulting from his own fatigue-induced inefficiency. By burying the bodies, he was trying to bury his mistakes. And now, with rest and victory, his hyperaggressive, super-efficient Stonewall self was waking up, foul-tempered as a grizzly bear emerging from hibernation.

A minor comic incident illustrates the point: Two days after the battle, Jackson called his staff together and ordered them to be breakfasted and on the move next morning by "early dawn." Jim Lewis prepared the meal and tried to rouse the sleepers. He was unsuccessful, with one exception: Kyd Douglas, who had caught the general's mood the night before and was up and dressed immediately, "as if to catch a comet." Arriving on the scene, a wrathful Jackson ordered Lewis to pack up and be ready to move in ten minutes: "If my staff will not get up, they must go without their breakfast; let's ride!"

Lewis—who had already eaten—poured out coffee, stowed away biscuits, and scrupulously obeyed the general's orders by thwarting a disheveled Dabney, who appeared and "tried to save something for himself from the wreck."

The remains of breakfast drove off in the wagon with Lewis, followed by the staff's "inverted blessings." Shortly thereafter, Jackson ordered Douglas to help get Ewell's division in motion. He was able to obtain "an excellent breakfast" before the soldiers moved out. In the afterglow of a good meal, the whole episode started to seem funny, but when he told the story after rejoining his comrades, "they apparently didn't see the humor of it." The "grim and funereal staff" would not get anything to eat until afternoon.[1]

The Confederates made a stab at attacking McClellan at his new base on the James River, but by the time they got there, he had dug in. His fortifications—and his gunboats—made them abandon the endeavor. McClellan, reverting to type, started calling for reinforcements almost immediately. Lincoln stood it until August, when he relieved him from command and brought the Army of the Potomac back to northern Virginia.

Confederates also remained in character. Already refighting the war, A. P. Hill challenged Longstreet to a duel over publicity surrounding their respective roles in the battles. Lee stepped in as peacemaker, probably rolling his eyes. Afterward, the two men tolerated each other—barely. The conflict prefigured an even more consequential feud between Hill and Jackson that would get under way later in the summer.

Boteler trod the well-worn path to Davis's office with yet another request from Jackson for troops to undertake an invasion of the North. This time, after his customary refusal, Davis thought long and hard. A few weeks later, Confederate policy shifted from defense to offense, with an invasion of Maryland that ended with Antietam in mid-September.

Surgeons and gravediggers worked overtime. Richmond became a city of hospitals. North and South both suffered from heat and humidity, not to mention the hordes of flies, mosquitoes, ticks, and other vermin native to what Jackson and many others called a "malarious region."[2] Diarrhea—"the Chickahominy two-step"—afflicted more than a few and was sometimes fatal. I recall a relic hunter's story about finding a dozen or so Union belt buckles near McClellan's James River camp. The buckles were in a long row about two feet apart. The hunter racked his brain for an explanation, finally coming up with the theory that the buckles were from diarrhea-soiled pants hanging on a long-vanished clothesline. By purpose or by accident, the pants were left in place when the army decamped. The clothesline rotted, dropping them in a row on the ground. Eventually the pant cloth and belt leather also decayed, leaving only the buckles to puzzle the lucky finder years later.

The Confederate soldiers—those not ill or wounded—got some badly needed rest. They were heroes to civilians when they could make it into town. Jackson set the tone by only visiting the capital for meetings and a single service at Second Presbyterian Church.

I was informed that the congregation calls the church "Second" or "Second Prez" by a friend who attended in her youth, and still remembers the almost physical pain she experienced from irritation caused by the white gloves young ladies were expected to wear in those days. Second was famously founded and pastored by Moses Drury Hoge, an ardent Confederate as well as a noted orator. Later in the war, he would run the blockade to England to obtain Bibles for the soldiers. Preaching before Queen Victoria, he impressed her enough to be offered the gift of "a handsome Bible," which he refused, requesting instead "a slip of ivy from Westminster Abbey," which he planted outside his church. The ivy is still growing today in planters near the doors.[3]

Hoge was instrumental in the design of Second Presbyterian, and had to have been responsible for the pulpit. The minister mounts stairs that put him—or her; a woman was preaching the day I visited—head and shoulders above the congregation. Behind them, a stained-wood edifice soars in Gothic splendor halfway to the roof. A pastor could pronounce his grocery list from such a setting and have it weighted with the full gravity of scriptural authority.

Notwithstanding the architecture, or the art of Hoge's sermon, Jackson did as he always did when he felt completely at home and secure in church: He fell fast asleep. Recognized in his unobtrusive rear pew at the end of the service, he was either enthusiastically mobbed or able to quietly escape just ahead of the crowd, depending on who is telling the story. Today, a small plaque identifies the pew he sat in.

Lee was busy administratively. He reorganized the army, dividing it into two "wings" or "commands," one under Longstreet, the other under Jackson. Longstreet's, designed to oppose McClellan, was larger, consisting of five divisions. Jackson's, designed to be mobile, contained two: one under Winder, and one under Ewell. Lee kept A. P. Hill under his own command, a move reminiscent of the elementary school teacher who makes the most difficult student sit beside her desk. He also politely got rid of commanders who, like Magruder and Holmes, had fought ineffectively during the Seven Days.

Jackson's "wing" left Richmond after he attended Second Prez on July 13. The soldiers, who thought they would be heading east toward McClellan, cheered when they turned west toward the mountains, happy to be leaving the swampy, malarious Tidewater behind. Jackson's area of operations was central Virginia. His job: Protect the railroads and counter the moves of the enemy, attacking if he could see the least chance of success with his outnumbered forces.

The area's two main railroads, the Orange and Alexandria and Virginia Central, intersected at Gordonsville, a small town noted mostly for the fact that two railroads intersected there. Jackson and his men arrived in Gordonsville on July 19, having covered the sixty-plus miles from Richmond in a combination of marching and riding on a cobbled-together railroad crippled by raids and wartime shortages. He pitched his tent in the front yard of a kinsman of the town's Presbyterian minister, Reverend Daniel Ewing, aligning it so that he could see the Blue Ridge Mountains from its front.

Lincoln, in the meantime, had summoned John Pope from the west to take command of most of the forces that had fought against Jackson in the Valley Campaign. The blustery Pope seems to have offended everyone, Union and Confederate alike. He signed his dispatches "Headquarters in the Saddle," which gave rise to the war's most famous joke: "Pope has his headquarters where his hindquarters ought to be."

"I have come to you from the West, where we have always seen the backs of our enemies," he boasted in an opening proclamation. There was more in the same vein, much more, and it didn't go over well with veterans of the hard-fought Valley Campaign. Frémont actually resigned rather than serve under him.

The Confederates were incensed at the harshness of Pope's version of martial law. After he authorized the execution of guerrillas and the seizure of rebel property, "On July 23 Pope's generals were instructed to arrest every Virginian within the limits of their commands, to administer the oath of allegiance to the Union, and to expel from their homes all those who refused to take it."[4] While not all of his talk translated into action, "His policy concerning southern property was carried out by privates as well as officers, with or without orders. Large portions of the South were becoming a wasteland.... Soldiers have pillaged civilian property since the beginning of time. But by midsummer 1862 some of the destruction of southern property had acquired a purposeful, even an ideological dimension." Suddenly it seemed like everyone, from the administration on down, was "taking off the gloves." If you couldn't get to the rebelling soldiers, you could at least make life miserable for the civilians supporting them. "Take up all active [Rebel] sympathizers, and either hold them as prisoners or put them beyond our lines," Grant was ordered in the west about this time. "Handle that class without gloves, and take their property for public use."

"Property," of course, included slaves. African Americans left their masters by the thousands, in Virginia and elsewhere, for the safety and relative freedom of Union-held territory, where they worked as everything from teamsters to nurses. It was during this period that the idea of emancipation took hold. Lincoln presented it to a couple of surprised cabinet members on July 13, saying it had "occupied his mind and thoughts day and night" for several weeks.[5]

"Neither of us had any special concern for slavery," Jackson told his brother-in-law Captain Rufus Barringer, after summoning him to his camp while en route to Gordonsville on July 14, "but both of us agreed that if the sword was once drawn, the South would have no alternative but to defend her homes and firesides, slavery and all."

Jackson outlined to Barringer, whom, in spite of their relationship, he knew only slightly, just what he planned to do if he were granted the 40,000 men he was always calling for: Invade the North as a strike force, ranging perhaps as far as Kansas—"bleeding Kansas," he said, with what must have been some relish—or even Chicago. His column would be only one of several, all dedicated to quick, lethal attacks in the heart of the Union. Jackson had heard good things about Barringer from Stuart, and wanted to couple his relative's military skills with the business and administrative experience the North Carolina cavalryman had acquired before the war: "I would seek to reorganize my whole staff, and I should want you as quartermaster-general." Barringer would requisition supplies from the local citizenry so that the fast-moving soldiers wouldn't be encumbered by wagon trains and herds of cattle. He would also take command of troops if that were needed.

The two talked late into the night before finally falling asleep. At some point, Jackson woke up, saying he'd heard cannon fire, but it turned out he'd only been dreaming of the sound of the guns. His strike-force plan never came to fruition, and Jackson and Barringer saw each other only a few more times during the war.[6]

The incident is important because it opens a window into Jackson's thoughts, and serves as a reminder of just how much was always going on beneath the seemingly imperturbable surface. It also brings to mind the speech that shocked and electrified the VMI cadets on the eve of the conflict in 1861: "The time for war has not yet come, but it will come and that soon, and when it does come, my advice is to draw the sword and throw away the scabbard!"[7]

Jackson still hadn't recovered from the Seven Days. When mapmaker Jed Hotchkiss reunited with him in Gordonsville on July 19, he noted that the general looked "the worse for his trip to the Peninsula."[8] Staff member Charles Minor Blackford was in the midst of reporting to the general on a dangerous reconnaissance near Fredericksburg when Stonewall fell asleep. Blackford was taken aback. He thought his mission had been vital, that headquarters anticipated it with bated breath. "I stopped and waited several minutes. He woke up and said: 'Proceed.' I did so for a few minutes when I noted he was fast asleep again so I stopped. He slept longer this time and when he awoke he said without explanation, apology or further questioning 'you may proceed to your quarters.' I did so although I felt somewhat put out."[9]

Reports of the general's debilitated state reached a worried and pregnant Anna, who appealed to Dr. McGuire to ask him to rest: "Sixteen months of uninterrupted mental & physical labor is enough to break down the strongest constitution, but he is *self sacrificing*, & such a *martyr to duty*, that if he thinks he cannot be spared from the Service, I am afraid he would sacrifice his life before he would give up."[10]

Apparently, McGuire didn't share her concerns with Jackson, nor did the general do much to spare himself or change his routine. As was his custom, even before the war took this latest, harsher turn, he approved the execution of three deserters. He also disapproved leave for a young aide whose father was gravely ill, telling him, "Be patient and do your duty."[11]

Winder, who was always too much like Jackson for much of a relationship to develop between them, ordered thirty men from the Stonewall Brigade "bucked and gagged." The painful, humiliating punishment involved tying the victims' hands and looping them over their knees, then shoving a stick under their knees and over their arms to render them almost immobile. A second stick or a bayonet was put in their mouths and tied behind their heads. Their crime? Straggling on the march to Gordonsville.

Jackson intervened, telling Winder to back off, but it was too late—the damage had been done. Half of the punished men deserted that night after being untied. Much of the brigade subsequently turned against Winder, many saying darkly that the next fight he participated in would be his last. Noted James I. Robertson: "This extraordinary statement is the only known instance in all of Civil War history where soldiers reportedly vowed to kill one of their own officers in the confusion of the next engagement."[12]

While Winder was always a strict disciplinarian, the sudden severity of this lashing out is an aberration. Perhaps he had an unconscious knowledge of his own impending death—he could feel something ominous on the horizon—and so behaved erratically.

CHAPTER 23

Jackson Is with You!

Lee sent A. P. Hill to reinforce Jackson with six brigades. In a letter accompanying the transfer, Lee called Pope a "miscreant"—a notable escalation from the term "these people" with which he habitually referred to the Yankees—and said he had to be "suppressed." He also offered, in his polite, deferential way, some advice: "A.P. Hill you will find I think a good officer with whom you can consult and by advising with your division commanders as to your movements much trouble will be saved you in arranging details as they can act more intelligently."[1]

Talk to your men, in other words: It's good for you; it's good for them. But not even Lee could break Jackson's habit of secrecy.

Another downside of Jackson's character was highlighted on August 5 when General Richard Garnett was finally brought to trial for dereliction of duty at Kernstown. The court-martial was well under way by August 7, and signs were pointing to Garnett's vindication, when word came that Pope was on the move. What's more, he had made a mistake, exposing the forefront of his army in an advanced position. The trial was postponed, and would never be resumed. Jackson's soldiers were marching north that afternoon. Historian Robert K. Krick speculates that the case may have been a bit too conveniently interrupted: "It is hard, though, to avoid wondering whether Mighty Stonewall was not encouraged, at least subconsciously, to move into action as an alternative to suffering further probing by a court-martial that was not working out at all well."[2]

Pope had about 50,000 widely scattered men, Jackson less than half that. But he was moving against his old adversary from the Valley, Nathaniel P. Banks, who had only about 8,000.

The first day's march went relatively well, in spite of the murderous Virginia heat. The second day was something else entirely. Lee had told Jackson to confer with A. P. Hill and other officers. He didn't, and the repercussions started almost immediately.

The marching order for the second day was to be Ewell first, Hill second, and Winder third. But Jackson changed his mind overnight, deciding to send Ewell on a roundabout route north. He didn't inform Hill, who had his Light Division ready to follow Ewell at dawn. In the small town of Orange, Hill waited by the street up which he expected Ewell to march. Troops began passing. All seemed to be going according to plan until he realized the soldiers were Winder's, not Ewell's. Rather than break the column, he waited for it to pass. Jackson rode up, furious, and asked what he was doing. Hill replied with a few curt sentences and Jackson galloped angrily away, possibly remembering earlier friction between the two at West Point. Hill's anger had a more recent provocation: Jackson had been late over and over during the Seven Days, and his tardiness had contributed to major losses in the Light Division. The relationship between the two generals would not improve.

The day wore on, with dust and near-triple-digit heat compounding frustration. Soldiers' accounts mention men straggling and collapsing, even dying of sunstroke. Riding forward, Hill discovered that Ewell and Winder had gotten tangled up after fording the Robinson River, a tributary of the Rapidan a few miles to the north. His men would cover only a single mile on August 8, "the poorest one-day march in the history of Jackson's forces."[3]

According to Jim Lewis, Jackson prayed even more than usual that night, and woke—if he had slept at all—with his issues unresolved.

He sent an uncharacteristically gloomy message to Lee: "I fear that [my] expedition will, in consequence of my tardy movements, be productive of but little good."[4]

In spite of his pessimism, he was prepared to fight. And the army sensed combat. Hill, determined that there would be no repetition of the previous day's performance, had his men up and moving shortly after 2 a.m. Winder had spent the march in an ambulance, after having been told by Dr. McGuire that he was too ill to march or fight. Now, according to Jackson, "his ardent patriotism and military pride could bear no such restraint"[5] and he was mounted and moving with his men.

The heat must have seemed personal to the Valley soldiers. They had just escaped the swampy Tidewater. Now here they were, with home almost in sight on the other side of the Blue Ridge, but it was hotter than ever—eighty degrees at 7 a.m.—without even the hint of a breeze to blow away the dust.

Jackson was moving north, Banks was moving south. The inevitable collision occurred at Cedar Mountain, a squat conical protuberance a few miles below Culpeper in the beautiful rolling country of the Piedmont.

Jubal Early was the tobacco-chewing, whiskey-drinking, hard-swearing antithesis to the pious and fastidious Jackson. Some say that he was the inspiration for the popular "Forget, Hell!" caricature of a Rebel soldier. Lee called him his "Bad Old Man," but no one would fight harder for his legacy during the years of the Lost Cause. Now, having been among the first on the field, he was at the center of the Confederate line, which stretched two miles from northeast to southwest with its right anchored on Cedar Mountain. Early was supposed to press the Federals in the center while the Confederates enveloped them on the left and right. The plan was solid, except for one thing: 1,700 Federals under General Samuel W. Crawford on the Union right, invisible to the Southerners behind a ridge in thick woods.

The battle started about 1 p.m. The Confederates deployed as they came up. Before half of them were in place, Jackson seemed to disengage. He played with some children at the home of the local family that was his headquarters, then lay down on the porch and took a nap. He was going into battle, a situation in which he felt completely comfortable. It must have been like dozing off in church, another place he felt totally secure. Ewell, companionably, lay down beside him for a short rest as well.

For several hours, Confederate artillery dueled with Federal cannon. Like Winder, artilleryman Edward A. Moore had been riding in an ambulance because he was too ill to march. Also like Winder, Moore had roused himself to participate when the fighting started. Moore was manning his gun when Winder rode up and dismounted. He began observing the battle through his field glass from a vantage point a little to the left of the battery. Between them, wrote Moore, "was a constant stream of shells tearing through the trees and bursting close by."

Winder said something that no one could hear because of the battle noise. Moore walked toward him to hear what he said. "As he put his hand to his mouth to repeat the remark, a shell passed through his side and arm, tearing them fearfully," wrote Moore. "He fell back at full length, and fell quivering on the ground."

Winder himself had given orders earlier in the day that no one was to help the wounded except those specifically detailed for the purpose. Obediently, Moore returned to his gun.[6] Winder was placed on a stretcher. The shell had lacerated his side all the way back to his spine. When his aide-de-camp and distant cousin, McHenry Howard, found him moments later, "it was evident that the wound to the body was mortal...[but he] was not suffering as much pain as he would have suffered if the shock had not been so great." Leaning over him, Howard asked the general if he knew him. "Oh yes," said Winder. Then the fact that Howard was a kinsman made Winder start to talk about his wife and children. Surgeons agreed that there was nothing to be done except make his last hours comfortable.

A chaplain arrived, bent over him, and said, "General, lift up your heart to God."

"I do," said Winder. "I do lift it up to Him."

The stretcher bearing Winder was borne to the rear. Walking beside him, holding his hand, Howard felt the fingers slowly grow cold. They stopped in a grove of trees. Howard kept vigil. "At sundown, with my arm around his neck and supporting his head, he expired, so quietly that I could scarcely mark the exact time of his death."

Moments after Winder was wounded, a courier from Early had galloped up: Federals were moving toward the exposed Confederate left. These were Crawford's men, hitherto concealed from the Southerners. The courier reported to Jackson in Winder's absence. Stonewall sent word to Thomas Garnett, the brigade commander in that sector, to "look well" to his left. (Thomas Garnett was not related to the court-martialed Richard B. Garnett.) But Garnett was looking elsewhere when Crawford's men slammed into him. Some of the Federals were actually able to attack the Confederate rear. Remembered John Worsham of the 21st Virginia: "There was such a fight as had not been witnessed during the war; guns, bayonets, swords, pistols, fence rails, rocks, etc. were used all along the line. I have heard of a 'hell spot' in some battles; this surely was one. Our color bearer knocked down a Yankee with his staff, and was shot to death at once." Three more men were killed trying to carry the colors; the fifth survived.[7]

"The isolated efforts of the Confederates were of no avail," wrote G. F. R. Henderson. "The first line was irretrievably broken; the troops were mingled in a tumultuous mass, through which the shells tore shrieking; the enemies' bayonets were surging forward on every side.... [The Southerners became] an ungovernable mob, breaking rapidly to the rear, and on the very verge of panic."[8]

Crawford's Federals kept up their momentum, swinging to the left and attacking Taliaferro, then collapsing Early's left. The unthinkable was happening: Outnumbered Yankees, under "Commissary"

Banks, the laughingstock of the Valley, were driving the Confederates, even elements of the vaunted Stonewall Brigade itself.

Jackson, watching near the Confederate center, sensed a change in the flow of hostilities. "That firing is very heavy," he said. He galloped to the breakthrough, assessed the situation, then rode to the rear and found A. P. Hill, telling him he was late and to move forward. Then he rode again to the breakthrough. He tried to draw his sword, but it was so little used that it had rusted in the scabbard. He unhooked the sheathed blade and brandished it, then grabbed a flag from a color bearer. "Rally, men! Forward!" He galloped toward the front with flag and sword. "Jackson is with you! Your general will lead you! Follow me!"

The retreat halted and changed course as the men followed Jackson to the front, where the fire, according to one witness, resembled a "tornado." His officers were astonished that he wasn't hit, particularly since he was the most conspicuous target on the most dangerous part of the field. Taliaferro rode up and reminded Jackson that this was no place for the commander of an army. Jackson agreed with his customary "Good. Good." and returned to a position of relative safety.

His personal bravery changed the tide of the battle. He was so inspiring that even a group of Union prisoners cheered him as they were herded toward the rear. Hill came on the scene moments later and started driving the Yankees, whose impetuous attack had been unsupported. Ewell, on the right, moved forward as well. Banks retreated. Jackson ordered Hill to pursue, but darkness fell before he could follow him very far.

The artillery duel had been horrific; the infantry fight had lasted scarcely ninety minutes. Union casualties totaled 1,400, Confederate 1,307. Banks was reinforced so that he outnumbered Jackson two to one. Jackson, unwilling to fight with those odds, returned to Gordonsville. Pope, bloodied now and cautious, showed no inclination to pursue.

Cedar Mountain itself is not accessible to tourists, but the Civil War Trust has saved 154 acres of the battlefield. Interpretive trails with an abundance of signage wind pleasantly through woods and fields, all within sight of Cedar Mountain, a feature of the landscape rather than a dominating presence. Douglas Freeman poked gentle fun by calling it one of the Piedmont's "rounded eminences, exalted with the name of mountains."[9] It certainly was a formidable artillery position for Jackson during the battle.

A. P. Hill fought only six miles south of his boyhood home in Culpeper, and got even closer during his evening pursuit of Banks. Civil War Trails signs mention a couple of Confederate soldiers who actually fought on their farms. On the edge of the battlefield, there is a small obelisk next to someone's garage. Dedicated to Wisconsin soldiers, it was placed there "by the survivors." The approximate spot where Jackson rallied his troops has a marker titled JACKSON IS WITH YOU in a grassy spot sheltered by young pines. In contrast to the act it commemorates, it has the quiet, contemplative aura of a shrine. No one has been able to pinpoint the place behind the lines where Winder died.

Rocky red soil; no footprints on the trail; an old house site with big oaks and daffodils; adjacent cemetery with family markers and a tombstone for a Georgia Confederate. Four hundred and five burials on the battlefield. I didn't have to go searching for a cemetery associated with the battle—it was right under my feet, though many were probably moved after the war. "The Federal commander asked for a truce to bury his dead," wrote Confederate cavalryman Major Daniel Grimsley, "and all that day the Federal and Confederate soldiers mingled freely together, engaged in the pious work of burying their dead and caring for their wounded."

Grimsley made the battlefield his project in the years after the war. He wrote about the battle, organized Blue and Grey reunions, and marked unit positions with granite blocks, most of which are still in place. In 1902, he gave a tour to President Theodore Roosevelt, afterward presenting him with an excavated cannon shell as a memento.[10]

It was blessedly cool the March day I visited, a contrast to the ninety-eight degrees the day of the battle. I had the field to myself for almost two hours. One exception: a couple who were switching drivers. The man walked over and read some markers. His wife didn't. It brought back a common sight from my ranger days: an oppressed-looking wife in the car, waiting in the AC while her husband pored over the exhibits.

While there are, of course, exceptions, interest in the Civil War is a middle-aged white guy kind of thing. Which always makes me sad—the subject is too rewarding to be race- and age-restricted. A shrinking demographic, I thought glumly. What will happen in the future?

The drive into Culpeper took only ten minutes. I had a hearty appetite from walking and quickly devoured the beef stew/hamburger special at the Frost Restaurant. Walking past olde quaint shoppes, I found the Culpeper History Museum a few blocks away. I was the only visitor. The docent didn't know where A. P. Hill had lived. Irritated, I found the information myself by looking around the museum.

The house turned out to be across the street from the restaurant, almost exactly the same distance from the History Museum as Jackson's headquarters had been from the visitor center in Romney, and Manassas Junction from that town's museum.

A marker on the outside of the big three-story building directed me upstairs. I didn't see any stairs. In the hair salon on the first floor, a stylist with scissors tattooed on her wrist used her comb to indicate an entrance outside and in the back. She let me know, politely, that this wasn't the first time she'd been asked.

The upstairs exhibit talked a lot more about the building than about Hill, who had lived there from the time he was seven until he went off to West Point. I guess they didn't want to seem to be celebrating anything Confederate...

Sadness over Hill's neglect merged with irritation at the locals for not knowing the location of such a significant building two blocks away. History is important, a guide to the present and a furnisher of context for practically everything. Patrick Henry said it wonderfully: "I have but one lamp by which my feet are guided, and that is the lamp of experience." And again: "I know of no way of judging the future but by the past."

His words bring back our shockingly divided present. If the Civil War teaches us anything, it's that conflicts sometimes get far worse before they get better. Could we possibly be going down that road again?

Worrying, I started toward home.

CHAPTER 24

A Strange, Mysterious Splendor

J eb Stuart, amid the easy relaxation of the truce following Cedar Mountain, lunched, visited, and joked with a couple of Union generals, George D. Bayard and Samuel W. Crawford. The three, all cavalrymen, talked of their recent exploits, then moved to other topics, chiefly about how the Yankee papers declared all battles Union victories. Stuart bet Crawford a hat that the Northern papers would claim Cedar Mountain a Union win. Crawford must have thought his odds were good, standing on the battlefield surrounded by Federal dead. He took the bet, saying that not even the notoriously jingoistic *New York Herald* would declare Cedar Mountain a Union success.

He lost the wager a few days later. The hat, along with a copy of the *Herald*, came through the lines for Stuart under a flag of truce.[1] Proving himself an early master of spin, Pope also trumpeted Union success, sounding more and more aggressive as Jackson moved south and the distance between them increased. He did not, however, march toward Gordonsville to follow up on his "victory."

McClellan, meanwhile, had been ordered to leave the Peninsula and return to northern Virginia. But Lee had already decided to shift the game north. He started Longstreet for Gordonsville on August 13—before McClellan's men were loaded onto transports. Lee was gambling that McClellan wouldn't break character and attack Richmond. He also knew that it would be hell to pay if the eastern Federals united. And there was opportunity near Culpeper: Pope had encamped between the Rapidan and the Rappahannock in a spot where their confluence resembled a V with its base pointing east. If the Confederates could trap Pope between the rivers he could be crushed in the corner where the V narrowed down.

Railroads were the key to the campaign. Pope's objective had been the railroad hub of Gordonsville. Confederates in Richmond were supplied from the west by the Virginia Central, which ran through the town, just as Pope was supplied from the north by the Orange and Alexandria, which ran through Culpeper and Manassas.

The tracks of the O&A formed the base of a triangle between the wings of the Rappahannock and Rapidan's V. The northernmost part of the triangle was the railroad bridge near Rappahannock Station. If Lee could destroy it, he would break Pope's supply line and block his easiest route of retreat.

Lee held a council of war in Gordonsville on August 15. Jackson wanted to march north immediately and attack Pope; Longstreet wanted to wait for his supply wagons so he could feed his men. Jackson offered to share his food. Even with that, Longstreet thought they would still be rushing things. He was also certainly remembering Jackson's tardiness during the Seven Days. This was supposed to be a joint operation, and he didn't want to bear the brunt of the fighting alone.

Success depended on the destruction of Pope's escape route, the Rappahannock railroad bridge. The cavalry was not present to do this. Siding with Longstreet rather than Jackson, Lee decided to wait.

Frustrated, Stonewall lay down on the ground and "groaned most audibly." Longstreet admonished him sternly that such behavior disrespected the council.[2] Lee, certainly appalled that his powerful lieutenant was channeling his inner twelve-year-old as well as remembering that he had only recently restrained Longstreet from fighting a duel, was probably thanking God that there was a grown-up in the room.

He directed Jeb Stuart to burn the bridge as soon as his troopers arrived. Jackson and Longstreet marched north to a place of concealment behind Clark's Mountain. They were poised to hit Pope on the flank as soon as Stuart acted.

Things didn't go according to plan. On the night of August 17, Stuart was sleeping on the porch of a house in the small hamlet of Verdiersville, waiting for his men to arrive from the south. Hearing a column of riders approach, he went out to meet them. Suddenly, there were pistol shots—these were Yankees! Stuart leapt onto his horse and galloped away. Federal cavalry pursued. He barely escaped. His staff officer, Captain Norman Fitzhugh, wasn't so fortunate. When Fitzhugh was captured, the Federals found papers in his possession that revealed Lee's plan.

The fact that Stuart had left his new plumed hat on the porch made the fiasco all the more humiliating. News of his loss spread quickly through the ranks. "Where's your hat?" delighted infantrymen called wherever he went.

The information, of course, was of far more consequence than Stuart's lost hat. Pope, now cognizant of the trap, retired northward to a position of strength behind the high northern banks of the Rappahannock. Confederates moved upstream probing for a crossing. Federals waited at every ford. There were inconclusive artillery duels and much wasted time.

Still trying to cut the supply line, Lee agreed to a request from Stuart a few days later for an attack on Catlett's Station farther north on the O&A. The raid took place on a proverbial dark and stormy night—"the darkest night I ever knew,"[3] according to Stuart, and so violently stormy that the soaked bridge wouldn't catch fire. But the Confederates had stumbled onto Pope's headquarters. They would have captured the man himself if he hadn't actually had his "headquarters in the saddle" and been away on reconnaissance. As it was, they netted some 300 prisoners, numerous fine horses, a spectacular amount of U.S. currency and gold—as well as Pope's uniform coat, thus avenging the loss of Stuart's hat. The cavalier sent a note through the lines proposing "a cartel for a fair exchange of the prisoners"—coat for hat—but Pope, who, like most men of vast self-importance had little sense of humor, ignored the request.

The raiders also captured Pope's dispatch book. Now it was Lee's turn to find out his enemy's plans. Fitz-John Porter's corps, McClellan's advance guard, had disembarked on August 22, the day of the raid, and was already heading west. More Union forces would follow. Time was running out.

Jackson, meanwhile, was underoccupied. Having finally rested, he had grown restless, the great war machine inside him idling with nothing to do. He snapped at subordinates, was rude to colleagues, and even insulted a man of the cloth, a minister who had come begging clemency for three men sentenced to die for desertion. The cleric found Jackson in his tent, watch in hand, shortly before the time scheduled for the executions. Jackson paced while he pleaded his case. "General," the minister said finally, "consider your responsibility before the Lord. You are sending these men's souls to hell!"

Jackson snapped. He took the minister by the shoulders. "That, sir, is my business," he said. "Do you yours!" And he pushed him from the tent.[4]

Still agitated that night, probably by both the executions and the general inactivity, Jackson went on a personal reconnaissance. Accompanied by a couple of staff officers and twenty cavalrymen, he wandered through woods and fields, spending pent-up energy and doubtlessly praying. Charles Minor Blackford, one of the staff officers who accompanied him, lamented in a letter to his wife about losing a good night's sleep investigating "by-paths and unused roads in places where neither friend nor foe would ever pass...hog paths and cow tracks....He was wandering in another world."

Jackson must have come to some resolution by "early dawn." At least he managed to exhaust himself physically. "About daylight the general stopped and laid down on the ground, without a word to anyone, using his canteen for a pillow, and was or appeared to be asleep in a moment." Following the example of their leader, the entire party was slumbering in five minutes. Even Blackford's horse lay down on the ground for a nap.[5]

The armies skirmished and probed. Then, in the early afternoon of Sunday, August 24, Lee summoned Jackson to a council of war. The meeting took place near Jeffersonton, an unincorporated community a dozen miles northeast of Culpeper. Secrecy was imperative. "A table was placed almost within the middle of a field, with not even a tree within hearing." Lee sat in the center, flanked by Longstreet on his right and Stuart on his left. Jackson stood opposite his friend Stuart. Set off by such strong personalities, Lee must have looked even more impressive than usual. The gravitas of his presence was in contrast to the reckless gamble he proposed.

Jackson, with 23,500 men, would make a third attempt on Pope's supply line, combining it with the old Valley strategy of a threat to D.C. Stuart's troopers would accompany the foot cavalry. The column would swing surreptitiously to the west, then back to strike the Orange and Alexandria. In the meantime, Longstreet would take over Magruder's role from the Seven Days, bristling and threatening Pope. He would keep him pinned down and distracted, then slip away in the wake of Jackson and Stuart, uniting with them for a fatal surprise attack on the Union rear.

What could go wrong? Everything: A reinforced Pope could attack first one segment of the outnumbered Confederate army, then the other, annihilating them in detail. But Lee had to take the chance. He would be vastly outnumbered soon, and then it would be only a matter of time.

Now Jackson had a task equal to his powers. Overambitious, he said he would have the army moving in an hour.[6] But getting 23,500 men moving in an hour was too much even for him. Instead, they started at the usual 3 a.m., with three days' cooked rations and sixty rounds of ammunition. There would be no knapsacks and no rest— the prescribed halt of ten minutes per hour was suspended. A herd of cattle, an ordnance train, and ambulances accompanied the column.

Secrecy, of course, was paramount. A man was posted at each crossroads to point the way. Neither he nor the column was informed of the next stage of the journey. That would be revealed only by the man posted at the next crossroads up the route.

It was dusty and hot, but not terribly so. The pace was three miles per hour. Apples and green corn from the fields supplemented the meager supplies in the soldiers' haversacks. In spite of the exertions required of them, they were by all accounts in excellent humor. "There was excitement in the swift motion and pleasure in hailing friendly strangers," wrote South Carolina sharpshooter Berry Benson. "Jests were in constant play, and often bursts of song."[7]

Toward sunset, Jackson stopped and climbed up on a large rock by the roadside. The passing column started to cheer. Fearful of alerting the enemy, he sent an officer to shush them. Word for quiet went down the line. "But as they passed him," writes Dabney, "their eyes and gestures, eloquent with suppressed affection, silently declared what their lips were forbidden to utter."

Jackson, deeply moved, turned to his staff, and said, "Who could not conquer with such troops as these?"[8]

The soldiers made twenty-six miles that day. Most fell asleep on the ground as soon as they halted. Some who didn't sleep tried buying food from nearby houses—or begged outright. Berry Benson relates the case of one poor soul who was so weary or inept that he garbled his spiel: "Please ma'am, give me a drink of water, I'm so hungry, I ain't got no place to sleep."

The second day was more of the same: no rest, little or no food, three miles an hour, and Jackson urging constantly, "Close up, men, close up!" They were behind the Bull Run Mountains, the easternmost front of the Blue Ridge, screened from watchful Federals. To get back to the Piedmont they had to pass through Thoroughfare Gap. It was the ideal place for an ambush, a fight that would alert the whole Union army to their presence.

Jackson sent cavalry ahead to scout the gap. They brought back word that it was unguarded. The army would fight hunger and fatigue rather than Yankees until they arrived at Bristoe Station on the Orange and Alexandria. There, in late afternoon, they quickly bested the small Union garrison and cut the telegraph line. Then they heard a train. This was the hour when engines pulling empty boxcars rattled north to be resupplied at Manassas or Alexandria. The Confederates piled ties on the tracks, but the locomotive boomed through them and continued north, doubtless to spread the alarm that Bristoe was under attack. Shortly thereafter, another train whistle was heard from the south.

More savvy this time, the Confederates threw a switch that would send the train plunging into Broad Run. Beside the tracks, North Carolina infantry waited to fire a volley into the train crew. All things went as planned: first the volley, then the switch. "Down the embankment rushed the engine, screaming and hissing," wrote Colonel Blackford, "and down upon it rushed the cars, piling up one upon another until the pile reached higher than the embankment, checking further additions to its confused heap, and arresting the rear half of the train upon the track."

The fact that the wrecked engine was named *The President* and was fronted with a portrait of Lincoln added to the Confederates' satisfaction. And soon there would be more spectacular fireworks: Two red lights on the last car indicated that another train was following close behind. These lights were smashed, so that when the third train approached the station it had no warning of what was ahead and plowed into the waiting cars. Some of these actually wound up crossways on top of the speeding locomotive, while others were added to the pileup down the embankment.

There were red lights on the back of this train also. Blackford destroyed them with his saber; then "we placidly awaited the coming of the train which they indicated was yet to come." But the fourth engineer somehow ascertained the danger and applied his brakes before coming into musket range. He backed up south, taking word to Pope that the Rebels were in Bristoe and the main army some twenty miles away.

Jackson ordered his soldiers to burn the railroad bridge over Broad Run. He had cut Pope's supply line and was between the Federals and their main supply depot at Manassas Junction.

Federals had seen Jackson leaving Jeffersonton to begin his march, but Pope had wrongly deduced that he was headed for the Valley and, from there, to threaten Washington. Now he understood that Lee's army was split and, to his credit, saw it for the opportunity it was. He started north to do battle, sending word of Confederate troop dispositions to Lincoln's general-in-chief, Henry Halleck, who ordered yet more Federal soldiers to move against Jackson. All in all, the Southerners had some 80,000 Union troops headed toward their 55,000-man divided army, with Jackson's 23,500 the main target.

If some brave soul were to undertake to write *The Humor of Stonewall Jackson* it would be a very slim volume indeed. But there was a significant amount of humor *about* the stern general. One of the more famous incidents occurred that night. A Northern politician who had been on one of the wrecked trains was beside a campfire nursing a broken leg. When his captors told him whose soldiers they were he said he'd like to see the famous Stonewall. He's right across the campfire, they replied. The man asked to be raised. Wrote an Alabama soldier, "He surveyed the great Confederate general in his dingy gray uniform, with his cap pulled down on his nose, for half a minute, and then in a tone of disappointment and disgust exclaimed, 'Oh my God! Lay me down!' "[9]

After their first appreciative laughter, his soldiers appropriated the expression, using it "in almost every conceivable situation... whether confronted with an issue of meager rations or a charging Union line: 'Oh my God! Lay me down!' "[10]

Jackson, cool as always in the midst of danger, allowed his soldiers to lay themselves down for the night. They had marched an incredible fifty-six miles in two days.[11] But Manassas Junction was only four miles away. Was it heavily garrisoned? And were the stores there as vast and lavish as area civilians affirmed?

General Isaac Trimble, who had barely been dissuaded at the last minute from leading his soldiers into the death trap of Malvern Hill, volunteered those men now for a late-night march up the tracks to Manassas. He took his two favorite regiments, the 21st North Carolina and the 21st Georgia: "Give me my two Twenty-ones and I'll charge and capture hell itself!" he said. Jeb Stuart was sent to help after Trimble was dispatched.

The four miles must have seemed like forty after their exertions, but when the soldiers arrived it turned out that the rumors were true: Manassas Junction was lightly guarded, and the supplies there were abundant beyond belief.

Rumors of Confederate guerrillas had reached Manassas commander Captain Samuel Craig of Pennsylvania. He deployed his men but was himself asleep when the first of his pickets were attacked around midnight by Stuart's horsemen. The Confederates backed off, lulling the Federals into thinking it was a false alarm. They found out the truth shortly thereafter when Trimble's men came on "like an avalanche." Union soldiers fled; the Confederates swept ahead, capturing some 300 prisoners—plus a cornucopia of supplies that seemed even more incredibly rich after the privations of their march. "It would be impossible to tell the variety of provisions and other goods we found here," wrote Berry Benson.[12] A. P. Hill reported two miles of railroad cars.[13] John Worsham wrote of "vast storehouses filled with everything to eat, and sutler's stores filled with all the delicacies, potted ham, lobster, tongue, candy, cakes, nuts, oranges, lemons, pickles, catsup, mustard, etc."[14]

Dawn revealed the full extent of the treasures. Stuart's cavalry helped themselves. "The quantity of booty was very great," wrote Heros von Borcke of Stuart's staff, "and the amount of luxuries absolutely incredible. It was exceedingly amusing to see here a ragged fellow regaling himself with a box of pickled oysters or potted lobster; there another cutting into a cheese of enormous size, or emptying a bottle of champagne; while hundreds were engaged in opening the packages of boots and shoes and other clothing, and fitting themselves with articles of apparel to replace their own tattered garments."[15]

"Fine whiskey and segars circulated freely," elaborated the South Carolinian J. F. J. Caldwell, "elegant lawn and linen handkerchiefs were applied to noses hitherto blown by thumb and forefinger, and sumptuous underclothing was fitted over limbs sunburnt, sore and vermin-splotched."[16]

Trimble placed guards over the stores. When the Stonewall

Brigade marched in from Bristoe, hungry soldiers pushed past these sentries, whose numbers were strengthened to push the men back. A bloodless, intra-Confederate battle began. In a flanking maneuver, some of the famished soldiers discovered a commissary depot. According to John O. Casler of the Stonewall Brigade:

> I soon found, in one corner of the second story, a room full of officers' rations and several soldiers supplying themselves with coffee, sugar, molasses, etc. When we had appropriated all that we could carry, we found a barrel of whiskey, which we soon tapped; but as our canteens were full of molasses, and our tin cups full of sugar, we had nothing to drink out of. We soon found an old funnel, however, and while one would hold his hand over the bottom of it, another would draw it full.
> In this way it was passed around.[17]

Hill's soldiers followed the Stonewall Brigade. Sounding personally affronted, General Trimble wrote in his report: "It was with extreme mortification that, in reporting to General A. P. Hill about 10 o'clock, I witnessed an indiscriminate plunder of the public stores, cars, and sutler's houses by the army which had just arrived, in which General Hill's division was conspicuous, setting at defiance the guards I had placed over the stores."[18]

Jackson's foremost concern was the whiskey: "I fear the liquor more than General Pope's army," he said.[19] He ordered casks and barrels stove in and their contents poured out. Soldiers threw themselves on the ground and tried to lap up the spirits before they seeped into the earth.

Long-range shelling from a Union battery interrupted the festivities. It would have to be silenced—along with its probable accompaniment of Federal infantry. Around 9,000 Confederates were sent eastward to meet the threat, first from New York soldiers under Colonel Gustav Waagner, next from a New Jersey brigade under General George Taylor. Unbeknownst to each other, they had both been sent to retake the junction from what was assumed to be a small force of Confederate guerrillas.

Waagner wisely retreated when he discovered the "guerrillas" outnumbered him nine to one. Taylor was less perceptive. He deployed his regiments in a line of battle that the Confederates remembered as a "grand sight," until it was ripped apart by shot and canister from twenty-eight cannon along with massed volleys from Confederate infantry. But the Federals still came on, brave and too inexperienced to realize just how extensively they were outmanned and outgunned.

Being out of character was becoming characteristic for Jackson. But here he did something really odd: He ordered his men to cease firing. Next, he rode out in front of the line waving a white handkerchief, calling on the Yankees to surrender. In response, a New Jersey infantryman fired his musket at the general. Jackson turned back. The uneven contest continued, turning into a rout a few minutes later. Hundreds of Union soldiers were killed or wounded.

By the time the Confederates returned from their victory, the junction's warehouses had settled into a somewhat more orderly scene. Stores were now being officially distributed, and each man was ordered to take four days of rations. The order was obeyed, after a fashion. "What do you think they did?" Worsham wrote. "Begin to eat. Oh no. They discussed what they should eat and what they should take with them....I know one that took nothing but French mustard, filled his haversack and was so greedy he put one more bottle in his pocket. This was his four days' rations, and it turned out to be the best thing taken, for he traded it for meat and bread, and it lasted him until we reached Frederick City"—ten days later.[20]

That evening Jackson ordered his men to destroy what could not be carried away. "All the storehouses and depots were filled with straw and hay," von Borcke wrote, "and combustibles were also placed in forty-six railway cars, which had been pushed closely together.... Just as the sun was disappearing behind the range of distant hills, the flames were rising from a hundred different points of the plain." The sight, he continued, was one of "strange mysterious splendor."[21]

South Carolina's Benson remembered sleeping in an open field the night before, huddled together with other soldiers to keep warm. He contrasted that with the night of August 27: "Now we had blankets, and the whole field was lit up by burning cars. Shells and ammunition boxes were bursting in the flames, the pieces every now and then dropping amongst the sleeping men. But the chance of getting hit kept nobody awake."[22]

The men started north that night. "The appearance of the marching columns was novel and amusing," recalled Kyd Douglas. "Here one fellow was bending beneath the weight of a score of boxes of cigars, smoking and joking as he went, another with as many boxes of canned fruits, another with coffee enough for a winter's encampment, or perhaps with a long string of shoes around his neck, like beads."[23]

Jackson, austere even amid such bounty, allowed his men their fun, likely foreseeing the coming cataclysm of Second Manassas, a rematch far bloodier than its predecessor of nearly the same name the year before.

CHAPTER 25

A Trail of Cemeteries

I'd imagined a pristine field in Jeffersonton with a historic marker talking about Lee's top-secret council of war. Instead, there was an ancient Baptist church surrounded by a cemetery where every other stone seemed to read UNKNOWN CONFEDERATE SOLDIER.

"Unknown to us, but not to God," I read later on the church's website, which went on to say that they were "a conservative Bible-believing church that God has preserved for over 240+ years in the village of Jeffersonton." A facsimile of the Ten Commandments on the front of the church gave the statement added emphasis.

The building was used as a hospital in 1862. I didn't even realize there had been fighting nearby—but if Jackson was there, there was fighting.

The graves were a sobering sidebar to the opening of my quest to follow Jackson's flank march. The maps in my books didn't correspond to roads on the ground. From the church, I wended my way to Amissville on what I hoped was a Jacksonian path, then to nearby Hackley's Store on Route 211, "The Lee Highway." Hackley's, despite several "No Public Restrooms" signs, was a friendly place, its stock of typical country store merchandise augmented by stuff that looked like the owner had brought it in after he cleared out his garage. I ordered a chicken salad sandwich, drink, and chips, and ate on the front porch watching the intermittent traffic on 211.

The sandwich was good. When I went back inside to pay, I asked how to get to Orlean, the next town on Jackson's itinerary. The woman behind the counter told me the quick way; when I asked for the country roads way, the man next to her consulted his computer—which doubled as the cash register; he held up the line to do it—and directed me to Hinson's Ford, where Jackson crossed. The road ended there—I would have to cross elsewhere—but he told me how to drive down and see it.

Hinson's Ford Road went from a paved two-lane, to an unpaved two-lane, to an unpaved one-lane, to a driveway, then ended altogether at someone's house, where I was greeted by two big, curious dogs with tentatively wagging tails. I was making a U-turn when a man with a shaved head, feather tattoo, and orange-red sunglasses pulled up. Bracing for a confrontation, I was surprised at the man's friendly expression as he rolled down his window and moved his glasses to the top of his head.

"I'm looking for the place where Stonewall Jackson crossed the river," I said.

The man put his head back in a silent laugh. Then he said the river was a quarter of a mile away and you couldn't get there from here. I had to go back up to 211 and take the next road west to cross.

Yet another friendly dog, midsized this time, put his front paws up on the car door and waited for me to pet him. "No, Jake!" said the man. "No, Jake!"

Jake wagged his tail. "He's okay," I said, petting him. "I'm sorry to trespass."

"No problem!" said the man. "You're not the first."

I retraced my route back to 211, reflecting that where I'm from in the Tidewater, I was more likely to have been met with snarling dogs and a shotgun rather than friendly directions.

I crossed the Rappahannock on a one-lane steel bridge. I was doing my best, but most of the time it was really hard to tell if I was on the right route or not. I decided that if I was on a quiet country lane, I was probably on the trail—even more likely if the road was unpaved. I'm not sure if it was true, but it was comforting.

The established theme continued: country roads, churches, and dead Confederates. Leeds Church was heartbreakingly beautiful. A plaque on the front enumerated the Confederate officers associated with it, Richard and Turner Ashby prominent among them. Inside, Christ the Good Shepherd herded sheep on a stained-glass window. The motif continued with a cute lamb heading a handout on children's participation in the service.

St. Paul's in Haymarket started life as a courthouse, and the ghosts of its double chimneys can still be seen on the front brickwork. The Yankees burned it in 1862, along with the whole town after bushwhackers fired on Union soldiers. Although the church afterward was "a mere shell," according to the Civil War Trails sign, citizens took refuge there and on nearby farms. It was next used as a Union stable. But before all that as a hospital. There's a commemorative stone beside the front door: IN THIS AREA ARE BURIED EIGHTY UNKNOWN CONFEDERATE SOLDIERS WHO DIED OF WOUNDS AFTER THE BATTLE OF MANASSAS JULY 21 1861.

The church had been doing some repairs, and there were water-filled tracks from a piece of heavy equipment beside the front walkway. I remembered Charles Minor Blackford, quoted earlier talking about his sleepless night in the woods with Jackson. In a previous letter, he wrote about a much harder night when he was so thirsty he drank water that had collected in a horse's hoofprint, then lay down in the dark beside what he thought was a sleeping soldier. In the morning, the man beside him turned out to be a corpse. Then he saw that blood was mixed with the water he had drunk the night before.[1]

"Who would drink bloody water in defense of slavery?" I thought bitterly. Then, thinking of Lieutenant T. J. Michie, who had fallen in the hand-to-hand fighting around Randol's battery at Glendale: "Who would take a bayonet in the face for slavery?"

It had been a particularly bad week for the South, full of self-righteous rhetoric reinforcing the equation that the Confederacy equaled slavery and nothing more. The soldiers were all one-dimensional evildoers, their monuments symbols of hatred and oppression.

Politicians exploited the sentiment. In New Orleans, Mayor Mitch Landrieu congratulated himself on the removal of the last of four Confederate statues, that of Robert E. Lee, with a speech that called the monuments "terrorism, as much as a burning cross on someone's lawn." In the *New York Times*, Frank Bruni hailed the speech in a headline as "eloquence," and in his column as a "masterpiece," before enthusiastically confiding that Landrieu had been mentioned as a Democratic presidential hopeful for 2020.[2]

"New Orleans has the fourth-highest murder rate in the country," I groused aloud. "Landrieu can't fix his potholes or solve his parking problems, but the *Times* has him riding 'Confederate Terrorism' all the way to the White House."

I stared at the tombstone-shaped monument. Eighty soldiers. If they had been here in the hospital, they hadn't died easy. Who would die for slavery? Yes, it was the cause of the war, and absolutely indefensible, but there was so much more to the struggle and to the men themselves than that one fact.

Jackson, who had before the war founded an African American Sunday school, perfectly mirrored the contradictions of my internal debate. I remembered the conversation with his brother-in-law Barringer: "Neither of us had any special concern for slavery, but both agreed that if the sword was once drawn, the South would have no alternative but to defend her homes and firesides, slavery and all." Of course, being Jackson, he took the whole thing to the next level. He advocated raising "the black flag, viz. 'No quarter to the violators of our homes and firesides!' "[3]

Then, just a little over a month later, the man who advocated "no quarter" rode out in front of his soldiers waving a white handkerchief, trying to save a vastly outnumbered band of Yankees from being slaughtered.

The armies left a trail of cemeteries. Eighty dead in the churchyard. Eighty-six at my own church, Emmanuel Brook Hill north of Richmond. Probably one, maybe more, in front of my house—I'd found the shovel but not, thank God, the body.

Virginia is one vast graveyard.

To get to Manassas Junction, the Confederates marched fifty-six miles in two days. They barely ate except for green corn and apples. They carried no knapsacks, but their muskets still weighed nine pounds, a weight that would have multiplied with the march. Some were barefoot. A South Carolina soldier remembered seeing bloody footprints in the dirt, then flashed forward to the image of the blistered bare feet of dead soldiers on the battlefield.[4]

Forty years ago I might have kept up—and that's a big maybe. In my sixties it was tiring just to drive it.

I hadn't gone far through Thoroughfare Gap before I hit Sprawl Nation, miles and miles of town houses, big-box stores, and hideous traffic. I found Bristoe—currently Bristow—Station, where Jackson's men had had so much fun wrecking trains. Now it was a commuter stop for people working in the District. Most of these commuters worked directly or indirectly for the federal government, its growth and power an ultimate result of the Union victory over the agrarian South.

I chuckled, thinking what a bad agrarian I would make: I would far rather work a desk job than dig a row of potatoes or even drive a tractor.

Then I contradicted myself again as I got lost trying to find my way out of the endless rows of vehicles: "I'd always prefer woods and fields to this."

I located Broad Run nearby, which lived up to its name by being wide and fast, up over its banks from recent rains. I could easily imagine an antique train plunging headfirst into its depths. I drove back to the main road, took one look at the congestion, and decided not to fight the traffic to revisit Manassas, the town, and instead headed toward Manassas, the battlefield.

CHAPTER 26

A Brief Pursuit

Jackson's army was divided into three parts as it marched north in the night, the "strange mysterious splendor" of the glow from burning supplies receding behind it. Stonewall wanted a convergence on Stony Ridge on the Manassas battlefield, but darkness, vague orders, and inept guides caused the two commands not under his direct supervision to go astray. A. P. Hill marched all the way to Centreville, ten miles to the north. The fiery Hill, not to mention the profane Ewell, probably had some choice words for their secretive commander when the errors were discovered. But even Jackson's mistakes were working in his favor.

"Pope would always have trouble perceiving the obvious,"[1] wrote S. C. Gwynne. Far from obvious, the clues coming in from three meandering Confederate columns were subtle and contradictory. Mixed with wishful thinking—Pope wanted to believe that Jackson was fleeing to the Valley—they led first to a Union convergence on Manassas Junction, then on Centreville, both places the Confederates had already vacated. Worst of all, Pope seemed to have simply forgotten about Lee and Longstreet, who were following Jackson's route behind the Bull Run Mountains for a rendezvous with Stonewall.

Jackson, from his sojourn in the area the previous year, certainly remembered a salient feature of the Manassas battlefield, an unfinished railroad cut that ran northeast to southwest, in places paralleling Stony Ridge and the Warrenton Turnpike. It's formidable even today, a more than head-high causeway or ditch, depending on the terrain. From its shelter, the Confederates would have a decided advantage if the belligerent Pope could be persuaded to attack. But in the meantime, sections of his army were on the move.

On the afternoon of August 28, Jackson's soldiers were in the woods behind the railroad cut, "lounging...snoozing, playing cards and munching at more of the good things they had in their haversacks by courtesy of Commissary Pope."[2] Stuart's aide-de-camp, W. W. Blackford, says that though they were "packed like herring," they were content, laughing and talking so that "the woods sounded like the hum of a beehive in the warm sunshine of the August day."[3] Jackson had been in a foul mood until, toward evening, he got word that Lee and Longstreet were at Thoroughfare Gap and would cross through in the morning. "Old Stonewall's face beamed with pleasure," writes Blackford. Still, Jackson remained restless. Then the "ever-kind Providence" he was always invoking sent a column of Yankees straight into the ambush he had so painstakingly prepared.

They were "a handsome parade...with everything in compact order" as they marched northeast on the Warrenton Pike. Careless, as usual, for his own safety, Jackson rode down within easy musket range to observe. His officers, on the ridge, were watching him; his soldiers, in the woods, watched the officers. "We could almost tell his thoughts by his movements," wrote Blackford. "Sometimes he would halt, then trot on rapidly, then halt, wheel his horse and pass again along the front of the marching column, or rather its flank."

Suddenly Jackson stopped, wheeled his horse, and galloped toward his officers. "Here he comes, by God!" said several. All knew he had made up his mind. "Jackson rode up to the assembled group as calm as a May morning and, touching his hat in military salute said, in as soft a voice as if he had been talking to a friend in ordinary conversation, 'Bring out your men, gentlemen!'"

The officers wheeled their horses and galloped toward the woods. The soldiers knew exactly what this meant. "From the woods arose a hoarse roar like that from cages of wild beasts at the scent of blood."[4]

Some of the best fighters of the South were about to meet some of the best fighters of the North. The difference between them was that the Southerners were veterans; with the exception of one of their four regiments, the Northerners had never fought before. They were westerners, tough frontier farmers and loggers from Wisconsin and Indiana, and were about to get a uniquely intense baptism by fire.

Southern artillery opened on them from the ridge. The Federals took shelter from the screaming shells. Thinking it was only Jeb Stuart's horse artillery, the commander, the former regular army officer John Gibbon, ordered his own artillery to fire in opposition, then sent infantry forward to take the batteries. The guns fell silent when they came close, then Rebel skirmishers rose and fired on them from the grass. What was infantry doing with cavalry? The answer came moments later when waves of Confederate soldiers emerged from the woods with flags flying. Stonewall Jackson, for whom Pope had been fruitlessly searching for days, was now indisputably *found*.

The Southerners fired volleys at the western soldiers, who were outnumbered and should have run. They didn't. Instead, they held their ground and fired right back at the Confederates. Wrote William B. Taliaferro, who commanded both the Stonewall Brigade and the Stonewall Division: "They stood, and although they could not advance, they would not retire. There was some discipline in this, but there was much more of true valor." It was everyone's nightmare of an early-war battle: two sides, almost completely without shelter, shooting at each other at close range, less than a hundred yards apart—only thirty in one place near the battle's end.

Jackson had 20,000 men close by. Despite frantic personal efforts, he was unable to get more than a fraction of them into action. The Union men remained outnumbered even after both sides were reinforced.

They kept at it, up close and personal, until dark. "In this fight there was no maneuvering, and very little tactics," continued Taliaferro, "it was a question of endurance, and both endured."[5] Taliaferro himself endured, finishing the battle in spite of being wounded three times. His Stonewall Brigade suffered an astonishing 340 casualties out of the 800 who went into action. On the Federal side, the 2nd Wisconsin stands out: Of its 430 men, 276 were casualties. The 2nd formed part of what was called "the Iron Brigade," a name acquired shortly after this fight. Wrote Shelby Foote: "Few men anywhere were inclined to question their right to call themselves by any name they fancied."[6]

General Ewell went into action with Trimble's beloved "two 21s." When the 21st Georgia cheered him by name, Yankee soldiers picked up on it and fired at the noise, bringing down the man most commentators rate as the ablest of Stonewall's lieutenants. Wounded in the leg, he would suffer amputation and be out of the war until two weeks after Jackson's death. Returning, strapped into the saddle, he would never be quite the same. The 21st Georgia's casualties: 173 out of 242, a shocking 71 percent.

Brawner's Farm or Groveton was a costly and bloody two hours, with one out of three men engaged on either side killed or wounded. Despite his losses, Jackson reportedly slept well. After his prayers, he no doubt consoled himself with the thought that Pope now knew where he was and would certainly attack him along the formidable railroad cut, where the terrain itself created a sort of killing machine for the defenders. Also, the Army of Northern Virginia would soon be reunited—Longstreet and Lee were on their way.

Pope continued to play Wile E. Coyote to Jackson's Roadrunner. After Groveton, you can almost hear a stentorian voice on the soundtrack: "And now the hunter became the hunted." Pope thought he was trapping Jackson, but all along Jackson was trapping him, waiting behind the railroad cut like a cat at a mouse hole. Then, when Lee and Longstreet brushed aside resistance at Thoroughfare Gap, Pope had further bad luck in that his subordinates neglected to tell him that the two parts of the Southern army were about to reunite. Completely focused on "bagging Jackson," he even ignored his own men's need for rations.

The Northern soldiers had been marching and fighting as hard as Jackson's, and, because the Confederates had stolen or destroyed so many Yankee provisions, were arguably even hungrier, but when Pope's commissary captain told him he had a trainload of rations available, he couldn't be bothered. "Return to your post," he snapped. "When I want rations I will send for them."[7]

Pope's visions of "crushing Jackson in a vise" came to nothing when it turned out that one of the vise's jaws was unavailable: McDowell had managed to get himself lost in some woods and his command was scattered. The absence of McDowell, for whom no one seems to have had a kind word, prompted Pope to growl, "God damn McDowell. He's never where I want him."[8]

Unable to implement his pincer movement, Pope opened on Jackson with an artillery barrage, which the Confederates answered in kind. It was around 10 a.m. on Friday, August 29. Infantry assaults followed. Valiant but uncoordinated, these were beaten back by the Confederates. Because it passed intermittently through woods and varied terrain, the Southerners used the railroad cut as a general guide rather than a rigidly adhered-to battle line. They also sallied forth or retired as the tide of battle dictated.

John Worsham's 21st Virginia, on the Confederate right, suffered artillery fire, then came under attack by Federal infantry. They repulsed the attack, then pursued the Yankees, then retired to the railroad. Shortly afterward, they were attacked by three lines of infantry in succession. These were all repulsed. The Confederates again left the railroad cut, this time coming under artillery fire as they moved forward. The Southerners turned and faced the cannon. "As we did so," writes Worsham, "I heard a thud on my right, as if one had been struck with a heavy fist. Looking around, I saw a man at my side standing erect, with his head off, a stream of blood spurting a foot or more from his neck."

Behind him, Worsham saw three more men who had been killed by that cannon shot. It was not the first time he had seen such a sight. In both instances, the ball had been descending: "The first man had his head taken off, the next was shot through the breast, the next through the stomach, the next had all his bowels torn out."

This grisly event, which in a fictional narrative would foreshadow complete disaster, was instead a harbinger of good fortune for the Confederates. Shortly afterward, Worsham wrote that he could see soldiers massing to his right: "What did this mean? Were the enemy making preparations to storm us again?" His commander sent a courier to find out the answer. The man came galloping back with the news: "It is Longstreet!" Cheering spread quickly up and down the line. Even better: Lee himself had seen one of their sorties against the Yankees and pronounced it "splendid."[9]

Longstreet deployed at a right angle to Jackson. The four-mile-long Confederate battle line was in place by noon, which, coincidentally, is about when Pope himself arrived on the scene. Extraordinarily, he took no notice of Longstreet, and actually did not appear to know he was there.

The attacks continued. Wrote Kyd Douglas: "Time and again the heavy lines of the enemy rolled against us, like roaring waves of the sea, but they were broken and thrown back. Each attack was weaker, each repulse more difficult—the Federals dispirited, the Confederates worn out."[10]

On the Confederate left, Hill was particularly hard hit. A mid-afternoon clash shows the intensity of the fighting. At three o'clock, Union brigadier Cuvier Grover directed his men in a bayonet charge, which found a gap between Maxcy Gregg's South Carolinians, on the farthest left, and Edward Thomas's Georgians. Federals poured through the gap, collapsing the Rebels' front line, which fell back on the second. There was close-range fighting with bayonets and clubbed muskets. The second line fell back on the third. By this time, the Federals were exhausted, their numbers depleted. The third line rallied and held, then they chased the Federals. The Yankees came under cannon fire as they recrossed the railroad cut on their way back to their starting point. Grover lost almost one-third of his men in the attack—486 out of 1,500 were killed, wounded, or captured.

The Confederates were victorious, albeit damaged and exhausted. Hill sent a message asking Gregg if he could hold out. Gregg sent back word that he thought he could but added, "as if casually, that his ammunition was about expended, but he still had the bayonet." It didn't take much to read between the lines. While tired Confederates scavenged the cartridge boxes of the dead and wounded of both sides, Hill sent Kyd Douglas to Jackson, saying that "if he were attacked again, he would do the best he could, but he could hardly hope for success." Added Douglas: "Such a message from a fighter like Hill was weighty with apprehension."

Jackson, who was always talking about using the bayonet, was not happy when he was actually confronted with its inevitability. "Tell him if they attack him again he must beat them!" he told Douglas, then followed him to deliver the message in person. Hill, meanwhile, was coming the other way to speak to Jackson. "General, your men have done nobly," said Jackson when the two met, "if you are attacked again you will beat the enemy back."

Hill, no doubt thinking something along the lines of "Easier said than done," cut the conference short when he heard the sound of musket volleys along his front. "Here it comes!" he said.

"I expect you to beat them!" Jackson called after him as he galloped away.

If anyone could have beaten the Southerners that day, it should have been Phil Kearny. The beau ideal of the dashing officer, Kearny seemed undiminished by the loss of an arm in Mexico. "He is the bravest and most perfect soldier I ever knew,"[11] said General Winfield Scott, who had known more than a few brave soldiers.

At first, Kearny's attack looked like it was going to be successful. Assault after assault pushed back the Confederate left. Gregg retired to a ridge three hundred yards behind the railroad cut. "Let us die here, my men, let us die here," he said, marching back and forth with a saber that had come down to him from the Revolutionary War. Many did just that—his casualties numbered over 600—but many more were saved when Jubal Early launched a counterattack that drove Kearny's men back to their starting point.

Kearny was waiting for them. He wept when he saw the remnant of what had been the 3rd Michigan. "My valiant lads, what have they done to you?" he sobbed.[12]

Both sides suffered long and terribly. "The sun went down *so* slowly," lamented a Confederate.[13] While there was more fighting, this sixth attack was the final one Hill faced that day. Jackson in general and Hill in particular paid heavily for their successful defense at the railroad cut on August 29. Longstreet, on the other hand, remained in position and did not help. Three times Lee urged him to attack and three times he refused, citing this or that extenuating circumstance. His major argument was irrefutable: Fitz-John Porter was on his right flank. But even taking that into account, the damage being done to Jackson should have outweighed the risks.

Oddly enough, on the other side, Porter was hesitating too. Dislike and distrust of Pope doubtlessly slowed him down. Earlier, he had been bamboozled by Jeb Stuart's cavalrymen dragging branches back and forth across a dusty road, creating the illusion of a vast, menacing host raising dust on the march. Now, south of the battlefield, he still didn't know what was in his front. He was so unsure that he disregarded a written order from Pope to go forward. It was 6:30 p.m., he rationalized—too late in the day to attack.

Although it must have made sense at the time, Porter would later be court-martialed for not obeying that order and would spend much of his postwar life trying to clear his name. Longstreet remains controversial. Aficionados debate his pros and cons with a fervor only exceeded by the debate over the causes of the war. Douglas Freeman was not a fan. In his four-volume, Pulitzer Prize–winning biography of Lee, he talks about Longstreet's August 29 hesitation and Lee's concurrence with it, saying darkly: "The seeds of much of the disaster of Gettysburg were sown in that instant—when Lee yielded to Longstreet and Longstreet discovered that he would."[14]

A final absence: At the time, McClellan was in charge of some 25,000 men in the vicinity of Washington. Halleck ordered him to Manassas to aid in the fighting, but McClellan hesitated with all the stubbornness and ingenuity he had shown on the Peninsula. Suppose there was an attack on Washington? The soldiers weren't ready! Pope already outnumbered the Confederates...

While McClellan loathed Pope, and was undeniably jealous, whether he was trying to harm his rival, or was just being himself, is moot. No matter the reason, the result was the same: A force that outnumbered Jackson's never made it to the battlefield.

Jackson came to Lee's headquarters for a conference around nine that evening. Lee wasn't there when he arrived, but one of his staff members, Captain Charles Venable, impressed by how worn down Jackson looked, offered him a couch in his own tent. Jackson was soon asleep. When Lee returned, he refused to awaken him and gave orders that he not be disturbed. Jackson slept through the night, saved by Lee from his tendency to stint himself on sleep as he tended to details. The well-rested Jackson had his conference with Lee in the morning.

Lee still wanted to destroy Pope and thought he could do so if the latter could be persuaded to attack. If he didn't, Jackson needed to make another flank march to get between Pope and Washington. Jackson agreed. It was fortunate it didn't take place. Neither man seemed to take into account just how worn down Jackson's men were after the hard marching and even harder fighting of the campaign.

On the Union side, Pope still didn't know that Longstreet had arrived and he still thought he had Jackson on the run. He would pounce on Jackson's rear when Porter finally carried out his orders and attacked. He dashed off a self-congratulatory message to Halleck to that effect, then sat in the shade with his staff, smoking a cigar, waiting for his plans to reach fruition.

"It was probably the briefest pursuit in history," wrote Bruce Catton of the massive Union assault that finally went forward in midafternoon.[15] Three huge columns came at Jackson, stronger than anything the day before. The ill-conceived attack was uncoordinated and unsupported. Still, it was all the exhausted Southerners could do to hold on. Some attackers gained a lodgment on the near side of the railway embankment; others fought their way beyond it. Fighting was at close range. On the Confederate left, some men, out of ammunition, resorted to throwing rocks.

"We slaughtered them like hogs," remembered one Southerner. "I never saw the like of dead men in all my life."[16] Bodies piled up, but still they came.

The day before, the hard-fighting Hill had sent to Jackson for aid, alarming the latter because the tenacious and aggressive general never asked for help. Now Jackson played the same role, appealing to Longstreet, again using Kyd Douglas as an envoy: "Ride rapidly to General Longstreet and ask him for a division." Douglas found Old Pete ready for battle. "Certainly," he said to Jackson's request, "but before the division can reach him, that attack will be broken by artillery."

Things often happened a bit too conveniently in Douglas's narratives. He was always at the crossroads of history, the pivotal point in every battle. Now, at that very moment, as if on cue, two batteries of artillery galloped up; Douglas himself had a hand in placing one. "They were soon at work, sending a storm of shell through the thickets into the front and flank of the assaulting column."[17] The bombardment turned the tide. Porter retreated; his soldiers faced more concentrated artillery fire as they moved back through the shooting gallery. The effect was terrible. Recalled a Louisiana soldier: "The Yankees in front of the RR...were lying in heaps; some with their brains oozing out; some with the face shot off; others with their bowels protruding; others with shattered limbs."[18]

McDowell, seeing Porter's distress, sent 7,000 men under John Reynolds to his aid. This would seem a good, solid, logical decision, except that now Longstreet, whose 25,000 men astonishingly still did not figure into the equations of the Union high command, was only opposed by 2,200 Union troops, barely a speed bump for his fresh Confederate soldiers when Old Pete finally ordered them forward.

Seemingly from nowhere, the Confederates slammed into the Union flank. Stunned Federals reeled in confusion. Jackson's men, sensing weakness, went forward. Fifty thousand soldiers moved against the Yankees, sweeping inexorably forward in a five-mile arc.

Now it was the Federals' turn to long for sundown. Pockets of resistance at Chinn Ridge and Henry House Hill—center of the first Manassas battle—slowed the pursuit. Night fell. As with many other Southern victories, the Confederates could not press their advantage because of darkness. Then the rains came and turned the roads and fields to mud.

Most of the war narratives pause here to assess the overall situation, and indeed, it is a convenient and logical place to do so. Three months before, Richmond was under siege from the massive, seemingly unbeatable Army of the Potomac. Now Washington was threatened. Wrote Douglas Freeman: "Except for the troops at Norfolk and at Fort Monroe, the only Federals closer than 100 miles to Richmond were prisoners of war and men who were busily preparing to retreat from the base at Aquia Creek."[19]

Lee, and especially the Lee/Jackson partnership, were responsible for the change. But not according to Jackson. On the night of August 29, after a lengthy and heartbreaking enumeration of the day's casualties, Dr. Hunter McGuire said, "General, we have won this battle by the hardest kind of fighting."

"No, no," said Jackson. "We have won it by the blessing of Almighty God."[20]

Rain and mud. The Union soldiers were in a gloomy mood as they retreated toward the shelter of the Washington defenses. Lee, in pursuit, revived his plan for a flank march, but Jackson's worn-out "foot cavalry" could only cover ten miles on August 31. The following day,

September 1, Jackson encountered Union patrols. His presence no longer secret, he halted and waited for Longstreet.

Kearny and General Isaac Stevens attacked Jackson around five. It was pouring rain. The fighting was confused. At one point, Kearny galloped directly into Confederate lines. Called upon to surrender, he realized his mistake and started back. Shot from his horse, he fell dead in the mud. Wrote a Southern cannoneer: "As he galloped off lying prone on his horse's neck [he] was killed. No trace of a wound was to be found, the bullet having entered the anus."[21]

That night, A. P. Hill visited the body, which was on the porch of a cabin near where he had died. "Poor Kearny," he said. "He deserved a better death than that."[22] Lee later sent his body through the lines under a flag of truce, "thinking that the possession of his remains may be a consolation to his family." Kearny had wept for the 3rd Michigan as he watched their remnant return from the battlefield. Now the 3rd Michigan wept for him.[23]

Jackson doesn't seem to have wept or celebrated except by praying more than usual—a September 1 letter to his wife contained the overflow, mentioning God ten times in sixteen lines[24]—and continuing his military duties with his customary zeal. This was not a time for remorse or reflection—he had his eyes on the prize. The long-hoped-for invasion, for which he had agitated since the first victory at Manassas thirteen months before, was finally under way.

CHAPTER 27

The Fortunes of War

A fter the war, Lee gave a simple explanation for his first invasion of the North: "My men had nothing to eat."[1]

To stay where he was after Second Manassas was to invite disaster—and not just because of scarce rations. Lincoln had brought McClellan back to head the Army of the Potomac. Deliberate as McClellan was, he would eventually sally forth from the Washington defenses to crush Lee with overwhelming numbers. The Southerners had to go somewhere, and the logical direction was north.

It was a process of elimination. To the south was countryside that one or both armies had already depleted; beyond that, Richmond and the possibility of another siege. To the east, Washington, with a strong and now united Federal force behind formidable fortifications. The Shenandoah Valley was to the west, but its rich, ripening croplands were already mostly Confederate—there was nothing much to be gained in that direction. No, the prize was to the north: hitherto untouched Maryland, and beyond that, the house-dwarfing barns of Pennsylvania already awaiting the season's harvest.

But the main reason that Lee crossed into Maryland that first week of September was momentum. He had "won a signal victory on the plains of Manassas," decisively suppressing the miscreant Pope, and it would have been unthinkable to go any direction but forward. And he and Jackson had become of one mind now, and this is what Jackson had wanted all along, sending Boteler to Jefferson Davis with request after request for 40,000 men "to raise the siege of Richmond and transfer this campaign from the banks of the James to those of the Susquehanna."

The Confederates cheered and gave the Rebel yell as they crossed the Potomac at White's Ford. Heros von Borcke, who could always be depended on for a poetic rendering of military events, wrote of the cavalry's crossing: "It was indeed a magnificent sight, as the long column of many thousand horsemen stretched across this beautiful Potomac. The evening sun slanted upon its clear placid waters, and burnished them with gold, while the arms of the soldiers glittered and blazed in its radiance."

He spoke of his excitement and exhilaration, especially when he mounted the opposite bank and heard a military band play "the familiar but now strangely thrilling music of 'Maryland. My Maryland.'" But then he added ominously: "I little thought that in a short time I should recross the river into Virginia, under circumstances far different and far less inspiring."[2]

If there had been a soothsayer among the Confederates, there would have been no shortage of omens to give him pause. Lee, the mighty chieftain, had injured both hands in a fall. They were splinted. He had to move north in an ambulance instead of riding majestically on Traveller. Jackson had lost Little Sorrel. Shortly after he crossed into Maryland, an admirer gave him a huge gray mare, saying she was the finest horse in the state. Jackson accepted the gift. The next day the mare reared and fell over backward on him. He was stunned and bruised and also had to ride in an ambulance for a while. To complete the sorry picture of high command, Longstreet had a badly blistered heel and wore a carpet slipper, noticeably detracting from the imposing military persona of the man Lee styled his "war horse."

Also at about this time, misguided and petty discipline led to the arrest of two of the army's finest fighters. John Bell Hood, head of the Texas Brigade, leader of the breakthrough charge at Gaines' Mill, was arrested by Longstreet over a disagreement about captured ambulances. And Jackson arrested A. P. Hill after the two quarreled over soldiers taking a rest period during the march.

The army itself was ragged to an astonishing degree. Thousands didn't have shoes. Their overall numbers had diminished. Some, worn out by hard marching and fighting, simply slipped away; others left because they objected on principle to invasion—they had signed up to protect homes and families, not carry the war to homelands in the North.

"Lee approached the river," wrote S. C. Gwynne, "with fifty thousand to fifty-five thousand men, a force that had been replenished by Richmond after Second Manassas. Twelve days later he had less than forty thousand."[3]

"None but heroes are left," wrote a South Carolina staff officer a couple of weeks later.[4]

Just after the turn of the century, Marylander Leighton Parks looked back on seeing the Southern army as a young boy. The vivid word picture he painted of the Confederates is justly quoted in multiple sources: "They were the dirtiest men I ever saw, a most ragged, lean, and hungry set of wolves. Yet there was a dash about them that the Northern men lacked. They rode like circus-riders. Many of them were from the far South and spoke a dialect I could scarcely understand. They were profane beyond belief and talked incessantly."[5]

Parks noted their laughter and "good-natured banter"—this in spite of bare feet, ragged uniforms, and scarce rations. None of that was as important as the fact that they had won victory after victory against larger numbers of better-equipped opponents. And they had no reason to think their successes would not continue.

Already gambling with the invasion, Lee was getting ready to make another long-odds move. This one would pay off—for McClellan.

There were Federal garrisons at Martinsburg and Harpers Ferry to the west. Lee couldn't leave them in his rear as he moved north. At Harpers Ferry, there was also the prize of weapons and supplies. The Confederates badly needed muskets. Even this far into the war, about

30 percent of the Southerners were still using outdated smoothbores, barely accurate at a hundred yards. The Federals were mostly equipped with rifled muskets that were accurate at three hundred yards—and there were thousands of such weapons at Harpers Ferry.[6]

Harpers Ferry was surrounded by hills. Lee decided that Stonewall would attack from three of them—Loudoun, Maryland, and Bolivar heights. Jackson's 25,000 men would travel on different roads, then convene to attack the town from above. Longstreet, meanwhile, with D. H. Hill as a rear guard, would cross South Mountain, the north–south extension of the Blue Ridge. The army would be divided into four widely separated parts, each one vulnerable to attack; but the Confederates, betting on McClellan's slow, deliberate movements, thought they could take Harpers Ferry and reunite at Boonsboro, just west of South Mountain, before Little Mac came after them.

On September 9, Lee had his instructions written up as Special Orders 191. It told in great detail where each part of the divided army was to march, when it was supposed to arrive, and what it was supposed to do when it got there. Through an oversight, two copies of the order went to D. H. Hill. Someone—there's been speculation for a century and a half as to who—saved one copy for a souvenir. The unknown person wrapped it around three cigars, then put the order and the cigars into an envelope, which he subsequently lost.

The envelope was found on September 13 by a couple of Indiana soldiers who had just made camp at a site occupied by Confederates a few days before. They turned it over to their commanding officer and it shot like a rocket up the chain of command. "Now I know what to do!" McClellan exulted when he read it. Later, talking to his old army friend Brigadier General John Gibbon, he added, "Here is a paper with which if I cannot whip Bobbie Lee I will be willing to go home."

He had even more of an advantage than he realized. West of South Mountain, Lee got word that Federals were approaching from Chambersburg, some twenty-five miles to the north. He sent Longstreet north to Hagerstown to counter the threat, leaving D. H. Hill in Boonsboro as a rear guard and/or reinforcement for Harpers Ferry.

Now the even more vulnerable army was divided into five rather than four parts. In addition, he and Jackson had vastly underestimated the time it would take to march to Harpers Ferry and subdue its garrison. Stonewall was just getting there on September 13, the day the "Lost Order" was found.

Major General Lafayette McLaws was to attack from the northeast, Jackson from the southwest, Brigadier General John Walker from the south. Jackson, on a roundabout route through Martinsburg, whose 2,500 men fled to the Ferry at his approach, marched fifty-one miles in two days. McLaws, who only covered twenty, was already at Harpers Ferry when Jackson arrived. McLaws's veterans pushed back the Federals on Maryland Heights, green troops who had only been in the army twenty-one days.

Maryland Heights, at fourteen hundred-plus feet the highest elevation above the town, was key to the defense of Harpers Ferry. Colonel Dixon S. Miles manned it with inexperienced soldiers. He also left Loudoun Heights undefended, reasoning that it was dominated by Maryland Heights' artillery. Miles, a thirty-eight-year veteran of the old army, had been reprimanded for being drunk at First Manassas. After an eight-month leave of absence, he was given command of Harpers Ferry, which everyone must have assumed was a quiet backwater.

McLaws attacked again at midafternoon. Deciding that discretion was the better part of valor, the outnumbered Federals retreated downhill to Harpers Ferry, leaving McLaws free to place his guns on the ridge. Jackson and Walker were busy with the same task on their respective heights, encountering varying degrees of difficulty as they dragged cannon uphill through brush and over boulders. Sometimes two hundred men pulled a rope attached to a single gun.

The terrain had been extremely difficult for the infantry as well. One of McLaws's men reported they used bushes to pull themselves uphill. Some fired with one arm while they braced themselves with the other to keep from rolling down the slope.[7]

Jackson communicated with his far-flung soldiers using signal flags, an effort that was only partially successful. Envisaging a sort of grand artillery apocalypse, he messaged them to wait for his signal before raining shells down on the hapless garrison. But Walker drew enemy fire—it would turn out later he did it on purpose—and when he returned it, Jackson and McLaws joined in. The bombardment continued until after dark on September 14.

Meanwhile, a beleaguered Lee, having not heard from Jackson, was close to calling things off. "The day has gone against us," he wrote McLaws. "This army will go by Sharpsburg and cross the river."[8] McClellan, galvanized by the Lost Order's intelligence, had pressed the Confederates, with overwhelming numbers, throughout the day at South Mountain.

A Confederate sympathizer had been outside McClellan's tent when he read the Lost Order. Historians debate just how much the man learned, but it was obvious that a game-changing shift had occurred. The sympathizer—whose name, like so much in this episode, is lost to history—got word to Stuart, who got word to Lee.

It looked like the end of the Maryland Campaign until Lee received a message from Jackson. He must have known the gist of it from the first three words: "Through God's blessing…"

The siege had begun and would be finished successfully in the morning, Jackson continued. Taking a watch-and-wait approach, Lee canceled the retreat.

Jackson placed ten more cannon at the base of Loudoun Heights. Fog covered the town. Dawn came. The fog "began rising like a theater curtain."[9] The lower guns began the bombardment. Fifty more opened from three directions above as soon as they could see their targets. Jackson's infantry, outnumbering the Federals two to one, waited in the wings.

The defenders stood it as long as they could. The white flag went up around 8 a.m. Miles was mortally wounded shortly thereafter by an exploding shell from a Southern artilleryman who didn't realize things were over. No one seems to have much mourned his passing.

Some insinuated he had been drinking again; there were even rumors that he had been shelled by his own men.

- Jackson received the surrender of more than 12,400 Union prisoners—the largest surrender of Federals in the Civil War and a number so humiliating that Union censors cut it in half before they allowed it to be published.[10] In addition to the prisoners, Jackson also captured about thirteen thousand small arms, seventy-three cannon, and a plethora of other badly needed supplies.

In the wake of Miles's wounding, Brigadier General Julius White, who had been in charge of the recently arrived Martinsburg garrison, assumed command and unconditionally surrendered to Jackson. According to Kyd Douglas, "There was nothing strikingly military about his looks, but he was mounted on a handsome black horse, was handsomely uniformed, with an untarnished sabre, immaculate gloves and boots, and had a staff fittingly equipped." He contrasts him with Jackson, "the worst dressed, worst mounted, most faded and dingy-looking general he had ever seen anyone surrender to."[11]

A *New York Times* reporter carried it even further: "He was dressed in the coarsest kind of homespun, seedy and dirty at that; wore an old hat which any northern beggar would consider an insult to have offered him, and in general was in no respect to be distinguished from the mongrel, barefoot crew who follow his fortunes. I had heard much of the decayed appearance of the rebel soldiers, but such a looking crowd! Ireland in her worst straits could present no parallel, and yet they glory in their shame."

Americans cherish the idea of ragged underdogs defeating the smartly attired minions of government might. Sadly, the correspondent was carried away on the wings of his own rhetoric. Jackson's hat, which "any northern beggar would consider an insult," was actually brand-new—Jedediah Hotchkiss had given it to him as a gift just three days before. The takeaway is that it's a lot more fun to write—and in this case write very well—about Jackson the legend than it is to be accurate about Jackson the man.

Accuracy of a different kind occupied artilleryman George Neese, high on South Mountain on the east side of Crampton's Gap. He was shooting at the Yankees, who at that point were two miles away. Then his rifled gun, "a vicious little recoiler," bounded back into the steep slope behind it, breaking two bolts on its mounting and disabling it for the day. Momentarily inactive, he had an ideal vantage point from which to observe the advancing foe. William Franklin's 12,000-plus Federals outnumbered the Confederates better than twelve to one. From above, Neese admired "the magnificent splendor of the martial array that was slowly and steadily moving towards us." Glittering sidearms and shiny musket barrels brought to mind "a silver spangled sea rippling and flashing in the light of a mid-day sun."[12]

To the north near Turner's Gap, D. H. Hill watched an even larger number of soldiers file into place. "The vast army of McClellan spread out before me. The marching columns extended back far as eye could see in the distance.... It was a grand and glorious spectacle, and it was impossible to look at it without admiration.... I had never seen so tremendous an army before, and I did not see one like it afterward."

Hill's rear guard was so small that the Federals "might have brushed it aside almost without halting." But they hesitated. And to the south, at Crampton's Gap, Franklin's unit moved so slowly that it reminded Neese of "a lion, king of the forest, making exceeding careful preparations to spring on a plucky little mouse."[13] Because of the Lost Order, the Federals believed that Longstreet—with most of Lee's army, which McClellan still thought totaled 120,000—was lurking invisibly somewhere nearby. So they waited—but only for a while.

Federal reinforcements poured in; Confederate reinforcements arrived in a slow trickle. Fox's Gap was just south of Turner's. Defenders there were overwhelmed by 11 a.m. Contrasting his tiny numbers with the advancing host, D. H. Hill later admitted, "I do not remember ever to have experienced a feeling of greater loneliness. It seemed as though we were deserted by 'all the world and the rest of mankind.'"

He had only two cannon, but he "opened a brisk fire on the advancing foe. A line of dismounted staff-officers, couriers, teamsters, and cooks was formed behind the guns to give the appearance of battery supports.... By moving about from point to point and meeting the foe wherever he presented himself, the Confederates deluded the Federals into the belief that the whole mountain was swarming with rebels."[14]

It bought the Southerners time. The rest of the rear guard marched in from Boonsboro, slowing the advance. Then Longstreet's men arrived from Hagerstown, stalling the attackers until dark. While the Southerners still held the gap, Federals had taken the high ground on both sides.

At Crampton's Gap, Franklin had finally started moving by mid-morning. Northern skirmishers were within two hundred yards of the Confederates when the roar of Jackson's guns from Harpers Ferry suddenly ceased. Both sides were puzzled. The advance halted. Wrote cavalryman W. W. Blackford: "Then from away down the valley came rolling nearer and nearer, as the news reached the troops, ringing cheers and we knew the Ferry had surrendered, and soon a courier came spurring in hot haste with the official information of the fact."

One of the Federal skirmishers jumped up on a stone wall. "What the hell are you fellows cheering for?" he yelled.

"Because Harpers Ferry is gone up, God damn you."

"I thought that was it," the man yelled as he jumped down.[15]

The fall of the Ferry stymied Franklin. Wouldn't the besiegers come for him next? Finally, in late afternoon, elements of his command went forward on their own and pushed the Confederates off the mountain.

Crampton's Gap had fallen. Turner's Gap would do so in the morning. The handwriting was on the wall. Lee decided to abandon South Mountain.

CHAPTER 28

The Most Deadly Fire

The pieces of the army moved northwest toward Sharpsburg. "We will make our stand on those hills," said Lee. He began placing his men on the low ridgeline behind Antietam Creek. It was Monday, September 15. Jackson's men were completing their work at Harpers Ferry. Until he arrived, Lee had Longstreet's I Corps and D. H. Hill's II Corps, a total of 18,000 soldiers. McClellan pursued with 87,000.

The ground Lee chose was good but could have been better. He was on a peninsula formed by the Potomac River's juncture with Antietam Creek, both of which at this point ran roughly north to south. A worst-case scenario would have him falling into a trap like the one Pope had avoided back in mid-August, when Lee almost caught him in the V formed by the confluence of the Rappahannock and Rapidan rivers. But Lee was never one to dwell on the downside. He had lost his hopes of a spear thrust into the heart of the North. Now he just wanted to hurt McClellan as badly as he could. Wrote Shelby Foote: "With the situation thus at its worst and his army in graver danger of piecemeal annihilation than ever, Lee displayed for the first time a side to his nature that would become more evident down the years. He was not only no less audacious in retreat than in advance, he was also considerably more pugnacious, like an old gray wolf wanting nothing more than half a chance to turn on whoever or whatever tried to crowd him as he fell back."[1]

McClellan didn't crowd him. He could have attacked with better than three-to-one odds, but he planned and pondered, surveying the ground and working out details. Jackson, meanwhile, arrived mid-morning on the sixteenth from Harpers Ferry. Starting at midnight, he had pushed his men on a severe, seventeen-mile march that dribbled stragglers all along the route. Nor was he the last to arrive.

McLaws had to push his way through 12,000 paroled Yankees and only reached his goal on the day of the battle. A. P. Hill arrived after McLaws.

McClellan continued his ruminations, announcing at midafter-noon that the attack would begin at dawn the next day. It would start on the Confederate left—Jackson's position. He chose to attack there because it was accessed by the Upper Bridge over the Antietam, the northernmost of three and the only one that was out of range of Con-federate artillery. That was pretty much his whole plan: Start on the left, feint on the right, then hit the center with whatever he had left if either attack succeeded.

The most striking landmark on this part of the line was the Dunker Church, a whitewashed, steepleless structure, as plain-looking as its congregants were plain-living. The Dunkers were pacifists, part of the area's indigenous German farming culture. Officially called the German Baptist Brethren, they believed in baptism by total immersion, hence the nickname.

Other salient features of this part of the battlefield were patches of forest called consecutively the West Woods, North Woods, and East Woods, and a big field of tall, ripening corn owned by a farmer named Miller. As with many Civil War facts, the Cornfield changes size depending on who is describing it. The Park Service says it was twenty-four acres; other authorities have it ranging up to forty-plus.

General Joseph Hooker, "Fighting Joe," began moving his I Corps into position at four in the afternoon. They crossed the Upper Bridge and nearby shallows and made their way to a jumping-off point on the Poffenberger Farm near the East Woods, brushing up against some of John Bell Hood's men in the process. Skirmishing ensued. Union and Confederate artillery joined in, but the action was short-lived. "The fight flashed, and glimmered, and faded, and finally went out in the dark," summarized a reporter for the *New York Tribune* who was part of Hooker's retinue.[2] The main thing Hooker had done, besides get into position, was telegraph to Lee where the attack was going to open. He shifted his right to meet the incoming threat from the north and sent urgent messages to hurry to both McLaws, who was still in transit, and A. P. Hill, who had not yet left.

Hooker attacked at dawn, his objective the Dunker Church. Confederate artillery met his advance. It was immediately countered by Federal cannon fire.

In every Civil War battle, there are accounts that say it was the most intense fire, the most deadly action, the most terrible casualties of the entire war. Antietam is no exception—except in this case, it's true. Account after account from soldiers on both sides attest to its horror. John H. Worsham had been with Jackson since the Valley and would stay with the army until wounded in 1864. "The enemy's shells dropped in our midst from batteries in front and flank, and soon this became the fiercest artillery fire of the war!" Over five hundred well-placed cannon took part in the battle. Continued Worsham, "It seemed that the air was alive with shells!"[3]

"It was artillery hell," wrote Southern artillerist Stephen D. Lee.[4] The most iconic Antietam photo, of dead bodies in front of the Dunker Church pockmarked by cannon fire, was taken after the battle near the position of Lee's batteries. Infantry did their part to add to the infernal action. Driving forward through the Cornfield, the 12th Massachusetts advanced through deadly musket and artillery fire before encountering the 13th Georgia behind a fence. "Rifles are shot to pieces in the hands of the soldiers, canteens and haversacks are riddled by bullets, the dead and wounded go down in scores. The smoke and fog lift; and almost at our feet, concealed in a hollow behind a demolished fence, lies a rebel brigade pouring into our ranks the most deadly fire of the war."[5]

That "most deadly fire" resulted in 67 percent casualties, 224 of 12th's 334 men, the worst loss of any Union regiment that day.

The unit behind the fence, the 13th Georgia, was punished in return. According to the chronicler of the 12th Massachusetts, burial parties the next day wrote on the board that marked their mass grave: "In this trench lie buried the colonel, the major, six line officers, and one hundred and forty men of the [13th] Georgia Regiment."[6]

All told, Jackson lost at least 40 percent of the approximately 5,500 men he took into battle, though the National Park Service's website cautions: "Because of the catastrophic nature of the Battle of Antietam, exact numbers of casualties were virtually impossible to compile."

After an hour, the Confederates were being pushed back. Jackson sent in John Bell Hood and the Texas Brigade, who had been behind the lines cooking their first hot rations in days. They were shock troops already, but their usual ferocity was undoubtedly compounded by the interruption of their meal. Like the others, Hood said that it was the fiercest fighting he had ever seen. "It was here," he wrote, "that I witnessed the most terrible clash of arms, by far, that has occurred during the war."[7] Less than three months before, he had led the charge that broke the line at Gaines' Mill, a "terrible clash of arms" by anyone's reckoning.

"The air was full of shot and shell," wrote a Texas Brigade soldier. "It seemed almost impossible for a rat to live in such a place."[8] Neither rats nor men. The 1st Texas, which advanced farther than any other unit in the brigade, suffered a shocking 82.3 percent casualties, "the greatest loss suffered by any infantry regiment, north or south, during the war," according to their pink granite monument at Antietam. I vividly remember the frisson it gave me when I found the marker on my first visit to the battlefield years ago.

Punch and counterpunch, advance and retreat. According to one battle history: "It was later estimated that the opposing lines surged back and forth across the Cornfield no fewer than fifteen times in the course of this awful day."[9]

Hood's arrival saved the Confederate left, but soon he himself was in trouble. Unable to see through the battle smoke, Jackson sent aide Sandie Pendleton to see how things were going. Hood shouted to be heard above the gunfire: "Tell General Jackson unless I get reinforcements, I must be forced back, but I am going on while I can!"

Pendleton galloped back to Jackson, who sent him galloping off to Lee for more men. "Such a storm of balls I never conceived it possible for a man to live through," Pendleton said later about the harrowing ride. Jackson, in contrast, felt divinely protected. He told brother-in-law D. H. Hill afterward that he never felt safer in battle than at Antietam. He believed that "God would protect him & that no harm would befall him. This security he said extended to him throughout the day."[10]

Jackson and Lee sent what reinforcements they could. Lee, ever the gambler, weakened his right to shore up his left. Once on the field, Southern reinforcements met Northern reinforcements, the Union XII Corps under General Joseph Mansfield. That venerable commander, a distinguished-looking veteran with white hair and beard, personifies the saying "Be careful what you wish for." Mansfield had lobbied hard for a field command to crown his forty years of service, most of which had been spent in engineering and administrative duties. He was given leadership of the XII Corps on September 15, and mortally wounded two days later while deploying his men.

In all, six generals would be killed at Antietam, three Union and three Confederate. With more eerily corresponding symmetry, twelve generals would be wounded, six from each side; in addition, total casualties in the Cornfield were more or less equally distributed: 7,280 Union and 6,580 Confederate, according to the National Park Service website.

Among the Federal wounded was Hooker, who was shot in the foot and removed to the rear. Later, in his official report, he added to the list of negative superlatives: "It was never my fortune to witness a more bloody, dismal battle-field."[11]

There was more to come. With Mansfield down, General Alpheus Williams took command of the XII Corps. They advanced, losing nearly a quarter of their men, finally stalling near the Dunker Church. Then General Edwin Sumner's 15,000-man II Corps crossed the Antietam. Sumner was the oldest general in the Army of the Potomac. His nickname, "Bull," not only referenced his courage and forcefulness, it also reflected a certain hardheadedness as well—literally: Part of his legend involved a Mexican musket ball bouncing off his head at Cerro Gordo. Admired for his courage if not his intelligence—McClellan thought him a "fool"[12]—he lived up to his reputation for headstrong impetuosity by not reconnoitering or listening to advice from General Williams before he entered the fight. Nor did he send out scouts or skirmishers.

He would have done well to know what he was getting into. Although by this time the Park Service's sequential map of the action shows only "Remnants of Jackson and Hood" in his direct path, those battered units were about to be reinforced by McLaws and Walker, who were finally on the field following a hard march from Harpers Ferry.

Sumner's men moved directly into an ambush. The Southerners didn't plan it—they were just in the right place at the right time. Their surprise attack slammed into the left flank of the ponderously moving, closely packed blue mass. A few Federals were able to retire in good order, but most fled. In the confusion, some fired into the backs of their own men. "My God!" shouted Sumner. "We must get out of this." He furiously attempted to turn his men to face the attackers, then to retreat. In the meantime, the Confederates worked their way around to deliver converging fire from three directions. In twenty minutes, Sumner lost 2,200 of his 5,400 men.

Confederate casualties were light—until they pursued the fleeing Federals. They then took heavy losses in their turn, and the fighting continued for a while, with more backing and forthing, until midmorning when both sides were back in their respective starting points, like two evenly matched and bloodied fighters resting in their corners.

Jackson got a visit from Hunter McGuire around noon. The doctor had some peaches that he shared with the general, who fell on them ravenously, explaining that he hadn't eaten all morning. McGuire, contrasting the nearby Confederate remnant with the "overwhelming strength of the Federal masses" across the way, asked Jackson, "Can our line hold against another attack?"

Jackson answered calmly, "I think they have done their worst and there is now no danger of the line being broken."[13]

He was correct, once again exhibiting an understanding of the military situation that bordered on the preternatural.

Though the Battle of Antietam would continue for another eight hours, shifting first to the center, then finally ending on the Confederate right, Jackson's part in it was mostly over. Fighting in the center focused on an old road at the foot of a slight ridge. Generations of farm traffic had worn it into the earth until it resembled a trench. Confederates used this natural fortification to repulse attacks from elements of the II Corps that had been left behind in Sumner's headstrong rush to the West Woods. Volley after lethal volley crashed into succeeding waves of Federals, who charged down the ridge "outlined target sharp against the eastern sky." According to Shelby Foote: "The rebels jeered and hooted at the dark-clothed attackers coming over the rise, silhouetted against the glare of the sunlight."

Secure in their trench, made even more formidable by a breastwork of piled-up fence rails, the Confederates kept killing Yankees—but the Yankees kept coming. Dead Southerners started to accumulate in the road. Then pressure on the left necessitated the line's "refusal"—a turning to the side to repulse attackers. A Confederate colonel gave the wrong command: "About face; forward march." The soldiers headed toward the rear, as did those beside them, five regiments' worth. Federals rushed in to fill the vacuum, then poured an enfilading fire down the road. The secure position was suddenly a death trap. Shelby Foote: "Dead men filled whole stretches of the road to overflowing. Horrified, unit by unit from left to right, the survivors broke for the rear, and now it was the Yankees doing the hooting and the shooting."[14]

Witnesses said that dead Confederates were piled three deep in the sunken road. Afterward, it was renamed "Bloody Lane."

Longstreet tried to contain the breakthrough. Still wearing the unmartial carpet slipper, he scraped up enough artillery to make a small battery. It barked aggressively at the advancing Federals, spewing canister that slowed their attack. D. H. Hill, still full of fight after having three horses shot from under him, rallied some 200 of his men and mounted a countercharge. It bought time for Longstreet to assemble more cannon. One of their shells exploded near enough to General Israel Richardson to give him a mortal wound.

McClellan had more than enough reserves—22,000 infantry and 3,500 cavalry—to punch through what remained of Confederate resistance, but in an afternoon council of war, Sumner, who had had quite enough of Antietam facing Jackson that morning, convinced him instead to hold his position, and the battle shifted to its final phase on the Confederate right.

September 17 saw a new name for the Sunken Road. Rohrbach's Bridge, the southernmost crossing of the Antietam, would also be renamed, for Major General Ambrose Burnside, who fought there famously that afternoon.

Burnside's IX Corps, 10,000 strong, was to the east of Antietam Creek. The bridge, a picturesque stone structure with three arches, was a narrow bottleneck negating his advantage in numbers. Rocky outcroppings and an old quarry on the western side sheltered about 400 mostly Georgian soldiers who, along with twelve cannon, contested the crossing.

George Crook's 2nd Brigade attacked first, went astray, and spent the next several hours sniping at the Southerners from north of the bridge. James Nagle's 1st Brigade came next. Hit by Confederate fire in flank and in front, they never made it to the bridge. General Edward Ferrero's 51st New York and 51st Pennsylvania were to lead the third assault. Because of misconduct on the march, they had been deprived of their whiskey ration. A man from the ranks asked if it would be restored if they took the bridge. "Yes, by God!" said Ferrero.

The Southerners were taking casualties and running low on ammunition. In addition, they were in danger of being flanked by Union soldiers trying to force a crossing downstream. They pulled back under pressure from the two 51sts.

With the bridge secured, Burnside took two hours to get the IX Corps across. Constructed for wagons and carriages, the 125-foot-long bridge was only 12 feet wide—an obstruction to troop movements even without Confederate defenders, though generations of battlefield visitors have wondered, when looking at the shallowness of the stream on both sides of the structure, why the Federals didn't simply wade across.

With his men finally in line of battle at 3 p.m., Burnside moved against the Confederate right, which Lee had stripped earlier to support other parts of his beleaguered line. Burnside's 10,000 faced a quarter of their number. Brushing aside Confederate resistance, they were on the verge of victory when A. P. Hill's men arrived from Harpers Ferry. Like the cavalry in an old Hollywood western, they came on the scene in the nick of time, rolled up the inexperienced soldiers on the Union left flank, and saved Lee's army to fight another day.

By almost all accounts, Antietam was a stalemate. The Confederates had fewer casualties—10,320 versus 12,400—but could ill afford to lose them because of lower numbers overall. Lee remained in place, ready for battle the next day, then abandoned the campaign and returned to Virginia, leaving McClellan in possession of the field. Declaring a victory paved the way for Lincoln's Emancipation Proclamation, a game-changer whose long-range repercussions proved that there was more to waging war than what happened on a battlefield.

Jackson, who had arguably fought the hardest and unarguably suffered the most casualties of the war's bloodiest day, was, incredibly, still spoiling for a fight in early afternoon. He and Stuart were scouting their left flank, looking for counterattack opportunities, when they halted in front of Colonel Matt Ransom's 35th North Carolina. A Federal battery was firing at the Carolinians; Jackson asked Ransom if he thought he could silence it. Ransom replied that he had just tried, but when he got to the top of the rise on which the battery was placed, it looked like most of McClellan's army was there backing it up.

A skeptical Jackson called for a tree climber. Private William S. Hood volunteered eagerly and shinnied up a nearby hickory tree "like a squirrel."

"How many troops are over there?" asked Jackson.

"Oceans of them!" replied Hood.

"Count the flags, sir!" Jackson sternly admonished.

Each flag signified a regiment. Hood, despite sniper fire, counted. Jackson repeated each number. When he got to thirty-nine, Stonewall said, "That will do, come down, sir."[15]

Unlike Jackson, most men on both sides had had their fill of killing. Many Southerners spent the night searching for fallen comrades. Kyd Douglas, who had used up two horses during the day and fainted when he was mounted on the third, rode behind the Dunker Church carrying a message from Jackson to Early after dark. "It was a dreadful scene, a veritable field of blood," he wrote. "The pitiable cries for water and appeals for help were much more horrible to listen to than the sounds of battle.... Men were wiggling over the earth; and midnight hid all distinction between the blue and the grey. My horse trembled under me in terror, looking down at the ground, sniffing the scent of blood, stepping falteringly as a horse will over or by the side of human flesh; afraid to stand still, hesitating to go on, his animal instinct shuddering at this cruel human mystery."

The horse stepped into a puddle of blood; some splashed on Douglas. "I had had a surfeit of blood that day," he wrote. He left the horse with his courier and continued his mission alone.[16]

CHAPTER 29

The Certainty of Death

At first, I drove at the speed of a marching column because of northern Virginia traffic. Later, after making the turn to White's Ford in Loudoun County, the spot where the Confederates had crossed into Maryland, I still drove at the speed of a marching column, but now it was because of the accordioned dirt-and-gravel road, which wound scenically through woods and fields as it dropped slowly toward the Potomac.

The parking lot was set amid acres of magnificent eight-foot-high corn. I parked and walked to the boat ramp. An angler was stashing gear into the Pescador fishing kayak he'd unloaded just before I arrived. A young man, he met my gaze forthrightly and spoke in a low voice so as not to alarm the fish. He was going after smallmouths, he told me. They liked the deeper water up- and downstream. He pointed out a grassy inlet across the river where he'd had some luck. He was surprised when I said I wasn't going fishing. Civil War? You might find something out there...

I went back to the car and put on my swimsuit and river shoes. The angler parked his pickup, waved, and headed back to the river. He was far upstream by the time I started wading, which was good, because he didn't see me slip and fall, an action I repeated several times both on the way out and the way back.

The water was slightly chilly but not unpleasant. My soaked T-shirt stuck to my body. The day was overcast, with incredible blue-gray clouds and intermittent sun. Long weeds waved like mermaid hair on the river bottom—I didn't want to walk through them because anything could be under there, but I had to, so I did.

The angler disappeared. I was halfway to Maryland, alone with the river, which by now was up to my waist. I looked back. I'd left no impression on the water. Fifty thousand men crossed here without leaving a trace—just as I wouldn't leave a trace.

Sharp mussel shells and stones on the other side of the weeds. I thought of barefoot Confederates. How did they do it? Twenty-plus miles a day; nasty food or none at all; death waiting up the road. And for what? Glory? The Cause? Slavery? And what did it matter now anyway? They were all dead and gone, just like I'd be dead and gone...

My dark mood lessened somewhat after I reached the opposite bank. Such a beautiful day—why be melancholy? Then an interesting thought: Maybe solitude and natural beauty allowed me to tune in to a psychic impression from the past, a remnant of what the soldiers were really thinking.

I turned around and headed back to Virginia. I swung downstream to avoid the weed patch, then climbed out on the muddy bank.

Maybe the angler was right. Maybe I had found something out there.

He might have been an apparition except for the cell phone. A middle-aged man in a dust-colored Confederate uniform, sitting on a stump beside the ashes of a campfire.

"Are you an old Rebel soldier?"

"Oh, hey," he said, extending his hand. "Tudd Dean. We were up here cleaning the monument, spent the night, and had breakfast." I noticed eggshells in the ashes. "I was just trying to get hold of a fellow that was supposed to meet me to go to the reenactment."

It was the day before the weekend commemorating the 155th anniversary of Antietam. Touring South Mountain between White's Ford and the battlefield, I'd stopped at Fox's Gap and walked up a path through the woods. I had never been there. One of my ancestors had, and I wanted to see where he'd fought.

"Tudd?" I asked.

He helpfully spelled it out: "T—U—D—D." He beckoned me to another stump. I sat down and we chatted. He was from North Carolina, came up for Antietam, traveled around the country following his hobby. Saturday he was going to reenact A. P. Hill's march from Harpers Ferry, all seventeen miles.

"You must be in good shape."

"I've been walking around my mountain, four and a half miles. Sometimes I do it two times a day. Sometimes three."

"I admire you," I said. I complained about my bad knee. He showed me a scar that went from above his knee to below it and recited a list of other injuries that made me feel both lucky and lazy. I resolved to do better, especially after he revealed he was four years older than me.

"Have you seen the monument?"

It was another short walk through the woods. We stood and admired the life-size rendering of a North Carolina color bearer holding his flag aloft despite a mortal wound. The conversation drifted naturally to current events.

Recently, the anger and division roiling the country had focused on Confederate monuments. Close to home, the Charlottesville City Council decided to remove downtown statues of Lee and Jackson and rename their respective parks "Emancipation" and "Justice." White supremacists made keeping the statues a cause célèbre and descended on the quiet college town for a rally that surprised authorities by starting as a torchlight parade on the grounds of the university. Supremacists clashed violently with protesters and Antifa—anti-fascist—activists, who had also come spoiling for a fight. The police, by all accounts, did very little. Events turned tragic when a supremacist rammed his car into a crowd of protesters, injuring dozens and killing a young woman, Heather Heyer. My hometown paper featured a horrifying front-page picture of the car plowing into the crowd, victims head over heels from the impact. The photo later won the Pulitzer Prize.

Anger erupted nationwide, with collateral fury against the Confederacy and all its memorials. "Confederate Monuments Must Fall" declared Karen L. Cox in a *New York Times* op-ed, one of many. There were bushels of like-minded letters to the editors. Facebook sizzled with condemnation. "RACISTS!" and "TRAITORS!" and "TEAR THEM DOWN!" were among the frequent comments from my friends.

President Trump weighed in, condemning both sides, then only the supremacists, then both sides again, leaving those not scratching their heads even more outraged.

A new orthodoxy emerged, advanced by eminent professors, that the monuments had nothing to do with the war. They were instead tools of white supremacy and segregation. Hadn't they been put up during the time of poll taxes, disenfranchisement, and lynching?

Then there were a couple of hurricanes and people seemed to lose interest. The Charlottesville City Council shrouded Lee and Jackson with black plastic tarps "in mourning for Heather Heyer." They were pulled down in protest. The council tried and failed to arrest the perpetrators. The plastic went up again, then came down, then went back up. With each reshrouding, articles chronicling the event got smaller and retreated farther inside the newspaper. The last time I noticed, the council had put up plastic fences around the statues so they could arrest anyone crossing them over "safety issues."

A year later, supremacists tried to hold a second rally on the anniversary. It was a nonevent by all estimations. After the governor of Virginia declared a state of emergency, focus switched from the demonstration in Charlottesville to one in D.C. An army of anti-supremacists assembled, restrained by a somewhat smaller army of police—but only a couple of dozen demonstrators showed. "The Moving Finger writes; and having writ, moves on..."

I took pictures of the North Carolina monument with my phone. "A lot of the guys I know are really upset," Dean confided. "For us it's like family. Our ancestors fought for these men."

I had to agree, thinking of my own ancestor fighting on that very spot.

"They just poured red paint on Francis Scott Key's statue in Baltimore and wrote 'Racist Anthem' on it."

"Francis Scott Key? 'The Star-Spangled Banner.' Francis Scott Key?"

" 'Racist Anthem.' "

The conversation had reached a stopping point. Dean went to his pickup to charge his cell phone. I said goodbye and walked back through the woods to my car.

"How are you today?" I asked, opening my wallet.

"Crazy!" The volunteer manning the welcome desk at Antietam looked harried but cheerful. "There were fifty people waiting to get in this morning when I opened up."

I handed over the five-dollar entrance fee—a bargain for the whole weekend—and commiserated before asking about the Cornfield Tour. It started at 10:30, right outside the visitor center.

The line of visitors behind me stacked up when I asked the question. I made haste to get out of the way and wiled away the next half hour in the museum. An exhibit on battlefield archaeology said that the last body found at Antietam was in 2008. A visitor noticed bone fragments in the dirt thrown up by a groundhog and alerted the rangers. An excavation discovered the remains of a soldier in his late teens. Buttons told the archaeologists he was from New York. He was eventually reinterred, with full military honors, in the Saratoga National Cemetery.

"Hi, I'm Jess, and I'll be your tour guide today." Ranger Jess Rowley had a great nineteenth-century beard. He sketched the background of the battle. "The men who fought here had been fighting each other all summer. They started down around Richmond, and they didn't get here by getting in a car and driving up I-95." The fifty or so people on the tour gave an appreciative chuckle. "No," Rowley continued. "They had been marching and fighting almost the entire time. Brigades that started with a thousand men were down to forty by the time they got here."

A few more facts and we started toward the Cornfield. We paused on the edge of a harvested swath. The crop here was even more impressive than the one at White's Ford: ten feet high, with big fat ears on every stalk. Ghoulish thoughts about the manuring benefits of dead bodies; then, irreverently, that ranger talks had the same effect—though Rowley was actually doing quite well, leavening his facts with a dark humor that must come naturally to anyone who works at Antietam.

"Watch your step," he said, stopping the group on the edge of the field. "We have groundhogs here the size of small children—and their holes probably could swallow a small child if you have one, so be careful."

I examined a groundhog's mound of thrown-up earth as we passed. Impressive, but no bones...

The harvested cornstalks were all cut off neatly a few inches above the ground. I remembered Hooker's quote: "In the time I am writing every stalk of corn in the northern and greater part of the field was cut as closely as could have been done with a knife."

Canister cut the corn. "It turns the cannon into a giant shotgun," reenactors always say at artillery demonstrations. Rowley would later read a quote about it melting charging attackers "into a pink mist."

Artillery hell; infantry hell. How did the soldiers stand it?

People stopped to take pictures of the stalks. I realized then that they had never seen corn growing. The group halted under a big walnut tree.

"The field was a vortex. Men fought back and forth across it for three hours. One American was killed for every second of the fighting."

Jackson had presided over the bloodiest hours of the bloodiest day in American history. Men falling all around him, but he "never felt safer in battle." And at the end, he was eager for more.

Unlike Jackson, I'm afraid of death. Saddened and afraid. Here in this outdoor temple of mortality, all I could think about was how much I didn't want to die. I asked myself again: How did the soldiers stand it? I didn't want to leave these beautiful fields, the lovely river I waded through yesterday; work, family, friends...

Ready to move on, Rowley asked for questions. I shook off my mood when the opportunity presented itself to nail down some details for my writing. A handful of us surrounded him, asking this and that, while the rest of the group dispersed, spoiling his chance for a wrap-up back at the visitor center. He seemed all right with it, though, and generously spent time with us until we were all questioned out.

At the Battleview Market that evening, I ordered a Stonewall Jackson— a variation on the classic reuben sandwich—and contemplated buying a six-pack of Little Mac IPA, named after General McClellan and with his picture on the cans: ADORED AND RESPECTED BY HIS MEN, HE WAS PROBABLY THE KIND OF BOSS YOU'D DRINK A BEER WITH. Tudd Dean tapped me on the shoulder.

"Hey man!" I said. "You made it!" His group had actually beaten A. P. Hill's time from Harpers Ferry. "Seventeen miles! All right!"

Though he shook my hand warmly, my congratulations seemed oddly hollow. The march must have been an ordeal.

"Never again!" he said darkly. "Never again."

The early morning Cornfield Tour felt almost like a church service. It took place at the same time and on the same ground as the fighting, with thick fog—authentic to the battle—adding a further atmospheric touch. The group of visitors waited quietly, speaking in hushed tones, then wordlessly followed the rangers when they appeared, each with a loose-leaf notebook under his or her arm.

There were eight rangers at the first stop. They stood in a line, with a creaky portable sound system and a mike they passed from hand to hand. I squashed sarcastic thoughts that arose from seeing eight Smokey hats in a row, and became absorbed in the program as soon as it began.

It was done with a "less is more" philosophy, consisting almost entirely of quotes. The soldiers woke up. There was dew on the gun barrels. "The certainty of death never seemed so near." Opening salvos; first casualties; attack and counterattack.

"Onward into the Cornfield," said an older ranger who seemed in charge. Again, people snapping photos of stalks and ears as we walked. Lots of silver-haired men in the crowd, but a substantial number of women and young adults too; only one African American.

We halted at a snake-railed fence. A reverberant boom came from the visitor center just as the ranger was reading about artillery. I knew it was the gun crew rehearsing for a demo later in the day, but the synchronicity combined with the fog, the crowd's somber mood, and the vivid quotes made me feel like I was on the verge of a time slip. I withdrew inward, aware that the program was going on and that it was good, but, like yesterday, absorbed in my own thoughts about the preciousness of life and the inevitability of death.

Suddenly I was aware that the presentation was almost over. A ranger read Kyd Douglas's story of his horse encountering the "cruel human mystery" of the battle's aftermath. I envisioned the poor beast trembling as it picked its way among the bodies.

The rangers finished a few minutes later and we all walked back to the visitor center.

CHAPTER 30

Pain and Happiness

A comparatively quiet interlude followed the return from Maryland. Jackson's men—filthy, lice-infested, ill shod or not shod at all—bivouacked in a series of camps near Winchester. Jackson allowed them some rest, and, to the extent that it was possible, saw to it that they were reequipped. They bathed in a nearby creek. Stragglers returned, along with the men who had slipped away because they didn't want to invade the North. Jackson arrived in late September with a little over 10,000 soldiers. That number more than doubled in less than a month.[1]

As always, the period of nonfighting highlighted a different set of Jacksonian qualities, both good and bad. Reinstating strict discipline, he ordered the execution of deserters. One would like to think that he was doing it for the good of the service, but he seemed to relish it just a little too much.

At least one disciplinary action backfired. Jackson had ordered A. P. Hill arrested on September 4 over a disagreement about how the Light Division should march. Afterward, Hill's conduct had been exemplary, his fighting even better. He had actually saved the day at Antietam when he charged in from Harpers Ferry at midafternoon.

Jackson was content to let the disciplinary matter drop, but Hill, considering his honor besmirched, insisted on a court of inquiry. Lee's attempts to smooth things over were unsuccessful, and the relationship between Hill and Jackson settled into one of icy formality, a potential detriment to the fighting partnership vital on the battlefield.

Other relationships fared much better. Jackson's friendship with Stuart deepened. The improbable pairing of the most austere and self-effacing man in either army with the most colorful and flamboyant was much remarked on. In a few cases, it actually caused Old Jack to assay a few jokes.

One night Stuart arrived late in camp after Jackson had gone to sleep. The cavalryman removed his saber, but left on his boots and spurs, and got into bed with Jackson, unconsciously taking more and more of the covers as the night cooled down.

Jackson was up and standing by the campfire next morning when Stuart awoke. After they greeted each other, Jackson, "in tones as nearly comic as he could muster, said, 'General Stuart, I am always glad to see you here. You might select better hours sometimes, but I am always glad to have you. But General'—as he stooped and rubbed himself along the legs—'you must not get into my bed with your boots and spurs on and ride me around like a cavalry horse all night!' "[2]

Another good-humored story comes from Stuart's chief of staff, Heros von Borcke. Jackson, of course, was famous for his unassuming—some would say threadbare and ragged—mode of dress. To remedy the situation, Stuart had a beautiful uniform coat made by a tailor in Richmond, dispatching it with von Borcke to be delivered at the end of some other official business.

It was close to dinnertime when von Borcke arrived at Jackson's tent. When their business was over, von Borcke gave Jackson the coat. "I was heartily amused," writes the cavalryman, "at the modest confusion with which the hero of many battles regarded the fine uniform from many points of view, scarcely daring to touch it, and at the quiet way in which, at last, he folded it up carefully and placed it in his portmanteau."

Jackson thanked the major, but said the coat was too fine for him and that he would keep it as a souvenir. The Prussian protested. Stuart had to know if the coat fit. Von Borcke would regard it as a personal favor if the general would at least try it on.

Jackson put on the coat and went to dinner, which was being served outside. "The whole of the Staff were in a complete ecstasy at their chief's brilliant appearance," wrote von Borcke. Jim Lewis "gazed in wonderment.... Meanwhile, the rumor of the change ran like electricity through the neighboring camps, and the soldiers came running by hundreds to the spot, desirous of seeing their beloved Stonewall in his new attire."[3]

The coat would be retired for months after this first appearance.

That fall, the army was reorganized into two corps. Jackson was promoted to lieutenant general in charge of the second. It would have been odd if he had not been elevated, given his fame and the all but universal esteem in which he was held. But someone must have criticized him, causing Anna to send a letter asking if she should come to his defense.

"Don't trouble yourself about representations that are made of your husband," he wrote back. "These things are earthly and transitory. There are real and glorious blessings, I trust, in reserve for us beyond this life."[4] There was more, much more, as the letter went on, its obvious sincerity giving the lie to Taylor's statement that Jackson possessed "an ambition boundless as Cromwell's, and as merciless."[5] If he was guilty of anything, it was of prattling on ecclesiastically, unconsciously hoping to impress his wife with the fact that he could write like a minister, the profession he had always admired and, wisely, not pursued.

A great religious revival occurred in Lee's army that fall. Preachers plying their trade found a ready audience for their message. Jackson often led prayers or attended services in nearby camps, though Douglas relates that while the soldiers participated wholeheartedly, they did not become so pious as to give up the normal amusements of camp life. When Jackson arrived, "A runner sprinted on before and gave the news. I noticed as we approached the tents, in many of them were sitting squads of fours, around a candle in an inverted bayonet stuck in the ground as a candlestick, absorbed in games of cards. As the General approached the light would go out, the cards would be put down in place just as they were held, the players would crawl out and fall in behind; and when he had reached the place of prayer, lo, the camp was there."

The petitions to the deity concluded, the soldiers followed Jackson to the edge of camp, then, "doubtless, returned to their cards."[6]

Jackson kept his hand in militarily by wrecking some twenty miles of the Baltimore and Ohio Railroad. Afterward, he made a reconnaissance from a devastated portion of the track. The "young and pretty wife" of a railroad section foreman approached with her eighteen-month-old baby and asked him to bless her child. Jackson saw nothing odd in the request. He took the child "with a pleasant expression on his stern face," held it close, and offered a silent prayer. "We took off our hats," wrote cavalryman Charles Minor Blackford to his wife, "and the young mother leaned her head over the horse's shoulder as if uniting in the prayer."

Blackford wrote that he wished he were a poet or painter so that he could do justice to the "solemn and unusual" scene, but he actually does an excellent job of describing the fading autumn foliage, the destroyed railroad, and "Jackson, the warrior-saint of another era, with the child in his arms, head bowed until his greying beard touching the fresh young hair of the child, pressed close to the shabby coat that had been so well acquainted with death."[7]

Jackson had to have also been thinking of his own situation, apprehension mingling with delightful expectation at the thought that Anna was eight months pregnant. His habitual secrecy applied, of course, and he strictly admonished her to write, rather than telegraph, information of the birth. There must have been something of superstitious dread as well, the fear of announcing the event before he knew the final issue. Some members of his staff did not know he had a daughter until a month after she was born.[8]

Julia Laura Christian Jackson was born on November 23, 1862.

Jackson wrote Anna on December 4, the first sentence of the letter revealing not only his joy and religious fervor, but the worries experienced by a man who had lost his first wife and a child from each marriage: "Oh! how thankful I am to our kind Heavenly Father for having spared my precious wife and given us a little daughter!"[9]

Jackson's first marriage, to Elinor Junkin in 1853, had been a roller coaster of pain and happiness, with odd twists at the beginning and end. In early 1853, then professor and later Confederate general Daniel Harvey Hill received a visit from his close friend Jackson that was anything but ordinary. Instead of their well-worn topics of teaching and religion, Jackson's conversation returned again and again to the subject of Elinor Junkin—Ellie—the daughter of Washington College president George Junkin. "I don't know what has changed me," he said, deeply puzzled. "I used to think her plain but her face now seems to me all sweetness." Hill wasn't puzzled at all. "You are in love!" he said, laughing. "That's what's the matter!"

Jackson pondered the phenomenon the way he would a difficult problem in Natural and Applied Philosophy, the subject that, along with Artillery, he taught at VMI. After determining Hill was right, he decided to get married.

Ellie returned his affection and the couple was soon—secretly, of course—engaged. Then Ellie broke off the engagement under pressure from her sister Margaret—Maggie—who was terrified of losing her best friend. Jackson was devastated. "He was excessively miserable," wrote Hill, "and said to me one day: 'I think it probable that I shall become a missionary and die in a foreign land.'"

Ellie finally found the courage to stand up to Maggie, and she and Jackson were married on August 4, 1853. It was a package deal. Maggie accompanied them on their honeymoon to New York, Niagara Falls, and points north.

Ellie became pregnant not long after their return. She delivered a stillborn son on October 22, 1854, and died almost immediately thereafter.[10] Jackson was disconsolate. Providing mutual support, the bereaved sister and the heartsick widower were drawn together in their sadness—closer than either was prepared for. According to James I. Robertson, "Indications are strong that by the autumn of 1856 each was in love with the other." But what could have ripened into a relationship that transcended grief was blocked by a Presbyterian canon law that forbade the marriage of a bereaved husband to his deceased wife's sister. Jackson, the pious deacon, and Maggie, the daughter of a prominent minister, were both extremely aware of the strictures placed on them by their denomination, and mutually backed away.[11]

Their union is one of the great might-have-beens of American history. While both Ellie and, later, second wife Anna were intelligent and formidable women, Maggie was something else entirely: an influential writer with prestigious publications and a national reputation, all of which was accomplished during a time when a literary career for women was rare and hard to come by.[12] She was as unique in her sphere as Jackson was in his. It's fascinating to speculate how history could have been different if they had not both been such strict Calvinists.

Two emotionally resilient people, both coped. Maggie threw herself into what had to have been a self-sacrificing union with Jackson's professorial colleague, VMI founder John Preston, a widower with seven children. She would forswear her literary career until the emotional intensity of the war brought her back to writing.

Shortly after Ellie died, Jackson tried to finally come to terms with earlier losses by searching out the site of his mother's grave and those of other family members in what is now West Virginia. He also sought solace in religion and religious endeavors, starting his famous Sunday school for African Americans in the fall of 1855. The somewhat controversial effort—it was in defiance of Virginia law[13] and at odds with at least a segment of popular opinion—was extremely successful and continued for many years after his death. Along with his sincere Christianity, the Sunday school highlights the complexity of the man who would later defend slavery as one of the South's greatest generals.

Continuing his efforts for healing and renewal, Jackson went to Europe in the summer of 1856, touring Britain and the Continent for three months. Starting at five in the morning and ending at nine in the evening, he pursued culture with the same avidity with which he would later hunt Yankees. He viewed statues and scenery, architectural gems and ecclesiastical landmarks. Curiously enough, with the exception of Waterloo, few military sites were part of his itinerary.[14]

Not long after his return, he began courting Mary Anna Morrison, another pious and passionate daughter of a college president/Presbyterian minister. Their engagement, secret like the first, culminated in a summer wedding on July 16, 1857. Interestingly, the couple's honeymoon trip paralleled Jackson's first, although this time, of course, no older sister went with them.

Trinity Episcopal Church on Wall Street in New York City was a literal high point of both trips. "The view was indeed grand," wrote Anna, "embracing the whole city—graceful, sparkling rivers; the bay and sound, studded with vessels in motion and at rest; and beautiful rural scenery stretching out as far as the eye could reach."[15]

The spire itself was off-limits during a recent visit to Trinity, which is known to most of us for its role as a refuge during 9/11. I was escorted "behind the scenes" along a labyrinthine path to the bell tower by three church volunteers, who were generous with their time as well as with information.

Trinity was the tallest building in the United States until 1869, and the highest point in New York City until 1883. Now it is dwarfed by surrounding buildings. Looking out through the narrow, neo-Gothic windows, I was able to catch a glimpse, down a shadowy Gotham corridor, of the "graceful, sparkling" water Anna saw in 1857, though nothing at all, of course, of rural countryside.

The main impression from the view today—as it must also have been then—is one of the commercial might of the city and of the United States. Jackson was very familiar with both, before and after his visit to Trinity. He was stationed in New York, at nearby Fort Hamilton, for years, and visited frequently from Lexington, almost up until the opening of hostilities.[16] He knew exactly what the South was up against, the "overwhelming numbers and resources" referenced by Lee in his farewell message to the army after Appomattox.[17]

The numbers were indeed overwhelming: "Just before the Civil War the slave South had a white population of 8,099,674, compared to 18,901,917 in the North." To cite just one example of the North's superior resources: The South had 8,541 miles of railroads in 1860; border states and the North had 22,085.[18]

Small wonder that Jackson was always advocating total war and shock tactics as the South's only hope for victory.

Regional differences are alive and well in both North and South today. When I was growing up in Richmond in the 1950s and '60s, the people I knew who visited New York invariably reported on their trip with a clichéd but heartfelt, "It's a nice place to visit, but I wouldn't want to live there." Or, more emphatically, "I don't see how people live like that."

Most were referring to the overcrowding, the crime, and the lack of simple politeness; but for a sad few, the liberties accorded the city's African Americans were also a factor.

Today, except for the marginal acceptance of the idea that racism is a national rather than a southern problem, not all that much has changed since my youth or, for that matter, since the days of Jackson. North and South are still, as George Bernard Shaw was reputed to have said about Britain and America, two nations separated by a common language.

Though not always that common. I vividly recall a northern acquaintance congratulating me for a story of mine that aired on National Public Radio. After saying she liked it, she put her hand on my arm, lowered her voice, and said pityingly, "Do you know you sound really *southern*?"

Southerners' angst is nothing compared to the howls of anguish I've heard from northern expats over the years. I remember sitting quietly at a party while a New York academic regaled her listeners with tale after tale of southern boorishness. My assertion that I was Virginian—which to a southerner would have stopped her diatribe immediately—did nothing to check the flow.

She was suffering through her tenure in a lucrative professorship at a beautiful campus in western North Carolina. Her final story involved a tearful meltdown in a grocery store parking lot, where even the store's logo was a symbol of regional heinousness: "There were dancing *pigs* on the front of the building!" She called a comrade in the city for support: "I told her I simply couldn't take it anymore," she lamented. "I *had* to come back to New York. She said, 'You can't do that. If you leave now, *they win.*'"

CHAPTER 31

War So Terrible

In northern Virginia, the mighty war machine of the North was creaking into motion yet again. Frustrated with his reluctance to pursue Lee, Lincoln removed McClellan from command on November 5, replacing him with the hirsute Ambrose E. Burnside, who, though he was neither as intelligent nor as capable as McClellan, would at least do what he was told. The resulting disaster, known as the Battle of Fredericksburg, would give Little Mac the best opportunity for anyone during the conflict to say, "I told you so."

Burnside started east, his movements giving notice of his intention to attack. He arrived north of Fredericksburg on November 17, then stopped, waiting for pontoons in order to build bridges over the Rappahannock. By the time they arrived—ten days later—Lee was dug in on the opposite bank, ready and waiting.

Responding to Burnside, Jackson started east from Winchester in late November. While the march was particularly brutal, both soldiers and historians make somewhat less of it than they do of earlier, equally arduous treks. Perhaps the commentators had exhausted their store of adjectives for describing hardship and heroism; maybe the soldiers had become so inured to Jacksonian discipline that another horrendous march was simply routine. Most of them probably agreed with the sentiments Major Andrew Wardlaw of South Carolina penned to his wife earlier that fall: "I must admit that it is much pleasanter to read about

Stonewall & his exploits than to serve under him & perform those exploits."[1]

There was snow, sleet, and freezing rain. The soldiers were so short of blankets that Jackson told Anna to donate theirs as well as the carpets from their Lexington home.[2] Many men were still barefoot. "They could not obtain [shoes]," wrote John Worsham, "and finally orders were issued in Jackson's division, that the men should get the hides of the cattle we daily killed, and make moccasins of them."

It is a sad irony that, the day after Jackson received news of his daughter's birth, he would ride through what would later become the Chancellorsville battlefield, where a few months later he would receive his mortal wound. At the march's end, he would establish headquarters at Guinea Station on the Richmond, Fredericksburg, and Potomac Railroad, the very place where he would spend his final hours.

Jackson was far from the only soldier for whom the journey foreshadowed an untimely end. Close to Chancellorsville were the later battlefields of the Wilderness and Spotsylvania, not to mention the more immediate objective of Fredericksburg. As James Earl Jones says during the video in the park's visitor center, "Of all the southern towns made famous by blood, none would become more famous than Fredericksburg. No population in any community in America would face calamity on a greater scale. The December 1862 Battle of Fredericksburg commenced an eighteen-month ordeal of four battles that left a hundred thousand men killed or wounded. This is the bloodiest landscape in North America."[3]

This sanguinary period started with Lincoln's very understandable urgings of haste, compounded by General-in-Chief Henry Halleck's lackadaisical efforts to get pontoons to Burnside. Then Burnside decided to cross at Fredericksburg, Lee's strongest point on the entire Rappahannock. "Many called [it] the strongest position he ever held."[4]

"[The attack]...was indeed too much to be hoped for," wrote Shelby Foote. "But Lee did hope for it. He hoped for it intensely."[5]

Burnside, on the other hand, hoped that daring to do the obvious, compounded by his superior numbers—115,000 Union versus 78,000 Confederate—would be both surprising and effective.

Anyone stepping outside the battlefield's visitor center today and looking up at the Southern position on Marye's Heights could tell him otherwise, all the while wondering to themselves, "What was he thinking?"

The formidable hill was crowned with superbly sighted-in artillery; near its base, layers of infantry sheltered behind a stone wall. Both infantry and artillery had a veritable shooting gallery: an almost shelterless, gently rising plane that extended some six hundred yards between the heights and the town.

Burnside's main assault would take place downstream, where Jackson and his foot cavalry were waiting on almost equally strong wooded hills. The commander of this sector, General William B. Franklin—who'd clashed with A. P. Hill at Crampton's Gap—was only intermittently aggressive and would soon be working actively against Burnside behind the scenes. Franklin's ambivalence dovetailed perfectly with the ambiguity in Burnside's orders, a vagueness and nonspecificity born of his newness to command. Franklin's decision to undercommit his troops on the left was only one in the series of blunders that upped the death count for the Federals on December 13.

The attack through the town, a "diversion" that took on a deadly life of its own, started while Franklin's halfhearted assaults on Jackson were petering out at midday. On the Federal left, Franklin barely got going; on the right, once he got started, "Bull" Sumner wouldn't stop. Confederates killed Yankees in truly shocking numbers, a testimony to the ineptitude of the Federal commanders as well as to the undeniable bravery of the men in blue.

Construction of the pontoon bridges started the night of December 11. Confederates in the town, Mississippians mostly, under Brigadier General William Barksdale, waited until the Federals had completed about half the structure before opening fire through the misty darkness. The bridge builders retreated, returned, were shot at, then retreated again. The dance went on until midmorning, when a frustrated Burnside called in the artillery. One hundred and fifty cannon pounded the town for two hours. At the end of the bombardment, the pontonniers resumed their work. So did Barksdale's marksmen, who miraculously popped out of the rubble to start picking off the bridge builders once again.

Federals finally manned the pontoon boats with infantrymen who paddled across under fire. After establishing a bridgehead, they fought the Southerners house to house through the town. Meanwhile, downstream, Union carpenters had a better time of it, completing two spans by midmorning.

Burnside crossed a few men immediately. More crossed that night. He could probably still have been successful if he had not moved with such McClellanesque deliberation—Jackson's men were spread out far downriver, anticipating an attack to the southeast, still not believing the Federals would do the most obvious thing. Burnside negated his advantage by sending his men across slowly. He took his time and refined his plan: Franklin would sweep around the Confederate right while Sumner hammered the left. Meanwhile, as Jackson's soldiers hurried to consolidate, idle Federals frolicked through the town, rooting through cellars for fine old wines, burning libraries, dressing up in the abandoned wardrobes of Southern belles, vandalizing and looting with great glee.

Jackson was equally happy the next morning, though for reasons far more grim. He was expecting the Federal tide to break against his all but impregnable defenses. There were some 39,000 men along his two-mile front. Though undeniably outnumbered by Franklin's 60,000, Stonewall was supremely self-confident, "serene and cheerful,"[6] as he awaited the coming storm. He had even donned a new uniform for the occasion. Stuart's beautiful new coat highlighted the ensemble, which was crowned by the hat with gold braid from Anna.

The wardrobe change was so out of character that many of

his soldiers didn't recognize him as he rode along the lines. Others responded with good-natured jibes as well as the usual cheers.

Their jaunty self-confidence was belied by the massing Federals to their front. But when Heros von Borcke expressed apprehension, Jackson replied, "Major, my men sometimes fail *to take* a position, but *to defend* one, never! I am glad the Yankees are coming!"[7]

Those Yankees started coming a little after ten, accompanied by a bombardment that killed so many artillery horses, gunners afterward referred to one part of Jackson's line as "Dead Horse Hill." The foggy December morning was turning into an unseasonably pleasant day. "The sun," wrote G. F. R. Henderson, was "shining out with almost September warmth." Morning mist lifted to reveal "three great lines of battle." Quoting an anonymous eyewitness, Henderson continued: "On they came, in beautiful order, as if on parade, their bayonets glistening in the bright sunlight, which relieved with warm bits of coloring the dull blue of the columns and the russet tinge of the wintry landscape."[8]

The inspiring panoply was soon disrupted by Major John Pelham, of Stuart's horse artillery, who advanced a half mile ahead of the Southern lines with a single cannon and blasted the Union flank. A second cannon joined him but was soon disabled. Employing "the flying artillery tactics that he had perfected"—firing rapidly and nimbly relocating—Pelham disrupted the Union advance for almost two hours. Ordered to withdraw three times by Stuart, Pelham refused to leave until he was out of ammunition. "It is glorious to see such courage in one so young," said Lee,[9] watching through binoculars from high ground near the center of the Confederate lines, a point afterward renamed Lee's Hill.

Pelham's bravery is currently commemorated with a couple of cannon and a state historic marker headed "The Gallant Pelham." The site is disconcertingly located between a Family Dollar and a CVS. If Pelham fired his Napoleon today, he'd take out a line of motorists on the ever-busy Route 17.

Pelham wasn't the only heroic artilleryman in Jackson's sector.

Willy Pegram's gunners were the target of both Union artillery and infantry during the attack. When successive volleys from attacking Federals drove the Southerners from their posts, Pegram draped a Confederate battle flag over his shoulders and walked among the deserted cannon, trying to inspire his men to return.[10]

A. P. Hill had left a six-hundred-yard gap, a projection of marshy woodland he probably considered impregnable. Jackson must have noticed it, as often as he rode the lines. Von Borcke even brought it to Stuart's attention. Jeb didn't think it was vulnerable, standing as it did behind the no-man's-land of converging Southern artillery. It was also backed up by Gregg's South Carolinians.

But it was vulnerable. Forty-five hundred men under George Meade sought refuge there as they swept forward under fire. Finding it undefended, they kept going, shocking Gregg's men who were idling unprepared with muskets stacked. At first, Gregg himself thought the attackers were Confederates. According to the Park Service marker titled "The Death of Maxcy Gregg," "He ordered his South Carolinians, atop this ridge, to hold their fire—a fatal mistake. A Union bullet struck him in the side, piercing his spine. Two days later he died, having assured the governor of his state, 'I yield my life cheerfully, fighting for the independence of South Carolina.'"

It was a crisp fall day when I visited the breakthrough site. The red leaves of an overhanging dogwood contrasted with the yellows and oranges of hardwoods in the woods behind. Although he made a good death, I could not warm to Gregg. He was one of the "Fire Eaters" who brought on the war, so radical that he advocated reopening the Atlantic slave trade.

A Renaissance man, Gregg owned his own observatory and was also an amateur botanist, ornithologist, and linguist. I've always believed that knowledge and intelligence lead inevitably to progressive values. Gregg proves me wrong—as do so many others of the antebellum South's educated elite.

My thoughts shifted, and I imagined someone in the future judging me like I was judging Gregg.

Autumn leaves fell. I pondered the general's likeness on the Park Service marker beside the deserted two-lane road.

The triumph of Meade's Pennsylvanians was short-lived. Confederate counterattacks drove them back. Their retreat turned into a rout after they left the shelter of the woods and again came under fire. Franklin didn't support their efforts going or coming, although he had 40,000 men he could have called on at any point. Meade was furious, and rightly directed his anger at Franklin, who looks even worse when one considers the cheery little messages he had been sending Burnside all morning boasting about his success.

Efforts on the Union right had been under way for some time when Jackson's sector quieted in early afternoon. There is a final word picture of Stonewall deep in prayer as he watched the Federals flee and fall. Staff officer William Williamson witnessed Jackson praying and decided that just being in the vicinity would bring a blessing. "I saw him raise his hand," he wrote later, "& the expression on his face & the gesture so impressed me that I rode on behind him saying to myself, 'I will get the benefit of that prayer.' "[11]

"One of the most ghastly and dramatic assaults of American War" was how Douglas Freeman described the attack on Marye's Heights.[12]

Brigadier General Nathan Kimball's men were first. Already under long-range artillery fire in the town, Federal infantryman Benjamin Borton heard an inspiring speech from Kimball before they advanced onto the plain. "No wild hurrah went up in response," wrote Borton. "Every face wore an expression of seriousness and dread....The artillerymen on the summit are turning their guns upon us....Screeching like demons in the air, solid shot, shrapnel, and shell from the batteries on the hills strike the ground in front of us, behind us, and cut gaps in the ranks."[13]

Massed volleys from Southern infantrymen added to the slaughter from the artillery. The men who survived were pinned down. More assaults followed. "Again they came," wrote Freeman, "again, again, till Confederates lost count of the advances."[14] The futile charges—eighteen of them, according to the visitor center's movie—continued until nightfall. "For seven hours the fighting raged," intones James Earl Jones with majestic sadness, "an average of a thousand men fell each hour."[15]

Wrote one of the wall's defenders: "We waited until they got within about 200 yards of us then rose to our feet and poured volley after volley into their ranks. It had a most deadly effect. Men staggered, reeled, and fell, but the others pushed on. From the wall and road came a living sheet of fire, each one of us fired over one hundred rounds."[16]

The Southerners ran low on ammunition. Rather than resupply them, their officers ordered more men to the wall. Soon they were four deep. Men in the rear loaded muskets and passed them forward. "Their fire was the most rapid and continuous I have ever witnessed," wrote Major General J. B. Kershaw,[17] in charge at the wall after Brigadier General Thomas Cobb was mortally wounded. Soldiers on the firing line complained that their shoulders were bruised from the multiple recoils and sore for many days.[18]

Although sheltered, Confederates also took their share of losses from musket and cannon fire. Cadmus Wilcox wrote that "as many as fifty" artillery rounds a minute were directed at his soldiers behind the wall. In addition, pinned-down Union infantrymen kept the air "swarming with bullets,"[19] as they fired from the few buildings or the scant shelter afforded by low places in the ground.

Southern suffering was slight compared to that of the Federals. "All that day we watched the fruitless charges, their fearful slaughter, until we were sick at heart," wrote Alexander Hunter. He continued, more thoughtfully, "I forgot they were enemies and only remembered they were men, and it is hard to see in cold blood brave men die."[20]

"It can hardly be in human nature for men to show more valor, or generals to manifest less judgment, than were perceptible on our side that day," wrote a correspondent for the *Cincinnati Commercial*. Quoting him, historian Douglas Freeman said there was "much truth and little exaggeration" in the statement.[21]

There was a final charge when the light had almost gone. Confederates guided their fire by the flashes from the Union guns. Then, finally, it stopped. "It was a night of dreadful suffering," wrote Union major general Darius N. Couch. "Many died of wounds and exposure, and as fast as men died they stiffened in the wintry air, and on the front line were rolled forward for protection to the living. Frozen men were placed for dumb sentries."[22]

Jackson slept fitfully. Boteler, sharing his tent, wrote of how he was awakened when Jackson rose to pray and read his Bible in the early morning hours. Feigning sleep, Boteler surreptitiously watched as Jackson stood a book on end in front of a candle to shield his friend's eyes from the light.

Hunter McGuire reported to Jackson around 4 a.m. He told him Gregg was suffering and sinking rapidly. Jackson rode to see the dying general at a nearby home called Belvoir. In a manner reminiscent of his stormy relationship with A. P. Hill, the two had clashed previously, and Gregg had recently written something to Jackson he thought offensive. The dying man spoke of it when the general went in to see him. Jackson stopped Gregg's protestations and took his hand. "The doctors tell me that you have not long to live," he said. "Let me ask you to dismiss this matter from your mind, and to turn your thoughts to God and to the world to which you go."

Gregg began to cry. "I thank you," he said. "I thank you very much." He died the following day.

Jackson was silent on the way back to headquarters. Then he stopped, looked up at the sky, and said, "How horrible is war!"

"Horrible yes!" said McGuire. "But we have been invaded. What else can we do?"

"Kill them, sir!" said Jackson. "Kill every man."

In what was probably the most famous statement of his career, spoken as he watched Meade's men streaming out of the woods when they were repulsed following the breakthrough, Lee commented: "It is well that war is so terrible—we should grow too fond of it." Later, he displayed no fondness at all when writing to his wife: "But what a cruel thing is war; to separate and destroy families and friends, and mar the purest joys and happiness God has granted us in this world; to fill our hearts with hatred instead of love for our neighbors, and to devastate the fair face of this beautiful world!"[23]

In a macabre twist, the color of the killing field itself had changed the following morning. Wrote Shelby Foote: "The ground in front of the sunken road, formally carpeted solid blue, had taken on a mottled hue, with patches of startling white. Binoculars disclosed the cause. Many of the Federal dead had been stripped stark naked by shivering Confederates, who had crept out in the darkness to scavenge the warm clothes from the bodies of men who needed them no more."[24]

That night there was a display of the northern lights, an extremely rare sight so far south, taken by some Southerners to be a heavenly blessing of their victory.

The following day, the Confederates fortified and prepared for renewed attacks that never came. Burnside pulled out the night of the fifteenth, under cover of a fierce rainstorm. His army, along with his bridges, was gone when the Southerners reconnoitered on December 16.

Cavalryman W. W. Blackford and two of his brothers were among the first into the town. Exploring, they went to their boyhood home, the house where their uncle had lived before the battle. His collections of rare books and art had been looted; the house had been used as a hospital. "The room in which we were born was [a] half inch deep in clotted blood still wet, and the walls were spattered with it, and all around were scattered legs and arms." They found out later that there was a dead sniper in the attic. "His body was not found for weeks in that dark, lonely place."[25]

It was a sparsely touristed day in early November. I exited the Fredericksburg NPS visitor center into a balmy eighty-degree-plus afternoon and looked up at the terraced hillside of Marye's Heights, now a national cemetery. According to a marker: "Of the 15,243 interments of Federal soldiers from the Civil War era, only 2,437 are known."

The slanting sunlight, "shining out with almost September warmth," showed the air above the graveyard filled with thousands of tiny dancing motes of light. Normally I would have seen whatever they were as a curiosity, pretty rather than spooky, but since I'd been meditating for hours on "the bloodiest landscape in North America," I was reminded instead of the Upside Down from the popular Netflix series *Stranger Things*. The Upside Down is a sinister companion dimension that exists concurrent with ours. Floating motes and slime are only one small part of it. "It is a place of decay and death...a place of monsters.... It is right next to you and you do not even see it."

That's certainly one definition of the Civil War past, and for a split second, I thought I might slip backward into it. I looked at the stone wall and imagined Confederates four deep, shooting until their shoulders hurt, slaughtering wave after wave of charging Yankees so desperate for cover they were using the dead bodies of their fellow soldiers as shields.

Then I came to myself and walked over to investigate. The gossamer motes were actually flying ants. They were emerging from invisible holes in the hillside, from a space about as big as a manhole cover, spreading their wings, and being wafted off on a breeze so gentle I could barely feel it on my face.

The final figure for the Union killed and wounded at the Battle of Fredericksburg was 12,653; for the Confederates, 5,309.[26] The armies went into winter quarters not long afterward.

CHAPTER 32

A Piece of Gold Braid

Jackson wouldn't settle in quite yet. There was a report that Burnside was forcing a passage downstream. Lee sent Stuart to observe. Jackson started southeast with the II Corps to resist. They had only been marching a short while when Stuart dispatched a message saying it was a false alarm. Jackson had to reverse course. In order to lead, he had to ride through four miles of soldiers. They cheered him the entire way.

"Men suffering from cold, hunger, and weariness forgot their miseries at the sight of Old Jack and added their voices to the acclimation," wrote James I. Robertson. "It was a grand moment never to be forgotten. Jackson was at the zenith of his career."[1]

The staff found a place to bivouac that evening, but importuned their leader to instead let them go to one of the comfortable plantation homes nearby. Jackson refused. The Hero of the South, at the zenith of his career, would sleep on the wet, cold ground.

The staff built a roaring fire beneath a big poplar tree and settled in as best they could. "Men and horses went to bed supperless," wrote aide James Power Smith. "It was not long before the general asked if I had any biscuits in my haversack. I regret now to say that it was with extreme pleasure that I told him I had none."

The two wrapped themselves in their overcoats and tried to sleep between a couple of saddle blankets. "After awhile Jackson stirred and sat up, saying he was cold and hungry." At almost the same moment, the tree, weakened by the flames, fell into the fire, scattering hot coals in every direction.

Smith's silent opprobrium, along with the dramatic rejection by Nature herself, caused Jackson to bend a little when Hunter McGuire appeared shortly thereafter. The surgeon had prewar connections with Moss Neck. He rode to the nearby plantation, returning with a basket of biscuits and part of a ham. The hungry soldiers feasted. "The couriers were called in, and we had quite a merry time by the fire."

Afterward, Old Jack tried to sleep again on the frozen ground. He stood it for half an hour until thoughts of a warm bed won out. He rose and said quietly, "Captain, let's go to the 'Moss Neck' house." Adds Smith: "I almost dared to say 'I told you so!' "

After a comfortable night, Mrs. Corbin, the mistress of Moss Neck, extended an invitation to Jackson to use the house as his headquarters. Instead, he returned to his spartan ways, pitching his tents nearby. One of the first things he did after settling in was to ask his soldiers for donations for the citizens of Fredericksburg. His appeal netted an astonishing $30,000, which he presented to the mayor of the town a week later.

When Jackson decided to hold a Christmas dinner, the catering duties, which revolved among the staff, fell on James Power Smith. The neighborhood had been generous to the general. Their gifts, supplemented by Smith's considerable scavenging abilities, enabled the aide to provide a sumptuous feast for about a dozen officers including Stuart and Lee. Not one but *three* turkeys, along with oysters, "a splendid ham," fresh-baked biscuits, even a bottle of wine provided fare for a rolling party in the mansion. The entertainment consisted of poking good-natured fun at Jackson. Lee, feigning outrage at the opulence of the meal and the comfort of the accommodations, insisted that Jackson was only playing at being a soldier and should come visit him to see how a soldier ought to live. Stuart was next. The cavalryman made much of the sporting prints on the walls, pretending they had all been selected by Jackson himself. He was shocked—shocked!—to discover the Presbyterian deacon secretly pursuing the pastimes of the Virginia gentry. The bottle of wine furnished more ammunition. The denouement was a "print of butter" stamped with "a gallant rooster." Stuart pronounced solemnly that it was Jackson's coat of arms. "If there is not the crowning evidence of our host's sporting tastes! He even puts his favorite gamecock on his butter!"[2]

Jackson remained under canvas following the party until he developed an earache and McGuire ordered him to move inside, out of the cold. Even then he only consented to occupy a plantation office building rather than Moss Neck itself. It didn't take long for him to develop a friendship with five-year-old Janie Corbin. The child would visit him in the afternoon and play around his feet while he did his paperwork. He always had a small gift for her, an apple or some other treat, and helped her cut out paper dolls, which they called her "Stonewall Brigade." At one point he even removed the gold braid from a cap—the present from Anna, no less—and gave it to her to bind up her hair. "Janie came often," wrote S. C. Gwynne, "and the stern general and the golden-haired girl passed the time happily together, and this continued through the winter."[3]

But all good things must come to an end. Janie and two of her young cousins contracted scarlet fever when Jackson moved his headquarters in mid-March. At first he heard she was out of danger. Then news came that she had died. Jackson "wept freely,"[4] reported James Power Smith. Janie's two cousins died not long after. "Another outburst of tears came when Jackson learned that members of the Stonewall Brigade had made three coffins from part of a fence enclosing the Moss Neck estate."[5]

A particularly onerous part of his duties consisted of writing official battle reports. He had been too busy marching and fighting to do them at the time. To help with the work, Jackson secured the services of Charles J. Faulkner, a former congressman and ambassador to France. While the two generally got along, there was inevitable conflict. Jackson favored prose that was terse and simple, "sparing in praise of both the living and the dead."[6] Faulkner, while hardly flamboyant, was not unopposed to a literary flourish now and then, and he chafed against Jackson's "severe Roman simplicity." Surprisingly, Faulkner often prevailed, probably a result of Jackson turning his attention elsewhere because he found the task of writing and editing so uncongenial.

Believing wholeheartedly in the Cause, Jackson had no trouble upholding severe sentences—even death—for deserters. He also generally denied furloughs, setting an example by not taking time off himself to see his wife and infant daughter. He met his match in unbending stubbornness in A. P. Hill, who continued to agitate for a hearing on Jackson's charges against him. Lee wrote Hill to let the matter drop. "Upon examining the charges in question, I am of [the] opinion that the interests of the service do not require that they be tried." Hill disagreed. The feud continued.[7]

Nationwide, ripples from the Emancipation Proclamation continued to spread. Although Lincoln had definite humanitarian motives in freeing the slaves, there was a practical corollary: Both sides needed blacks for their war efforts. Confederates used impressed slaves for building fortifications as well as all types of manual labor. If they fled to the Union armies and freedom, they did much the same work, although now they were being paid, and their work hurt the South and helped the North.

The North was slow to use African Americans as soldiers. Recruitment was sporadic even after the Proclamation. It picked up because of Union losses and manpower needs, getting fully under way on May 22, 1863, when the U.S. War Department established the Bureau of Colored Troops. These soldiers fought bravely and made a significant contribution to the Union cause. By the end of the war, one-tenth of all Federal soldiers were African American. While the South was far slower to use blacks as soldiers, enlistment and recruitment were actually under way by the end of the conflict.

In the west, the Federals made incremental progress during the winter of 1862–63. Ulysses S. Grant was only one of many generals in that theater, having yet to emerge as the forceful leader Lincoln would bring east to win the war. In Virginia, the Yankees were mostly quiescent until, on January 20, Burnside attempted a flanking maneuver.

The sun was shining when it started. Rain began shortly thereafter and continued steadily for several days. The roads turned to mud. Soldiers floundered through the quagmire. Guns and caissons got stuck and sank; men and animals labored to dislodge them with little result. A hundred or more soldiers would struggle to drag a cannon only to have it threaten to disappear when they let up on the rope. One account mentions the striking silence that descended when "the discordant, unmusical braying of the mules" was checked because they had sunk so deep that "their ears, wafting above the sea of mud, were the only symbol of animal life." Delighted Confederates, fully aware of the top-secret maneuver, shouted helpful suggestions from across the river.[8]

"The Mud March" was Burnside's swan song. He was replaced shortly thereafter by Joseph Hooker—"Fighting Joe." While his aggression was a given, what surprised everyone was his administrative ability. Northern morale, which for many had sunk as low as the storyteller's enmired mules, began to recover.

Jackson worked hard to attend to the spiritual needs of his soldiers. When a Lexington friend, the Reverend B. Tucker Lacy, volunteered his services as a regimental chaplain, Jackson wound up appointing him unofficial chaplain for the entire II Corps. He paid the cleric out of his own pocket and even gave him one of his own horses to use. Lacy worked zealously at his commission, holding prayer meetings and services and supervising other chaplains. Lee and Jackson both attended services; Jackson held daily devotionals. Even if he and Lacy had a prayer meeting together, Jackson would not neglect afterward to complete the personal prayers he always said.[9]

Jackson sometimes corresponded with his father-in-law, Reverend Robert Morrison, on spiritual topics. At one point he floated the idea of a Christian daily newspaper. It would, of course, be printed on Saturday and mailed on Monday so as not to violate the Sabbath. "If such a paper could be established, it might be the means of influencing the future course of our country." He also weighed in to Boteler about a law requiring Sunday delivery of the mails, going so far as to say that God would punish the Confederacy for the violation: "I do not see how a nation that thus arrays itself, by such a law, against God's holy day can expect to escape His wrath."[10]

While such a belief seems quaint, even laughable, in the secular present, the concern of Jackson for his family is completely understandable. A steady stream of letters traveled between Anna in North Carolina and Jackson in Virginia—though of course, never on Sunday. They are gentle and touching. He is ecstatic over a lock of the baby's hair, worried to a frazzle over a bout of the chicken pox, and always, always hoping to arrange a visit: "How I do want to see you and our darling baby!"[11]

The stars finally aligned on April 20, 1863. The visit would be one of his happiest interludes in the war, if not his entire life. The couple spent nine days together in a spacious second-story room at Belvoir, Confederate civilian J. B. Yerby's hilltop mansion, sadly well known to Jackson because of his earlier visit to Maxcy Gregg's deathbed. It was the first time Jackson saw his daughter, the five-month-old Julia.

Jackson met the train at Guinea Station in pouring rain. "His face was all sunshine and gladness," Anna wrote years later. He didn't hold Julia. "He was afraid to take her in his arms, with his wet overcoat; but as we rode in the carriage to Mr. Yerby's, his face reflected all the happiness and delight that was in his heart."

Behind closed doors at Belvoir, he took off his raincoat and took up the child. "He caressed her with the tenderest affection, and held her long and lovingly."

The mansion was only a mile from headquarters. Jackson continued working while the three were together, leaving before dawn and returning for family time in the afternoon.

The days slipped by pleasantly: Friends and acquaintances called; General Lee paid his respects; the baby was baptized.

A photographer came up from Richmond and prevailed on the general to sit for his portrait, one of only two taken during the war. The first is famous for his having a misplaced button on his coat. He stares full in the camera, and Anna said it "has more of the beaming sunlight of his *home-look*." The second was taken at Belvoir. Anna arranged his hair, "which was unusually long for him, and curled in large ringlets." Jackson looks off into the distance with an expression that could mean anything, but which Anna finds severe: "A strong wind blew in his face, causing him to frown, and giving a sternness to his countenance which was not natural."[12]

The family worshipped together on Sunday, April 26, in a solemn outdoor service. About a thousand Confederates attended. "In front of the tent, under the canopy of heaven, were spread out in dense masses the soldiers, either sitting on benches or standing," wrote Anna. Generals Kershaw, Early, and Lee were also there. "I remember how reverent and impressive was General Lee's bearing, and how handsome he looked, with his splendid figure and faultless military attire."

Afterward, the Jacksons spent a quiet afternoon together. "His conversation was more spiritual than I ever observed before," wrote Anna. For the deeply religious Jackson, that must have been spiritual indeed.

Then it was over. They were awakened before dawn on April 29 by a messenger from General Early. "That looks as if Hooker were crossing," said Jackson. He said a quick goodbye and hurried off to headquarters. Anna and the baby were to take the train south to Richmond. Jackson would send Reverend Lacy to help them get away.

"Scarcely had he gone when the roar of cannons began—volley

after volley following in quick succession—the house shaking and the windows rattling from the reverberations, throwing the family into great panic, and causing the wildest excitement among all the occupants of the place."

The house would function as a hospital during the battle. The first wounded soldiers were being brought into the yard as Anna left.[13]

CHAPTER 33

Moss Neck and Belvoir

Moss Neck, site of the fabled Christmas party and home to young Janie Corbin, was open for Garden Week. The woman in period dress at the entrance table would not sell me a single ticket, so I grudgingly sprang for the whole deal—forty-five dollars—which allowed access to "five magnificent properties" plus lunch. I consoled myself that it was for a good cause, though the thrifty Jackson would have been horrified.

The house has a central two-story section with white pillars and a veranda—where you could easily imagine Rhett and Scarlett sipping juleps—along with a couple of matching wings called "hyphens." The previous owners had done a $2.5 million restoration, then sold it to the W. H. D. Koerner family, who own it today. The Koerners have lots of impressive art and even more impressive friends. A hoop-skirted reenactor proudly pointed out the piano—she pronounced it "peeanner"—played by former secretary of state Condoleezza Rice during a recent visit. There was more about Rice and almost nothing about Stonewall as I toured through, although I was able to ascertain that the dining room with the giant table and stunning Garden Club flower arrangement was *the* dining room where Lee, Jackson, and Stuart had Christmas dinner in 1862.

"The party started in the office where Jackson was staying, then moved inside to the dining room and the parlor," said NPS historian Frank O'Reilly. Organizers had placed him at the end of one of the hyphens as a sort of afterthought. The office where Jackson actually spent the winter has vanished, he continued. It fell into disrepair, then was replaced by some tennis courts that are now themselves gone.

I thanked him and walked across the yard to stare reverently at the empty space where Jackson had lived, worked, and befriended little Janie Corbin, when I was startled to see an ape climbing the bars of a giant cage. Although I'm no wildlife expert, I think it was an orang-utan, and I have to confess that, for the moment, my curiosity about it eclipsed my interest in Jackson.

"We're actually asking the public not to go any farther," said a no-nonsense woman who appeared at my elbow. I tried to sweet-talk her, saying "the historian" had sent me to look for Jackson's office, but she shooed me away emphatically, saying Jackson's office had been in the backyard anyway. I believed O'Reilly rather than her, but argument was clearly futile, and I was left to nurse my regrets at not having stood on the actual ground, not to mention unanswered questions about the Koerners' exotic pet.

I did another turn through the house, trying to imagine the Christmas party from long ago. O'Reilly was being buttonholed by a war bore when I exited. I saw his look of patience, overheard "Gettysburg," and, knowing it was not going to be a short conversation, went off in search of a bathroom. There was only one big port-a-potty for the whole event, hundreds of people. Eavesdropping during the twenty-minute wait, I realized the well-heeled young couple behind me had been to at least two dozen houses. They were following Garden Week around Virginia the way people used to follow the Grateful Dead.

Belvoir burned in 1910. Only a ruin remains today. John Hennessy, the Fredericksburg battlefield's chief historian/chief of interpretation, was kind enough to show me the site. It's on private property, but he has standing permission from the owners to visit.

He hadn't been there in five years. The entrance he was accustomed to using was no longer available. He emailed that we'd come in by another way he was unfamiliar with: "We'll have to bushwhack."

"That's fine," I confidently emailed back. "I'm used to being in the woods."

As soon as we started I realized I wasn't as used to it as I used to be. My sedate mile or two on the Vita Course hadn't prepared me for scrambling over logs, up hills, and down into and out of ravines. Hennessy started off with mighty strides. I was soon huffing and puffing trying to keep up.

"So what is this book you're working on?" he asked over his shoulder.

"Basically, I'm trying to go places Jackson lived and fought and see what they're like today," I panted. "And parallel that with his story. Hopefully, I can be fresh and insightful with both. I'm also hoping the writing is better than standard history. I've been to some incredible places…"

I trailed off as we slid down into an old railroad bed and climbed out by grasping tree branches. "Well," said Hennessy at the top, "Belvoir is also a really incredible place."

There were no discernable landmarks after the railroad bed. As we wandered through thick woods, one knoll blended with another. I bobbed my head as I walked, looking down so I wouldn't step in one of the numerous relic hunters' holes, then up so as not to lose Hennessy.

"The vegetation has changed," he said thoughtfully, surveying our surroundings from the crest of a little hill. He must have perceived I was overextended: "Wait here." I marveled at how quickly his green Park Service uniform blended into the trees. And by the time I caught my breath, I could no longer hear his footsteps.

Alone, I felt oddly content. I sardonically quoted Lord Byron: "There is a pleasure in the pathless woods…" Then I amused myself by thinking there were worse ways to die than by having a heart attack on a history quest.

Hennessy reappeared. "Not over there," he said unnecessarily. We chatted briefly while he pondered our next move. I felt better about my level of fitness when he mentioned that cycling, hiking, and running were among his hobbies.

We explored in another direction. A couple of knolls later, we found a barely discernable track. "Is this *a* road, or *the* road?" he mused. *The* road went past Belvoir; *a* road could go anywhere. "Wait here," he said, again striding off.

The path he explored turned out to be *a* road. We found *the* road a half hour later. "It's either this way or that way," he said. I couldn't tell if he was trying to be funny.

First we went this way. Then we went that way and found it.

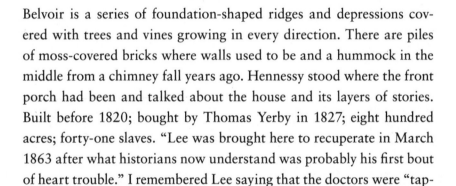

Belvoir is a series of foundation-shaped ridges and depressions covered with trees and vines growing in every direction. There are piles of moss-covered bricks where walls used to be and a hummock in the middle from a chimney fall years ago. Hennessy stood where the front porch had been and talked about the house and its layers of stories. Built before 1820; bought by Thomas Yerby in 1827; eight hundred acres; forty-one slaves. "Lee was brought here to recuperate in March 1863 after what historians now understand was probably his first bout of heart trouble." I remembered Lee saying that the doctors were "tapping me all over like an old steam boiler before condemning it."

Hennessy described the death of Maxcy Gregg after being wounded in the fighting on December 13; Jackson's blissful interlude with Anna and Julia; the famous photograph; Belvoir as a hospital; and the party held here for Ewell when he returned to the army after recuperating from his wounding at Second Manassas. It was a swank affair, I read later in a monograph Hennessy wrote on Belvoir, featuring "a delicious repast" and attended by "the flower of Virginia aristocracy." Some partygoers stayed up all night. Mr. Yerby sent them out mint juleps at dawn as they lounged on the porch. "These," one woman remembered, "helped us out until breakfast."[1]

I was moved by two other thumbnails from his monograph, both relating to Belvoir's time as a hospital. The first concerns Lieutenant

W. W. Cloninger, of the 28th North Carolina, who was wounded and brought to the yard on December 13. After some time without treatment, he called a friend to him and asked him why he had been neglected so long. Recounted a fellow soldier: "When told that he was mortally wounded, and the Surgeons considered it their first duty to attend to those whose lives might be saved, he replied, 'If I must die, I will let you all see that I can die like a man.' Folding his arms across his breast, that hero, far away from his loved ones, lay under that tree in Yerby's yard, and, without a murmur, quietly awaited death."

The second was a simple detail about how the first-floor parlor was a particular scene of suffering. "So many wounded were brought in this room that the floor was stained so that thereafter it had to be covered with carpet."[2]

They were worried about covering the bloodstains; now the floor itself is gone.

It was like visiting a physical parable on the passage of time. Gaiety, suffering, happiness, death—this is what all our passionate strivings come to in the end, returning to nature, like Belvoir itself. Even the "beautiful view" it's named for is barely visible through the undergrowth.

"All glory is fleeting," George Patton famously said at the end of the best war movie ever made. He neglected to add that so is everything else.

I took Hennessy's picture standing where the front porch used to be and thanked him for the tour. We chatted some more. Then I followed him as, completely oriented now, he made a beeline through the woods toward the parking lot. At the edge of the trees he tapped his Fitbit: "Four miles."

I thanked him again. We shook hands and said goodbye.

Thomas J. "Stonewall" Jackson, the elusive subject of this book. The photograph is from the Jacksons' nine-day idyll at Belvoir in April 1863. His wife, Anna, persuaded him to pose, and years later she remembered: "He sat in the hall of the house, where a strong wind blew in his face, causing him to frown, and giving a sternness to his countenance which was not natural." The photograph was taken a month before he died *(Library of Congress)*

Mary Anna and Julia, Jackson's wife and daughter, in a postwar photograph. "The pleasure he found in domestic life was almost pathetic," wrote a historian. Understandable when you consider the extent of his earlier losses: both parents and a brother before he was six; a brother in his teens; and, later, his first child and first wife, followed by the first child of his second marriage. The stern general was playful and loving in his home life, calling his wife pet names in Spanish that originated from his time in the Mexican War. He knew his daughter, Julia, only briefly before he died. *(Virginia Military Institute Archives)*

Belvoir. A comfortable plantation house in its heyday, Belvoir burned down about 1910. It was the scene of both gay parties and hospital horrors. Robert E. Lee convalesced here, Confederate general Maxcy Gregg died here, and Jackson spent what may have been the happiest days of his wartime life here: a little over a week with his wife and infant daughter. On private property in deep woods, a fallen chimney and fragments of the foundation are all that remain today, a physical parable on the passage of time. *(Courtesy of the Fredericksburg & Spotsylvania National Military Park, U.S. National Park Service)*

Robert E. Lee. There was a synergy between Lee and Jackson: The whole was greater than the sum of its parts. A study in contrasts—the Tidewater patrician and the mountain-born Puritan—they were nevertheless of one mind when it came to fighting. Lee was never as effective after Jackson's death.

The photograph shows a pugnacious Lee in Richmond shortly after Appomattox. One historian compared Lee in retreat to "an old gray wolf wanting nothing more than half a chance to turn on whoever or whatever tried to crowd him as he fell back." *(Library of Congress)*

James Ewell Brown "Jeb" Stuart. The improbable friendship between cavalryman Stuart, the most colorful and flamboyant man in either army, and Jackson, the most austere, was much remarked upon. Stuart wore a red-lined cape, yellow sash, and an ostrich plume in his slouch hat. Jackson was rumpled, his VMI cadet cap invariably described as "mangy." Stuart's entourage included a banjo player; Jackson's, a clergyman. Both men were teetotalers, deeply religious, and, as far as fighting went, highly effective. *(Library of Congress)*

Richard Ewell. Perhaps as much of a character as Jackson, he confided to Richard Taylor, a fellow general, that he was equally convinced of Stonewall's genius as of his lunacy and "never saw one of Jackson's couriers approach without expecting an order to assault the north pole." Like Jackson, Ewell was a dyspeptic who suffered through sleepless nights with indigestion. He was also, like Jackson, a fearless fighter. Well liked, he was also admired. Concluded Taylor: "Virginia never bred a truer gentleman, a braver soldier, nor an odder, more loveable fellow." *(Library of Congress)*

White's Ford on the Potomac. The Confederates cheered and gave the Rebel yell when they crossed here in September 1862, headed north. It was "a magnificent sight," wrote a cavalryman, who spoke poetically of bands playing and the setting sun burnishing the waters with gold. He added: "I little thought that in a short time I should recross the river into Virginia, under circumstances far different and far less inspiring." Intervening was Antietam, "the bloodiest day in United States history," a stalemate followed by a retreat. *(Author Photo)*

The Stonewall Jackson Shrine, off I-95 between Richmond and Fredericksburg. Jackson died here on May 10, 1863.

Gray and wet "Confederate weather" prevailed on many of my trips following Jackson, and this day was no exception. Rain from a nearby hurricane held off long enough for me to tour the shrine. Returning to the parking lot, I pushed a button in a brick column to hear a recording. It was as if the button started the rain, which came down suddenly in torrents, soaking me thoroughly before I could run to my car. *(Author Photo)*

CHAPTER 34

The Fallen Sword

Hooker was across the Rappahannock. Like a good boxer, feinting with his left to set up a hard right, "Fighting Joe" had crossed at Fredericksburg with a small but significant force while an almost simultaneous crossing with larger numbers was made upstream. Those upstream soldiers marched rapidly eastward down the south bank of the river, brushing aside resistance at the fords and opening them for crossings by yet more Federals. Their goal was to flank Lee, if not actually get behind him, then fight him in the open where their overwhelming advantage in men and matériel would come to bear. If the Confederates didn't retreat they would be crushed, vise-like, between the two wings of the Union army.

But first the Federals had to get through the Wilderness, a scrubby, tangled confusion of second-growth trees and briery underbrush. Their intermediate objective, Chancellorsville, was about midway. In spite of its name, Chancellorsville was a house rather than a village, standing in a clearing of roughly a hundred acres. It was the picture of a stately Southern mansion, complete with pillars, outbuildings, slaves—though almost all of them had fled to the Yankees by the time of the battle—and fiery secessionist females who had just been partying with Jeb Stuart[1] and would taunt the invading Federals that General Lee was just ahead waiting to offer them "the hospitality of the country."[2]

The situation was anything but clear to the Confederates. Where was Hooker and what was he doing? Still, Jackson was aggressive, energetic, and totally in character as the Southerners tried to understand the situation.

"Hold my horse," he told Jim Lewis before going alone into his tent. Lewis's long acquaintance allowed him to immediately discern what was going on.

"Hush!" he commanded. "The General is praying!"

Excited conversations of nearby soldiers respectfully ceased. A few reverent minutes later, Jackson emerged from his tent and rode off to join Lee.[3]

The two reconnoitered Union positions around Fredericksburg. As usual, Jackson's impulse was to attack. Lee demurred but then urged Jackson to study the situation. "If you think it can be done," he said, "I will give orders for it."

Jackson spent a rainy afternoon studying the 44,000 Union troops facing him as well as the ground on which he'd have to fight. "It would be inexpedient to attack here," he finally reported. By then Lee had another idea. It was obvious now that the main Union thrust was coming southeast along the Rappahannock. He sent Jackson and his men west to the Wilderness.

And here was the first of the long-shot gambles of Chancellorsville: Lee directed Jackson to detach 10,000 of his men to hold in place a Union force that outnumbered it by more than four to one. In the face of vastly superior numbers—Hooker totaled 135,000 against Lee's 55,000[4]—he divided his army. And he would do it again, just two days later, in even more dramatic form.

Confederate generals Anderson and McLaws were already in place east of Chancellorsville. Jackson arrived at Anderson's position around 8:30 a.m. following a night march. He had dug in on some high ground, Anderson reported, after encountering the enemy. Immediately dismissing the defensive, Jackson ordered him to abandon his entrenchments and advance on Chancellorsville. The Confederates, outnumbered five to one on this part of the field, attacked. Spirited fighting ensued. Then something strange happened: The Federals began to retreat.

Hooker had the men and the momentum, yet he suddenly surrendered the initiative, ordering his soldiers to fall back to Chancellorsville. He had been stunned by Jackson's attack—but this was only the final straw in a reversal that has puzzled historians ever since. Was it the Lee/Jackson mystique, abstract north of the river but more and more palpable the closer Hooker came to an actual battle? This was, after all, Lee, along with Stonewall Jackson and the army that had defeated every Union commander Lincoln sent against it. The list may have ticked through Hooker's mind: McDowell, removed after the debacle of First Bull Run; the charismatic McClellan, a brilliant organizer but diffident fighter; Pope, brash and arrogant, banished to the Dakotas after Second Bull Run; then McClellan again, in and out for Antietam's bloody stalemate; then Burnside, doing exactly what Lee expected and wanted at Fredericksburg—and finally Hooker himself. Why should he fare better than the others?

Or could it have had something to do with the fact that for the duration of the campaign, Hooker had famously forsworn whiskey? Did the unaccustomed internal clarity throw him off his game?[5]

Muddying the waters, there are some, including soldiers who were near him on the field, who asserted that Hooker *was* drunk.[6]

Probably the most important factor was the Wilderness itself. Unpleasant, hard to navigate, and disorienting, the tightly woven vines and trees augmented the fog of war, placing an almost impenetrable screen between Hooker and the actual situation on the battlefield. It allowed his imagination free rein; he took counsel of his fears.

The order to pull back surprised his generals. "Hurrah for old Joe!" the normally undemonstrative Meade exalted when the Union advance seemed to be sweeping inexorably forward. Then, when ordered to abandon an advantageous position he had reached while encountering no resistance, he grumbled, "If we can't hold the top of a hill, we certainly can't hold the bottom of it."

Others were angrier. Washington Roebling, who in postwar years would complete his father's work of building the Brooklyn Bridge, was sent from headquarters by Hooker with urgent orders to

General Henry Slocum to halt his advance and return with his soldiers to Chancellorsville. "Roebling, you are a dammed liar!" Slocum snapped furiously. "Nobody but a crazy man would give such an order when we have victory in sight!"

The skeptical Slocum rode back to headquarters himself for personal clarification, telling Roebling as he left, "If I find that you have spoken falsely, you shall be shot on my return." Slocum remonstrated with Hooker in vain. Within the hour he returned to begin his retreat, glaring at Roebling as he did so.[7]

From the beginning, Hooker had hoped that the Confederates would pull back—didn't Lee realize he was outnumbered two to one by this magnificent army?—or square off for a mano a mano on open ground where numbers would prove decisive. Now he abandoned both. He dug in, entrenching around Chancellorsville, hoping the Confederates would make a full frontal assault like Burnside's disastrous attack at Fredericksburg just four months before.

"Hope the enemy will be emboldened to attack me," he telegraphed General Daniel Butterfield. "I did feel certain of success."[8]

The discerning reader will note the past tense in the second sentence. Years later, General Couch wrote that at about this point, he knew that Hooker was "a whipped man."[9]

Lee and Jackson didn't waste time trying to analyze the reasons for the reversal. They accepted the gift at face value and prepared for the offensive.

Their May 1 rendezvous was at the intersection of the Orange Plank and Furnace roads, a spot known today as "The Lee Jackson Bivouac." The site is less evocative than it could be because of relentless traffic on what is now called the "Old Plank" Road. Still, you can catch your first glimpse of what the Wilderness must have been like in 1863. Stepping off the path, the going is rough through bushes, vines, and saplings. There's a plethora of greenbrier, fallen trees with

waist-high root balls—no wonder the Yankees thought the Confederates couldn't force their way through.

Park Service placards provide helpful narrative and art. My favorite painting shows Lee and Jackson, seated on cracker boxes discarded
during the Union retreat, earnestly plotting Hooker's destruction.

At first, Jackson misread the situation. Having fought retreating
Federals all day, he thought Hooker would pull back, recrossing the
Rappahannock to safety. "By tomorrow," he said definitively, "there
will not be any of them this side of the river." Lee disagreed, but he
sent out engineers to survey the strength of the Federals to their front.
His own thoughts were turning toward the Union right.

Then Jeb Stuart rode up to report that Hooker's right was dan-
gling "in the air"—anchored to no natural feature and vulnerable to
just the sort of flanking movement that Jackson found most congenial. Here then was the plan: Jackson would move swiftly and secretly
through the Wilderness and hit the Union right.

The engineers' report, received not long afterward, underlined
the correctness of this decision: Vast numbers of Federals were solidly
entrenched around Chancellorsville, their strength augmented with
artillery. Yes, the attack must be made on the right. But how could the
Confederates move quickly to that part of the battlefield without being
seen? Did the roads even exist that would make it possible?

Lee sat on the cracker box, staring at a rough map in the moonlight, speaking aloud the question in his mind: "How can we get at
these people?"

Jeb Stuart scouted; locals were awakened and quizzed. Details of
the route came together slowly through the night.

Jackson's aide, James Power Smith, tells of waking Lee to deliver
a report, then lying down himself to sleep with saddle and saddle blanket for pillow and bed: "Some time after midnight I was awakened
by the chill of the early morning hours, and, turning over, caught a
glimpse of a little flame on the slope above me, and looking up to see
what it meant I saw, bending over a scant fire of twigs, two men seated

on old cracker boxes and warming their hands over the little fire. I had but to rub my eyes and collect my wits to recognize the figures of Robert E. Lee and Stonewall Jackson. Who can tell the story of that quiet council of war between two sleeping armies?"[10]

Jackson was up before dawn. Colonel Armistead Long, of Lee's staff, saw him and made conversation. Warming his hands over the fire, Jackson complained of the cold. Long was able to get him a cup of coffee. The two continued talking. Then "the general's sword, which was leaning against a tree, without *apparent* cause fell with a clank to the ground."

Long was rattled: "It strongly impressed me at the time as an omen of evil—an indefinable superstition such as sometimes affects persons upon the falling of a picture or mirror. This feeling haunted me the whole day, and when the tidings of Jackson's wound reached my ears, it was without surprise that I heard this unfortunate confirmation of the superstitious fears with which I had been so oppressed."[11]

Lee arrived about dawn. Jackson's mapmaker, Jed Hotchkiss, rode up. He had conferred with locals, found a route, and sketched it on a map, which he placed on another cracker box between the two generals. The soldiers would march about twelve miles. It was not so far that it would exhaust them for battle, and, mostly, they'd be concealed.

The two studied the map. "General Jackson, what do you propose to do?" asked Lee.

The question had to be rhetorical, formalizing what they had already discussed around the small campfire just hours before.

Jackson traced the Hotchkiss route with his finger. "Go around here," he said.

"What do you propose to make this movement with?"

While Lee must have known the answer to his first question, he was probably surprised by the reply to the second.

"With my whole Corps."

Twenty-eight thousand men.

Though it is unreported, there must have been a pause. Then Lee, thinking aloud again, asked for information he already knew: "What will you leave me?"

"The Divisions of Anderson and McLaws."

Fourteen thousand soldiers. Outnumbered two to one, the Confederates would be divided into thirds: Early, holding Sedgwick in check at Fredericksburg; Jackson strung out and vulnerable on the march; and Lee with his 14,000, his head in the lion's mouth, between two wings of the Union army that could crush him at any time.

No hesitation was recorded: "Well," he told Jackson, "go on."[12]

Jackson got his men moving. He passed Lee at the bivouac around 7:30 a.m. They spoke, but no one heard what they said. Jackson pointed west, in the direction of his moving column, then rode on.

The Park Service preserves a little over four miles of Jackson's route. Of course, it's possible to walk the entire twelve, and if you did, you could somewhat reenact the experience of battle by dodging automobiles instead of bullets. To me, it's much more evocative to restrict my walking to the Jackson Trail.

It's a woodland road, unpaved and lightly traveled. I've walked all or part of it many times. The last was not atypical: I saw about as many deer as cars, less than a dozen of each. There are scattered houses and farms—and one jarring subdivision—but it's mostly just you and the woods, the walk a moving meditation "in the footsteps of history."

Sometimes I boyishly pretended to be one of Jackson's soldiers, marching tired and thirsty through the heat of the day, apprehensive yet confident. The experience was deepened for me when I thought of my ancestor who was with Jackson. Martin White, with the 1st North Carolina, was near the front of the ten-mile-long column.

I sat on a mossy bridge and ate a sandwich, then closed my eyes and tried to force a time slip. I opened my eyes. No Confederates, just a fine brisk afternoon.

Resuming my walk, I mused on the many lessons of Chancellorsville. The synergy of Lee and Jackson: how each one was vastly more effective when working with the other; also, how history intervened in their lives, raising them from relative obscurity to mythic status in a few short years. Lee would have remained a highly respected military man, but at best a historical footnote. Jackson would have continued doting on his family, fretting about his digestion, and driving generations of VMI cadets crazy. War brought out what they were both really good at: killing people.

Hooker is also a parable. In spite of all evidence to the contrary, he firmly believed the Confederates were retreating. That's what he wanted, so that's the way things had to be. Today we'd say he was in denial.

Concealing 28,000 men so close to the enemy was a little like trying to hide an elephant in your living room. Observed by scores of Federals, the reports went up the chain of command, then came back down again with the reassurance that the Confederates were actually leaving.

Incredibly, "Fighting Joe" himself seemed aware of what was really happening that morning. "We have good reason to suppose that the enemy is moving to our right," he wrote Slocum and Howard, his generals in the vicinity, at 9:30 a.m.[13] He directed them to be ready for a flank attack—yet his moment of clarity vanished. He didn't follow up. Howard posted only a token force, along with a couple of cannon, and by late afternoon, Hooker lapsed back into the idea that Lee was retreating. A little after four o'clock, he urged Sedgwick to take Fredericksburg: "We know the enemy is fleeing, trying to save his trains."[14]

It is also noteworthy that he wanted Sedgwick to attack rather than taking on Lee himself.

Not far from the small bridge there's a wayside exhibit discussing one of the Union forays against the "retreating" Confederates. A five-pointed star, denoting the Bloods gang, is scratched into several places on the metal. Why are they tagging out here? Drug deals on the battlefield? A good place to dump a body? There's certainly been bodies here before...

I wondered what Jackson would have made of our present-day

proliferation of gangs. I chuckled, imagining him trying to recruit some of my former students for his Sunday school.

Before retiring in 2016, I spent twelve years teaching teenagers—mostly African American—in a juvenile prison. A day didn't go by when I wasn't painfully confronted by the consequences of poverty and neglect, the legacy of the slavery that Jackson was fighting to defend—though he would have said he was fighting for his country. I'm deeply aware of this, yet when I study the Civil War, I'm not drawn at all to any Union personalities, those on the "right" side; it's always the Confederates with whom I have the chemistry. Especially Jackson. As I mentioned earlier, one reason is obvious: He was a fighter. And maybe the contradictions in me call out to the contradictions in him. "Real recognize real," my students often said.

Many of them were as familiar with death as any Confederate soldier. I remember once teaching a class with only three students and finding out that two of them had been shot, one on two separate occasions, the second time by his father.

"That's horrible," I told the young man. "I'm really sorry. What happened to your dad? Did he go to jail?"

"Nah. We never told nobody. I laid on the bed bleedin' till the next day. I thought if I laid real still the blood would stop but it didn't. I felt awful sick. The next evening I got somebody to take me to the hospital."

Kirby—another student—grew up in an East Richmond neighborhood close to where my grandparents lived before they retired. When I told Kirby that, he told me about his grandfather who had made sure he had boxing lessons growing up. The old man always kept his pistol nearby, he added. "Even if he was working up under his car, he had it right where he could put his hand on it."

Kirby did okay for a while after he was released. Then one evening he drove with his girlfriend to drop off her son for a visit with his father. Kirby was smoking. The father said he shouldn't be because the child had asthma. Things escalated from there. Kirby wound up getting shot seven times. Dead at twenty-one in a Rite Aid parking lot.

I didn't hear about it until the next day. I could tell something had happened by the way the students were huddled together talking in low voices. When I asked what was going on they closed ranks, except for Keshawn, with whom I was close. When he told me the story I started crying. He comforted me, rubbing my back as I sobbed, saying, "See, Cleary, this is why we need you. You can't leave us. You've got to stay."

I did stay, for three more years.

After Keshawn was released, I heard he was doing well. He had been locked back up but it wasn't anything serious, his cousin, another student, told me when he came into my class. Well, it actually was *kinda* serious, but he was doing okay. Later that same day, the cousin confided that his own ambition was to play European basketball. Just before the bell, he dropped and did a dozen one-handed push-ups, demonstrating a level of fitness that would be impressive in any league.

Another small watercourse crosses the road near the end of the trail. There's a gray sign with raised black lettering a few feet away. An artifact itself, part of an earlier generation of National Park interpretation, it opens a window into the past with the melodrama appropriate for war: "May 2, 1863. Hour by hour, the long gray columns of Jackson's Corps splashed through the shallow ford here, which was not stone paved then, stirring the crossing into a mud hole. Before the waters of this branch of Poplar Run ran clear again, in its course towards the distant York, 'Stonewall' Jackson and hundreds of his marchers were to fall dead or wounded. Many would never cross another earthly stream."

CHAPTER 35

Let Us Cross over the River

General Fitzhugh Lee, nephew of the Southern commander, was screening Jackson's column with his cavalry. Around 2 p.m. he discovered that a course correction was necessary: Hooker's flank was a mile farther west than had been anticipated. Fitz Lee galloped to find Jackson and brought him to the vantage point from which he had gleaned this information. Expecting praise, he conversationally noted just how relaxed and vulnerable the Union soldiers were. They talked, smoked, boiled coffee, played cards. Arms were stacked. Some butchered cattle.

After a few minutes, Lee realized that Jackson wasn't listening. He turned and studied the general. "His eyes burned with a brilliant glow," he wrote years later. "His lips were moving....From what I have read and heard of Jackson since that day, I know now what he was doing then. Oh, 'beware of rashness,' General Hooker. Stonewall Jackson is praying in full view and in rear of your right flank!"[1]

Jackson marched the necessary extra distance, then started forming his men into battle lines, which took some doing in the tangled Wilderness. Arrangements were far from perfect at 5:30—only ten of his fifteen regiments were deployed—but he was burning daylight. "Well, you can go forward then," he told General Robert E. Rodes.

Union soldiers were highly amused when terrified deer, rabbits, and turkeys started streaking through their camp. Their mood changed abruptly when they heard the Rebel yell. Some ran for their weapons; many simply ran, using pocketknives to cut the straps of their knapsacks rather than pause to unshoulder them. Federals who resisted were enveloped and obliterated. Wrote James Power Smith: "Leaving wounded and dead everywhere, on into the deep thicket again, the Confederate lines press forward, Jackson on the road in the centre [sic], with uplifted hand crying always: 'Forward men, forward: press forward.' "[2]

Confederates swarmed over Howard's two cannon, reversed them, and fired into the retreating Yankees.

General Howard, by all accounts a very brave man, clutched the staff of a fallen regimental flag under the stump of the right arm he had lost at Seven Pines and tried—unsuccessfully—to rally his men. "More quickly than it could be told," he wrote later, "with all the fury of the wildest hailstorm, everything, every sort of organization that lay in the path of the mad current of panic-stricken men had to give way and be broken into fragments."[3]

The Confederates themselves were disorganized by the speed and success of their attack. Units were fragmented and intermingled. Some soldiers gave in to temptation, disobeying the Jacksonian prime directive about looting on the battlefield, and paused to partake of the good cooked suppers and rummage through Union knapsacks and tents. Darkness fell. Momentum stalled.

Jackson was frustrated. There was a full moon. Surely more could be done. It was around nine in the evening when he rode out in front of his lines with a few aides to scout the Federal position. There was a shot, then a volley. They came from the 18th North Carolina Regiment, who mistook the general and his party for Union cavalry.

Jackson's horse bolted, charging into the trees. He checked him with difficulty. "Cease firing!" yelled Lieutenant Joseph G. Morrison, Jackson's brother-in-law and a member of his entourage. "You are firing into your own men."

"Who gave that order?" shouted Major John D. Barry of the 18th. "It's a lie! Pour it into them, boys!"

The North Carolinians obeyed with another volley. Jackson was hit. Little Sorrel bolted again. This time it took two aides to stop the horse. "How do you feel, General?" asked Captain R. E. Wilbourn when the animal was halted. "Can you move your fingers?"

Jackson could not. His arm was broken. He had been hit three times. A musket ball had broken two bones in his right hand; a second bullet hit the left forearm. The third wound was the most dire. The bullet struck him about three inches below the left shoulder, severing the artery and breaking the bone.

Jackson was helped from his horse in a near faint. His aides supported him as he staggered into the woods and lay down. They gave him a little whiskey, the teetotaling general hesitating before he drank. Next, they applied a tourniquet.

An attack seemed imminent. The general had to be moved. The officers tried to walk him back to Confederate lines. It quickly became obvious that he was too weak. They placed him on a litter. Union artillery opened fire. Canister and grapeshot ripped through the woods and struck sparks on the road. A litter bearer fell, wounded in both arms. An officer caught the handle of the litter. Jackson did not fall.

The firing continued. The soldiers lay around Jackson, shielding him with their bodies. Shortly thereafter, still under fire, they again tried to help the wounded general walk. Again he was too weak. They returned him to the litter. They had not gone far before one of the bearers tripped. This time Jackson fell. He groaned in pain.

Finally they procured an ambulance. Lieutenant Morrison got in to hold the general's wounded arm. Hunter McGuire joined them. "I am badly injured, Doctor; I fear I am dying," Jackson told him. "I am glad you have come. I think the wound in my shoulder is still bleeding."

"I found his clothes still saturated with blood," wrote McGuire, "and blood still oozing from the wound." McGuire put his finger on the artery. "Then I readjusted the handkerchief which had been used as a tourniquet, but which had slipped a little. Without this [having] been done, he would probably have died in ten minutes."

Jackson was in tremendous pain but controlled it, wrote

McGuire, "by his iron will." Still, the doctor noted that his lips "were so tightly compressed that the impression of his teeth could be seen through them."

McGuire administered whiskey and morphine, and rode with Jackson in the ambulance to a field hospital some four miles away. There, Jackson was stabilized in a hospital tent. A team of doctors assembled. Chloroform would be administered, McGuire told Jackson around 2 a.m. His wounds would be examined. Amputation was probable. Did the general consent?

"Yes, certainly, Dr. McGuire, do for me whatever you think best."

The anesthetic took effect. "What an infinite blessing!" said Jackson. He repeated the last word, "Blessing... blessing..." as he drifted off.

The musket ball was removed from his right hand; then his left arm was amputated. Afterward, he seemed to be doing well. He ate and drank and talked to visitors about military matters and theology. He also sent Lieutenant Morrison to Richmond to bring Anna to be with him as he convalesced. One puzzling and disturbing episode: a pain in his side. He told McGuire he had injured it during his fall from the litter the night before. McGuire examined him and found nothing.

Meanwhile, the Battle of Chancellorsville continued. May 3 was the war's second-bloodiest day. "The fighting was some of the most desperate of the war, exceeding, for the time engaged, both Antietam and Gettysburg," states one Park Service exhibit. Adds another: "In five hours of fighting, more than 17,500 soldiers were killed, wounded or captured—more than one soldier for every second of combat."

The woods caught fire. Many of the wounded were burned alive. "The scene as I marched through the burning woods was harrowing," wrote Confederate general James Lane. "Unexploded shells & muskets going off in all directions, the dead of both sides enveloped in flames, the appealing cries of the helpless, wounded Federals to be removed from the tracks of fire, the heavy pall of stifling sulfurous smoke, all added to the general roar of battle and made it a perfect hell on earth."[4]

Lee, fearing the hospital would be overrun, sent word for Jackson to be moved. He suggested Guinea Station, some twenty-seven miles southeast on the Richmond, Fredericksburg, and Potomac Railroad. From there, Jackson could easily be evacuated farther south.

The move was accomplished Monday, May 4. Wrote McGuire: "The rough teamsters sometimes refused to move their loaded wagons out of the way for an ambulance until told that it contained Jackson, and then, with all possible speed, they gave the way and stood with hats off and weeping as he went by." The country people brought such gifts of food as were to be had from their meager stores "and with tearful eyes they blessed him and prayed for his recovery."

At Guinea Station, Jackson did indeed seem to be recovering. He settled into the plantation office of "Fairfield," the Thomas Chandler House, and slept well the first night. McGuire was optimistic. He was also vigilant, strictly limiting the number of visitors and watching through the night while Jackson slept.

Reverend Lacy arrived the next day. He held a bedside prayer service. An odd and interesting footnote: After the amputation, Lacy had taken Jackson's arm to Ellwood, his brother's nearby home, and buried it in the family cemetery.

There were more pious conversations later that day with James Power Smith, who would become a Presbyterian minister after the war. Lacy returned the next morning for another prayer service. That evening, thinking that Jackson's recovery was under way, McGuire allowed himself to sleep on the couch in the sickroom.

Jackson awoke with nausea around 1 a.m. He directed Jim Lewis to wet a towel with cold water and place it on the painful area. Lewis wanted to wake McGuire. Jackson refused, knowing how much sleep the doctor had lost the last few nights. The hydrotherapy continued until dawn, with Jackson's pain increasing. When McGuire awoke and examined his patient, he diagnosed pneumonia, certainly resulting from his fall from the litter the night he was wounded.

Mrs. Jackson arrived with their infant daughter as the crisis was unfolding. She seemed to sense the prognosis immediately.

More doctors arrived. There were consultations, prayers, and hymn singing. Jackson drifted into and out of consciousness. Then he would rally, talking to his wife and playing with his daughter. "Little comforter," he called her, still insisting to those around him that he would recover.

Sunday, May 10: McGuire was certain that Jackson would not last the day. Mrs. Jackson went in to him and, weeping, broke the news. Jackson sent for McGuire.

"Doctor," he said, "Anna informs me that you have told her I am to die today; is it so?"

McGuire answered in the affirmative.

"Very good, very good," said Jackson. "It is all right."

He tried to comfort his wife. After he died, he said, she should return to live with her father, who was "kind and good." They discussed that he wished to be buried in Lexington, near where they had lived when he taught at the Virginia Military Institute.

There was a farewell visit with his daughter. "Little darling," he called her. "Sweet one."

"It is the Lord's Day," he said later. "I have always desired to die on Sunday."

He sank into delirium, talking as though he were still on the battlefield: "Order A. P. Hill to prepare for action! Pass the infantry to the front!"

He died at 3:15 p.m. His final words: "Let us cross over the river and rest under the shade of the trees."[5]

Afterword

The funeral in Richmond was monumental, attended by "the largest crowd ever assembled in the city."[1] A few writers try to turn it into an event symbolic of a lost hope for Confederate victory. For most mourners, however, it was simply an outpouring of grief for the man himself. Jackson didn't embody the ideals of the Confederacy, he transcended them.

Even the Federals expressed admiration. "I rejoice at Stonewall Jackson's death as a gain to our cause," said Grant's corps commander Major General Gouverneur K. Warren, "and yet in my soldier's heart I cannot but see him as the best soldier of all this war, and grieve at his untimely death."[2]

Grant himself happened upon Guinea Station on his way south during the Overland Campaign in 1864. Mrs. Chandler, of Fairfield, showed him the building and related the story of Jackson's death. Grant had served with Jackson in Mexico and spent a year with him at West Point. "He was a gallant soldier and Christian gentleman," he told Mrs. Chandler, "and I can fully understand the admiration your people have for him."[3]

The train bearing his body stopped in the Richmond suburbs, allowing Mrs. Jackson to disembark and avoid the crowds. "We were met by Mrs. Governor Letcher and other ladies, with several carriages, and driven through the most retired streets to the governor's mansion. Kind friends also had in readiness for me a mourning outfit."[4] The train drove the last couple of miles through throngs of mourners, the sound of its bell joined by minute guns and the tolling of "the few church bells that had not been moulded into cannon."[5]

Jackson lay in state in the governor's mansion for viewing by friends, family, officers, and officials. After the visitations were over, Richard Garnett, "the soldier whom Jackson most had wronged,"[6] appeared. Sandie Pendleton and Kyd Douglas met him at the door and led him into the parlor. "Jackson's treatment of Garnett was perhaps his worst moment," wrote S. C. Gwynne, "the charges he brought his least forgivable act. Yet now the brigadier stood before Jackson's casket with tears in his eyes."

In spite of all that had transpired, Garnett said, "I do wish here to assure you that no one can lament his death more sincerely than I do. I believe that he did me a great injustice, but I believe also that he acted from the purest motives. He is dead. Who can fill his place?"

When Pendleton asked him to be a pallbearer, Garnett "willingly consented."[7]

It was probably even later when Constance Cary visited. "We were admitted privately late at night into the hall," she wrote. "Two guards, pacing to and fro in the moonlight streaming through high windows, alone kept watch over the hero. A lamp burned dimly at one end of the hall, but we saw distinctly the regular white outline of the quiet face in its dreamless slumber."[8]

The following day, the funeral procession left the governor's mansion and made a circuit of a few blocks through the city before returning to Capitol Square. The military band near the front of the procession had trouble playing because so many of the musicians were weeping. The hearse was surrounded by generals. Garnett was included but not Lee, who had not even allowed himself to see Jackson's body depart from Guinea because he was afraid Hooker would cross the Rappahannock again.

Jim Lewis followed the hearse. Since Little Sorrel had been taken by the enemy, Lewis led Superior, another of Jackson's horses, with reversed boots in the stirrups. A carriage followed with Anna, Julia, and Jefferson Davis.

Back at the capitol, Jackson lay in state again. An estimated 20,000 people viewed his remains. The following morning, May 13, he was returned to the governor's mansion, where there was a brief, private service.

Afterward, Jackson started his final journey, first by rail through Gordonsville to Lynchburg, then by canal boat to Lexington. He lay in state for the last time at VMI. They couldn't maneuver the coffin up the circular stairs to his old classroom, so the viewing was in the lecture room. Visitors placed so many flowers onto the casket that it was hidden from view.[9]

There was a final service on May 15 at the Lexington Presbyterian Church. Jackson was buried in the nearby Presbyterian Cemetery, which was later renamed the Stonewall Jackson Cemetery.

Volumes of eulogies paid tribute. One of the most moving was among the simplest, written in a private journal that evening by Margaret Junkin Preston—Maggie—his first wife's sister, a woman who under different circumstances would have certainly been one of the great loves of his life. "Now it is all over," she wrote, "and the great hero is 'alone in his glory.' Not many better men have lived and died."

For the purposes of this project, I lived with Jackson four years, about as long as it took to fight the Civil War. I set out to understand him; in closing, I must confess that I do only slightly more than at the beginning. "Always mystify, mislead, and surprise the enemy," he said, and he still mystifies those who seek to understand him today. He was complex and contradictory in so many ways. Kyd Douglas noted on the death of little Janie Corbin and her two cousins that "General Jackson showed the tenderest sorrow at the death of these three children. A few days before he would not consent to remit the death penalty incurred by three soldiers who had gone home, perhaps to see their little girls.

Surely the ways of strong men in war are past finding out; and it must be so."[10]

◁══▷

It is hard winter as I write this, and I find myself daydreaming over pictures of places I visited in more seasonable weather. I can't imagine not going to the sites. Nothing compares with walking the ground, putting pieces of the puzzle together with the landscape—or just walking, wandering for the pleasure of being outdoors and seeing what you can discover. Battlefields are national treasures. I am always grateful for them, although it says something disturbing about our culture that great numbers of men have to die violently in a place for us to justify saving it from sprawl and commerce.

It'll be hard to stop the research. It seemed like every week I discovered a new person from the past that I enjoyed spending time with, or a new secondary source that helped my understanding.

◁══▷

In spite of the fact that he's buried there, Lexington is, for me, much more about Jackson living than Jackson dead. Of course you can visit his grave, and it is very moving—not to be missed. But his home is more compelling. His nightly meditation with his chair to the wall is one of the keys to his personality. I marvel at the fact that the warrior loved to garden. Catherine admired the tall, showy pink hollyhocks in the period flowerbed. The last time we went she took some seeds, but they didn't flourish far from their Valley home.

You can walk where he walked in the little town and see where he worshipped and taught. Looking at a taxidermied Little Sorrel behind plate glass in the VMI museum is an odd experience. But the raincoat with bullet holes from the night he was shot is somber and moving, particularly when you remember it must also be the one he wore when he met Anna and Julia at Guinea Station in the rain.

There's never been anyone else present when I visited the grave of Jackson's amputated left arm near Ellwood at the Lacy House, west of Fredericksburg. Once, when I came years ago, groundhogs had had a field day honeycombing the little cemetery with their holes. They weren't as active when I went there recently.

I have lived near Richmond nearly all my life, but I had never walked the route taken by Jackson's funeral procession. It's completely uncommemorated. So is the spot where he lay in state in the capitol building. A helpful security guard googled it for me, with inconclusive results; then a very knowledgeable docent told me exactly where the coffin had been: near the entranceway on the south side of the building.

I had to do the walk in stages because I was fearful of getting my car towed and needed to move it twice and feed the meter. As with many of my Jackson expeditions, the temperature was twenty-seven degrees—brutally cold for a southerner, making me think more of Romney than of the warm May day of the procession. Long winter shadows and the quickly falling dusk made for a melancholy mood as I walked down Governor Street to Main, then north on 2nd Street and back to Capitol Square on Grace. I passed Civil War and Jackson sites, like Second Presbyterian Church, where he worshipped and was mobbed after the Seven Days, along with places of personal association—the defunct department store where my mother worked most of her life, a restaurant where my son currently works, the library where I spent so much time as a teenager—all reinforcing the fact that pilgrimages are as much about the pilgrim as they are about the destination.

Back at Capitol Square, an equestrian statue of Washington points dramatically southwest with a gesture reminiscent of God reaching out to Adam on the Sistine Chapel ceiling. For years, the joke was that Washington was looking at the legislature and pointing toward the penitentiary.

The penitentiary was demolished in 1992, so the joke no longer works. As I walked across the grounds I pondered what it meant that Washington now points to the forest of communications equipment on the roof of the Verizon Building.

West of Fredericksburg, the actual site of Jackson's wounding is so close to busy Route 3 that it's hard to think of anything but traffic. Guinea, the "Stonewall Jackson Shrine," north of Richmond off I-95, is much more evocative. I often stop there. The last time was late on a winter afternoon. A train went by on the tracks that are just to the west. It blew for the crossing. Then it was gone and only the quiet stillness remained.

Acknowledgments

The National Park Service historians John Hennessy, Robert E. L. Krick, and Eric Mink were extremely helpful and generous. Writer Evans Hopkins has been a constant friend and advisor for over three decades. Author Lee Smith has consistently been kind and encouraging, even when I fell silent for years at a time. My son, Alexander, was always interested. He listened to me when I needed it most and encouraged me to dream big dreams. Special gratitude is due my patient editor, Sean Desmond, for believing in me and supporting me throughout. Finally, to my wife, Catherine—editor, advisor, and boon companion of many a battlefield trek—a heartfelt and loving thanks.

Bibliography

Adams, Shae. "Cultural Distortion: The Dedication of the Thomas 'Stonewall' Jackson Monument at Manassas National Battlefield Park." *Gettysburg College Journal of the Civil War Era*, vol. 2, article 3 (2011). https://cupola.gettysburg .edu/cgi/viewcontent.cgi?referer=https://www.google.com/&httpsredir=1&arti cle=1016&context=gcjcwe. Accessed May 13, 2016.

Alexander, Edward Porter. *Military Memoirs of a Confederate.* New York: Charles Scribner's Sons, 1907.

———. *Fighting for the Confederacy: The Personal Recollections of General Edward Porter Alexander.* Edited by Gary Gallagher. Chapel Hill: University of North Carolina Press, 1989.

Anderson, Carter S. *Train Running for the Confederacy.* Library of Virginia typed copies of eleven articles published in *Locomotive Engineering* between July 1892 and January 1898, July 20, 1949: Accessioned Memorandum.

Bailey, Ronald H. *The Bloodiest Day: The Battle of Antietam.* Alexandria, VA: Time-Life Books, 1984.

Benson, Berry. *Berry Benson's Civil War Book: Memoirs of a Confederate Scout and Sharpshooter.* Edited by Susan William Benson. Athens: University of Georgia Press, 1992.

Blackford, Susan Leigh, compiler. *Letters from Lee's Army.* New York: Charles Scribner's Sons, 1947.

Blackford, W. W. *War Years with Jeb Stuart.* New York: Charles Scribner's Sons, 1945.

Blanton, Wyndham B. *The Making of a Downtown Church: The History of the Second Presbyterian Church, 1845–1945.* Richmond, VA: John Knox Press, 1945.

Bluford, Robert Jr. *The Battle of Totopotomoy Creek: Polegreen Church and the Prelude to Cold Harbor.* Charleston, SC: History Press, 2014.

Borton, Benjamin. *On the Parallels: Or, Chapters of Inner History; A Story of the Rappahannock.* Woodstown, NJ: Monitor-Register Print, 1903.

Boteler, Alexander R. "Stonewall Jackson in the Campaign of 1862." *Southern Historical Society Papers* 40 (September 1915).

Caldwell, James Fitz James. *The History of a Brigade of South Carolinians: Known First as "Gregg's," and Subsequently as "McGowan's Brigade."* Philadelphia: King and Baird, 1866.

Carmichael, Peter S. *Lee's Young Artillerist: William R. J. Pegram.* Charlottesville: University of Virginia Press, 1995.

Carter, Robert Goldthwaite. *Four Brothers in Blue.* Washington: Press of the Gibson Bros., Inc., 1913.

Casler, John Overton. *Four Years in the Stonewall Brigade.* Dayton, OH: Morningside Bookshop, 1971.

Catton, Bruce. *Bruce Catton's Civil War.* New York: Fairfax Press, 1984.

Chamberlain, Joshua Lawrence. "Dedication of the Maine Monuments at Gettysburg, October 3, 1889." *Maine at Gettysburg.* Portland, ME: Lakeside Press, 1898.

Chesnut, Mary Boykin. *Mary Chesnut's Civil War.* Edited by C. Vann Woodward. New Haven, CT: Yale University Press, 1981.

Clark, Walter, compiler. *Histories of the Several Regiments and Battalions from North Carolina in the Great War, 1861–65.* 5 vols. Raleigh, NC: E. M. Uzzell, 1901.

Cook, Benjamin F. *History of the Twelfth Massachusetts Volunteers (Webster Regiment).* Boston: Twelfth Regiment Association, 1882.

Cozzens, Peter. *Shenandoah 1862: Stonewall Jackson's Valley Campaign.* Chapel Hill: University of North Carolina Press, 2008.

Dabney, Robert Lewis. *Life and Campaigns of Thomas J. Jackson.* New York: Blelock and Co., 1866.

Douglas, Henry Kyd. *I Rode with Stonewall.* Chapel Hill: University of North Carolina Press, 1940.

Dowdy, Clifford, and Louis H. Manarin, eds. *The Wartime Papers of Robert E. Lee.* New York: Bramhall House, 1961.

Early, Jubal Anderson. *Autobiographical Sketch and Narrative of the War Between the States.* Philadelphia and London: J. B. Lippincott, 1912.

Ecelbarger, Gary L. *Three Days in the Shenandoah: Stonewall Jackson at Front Royal and Winchester.* Norman: University of Oklahoma Press, 2008.

———. *"We Are in for It!": The First Battle of Kernstown.* Shippensburg, PA: White Mane Publishing Company, 1997.

Editors of Time-Life Books. *Lee Takes Command: From Seven Days to Second Bull Run.* Alexandria, VA: Time-Life Books, 1984.

Foote, Shelby. *The Civil War: A Narrative.* 3 vols. New York: Random House, 1958.

Freeman, Douglas Southall. *R. E. Lee: A Biography.* 4 vols. New York: Charles Scribner's Sons, 1934–35.

———. *Lee's Lieutenants: A Study in Command.* 3 vols. New York: Charles Scribner's Sons, 1945.

———. *The South to Posterity: An Introduction to the Writing of Confederate History.* New York: Charles Scribner's Sons, 1951.

Furgurson, Ernest B. *Chancellorsville 1863: The Souls of the Brave.* New York: Alfred A. Knopf, 1992.

Gallagher, Gary W., ed. *The Shenandoah Valley Campaign of 1862.* Chapel Hill: University of North Carolina Press, 2003.

Gordon, George Henry. *Brook Farm to Cedar Mountain: In the War of the Great Rebellion 1861–62.* Boston: Houghton Mifflin, 1885.

Graham, James R. "Reminiscence of General T. J. 'Stonewall' Jackson." In Mary Anna Jackson, *Memoirs of Stonewall Jackson.* Louisville, KY: Prentice Press, 1895.

Greene, A. Wilson. *The Second Battle of Manassas*. Fort Washington, PA: Eastern National Parks and Monument Association, 1995.

Gwynne, S. C. *Rebel Yell: The Violence, Passion, and Redemption of Stonewall Jackson*. New York: Scribner, 2014.

Harrison, Constance Cary. *Recollections Grave and Gay*. New York: Charles Scribner's Sons, 1911.

Henderson, G. F. R. *Stonewall Jackson and the American Civil War*. 2 vols. New York: Konecky & Konecky, n.d.

Hennessy, John. "Belvoir: The Thomas Yerby Place, Spotsylvania County." https://npsfrsp.files.wordpress.com/2010/06/belvoir2.pdf.

Hennessy, John, and Brad Graham. *Fredericksburg: A Documentary Film*. Lansing, MI: Media Magic Productions, n.d.

Holsworth, Jerry. *Stonewall Jackson and Winchester, Virginia*. Charleston, SC: History Press, 2012.

Holt, David. *A Mississippi Rebel in the Army of Northern Virginia: The Civil War Memoirs of Private David Holt*. Edited by Thomas D. Cockrell and Michael B. Ballard. Baton Rouge: Louisiana State University Press, 1995.

Hood, John Bell. *Advance and Retreat: Personal Experiences in the United States and Confederate States Armies*. New Orleans: Hood Orphan and Memorial Fund, 1880.

Hotchkiss, Jedediah. *Make Me a Map of the Valley: The Civil War Journal of Stonewall Jackson's Topographer*. Dallas: Southern Methodist University Press, 1973.

Howard, McHenry. *Recollections of a Maryland Confederate Soldier and Staff Officer Under Johnston, Jackson, and Lee*. Dayton, OH: Morningside Bookshop, 1975.

Hunter, Alexander. *Johnny Reb and Billy Yank*. New York: Neale, 1905.

Jackson, Mary Anna. *Life and Letters of General Thomas J. Jackson (Stonewall Jackson)*. New York: Harper and Brothers, 1892.

Johnson, Bradley T. *Maryland and West Virginia*. Vol. 2 of *Confederate Military History*. Edited by Clement A. Evans. 13 vols. Atlanta: Confederate Publishing Co. Reprint: Dayton, OH: Morningside Bookshop, 1975.

Johnson, Robert Underwood, and Clarence Clough Buel, eds. *Battles and Leaders of the Civil War*. 8 vols. New York: Century Co., 1887–88.

Johnson, Thomas Cary. *The Life and Letters of Robert Lewis Dabney*. Richmond, VA: Presbyterian Committee of Publication, 1903.

Jones, J. William. *Christ in the Camp: Or, Religion in Lee's Army*. Atlanta: B. F. Johnson and Co., 1887.

Jones, Terry L., ed. *Campbell Brown's Civil War: With Ewell and the Army of Northern Virginia*. Baton Rouge: Louisiana State University Press, 2001.

Jordan, J. P. "My Worst Three Days." *Confederate Veteran* 26 (1918).

Krick, Robert E. L. "Bobby Krick Describes the Battle of Gaines' Mill." Civil War Trust: Saving America's Civil War Battlefields.

Krick, Robert K. "Battle of Cross Keys: Ambush of the 8th New York." Video. American Battlefield Trust. www.battlefields.org/learn/videos/battle-cross-keys-ambush-8th-new-york.

———. *Conquering the Valley: Stonewall Jackson at Port Republic*. New York: William Morrow, 1996.

————. *The Smoothbore Volley That Doomed the Confederacy: The Death of Stonewall Jackson and Other Chapters on the Army of Northern Virginia.* Baton Rouge: Louisiana State University Press, 2002.

————. "The Metamorphosis in General Jackson's Public Image." In *The Shenandoah Valley Campaign of 1862.* Edited by Gary W. Gallagher. Chapel Hill: University of North Carolina Press, 2003.

————. *Civil War Weather in Virginia.* Tuscaloosa: University of Alabama Press, 2007.

Lee, Fitzhugh. "Chancellorsville Address of General Fitzhugh Lee Before the Virginia Division, A.N.V. Association, October 29th, 1879." *Southern Historical Society Papers* 7, no. 12 (December 1879).

Long, Armistead Lindsay, and Marcus Joseph Wright. *Memoirs of Robert E. Lee.* London: Sampson, Low, Marston, Searle and Rivington, 1886.

Long, E. B., with Barbara Long. *The Civil War Day by Day: An Almanac, 1861–1865.* Garden City, NY: Doubleday, 1971.

Mackowski, Chris. "Statues of Stonewall: Manassas." *Emerging Civil War.* December 26, 2011. https://emergingcivilwar.com/2017/08/16/statues-of-stonewall-2/. Accessed May 13, 2016.

Mackowski, Chris, and Kristopher D. White. *The Last Days of Stonewall Jackson.* El Dorado Hills, CA: Savas Baetie LLC, 2013.

MacLean, Maggie. "Fannie Lawrence Ricketts." *Civil War Women.* June 12, 2008. www.civilwarwomenblog.com/fannie-lawrence-ricketts/. Accessed May 16, 2016.

McDonald, William Naylor. *A History of the Laurel Brigade.* Baltimore: Sun Job Printing Office, 1907.

McGuire, Hunter Holmes. "Death of Stonewall Jackson." *Southern Historical Society Papers* 14 (January–December 1886).

————. "General T. J. ('Stonewall') Jackson: His Career and Character." *Southern Historical Society Papers* 25 (1897).

McGuire, Hunter Holmes, and George L. Christian. *The Confederate Cause and Conduct in the War Between the States.* Richmond, VA: L. H. Jenkins, 1907.

McPherson, James M. *Battle Cry of Freedom: The Civil War Era.* New York: Oxford University Press, 1988.

Miller, William J. *Mapping for Stonewall: The Civil War Service of Jed Hotchkiss.* Washington, DC: Elliott and Clark Publishing, 1993.

————. *The Battles for Richmond, 1862.* Eastern National Park and Monument Association, 1996.

————. "The Battle of McDowell." In *"If This Valley Is Lost, Virginia Is Lost!": Stonewall Jackson's Valley Campaign.* Edited by Jonathan A. Noyalas. New Market, VA: Shenandoah Valley Battlefields Foundation, 2006.

Moore, Edward A. *The Story of a Cannoneer Under Stonewall Jackson.* New York: Neale, 1907.

Neese, George M. *Three Years in the Confederate Horse Artillery.* New York: Neale, 1911.

Oates, William C. *The War Between the Union and the Confederacy and Its Lost Opportunities.* New York: Neale, 1905.

Old Homes of Hanover County, Virginia. Salem, WV: Walsworth Publishing Company, 1983.

Opie, John N. *A Rebel Cavalryman with Lee, Stuart, and Jackson*. Chicago: W. B. Conkey, 1899.

Otott, George E. "First Texas in the Cornfield." *The Maryland Campaign of 1862*. *Civil War Regiments: A Journal of the American Civil War 5*, no 3. Campbell, CA: Savas Publishing Company, 1998.

Parker, Kathleen, and Jacqueline Hernigle. "Portici: Portrait of a Middling Plantation in Piedmont Virginia, Manassas National Battlefield Park." Washington, DC: Occasional Report #3, Regional Archeology Program, National Capital Region, National Park Service, 1990.

Porter, Horace. *Campaigning with Grant*. New York: Century Company, 1906.

Richmond National Battlefield Park and Rural Plains Foundation. *Totopotomoy Creek at Rural Plains: Volunteer Information Guide*. Compiled August 2013; updated March 20, 2014.

Robertson, James I. Jr. *The Stonewall Brigade*. Baton Rouge: Louisiana State University Press, 1963.

———. *General A. P. Hill: The Story of a Confederate Warrior*. New York: Random House, 1987.

———. *Stonewall Jackson: The Man, the Soldier, the Legend*. New York: Macmillan, 1997.

Sears, Stephen W. *Chancellorsville*. Boston: Houghton Mifflin, 1996.

———. *Landscape Turned Red: The Battle of Antietam*. New York: Houghton Mifflin, 1983.

———. *To the Gates of Richmond: The Peninsula Campaign*. New York: Ticknor and Fields, 1992.

———, ed. *The Civil War Papers of George B. McClellan: Selected Correspondence, 1860–1865*. New York: Da Capo, 1992.

Smith, James Power, Capt. CSA. "With Stonewall Jackson in the Army of Northern Virginia," in Douglas S. Freeman et al., ed., *Papers of the Military History Society of Massachusetts 5*. Boston: The Society, 1906.

Stiles, Robert. *Four Years Under Marse Robert*. Marietta, GA: R. Bemis Publishing, Ltd., 1995.

Survivors Association. *History of the Corn Exchange Regiment: 118th Pennsylvania Volunteers*. Philadelphia: J. L. Smith, 1888.

Tanner, Robert G. *Stonewall in the Valley*. Garden City, NY: Doubleday, 1976.

Taylor, Richard. *Destruction and Reconstruction: Personal Experiences of the Late War*. New York: D. Appleton, 1879.

Trowbridge, John. *The South: A Tour of Its Battlefields and Ruined Cities*. Hartford, CT: L. Stebbins, 1866.

United States War Department. *The War of the Rebellion: A Compilation of the Official Records of the Union and Confederate Armies*. Washington, DC: Government Printing Office, 1880–1901. Abbreviated in the endnotes as OR.

Vandiver, Frank E. *Mighty Stonewall*. New York: McGraw-Hill, 1957.

Vickers, George Morley, ed. *Under Both Flags*. St. Louis: People's, 1896.

von Borcke, Heros. *Memoirs of the Confederate War for Independence: A Prussian Officer with J. E. B. Stuart in Virginia.* Nashville: J. S. Sanders & Company, 1999.

Watkins, Sam R. Co. *Aytch: A Side Show of the Big Show.* New York: Touchstone, 1997.

Wersteev, Irving. *Kearny the Magnificent: The Story of General Philip Kearny, 1815–1862.* New York: John Day Company, 1962.

Wert, Jeffry D. *General James Longstreet: The Confederacy's Most Controversial Soldier; A Biography.* New York: Simon & Schuster, 1993.

Worsham, John H. *One of Jackson's Foot Cavalry.* New York: Bantam, 1992.

MANUSCRIPT SOURCES

Virginia State Library, Richmond
Edgar Allan Jackson letters

Endnotes

CHAPTER 1. *The Soundtrack of Southern Victory*

1. Alexander, *Fighting for the Confederacy*, 50.
2. Don Lipman, "Bull Run Battle 1861: As Hot Then as Now?," *Washington Post*, July 21, 2011.
3. "Virginia Man Killed in Civil War Cannonball Blast," Fox News via Associated Press, May 2, 2008, www.foxnews.com/story/virginia-man-killed-in-civil-war-cannonball-blast. Accessed May 5, 2016.
4. Stiles, *Four Years Under Marse Robert*, 293–96.
5. *Bruce Catton's Civil War*, 547.
6. John Lyle, *Sketches from a Confederate's Desk*, quoted in Gwynne, *Rebel Yell*, 87.
7. Robertson, *Stonewall Jackson*, 44.
8. John D. Imboden, "Incidents of the First Bull Run," in Johnson and Buel, eds., *Battles and Leaders of the Civil War*, vol. 1, 236.
9. Gwynne, *Rebel Yell*, 88.

CHAPTER 2. *After the Battle*

1. Douglas, *I Rode with Stonewall*, 142.
2. Mary Anna Jackson, *Life and Letters of General Thomas J. Jackson*, 178.
3. Gwynne, *Rebel Yell*, 155.
4. Robertson, *Stonewall Jackson*, 191–92.
5. Adams, "Cultural Distortion." The article highlights the same similarities I noticed between Jackson and Superman while registering stern academic disapproval of any positive Jackson commemoration.
6. Parker and Hernigle, "Portici," vii.
7. MacLean, "Fannie Lawrence Ricketts."

CHAPTER 3. *All Things Work Together*

1. Mary Anna Jackson, *Life and Letters of General Thomas J. Jackson*, 180.
2. Robertson, *Stonewall Jackson*, 170, 186.
3. Porter, *Campaigning with Grant*, 133.
4. Gwynne, *Rebel Yell*, 15.

5. Ibid., 24–44.
6. McPherson, *Battle Cry of Freedom*, 100, 546.
7. Douglas, *I Rode with Stonewall*, 236–37; Robertson, *Stonewall Jackson*, 274, n. 838.
8. Mary Anna Jackson, *Life and Letters of General Thomas J. Jackson*, 187–91.
9. J. William Jones, *Christ in the Camp*, 89–90.
10. Mary Anna Jackson, *Life and Letters of General Thomas J. Jackson*, 110.
11. Taylor, *Destruction and Reconstruction*, 42.
12. Douglas, *I Rode with Stonewall*, 16–17.

CHAPTER 4. *Fearful Odds*

1. Freeman, *R. E. Lee*, vol. 1, 574.
2. Worsham, *One of Jackson's Foot Cavalry*, 30.
3. Opie, *A Rebel Cavalryman with Lee, Stuart, and Jackson*, 56.
4. Ibid., 57, 58.
5. Robertson, *Stonewall Jackson*, 294, n. 841; Holsworth, *Stonewall Jackson and Winchester, Virginia,* 49–50.
6. Robertson, *Stonewall Jackson*, 294.
7. *OR*, vol. 5, 398–99.
8. Mary Anna Jackson, *Life and Letters of General Thomas J. Jackson*, 215.
9. Ibid., 108.
10. Robertson, *Stonewall Jackson*, 305.
11. Ibid., 306.
12. Watkins, *Co. Aytch*, 31.
13. Robertson, *Stonewall Jackson*, 306.
14. Worsham, *One of Jackson's Foot Cavalry*, 44.

CHAPTER 5. *Icicles of Blood*

1. Watkins, *Co. Aytch*, 38.
2. Douglas, *I Rode with Stonewall*, 23.
3. Robertson, *Stonewall Jackson*, 309.
4. Worsham, *One of Jackson's Foot Cavalry*, 45.
5. Robertson, *Stonewall Jackson*, 309.
6. Gwynne, *Rebel Yell*, 182.
7. Robertson, *Stonewall Jackson*, 310.
8. Henderson, *Stonewall Jackson and the American Civil War*, vol. 1, 186.
9. Robertson, *Stonewall Jackson*, 313.

CHAPTER 6. *An Insubordinate Frenzy*

1. Mary Anna Jackson, *Life and Letters of General Thomas J. Jackson*, 236.
2. Robertson, *Stonewall Jackson*, 313–14; Tanner, *Stonewall in the Valley*, 82; Mary Anna Jackson, *Life and Letters of General Thomas J. Jackson*, 237.
3. Tanner, *Stonewall in the Valley*, 82.

4. Ibid., 83.
5. Robertson, *Stonewall Jackson*, 316.
6. Gwynne, *Rebel Yell*, 185.
7. Henderson, *Stonewall Jackson and the American Civil War*, vol. 1, 201–3.
8. Robertson, *Stonewall Jackson*, 317.
9. Graham, "Reminiscence of General T. J. 'Stonewall' Jackson," 497.
10. Robertson, *Stonewall Jackson*, 318.
11. Alexander R. Boteler, "Stonewall Jackson's Discontent," in Johnson and Buel, eds., *Battles and Leaders of the Civil War*, vol. 6, 109–13. Romney was reoccupied by the Federals on February 7; Tanner, *Stonewall in the Valley*, 104.
12. Ned Oliver, "Wilder Asks Pointed Questions as 12 Richmond Mayoral Candidates Appear at Forum," *Richmond Times-Dispatch*, April 6, 2016.
13. Freeman, *Lee's Lieutenants*, vol. 1, 309.
14. McDonald, *A History of the Laurel Brigade*, 22–24.
15. "Indian Mound Cemetery," Wikipedia, https://en.wikipedia.org/wiki/Indian _Mound_Cemetery. Accessed May 17, 2016.
16. Robertson, *Stonewall Jackson*, 67, 263.

CHAPTER 7. *A Dazzling Glimpse*

1. Conversation with historian Gary Ecelbarger, May 20, 2016; Gwynne, *Rebel Yell*, 162.
2. Jefferson Davis to Joseph E. Johnston, February 19, 1862, OR, vol. 14, 1077.
3. Freeman, *Lee's Lieutenants*, vol. 1, 305.
4. Historian Jerry Holsworth, lecture, May 20, 2016; Mary Anna Jackson, *Life and Letters of General Thomas J. Jackson*, 214.
5. Mary Anna Jackson, *Life and Letters of General Thomas J. Jackson*, 215.
6. Sears, *To the Gates of Richmond*, 16.
7. Ibid., 17.
8. Tanner, *Stonewall in the Valley*, 105–6.
9. Mary Anna Jackson, *Life and Letters of General Thomas J. Jackson*, 240.
10. Ibid., 243.
11. Ed Bearss, Valley Campaign Tour, May 21, 2016; Gwynne, *Rebel Yell*, 199.
12. Graham, "Reminiscence of General T. J. 'Stonewall' Jackson," 500–501.
13. McGuire, "General T. J. ('Stonewall') Jackson: His Career and Character," 97.
14. Foote, *Civil War*, vol. 1, 427.
15. Freeman, *Lee's Lieutenants*, vol. 1, 136.
16. Taylor, *Destruction and Reconstruction*, 26.
17. Gwynne, *Rebel Yell*, n. 591.
18. Robertson, *Stonewall Jackson*, 336
19. Ibid., 334–35.
20. Henderson, *Stonewall Jackson and the American Civil War*, vol. 1, 220.
21. OR, vol. 12, pt. 1, 164.
22. Ibid., 380; Robertson, *Stonewall Jackson*, 338.
23. Ecelbarger, *"We Are in for It!,"* 66.
24. Robertson, *Stonewall Jackson*, 338, 339.
25. Ibid., 340.

CHAPTER 8. *Following the Footsteps*

1. Robertson, *Stonewall Jackson*, 343; Gwynne, *Rebel Yell*, 223.
2. Worsham, *One of Jackson's Foot Cavalry*, 54.
3. Foote, *Civil War*, vol. 1, 269, 272.
4. *OR*, vol. 12, pt. 1, 335.
5. Henderson, *Stonewall Jackson and the American Civil War*, vol. 1, 247.
6. Ecelbarger, *"We Are in for It!,"* 204–5.
7. Johnson and Buel, eds., *Battles and Leaders of the Civil War*, vol. 2, 297.
8. Ecelbarger, *"We Are in for It!,"* 205–6.
9. Gwynne, *Rebel Yell*, 226.

CHAPTER 9. *Spirits of the Place*

1. Mary Anna Jackson, *Life and Letters of General Thomas J. Jackson*, 247.
2. Miller, *Mapping for Stonewall*, 11, 12, 52.
3. Gwynne, *Rebel Yell*, 259.
4. Douglas, *I Rode with Stonewall*, 37.
5. Robertson, *Stonewall Jackson*, 521.
6. Gywnne, *Rebel Yell*, 259.
7. Robertson, *Stonewall Jackson*, 349.
8. Chamberlain, "Dedication of the Maine Monuments at Gettysburg, October 3, 1889."
9. Matthew Brzezinski, "Hillbangers," *New York Times Magazine*, August 15, 2004.
10. Paul Bradley, "NVA Trial to Shed Light on MS-13," *Richmond Times-Dispatch*, August 10, 2005.
11. Freeman, *Lee's Lieutenants*, vol. 1, 309.
12. Robertson, *Stonewall Jackson*, 361.
13. Freeman, *Lee's Lieutenants*, vol. 1, 338.
14. Ibid., 309.
15. Douglas, *I Rode with Stonewall*, 40–41.
16. Gwynne, *Rebel Yell*, 262.
17. Tanner, *Stonewall in the Valley*, 149.

CHAPTER 10. *God Blessed Our Arms*

1. Robertson, *Stonewall Jackson*, 360.
2. Johnson, *Life and Letters of Robert Lewis Dabney*, 270.
3. Ibid., 264.
4. Foote, *Civil War*, vol. 1, 429.
5. Watkins, *Co. Aytch*, 27.
6. *OR*, vol. 12, pt. 3, 859, 860.
7. Gwynne, *Rebel Yell*, 239.
8. *OR*, vol. 12, pt. 3, 862, 863.
9. Gwynne, *Rebel Yell*, 242, 243.

10. *OR*, vol. 12, pt. 3, 865, 866.
11. Johnson and Buel, eds., *Battles and Leaders of the Civil War*, vol. 2, 297.
12. Robertson, *Stonewall Jackson*, 367.
13. Taylor, *Destruction and Reconstruction*, 26.
14. Foote, *Civil War*, vol. 1, 420.
15. Robertson, *Stonewall Jackson*, 367.
16. Taylor, *Destruction and Reconstruction*, 26.
17. Douglas, *I Rode with Stonewall*, 47.
18. Worsham, *One of Jackson's Foot Cavalry*, 61.
19. Ibid.
20. Douglas, *I Rode with Stonewall*, 48.
21. Ibid., 47.
22. *Mary Chesnut's Civil War*, 444.
23. Robertson, *Stonewall Jackson*, 372.
24. Miller, "The Battle of McDowell," 23.
25. Gwynne, *Rebel Yell*, 253.
26. Ibid., 253, 254.
27. Dabney, *Life and Campaigns of Thomas J. Jackson*, 345.
28. Johnson and Buel, eds., *Battles and Leaders of the Civil War*, vol. 2, 287–88.
29. Moore, *Cannoneer Under Stonewall Jackson*, 48.

CHAPTER 11. *An Unconscious Poet*

1. Robertson, *Stonewall Jackson*, 382–83.
2. Tanner, *Stonewall in the Valley*, 178.
3. Vandiver, *Mighty Stonewall*, 238–39.
4. Dabney, *Life and Campaigns of Thomas J. Jackson*, 364.
5. Moore, *Cannoneer Under Stonewall Jackson*, 50.
6. Freeman, *South to Posterity*, 85–86.
7. Robertson, *Stonewall Jackson*, 389, 390.
8. Taylor, *Destruction and Reconstruction*, 37, 38.
9. *OR*, vol. 12, pt. 3, 898.
10. Taylor, *Destruction and Reconstruction*, 39.
11. Robertson, *Stonewall Jackson*, 391.
12. Ecelbarger, *Three Days in the Shenandoah*, 42.
13. Douglas, *I Rode with Stonewall*, 271.
14. Johnson, *Maryland and West Virginia*, 69–70.

CHAPTER 12. *A Talent for Retreat*

1. Douglas, *I Rode with Stonewall*, 51–52.
2. Robertson, *Stonewall Jackson*, 395.
3. Henderson, *Stonewall Jackson and the American Civil War*, vol. 1, 317.
4. Johnson, *Maryland and West Virginia*, 70.
5. Holt, *Mississippi Rebel in the Army of Northern Virginia*, 73, 74.
6. Ecelbarger, *Three Days in the Shenandoah*, 56

7. Taylor, *Destruction and Reconstruction*, 41.
8. Worsham, *One of Jackson's Foot Cavalry*, 68.
9. Ecelbarger, *Three Days in the Shenandoah*, 58.
10. Ibid., n. 240. Dabney, *Life and Campaigns of Thomas J. Jackson*, 365–66, has Jackson making this statement when he sees Kenly retreating from Richardson's Hill. Ecelbarger, probably more accurate, places it about an hour earlier, then oddly has him saying it again during the retreat.
11. Taylor, *Destruction and Reconstruction*, 42.
12. Gordon, *Brook Farm to Cedar Mountain*, 192, 193.
13. Dabney, *Life and Campaigns of Thomas J. Jackson*, 372.
14. Gwynne, *Rebel Yell*, 286.
15. Taylor, *Destruction and Reconstruction*, 43.
16. Dabney, *Life and Campaigns of Thomas J. Jackson*, 373.
17. Ecelbarger, *Three Days in the Shenandoah*, 139.
18. Robertson, *Stonewall Jackson*, 366.
19. Foote, *Civil War*, vol. 1, 433.
20. Ecelbarger, *Three Days in the Shenandoah*, 153.
21. Cozzens, *Shenandoah 1862*, 338.
22. Robertson, *Stonewall Jackson*, 403.
23. Taylor, *Destruction and Reconstruction*, 44.
24. Robertson, *Stonewall Jackson*, 403.

CHAPTER 13. *The Lion's Mouth*

1. Taylor, *Destruction and Reconstruction*, 45–46.
2. Cozzens, *Shenandoah 1862*, 364.
3. Worsham, *One of Jackson's Foot Cavalry*, 72, 73.
4. Dabney, *Life and Campaigns of Thomas J. Jackson*, 381.

CHAPTER 14. *A Lost Battlefield*

1. Mary Anna Jackson, *Life and Letters of General Thomas J. Jackson*, 265.
2. Worsham, *One of Jackson's Foot Cavalry*, 74.
3. Krick, "The Metamorphosis in General Jackson's Public Image," 28.
4. Robertson, *Stonewall Jackson*, 411.
5. Dabney, *Life and Campaigns of Thomas J. Jackson*, 384–85.
6. Ibid., 385.
7. Gwynne, *Rebel Yell*, 298.
8. Ibid.
9. Ibid., 300.
10. Robertson, *Stonewall Jackson*, 414.
11. Howard, *Recollections of a Maryland Confederate Soldier and Staff Officer Under Johnston, Jackson, and Lee*, 114–15.
12. Hotchkiss, *Make Me a Map of the Valley*, 50.
13. Gwynne, *Rebel Yell*, 307.

14. Robertson, *Stonewall Jackson,* 419; Hotchkiss, *Make Me a Map of the Valley,* 50, 51.
15. Cozzens, *Shenandoah 1862,* 235.
16. Robertson, *Stonewall Jackson,* 421.
17. *OR,* vol. 12, pt. 1, 708.
18. Robertson, *Stonewall Jackson,* 422.

CHAPTER 15. *The Dead Thick as Blackbirds*

1. Douglas, *I Rode with Stonewall,* 74, 75.
2. Robertson, *Stonewall Jackson,* 425; Cozzens, *Shenandoah 1862,* 427.
3. Douglas, *I Rode with Stonewall,* 75.
4. Cozzens, *Shenandoah 1862,* 427.
5. Hotchkiss, *Make Me a Map of the Valley,* 53.
6. *OR,* vol. 12, pt. 1, 712.
7. Tanner, *Stonewall in the Valley,* 288.
8. Freeman, *Lee's Lieutenants,* vol. 1, 440.
9. Cozzens, *Shenandoah 1862,* 450.
10. Moore, *Cannoneer Under Stonewall Jackson,* 69.
11. Ibid.
12. Dabney, *Life and Campaigns of Thomas J. Jackson,* 413.
13. Robertson, *Stonewall Jackson,* 435.
14. Freeman, *Lee's Lieutenants,* vol. 1, 445.
15. McPherson, *Battle Cry of Freedom,* 330.
16. Krick, *Conquering the Valley,* 172.
17. Krick, "Battle of Cross Keys: Ambush of the 8th New York."
18. Krick, *Conquering the Valley,* 174, 175.
19. Ibid, 177, 179.
20. Ibid, 181.
21. Foote, *Civil War,* vol. 1, 460.

CHAPTER 16. *Their Backs to the Mountain*

1. Howard, *Recollections of a Maryland Confederate Soldier and Staff Officer Under Johnston, Jackson, and Lee,* 124, 125.
2. Krick, *Conquering the Valley,* 289.
3. Moore, *Cannoneer Under Stonewall Jackson,* 73.
4. Robertson, *Stonewall Jackson,* 443. Robertson says that this conversation is "another fabrication from the Taylor memoirs," but I disagree. To me, it has the flavor of one of many out-of-character moments produced by the campaign's stress and fatigue.
5. Krick, *Conquering the Valley,* 428.
6. Taylor, *Destruction and Reconstruction,* 62.
7. Krick, *Conquering the Valley,* 429.
8. Gwynne, *Rebel Yell,* 326.
9. Freeman, *Lee's Lieutenants,* vol. 1, 463.

10. Ibid., 483.
11. Gwynne, *Rebel Yell*, 326, 327.
12. Taylor, *Destruction and Reconstruction*, 65.

CHAPTER 17. *The Tired Man*

1. Foote, *Civil War*, vol. 1, 470.
2. Robertson, *Stonewall Jackson*, 453.
3. Dowdy and Manarin, eds., *Wartime Papers of Robert E. Lee*, 193.
4. Ibid., 194.
5. Johnson and Buel, eds., *Battles and Leaders of the Civil War*, vol. 2, 296–97.
6. Robertson, *Stonewall Jackson*, 57.
7. Freeman, *R. E. Lee*, vol. 2, 108.
8. Anderson, *Train Running for the Confederacy*, 3.
9. Ibid., 11.
10. Boteler, "Stonewall Jackson in the Campaign of 1862," 176–78.
11. Worsham, *One of Jackson's Foot Cavalry*, 82.
12. Anderson, *Train Running for the Confederacy*, 10.
13. Sears, *To the Gates of Richmond*, 191.
14. Robertson, *Stonewall Jackson*, 354.
15. Wert, *General James Longstreet*, 405.
16. Foote, *Civil War*, vol. 1, 401.
17. Gwynne, *Rebel Yell*, 353.
18. Freeman, *R. E. Lee*, vol. 2, 106.
19. Freeman, *Lee's Lieutenants*, vol. 1, 499.
20. Sears, *To the Gates of Richmond*, 189.
21. Gwynne, *Rebel Yell*, 354.
22. Sears, ed., *The Civil War Papers of George B. McClellan*, 309.
23. Robertson, *Stonewall Jackson*, 470.
24. Taylor, *Destruction and Reconstruction*, 72.
25. Robertson, *Stonewall Jackson*, 470.

CHAPTER 18. *Men Falling Continually*

1. *Old Homes of Hanover County, Virginia*, 28.
2. *OR*, vol. 11, pt. 2, 835.
3. Alexander, *Fighting for the Confederacy*, 95.
4. Ibid., 100.
5. M. T. Ledbetter in *Confederate Veteran* 1, no. 8 (August 1893): 234.
6. "Confederate Newspaper Correspondent" quoted on National Park Service interpretive sign at Beaver Dam Creek.
7. Sears, *To the Gates of Richmond*, 206
8. Edgar Allan Jackson to mother, July 1, 1862, Jackson papers, Virginia State Library.
9. Sears, *To the Gates of Richmond*, 211.

CHAPTER 19. *Bloody Ground*

1. Sears, *To the Gates of Richmond*, 213.
2. Worsham, *One of Jackson's Foot Cavalry*, 85.
3. Robertson, *Stonewall Jackson*, 477.
4. National Park Service marker, Gaines' Mill battlefield.
5. Editors of Time-Life Books, *Lee Takes Command*, 42.
6. Robertson, *General A. P. Hill*, 84.
7. Sears, *To the Gates of Richmond*, 229.
8. Robertson, *General A. P. Hill*, 84.
9. *Berry Benson's Civil War Book*, 10.
10. Freeman, *Lee's Lieutenants*, vol. 1, 530.
11. Krick, "Bobby Krick Describes the Battle of Gaines' Mill."
12. Robertson, *Stonewall Jackson*, 481.
13. Miller, *Battles for Richmond, 1862*, 43.
14. Hood, *Advance and Retreat*, 27.
15. Miller, *Battles for Richmond, 1862*, 43.
16. Hood, *Advance and Retreat*, 28–29.
17. Sears, *To the Gates of Richmond*, 249.
18. Robertson, *Stonewall Brigade*, 118.
19. Sears, *To the Gates of Richmond*, 244.
20. Ibid., 245.
21. Blackford, *War Years with Jeb Stuart*, 74.
22. von Borcke, *Memoirs of the Confederate War for Independence*, 42–43.
23. Telephone conversation between the author and Robert Giles, April 12, 2018.
24. M. J. Haw, "My Visits to Grandmother," *Christian Observer*, May 18, 1910, 22–23.
25. Hood, *Advance and Retreat*, 28.
26. Early, *Autobiographical Sketch and Narrative of the War Between the States*, 76.

CHAPTER 20. *The Prize Within Their Reach*

1. Freeman, *R. E. Lee*, vol. 2, 167.
2. Robertson, *Stonewall Jackson*, 488.
3. *OR*, vol. 11, pt. 2, 675.
4. Jones, ed., *Campbell Brown's Civil War*, 121.
5. Blackford, *War Years with Jeb Stuart*, 76.
6. *Berry Benson's Civil War Book*, 12.
7. Dabney, *Life and Campaigns of Thomas J. Jackson*, 459.
8. Sears, *To the Gates of Richmond*, 256.
9. Foote, *Civil War*, vol. 1, 449.
10. Miller, *Battles for Richmond, 1862*, 48.
11. Alexander, *Fighting for the Confederacy*, 108.
12. Ibid., 108–9.

13. Howard, *Recollections of a Maryland Confederate Soldier and Staff Officer Under Johnston, Jackson, and Lee*, 149.
14. Robertson, *Stonewall Jackson*, 495.
15. Alexander, *Fighting for the Confederacy*, 109–10.
16. Ibid., 107.
17. Sears, *To the Gates of Richmond*, 296–99.
18. Ibid., 303.
19. Ibid., 306.
20. Ibid., 307.

CHAPTER 21. *A Melancholy Field*

1. Vickers, ed., *Under Both Flags*, 136.
2. Freeman, *R. E. Lee*, vol. 2, 209.
3. Freeman, *Lee's Lieutenants*, vol. 1, 601, 612.
4. National Park Service wayside, Malvern Hill battlefield.
5. Freeman, *R. E. Lee*, vol. 2, 215.
6. Sears, *To the Gates of Richmond*, 327, 332.
7. Ashley Whitehead, "Malvern Hill: Edwin Jemison—Loss of Innocence and the American Civil War," video, American Battlefield Trust, www.battlefields .org/learn/videos/malvern-hill-edwin-jemison.
8. "Malvern Hill: Then & Now—An Interview with Robert E. L. Krick," video, American Battlefield Trust, https://www.battlefields.org/learn /articles/malvern-hill-then-now
9. Robertson, *Stonewall Jackson*, 502.
10. "Malvern Hill: Then & Now—An Interview with Robert E. L. Krick."
11. Freeman, *R. E. Lee*, vol. 2, 218.
12. *OR*, vol. 11, pt. 3, 590.
13. Ibid., 503; McGuire and Christian, *Confederate Cause*, 197.
14. Johnson and Buel, eds., *Battles and Leaders of the Civil War*, vol. 2, 432.
15. Blackford, *War Years with Jeb Stuart*, 80–81.
16. J. P. Jordan, "My Worst Three Days," *Confederate Veteran* 26 (1918): 210–11.
17. Veterans Administration wayside exhibit, Glendale National Cemetery, Henrico County, Virginia.
18. Private email communication with Robert E. L. Krick, April 17, 2018.
19. Trowbridge, *The South: A Tour of its Battlefields and Ruined Cities*, 184.

CHAPTER 22. *Leaving Richmond*

1. Douglas, *I Rode with Stonewall*, 111–12.
2. Robertson, *Stonewall Jackson*, 508.
3. Blanton, *The Making of a Downtown Church*, 79.
4. Henderson, *Stonewall Jackson and the American Civil War*, vol. 2, 82.
5. McPherson, *Battle Cry of Freedom*, 500–505.
6. Mary Anna Jackson, *Life and Letters of General Thomas J. Jackson*, 308–18.

7. Robertson, *Stonewall Jackson,* 210.
8. Miller, *Mapping for Stonewall,* 78.
9. Robertson, *Stonewall Jackson,* 517.
10. Ibid., 520.
11. Ibid., 518.
12. Ibid., n. 882.

CHAPTER 23. *Jackson Is with You!*

1. OR, vol. 12, pt. 3, 918.
2. Krick, *Smoothbore Volley That Doomed the Confederacy,* 54.
3. Ibid., 524.
4. OR, vol. 12, pt. 2, 181.
5. OR, vol. 12, pt. 2, 183.
6. Moore, *Cannoneer Under Stonewall Jackson,* 94–95.
7. Worsham, *One of Jackson's Foot Cavalry,* 96–97.
8. Henderson, *Stonewall Jackson and the American Civil War,* vol. 2, 94–95.
9. Freeman. *R. E. Lee,* vol. 2, 279.
10. Civil War Trust wayside exhibits, Cedar Mountain battlefield.

CHAPTER 24. *A Strange, Mysterious Splendor*

1. Blackford, *War Years with Jeb Stuart,* n. 98; Freeman, *Lee's Lieutenants,* vol. 2, 58; Susan Leigh Blackford, comp., *Letters from Lee's Army,* 110–11.
2. Robertson, *Stonewall Jackson,* 541.
3. OR, vol. 12, pt. 2, 731.
4. Robertson, *Stonewall Jackson,* 542–43; Henderson, *Stonewall Jackson and the American Civil War,* vol. 2, 365–66.
5. Blackford, *Letters from Lee's Army,* 113–14.
6. Douglas, *I Rode with Stonewall,* 132–33.
7. *Berry Benson's Civil War Book,* 17.
8. Dabney, *Life and Campaigns of Thomas J. Jackson,* 517.
9. Oates, *War Between the Union and the Confederacy,* 134.
10. Foote, *Civil War,* vol. 1, 617.
11. Robertson, *Stonewall Jackson,* 552.
12. *Berry Benson's Civil War Book,* 17.
13. OR, vol. 12, pt. 2, 670.
14. Worsham, *One of Jackson's Foot Cavalry,* 104.
15. von Borcke, *Memoirs of the Confederate War for Independence,* 97.
16. Caldwell, *History of a Brigade of South Carolinians,* 31.
17. Casler, *Four Years in the Stonewall Brigade,* 151–52.
18. OR, vol. 12, pt. 2, 721.
19. Robertson, *Stonewall Jackson,* n. 30, 888.
20. Worsham, *One of Jackson's Foot Cavalry,* 105.
21. von Borcke, *Memoirs of the Confederate War for Independence,* 98.
22. *Berry Benson's Civil War Book,* 20.
23. Douglas, *I Rode with Stonewall,* 136.

CHAPTER 25. *A Trail of Cemeteries*

1. Blackford, *Letters from Lee's Army*, 108–9.
2. Frank Bruni, "Mitch Landrieu Reminds Us That Eloquence Still Exists," *New York Times*, May 23, 2017; "Mitch Landrieu's Speech on the Removal of Confederate Monuments in New Orleans," *New York Times*, May 23, 2017.
3. Mary Anna Jackson, *Life and Letters of General Thomas J. Jackson*, 310.
4. Editors of Time-Life Books, *Lee Takes Command*, 127.

CHAPTER 26. *A Brief Pursuit*

1. Gwynne, *Rebel Yell*, 416.
2. Foote, *Civil War*, vol. 1, 624.
3. Blackford, *War Years with Jeb Stuart*, 117.
4. Ibid., 121.
5. William B. Taliaferro, "Jackson's Raid Around Pope," in Johnson and Buel, eds., *Battles and Leaders of the Civil War*, vol. 2, 510.
6. Foote, *Civil War*, vol. 1, 617.
7. Editors of Time-Life Books, *Lee Takes Command*, 144.
8. Ibid.
9. Worsham, *One of Jackson's Foot Cavalry*, 110–13.
10. Douglas, *I Rode with Stonewall*, 137.
11. Wersteev, *Kearny the Magnificent*, 13.
12. Ibid., 234.
13. Freeman, *Lee's Lieutenants*, vol. 2, 118.
14. Freeman, *R. E. Lee*, vol. 2, 325.
15. *Bruce Catton's Civil War*, 25.
16. Robertson, *General A. P. Hill*, 124.
17. Douglas, *I Rode with Stonewall*, 140.
18. Greene, *Second Battle of Manassas*, 38.
19. Freeman, *R. E. Lee*, vol. 2, 345.
20. Robertson, *Stonewall Jackson*, 569.
21. Gwynne, *Rebel Yell*, 445.
22. Robertson, *General A. P. Hill*, 128.
23. *Bruce Catton's Civil War*, 30–31.
24. Mary Anna Jackson, *Life and Letters of General Thomas J. Jackson*, 341.

CHAPTER 27. *The Fortunes of War*

1. Freeman, *R. E. Lee*, vol. 2, 349.
2. von Borcke, *Memoirs of the Confederate War for Independence*, 130.
3. Gwynne, *Rebel Yell*, 303, 452.
4. Freeman, *Lee's Lieutenants*, vol. 2, 149
5. Leighton Parks, "What a Boy Saw of the Civil War," *The Century Illustrated Monthly Magazine* 70, no. 2 (1905): 258.
6. Freeman, *Lee's Lieutenants*, vol. 2, 451; 229–33.
7. Ibid., 187.

8. Robertson, *Stonewall Jackson*, 603.
9. Ibid., 604.
10. Sears, *Landscape Turned Red*, 166.
11. Douglas, *I Rode with Stonewall*, 162.
12. Neese, *Three Years in the Confederate Horse Artillery*, 121.
13. Ibid., 122.
14. D. H. Hill, "The Battle of South Mountain," in Johnson and Buel, eds., *Battles and Leaders of the Civil War*, vol. 2, 560–66.
15. Blackford, *War Years with Jeb Stuart*, 145.

CHAPTER 28. *The Most Deadly Fire*

1. Foote, *Civil War*, vol. 1, 678.
2. Sears, *Landscape Turned Red*, 176.
3. Worsham, *One of Jackson's Foot Cavalry*, 125.
4. Alexander, *Military Memoirs of a Confederate*, 247.
5. Cook, *History of the Twelfth Massachusetts Volunteers*, 73.
6. Ibid.
7. Hood, *Advance and Retreat*, 45.
8. Otott, "First Texas in the Cornfield."
9. Bailey, *Bloodiest Day*, 81.
10. Robertson, *Stonewall Jackson*, 614–15; n. 898.
11. OR, vol. 19, pt. 1, 218.
12. Sears, *Landscape Turned Red*, 171.
13. Robertson, *Stonewall Jackson*, 617; Henderson, *Stonewall Jackson and the American Civil War*, vol. 2, 256.
14. Foote, *Civil War*, vol. 1, 693–94; Bailey, *Bloodiest Day*, 103.
15. Clark, *Histories of the North Carolina Regiments*, vol. 2, 603–4.
16. Douglas, *I Rode with Stonewall*, 175.

CHAPTER 30. *Pain and Happiness*

1. Robertson, *Stonewall Jackson*, 625.
2. Douglas, *I Rode with Stonewall*, 196.
3. von Borcke, *Memoirs of the Confederate War for Independence*, 206–7.
4. Mary Anna Jackson, *Life and Letters of General Thomas J. Jackson*, 363.
5. Taylor, *Destruction and Reconstruction*, 65.
6. Douglas, *I Rode with Stonewall*, 197.
7. Blackford, *Letters from Lee's Army*, 130–31.
8. Robertson, *Stonewall Jackson*, 645.
9. Mary Anna Jackson, *Life and Letters of General Thomas J. Jackson*, 375.
10. Robertson, *Stonewall Jackson*, 144–58.
11. Ibid., 174.
12. Gwynne, *Rebel Yell*, 566.
13. Robertson, *Stonewall Jackson*, 168.
14. Ibid., 171–72.
15. Mary Anna Jackson, *Life and Letters of General Thomas J. Jackson*, 104.

16. Ibid., 112.
17. Dowdy and Manarin, eds., *Wartime Papers of Robert E. Lee*, 934.
18. Long, *Civil War Day by Day*, 700, 713.

CHAPTER 31. *War So Terrible*

1. Robertson, *Stonewall Jackson*, 628.
2. Mary Anna Jackson, *Life and Letters of General Thomas J. Jackson*, 363.
3. John Hennessy and Brad Graham, *Fredericksburg: A Documentary Film*.
4. Ibid.
5. Foote, *Civil War*, vol. 2, 24.
6. Douglas, *I Rode with Stonewall*, 205.
7. Robertson, *Stonewall Jackson*, 655.
8. Henderson, *Stonewall Jackson and the American Civil War*, vol. 2, 212–13.
9. Virginia State Historic Marker N-2, "The Gallant Pelham," Benchmark Road, Spotsylvania County.
10. Carmichael, *Lee's Young Artillerist*, 77–78.
11. Robertson, *Stonewall Jackson*, 659.
12. Freeman, *Lee's Lieutenants*, vol. 2, 358.
13. Borton, *On the Parallels*, 66–67.
14. Freeman, *Lee's Lieutenants*, vol. 2, 367.
15. Hennessy and Graham, *Fredericksburg*.
16. Hunter, *Johnny Reb and Billy Yank*, 317; Hennessy and Graham, *Fredericksburg*.
17. *OR*, vol. 21, 589, quoted in Freeman, *Lee's Lieutenants*, vol. 2, 364.
18. Hennessy and Graham, *Fredericksburg*.
19. Alexander, *Fighting for the Confederacy*, 177.
20. Hunter, *Johnny Reb and Billy Yank*, 316.
21. Gwynne, *Rebel Yell*, 502; Freeman, *Lee's Lieutenants*, vol. 2, 368.
22. Johnson and Buel, eds., *Battles and Leaders*, vol. 3, 116.
23. Dowdy and Manarin, eds., *Wartime Papers of Robert E. Lee*, 380.
24. Foote, *Civil War*, vol. 2, 43.
25. Blackford, *War Years with Jeb Stuart*, 194–95.
26. Gwynne, *Rebel Yell*, 501.

CHAPTER 32. *A Piece of Gold Braid*

1. Robertson, *Stonewall Jackson*, 665.
2. Smith, *With Stonewall Jackson in the Army of Northern Virginia*, 35–38.
3. Gwynne, *Rebel Yell*, 511.
4. Mary Anna Jackson, *Life and Letters of General Thomas J. Jackson*, 410–11.
5. Robertson, *Stonewall Jackson*, 689.
6. Ibid., 673.
7. Ibid., 679.
8. *Bruce Catton's Civil War*, 274, 275.
9. Robertson, *Stonewall Jackson*, 684–85.

10. Mary Anna Jackson, *Life and Letters of General Thomas J. Jackson*, 402–3.
11. Ibid., 411.
12. Ibid., 427–28.
13. Ibid., 422–30.

CHAPTER 33. *Moss Neck and Belvoir*

1. John Hennessy, "Belvoir: The Thomas Yerby Place, Spotsylvania County," https://npsfrsp.files.wordpress.com/2010/06/belvoir2.pdf, 12–13.
2. Ibid., 5–6.

CHAPTER 34. *The Fallen Sword*

1. Blackford, *War Years with Jeb Stuart*, 188, 189.
2. Furgurson, *Chancellorsville 1863*, 107.
3. Robertson, *Stonewall Jackson*, 702.
4. Sears, *Chancellorsville*, 132, 151.
5. Johnson and Buel, eds., *Battles and Leaders of the Civil War*, vol. 3, 170.
6. Survivors Association, *History of the Corn Exchange Regiment*, 188; Carter, *Four Brothers in Blue*, 270–73.
7. Furgurson, *Chancellorsville 1863*, 129, 130.
8. *OR*, vol. 25, pt.2, 328.
9. Darius Couch, "The Chancellorsville Campaign," in Johnson and Buel, eds., *Battles and Leaders of the Civil War*, vol. 2, 161.
10. James Power Smith, "Stonewall Jackson's Last Battle," in Johnson and Buel, eds., *Battles and Leaders of the Civil War*, vol. 2, 205.
11. Long and Wright, *Memoirs of Robert E. Lee*, 258.
12. Henderson, *Stonewall Jackson and the American Civil War*, vol. 2, 432.
13. Gwynne, *Rebel Yell*, 533.
14. Furgurson, *Chancellorsville 1863*, 170.

CHAPTER 35. *Let Us Cross over the River*

1. Lee, "Chancellorsville Address of General Fitzhugh Lee Before the Virginia Division, A.N.V. Association, October 29th, 1879."
2. Smith, "Stonewall Jackson and Chancellorsville," 20.
3. Oliver O. Howard, "The Eleventh Corps at Chancellorsville," in Johnson and Buel, eds., *Battles and Leaders of the Civil War*, vol. 3, 198.
4. National Park Service wayside exhibits, Chancellorsville Battlefield.
5. Mary Anna Jackson, *Life and Letters of General Thomas J. Jackson*, 442–73; McGuire, "Death of Stonewall Jackson."

AFTERWORD

1. Robertson, *Stonewall Jackson*, 756.
2. Mackowski and White, *Last Days of Stonewall Jackson*, 92.
3. Porter, *Campaigning with Grant*, 133.

4. Mary Anna Jackson, *Life and Letters of General Thomas J. Jackson*, 473.
5. Freeman, *Lee's Lieutenants*, vol. 2, 684.
6. Ibid., 685.
7. Douglas, *I Rode with Stonewall*, 38.
8. Harrison, *Recollections Grave and Gay*, 141.
9. Robertson, *Stonewall Jackson*, 761.
10. Douglas, *I Rode with Stonewall*, 215.

Index

About the Author

Ben Cleary is a writer and teacher. He lives in Mechanics-ville, Virginia.